THE Home Recording HANDBOOK

Dave Hunter

The Home Recording Handbook
Dave Hunter

A BACKBEAT BOOK
First edition 2011
Published by Backbeat Books
An Imprint of Hal Leonard Corporation
7777 West Bluemound Road,
Milwaukee, WI 53213
www.backbeatbooks.com

Devised and produced for Backbeat Books by
Outline Press Ltd
2A Union Court, 20-22 Union Road,
London SW4 6JP, England
www.jawbonepress.com

ISBN: 978-0-87930-958-9

A catalogue record for this book is available from the British Library.

DESIGN: Paul Cooper Design
EDITOR: John Morrish
PHOTOGRAPHY: Jerry Monkman

Printed by Everbest Printing Co. Ltd, China

11 12 13 14 15 5 4 3 2 1

Contents

Introduction

You can skip most introductions, move on to the meat of the book, dig in, get your hands dirty. On this occasion, however, you will want to start right at the beginning. Yes, I will tell you a little bit about what lies ahead, what you will discover in more depth on your own as you read further into these pages; but more than that, I'm going to set the attitude for this adventure, to establish its philosophy. Remember how your middle-school gym teacher used to tell you it's only 10 per cent perspiration and 90 per cent determination? We are going to approach home recording with a similar attitude. You need the recording techniques, sure, and they are right here, but they will do little for you if you aren't determined to create great recordings come hell or high water, whatever your abilities, whatever you have to hand. That's what it's all about: you need to believe you can capture moments of magic, regardless of your limitations or technical shortcomings, and that you aren't going to let the lack of anything get in your way. That is where we really begin this thing.

The main thrust of *The Home Recording Handbook* is to convince you that you can use what you've got, here and now, to start making creative, expressive, and great-sounding recordings. You need a certain minimum of equipment, of course: an audio recording device, a microphone, a ... well, no, that's it really. Then you need whatever instrument or instruments you and your bandmates play. That is essentially all it takes to get started. Let's drop the excuse that you "need to wait until you buy that new compressor," or "can't possibly start recording until you save up for that tube mic pre." There's nothing wrong with investing a little cash in good and useful gear, and we will certainly explore an "essentials, and more" wish list of what is ideal to have, but don't let "if" and "when" stop you from making music right now. This is how recorded music began its run on this planet: one mic, one track. It stayed that way for a long time, and countless classic songs were recorded thus.

Add just a little more gear to the equation, so you have the kind of set-up that the most basic home studio is likely to include (as outlined in detail in Chapter One) and you are really rolling. But you still can't make broadcast-quality recordings at home, right? Well, that's what plenty of people might try to tell you, but this opinion is clearly and verifiably wrong. The recording fidelity and the quality of processing afforded by relatively inexpensive digital audio workstation (DAW) software these days offers, on paper at least, better-than-CD-quality audio. Its computer-based mixing and mastering capabilities are—in the virtual sense—equal to what any big studio of the 90s would give you as regards track count, outboard processing, and so on. Get quality recorded takes into the box in the first place and the sky's the limit. Even using the inferior home-recording solutions of the past, several bands created broadcastable, releasable master recordings. Check out the earlier work of lo-fi masters like Pavement or Guided By Voices, or solo artists like Bon Iver and early-era Elliott Smith (on his first couple of albums, at least), and you're hearing great, moving recordings that were made without professional facilities. I have recorded bands and projects in my own little old attic studio—not at all a "professional" space, believe me—that have been played widely, reached high positions in independent radio charts in the USA, used in film and TV scores, and even spun by the venerable "Whispering" Bob Harris on BBC Radio Two in the UK. You can't ask for much more "broadcast ready" than that.

The trick to it all lies in that unassuming little phrase in the previous paragraph: "Get quality recorded takes into the box." That is the key, and that is primarily what *The Home Recording Handbook* is here to help you with. You can own the best-equipped home studio on the planet, but if you don't capture viable tracks in the first place, all the 24-bit 96kHz digital love in the world won't give you a song that people want to listen to. Just as great chops, a dynamic touch, and an expressive playing voice will make a guitarist sound better than any amount of expensive hand-made guitars and amps, knowing how to get good-sounding instrumental and vocal takes into your recording device in the first place will take you a long way toward achieving master-ready recordings. Add solid mixing techniques, and a clued-in approach to mastering, all covered here too, and there's nothing to stop you.

When the publisher asked me to write this book, my first response was, "But I'm not a qualified studio engineer." Their reply: "Exactly!" I have recorded in several top studios, and even, at times, manned the controls to produce, engineer, and mix the bands I was playing with. But for the past decade and a half I have resolutely been a home recordist, and proud of it. To that end, *The Home Recording Handbook* addresses the musician who wants to make quality recordings, not the would-be engineer who dreams of a job in a big studio (a job that is getting harder and harder to find these days). Fortunately, musicians working today are in a new age of empowerment, and can turn their back on many of the traditional requirements of studio recording. High-quality home-recording equipment is both more powerful and more affordable than ever before, and as a result, a musician's ability to produce a creative product is no longer dependent upon landing a recording contract and affording expensive studio time. No more clock-watching, no more fretting over burning money while you struggle through "red-light fever" to capture takes that seem to be falling short of your hopes and dreams. The entire creative realm of music-making is now in your hands, and that's a great thing.

Entering into the realm of serious home recording requires a new skill-set, however, and a new mindset. Until now, recording techniques have most often been taught by recording engineers and producers, from the perspective of the high-end professional studio. Fully adopting that kind of instruction is often impossible, and intimidating at best, and the mere effort stops many musicians in their tracks (no pun intended). *The Home Recording Handbook* strips away the elitism and pretense from that approach, and tells independent musicians how to get powerful results from the most basic digital recording system and a handful of outboard essentials. The book is grounded in time-tested studio techniques, but it boils them down to real-world, at-home solutions and workarounds—a tool kit that enables you to get the job done, regardless of any equipment limitations. At the same time, it debunks the supposed barriers that others might put between you and your creative achievements. Ultimately, *The Home Recording Handbook* proves that you don't need a lottery-win's worth of gear to start getting good results. Just as any good musician makes the best music they can make on the best instrument they can afford—whether it's a $500 guitar or a $5,000 guitar—you can still make valid, lively, ear-catching recordings with a very basic home studio set-up.

Enough of the philosophy. Let's jump in and explore these crafts step by step, and we will be recording like pros in no time.

CHAPTER 1

HOME STUDIO SET-UP

As we might expect, a chapter such as this really needs to open with a question: "What do you need to start your own home studio?" The simple answer is: one computer loaded with digital audio workstation (DAW) software, one hardware interface or mic/instrument preamp (usually known as a "pre'), speakers or headphones on which to monitor sound, one microphone, one mic cable, one mic stand. That's it, and that is really what's at the heart of this book: if you have just invested in your first little bundle of recording gear, a bundle similar to this, great—get to work! Don't let its paucity stop you from getting started. You have got the bare minimum of ingredients necessary, so don't use the excuse that you are "waiting to get more gear" to delay your adventures in recording music.

If your set-up is as basic as this, your variables are minimal. Larger set-ups will require a little more thought, but can still be kept efficient and simple to use. Even with the bare minimum, you want to devote some care to the physical space used as your "studio," and the same effort made here will help with your final results whether you are starting with a recording package that cost you $500 or $5,000. That is another major topic for discussion, and one that we will tackle later in this chapter.

If you already have your home studio set up and ready to go, there's nothing wrong with skipping right to the following chapters to dig into discussions on recording techniques for specific instruments. Even so, you should find some topics of interest in this chapter, even if your gear budget is tapped out for now and your recording space all organized and ready for action.

Equipping your home studio

As I have already emphasized, the equipment with which you populate your home studio can be as sparse as the bare minimum necessary to plug in and record a voice or an instrument. If you are working purely with digital virtual and/or MIDI instruments, and recording only instrumental compositions, you can survive on even less and keep your recording truly "inside the box" (a phrase used to describe a recording process during which no audio signal ever leaves the computer after it has been recorded, until you burn it to a CD perhaps). For our purposes here, though, we will assume that you will occasionally want to record at least some external "live" sound sources, and will need at least a microphone and related accessories with which to do so. Also, you will want to read this chapter in conjunction with Chapter Two: Hardware, where I will provide necessary technical info on most of the gear found in a good home studio.

While I talk about getting down to business with the bare minimum, I have to admit that that's as much a pep talk as it is a working reality. If you hope to achieve master recordings that result in release-quality CDs or downloads and to have some chance of radio play, you will most likely need to equip your studio to a slightly more bountiful "minimum." I would call that the home studio core to aim for if you are starting with

BASIC COMPONENTS OF A DIGITAL RECORDING SYSTEM

Most home-studios will consist of these basic "work station" ingredients, in some form or other. These are the hardware and software components that work together to form a recording system that equates to the tape deck, mixer, and outboard processors used in the good old days of analog recording. As they will be referred to throughout this book, it is worth laying down some basic definitions at the outset.

Computer This one would seem obvious, but should be taken to stand for whatever system you work on, whether PC, Mac, desktop, or laptop. System and software requirements will differ depending which of these you use. I won't usually specify any one set-up because the variables would be too extensive to account for in each instance.

Audio interface An audio interface ("interface" for short) is the piece of hardware that translates analog audio signals from a microphone or electronic instrument into digital signals that your computer and DAW can work with, which it feeds to them via a USB or FireWire port. They invariably include a set of analog-to-digital and digital-to-analog (AD/DA) converters, and often have mic and/or instrument preamps with level controls so you can plug mics or instruments directly into them without need of further external preamp units. Basic entry-level small-box interfaces might have two channels (that is, two inputs with preamps, and two sets of AD/DA converters), while mid-level units might have eight analog inputs (with preamps on a pair, or all), plus other digital inputs that can be used simultaneously. Perhaps surprisingly, high-end interfaces often have no onboard preamps, because they are intended for use in better equipped studios that are likely to use external mic preamps.

Digital Audio Workstation Called a "DAW" for short, this is the software that provides the "virtual studio" in which you work. It allows the interaction of your hardware interface and your computer's hard drive, gives you essential tools such as an on-screen "mixer" and virtual processors for mixing and treating your recorded audio tracks, and in short, provides everything needed to go from audio input to finished product. Some basic DAWs, such as Apple's popular GarageBand, can even work directly with your computer's sound card, eliminating the need for a separate interface.

Hard-disk recorders/workstations Several units still exist—at the time of writing, at least—that take the place of the old analog cassette-based "portastudio," and might be used instead of the computer/DAW/interface combination. These usually incorporate some form of internal hard-disk-based multi-track recorder, with a multi-channel mixer that includes mic preamps for audio input and facilities for mix-down of recorded tracks, as well as onboard digital effects and processors. These workstations can offer a lot of features in one place for a reasonable price, and might be a good alternative for a recordist who can't invest in a computer around which to base a home studio. The flipside is that they will often pose limitations when compared to a computer-based recording system, which is inherently more expandable in most cases.

nothing, and it mainly includes expanding your microphone selection and the number of inputs in your interface so you are capable of recording more than one or two channels of independent audio at a time. Even so, let's start by exploring some of the options for that bare-minimum studio-on-a-budget, and we will move on to the ideal, and the dream, after that.

I won't go to great lengths to discuss the merits of specific makes and models of recording gear in this book, because the market and the technologies are changing so rapidly that such info is usually out of date pretty quickly. Some items will be mentioned as examples of their type, or because they have been market leaders for a significant amount of time; but I would ask that you to note the general feature-set of such products, and their approximate pricing position, and apply these to whatever semi-equivalent product will work best for you. Also, this book isn't the place for tutorials on how to use the software and hardware discussed in this chapter. We're here to learn recording technique itself, not system usage. Elements of using these systems will be covered in the course of things, certainly, but the manufacturer or seller of each product should provide any end-user instruction necessary for each specific product, via owner's manuals or online instruction.

Finally, there simply isn't scope here to discuss issues of software and hardware compatibility, computer systems and requirements, and all of the little details that enable modern digital recording systems to play nicely together. Before purchasing any such gear, ensure that the specifications of any other equipment with which you intend to use it meet the manufacturer's requirements, and that the systems are designed to work together.

Starter set-up: the bare minimum

In all instances here, the existence of a computer that is compatible with current system requirements of new DAWs and interfaces on the market will be a given. In generic terms, you could expect the gear that comprises your basic minimum starter system to offer the following.

YOUR STARTER INTERFACE At the time of writing, companies such as Behringer, Lexicon, Tascam, Cakewalk, Art, and others offer compact interfaces that retail for from under $100 street price (or the equivalent in pounds sterling) for a basic model, to a little more than $100 for a more advanced model with added features. The most popular of the breed, however, has possibly been M-Audio's Mbox, versions of which start at the upper end of this price range, and escalate from there, but come bundled with a starter version of Avid's (formerly DigiDesign's) popular Pro Tools DAW, known as Pro Tools LE.

Different preamps within different interfaces, and differing qualities in AD/DA conversion, might lead to some sonic differences between units. Professional and customer reviews—and online home-recording chatrooms—might help you to discern the leaders in the pack in this regard. Given the inherently generic nature of digital sound, however, which is to say 16-bit/44.1kHz files in one interface should have the same sound quality as 16-bit/44.1kHz files in another (or whatever bit rate and frequency you decide to work in), consumers are likely to decide on one unit over another by choosing the features they feel they need, or simply by going on reputation. Having said all that, some of these starter units are likely to limit your recording resolution to a maximum of 24-bit/48kHz, so there's an inherent ceiling on your fidelity in that sense.

Smaller units in this range might offer one mic input with mic-preamp level control, which doubles as a line-level input, and a second line-level-only input for a total of two inputs with respective AD converters. They also generally provide a pair of left/right monitor outputs fed by internal DA converters to send your audio out to powered speakers. Slightly more advanced units might carry two mic inputs with preamps and level controls. With most units in this range, however, if you want to record more than two audio sources at a time you will need to combine them with an external multi-channel mixer (the good old fashioned way) into a stereo signal fed to the interface's two inputs.

YOUR STARTER DAW If you don't receive a DAW packaged with your interface, there's no shortage of options for software that can be purchased separately. Popular DAWs come from Steinberg, Cakewalk, Ableton, Apple, Synapse Audio, Acoustica (Mixcraft), Propellerhead, PG Music, and several others. The functionality of Pro Tools LE, and its associations with its pro-standard bigger siblings Pro Tools 9 and Pro Tools HD, make it one of the more popular DAWs out there for starter studios, even though the version available at this level generally requires that it be used with M-Audio hardware (such as the company's interfaces mentioned above).

Most of these DAWs offer an impressive list of features for really very little money. You can expect to be able to work with anywhere from 48 to 64 audio tracks at a time (which might include limits to recording, say, eight tracks at a time, or whatever your interface limits you to—just two, in many cases). You will get a fully featured virtual mixing desk with level, pan, and insert functions and more, a bundle of "plug in" digital effects and processors, and extensive digital editing capabilities. Many also offer a bundle of virtual instruments so you can compose and record backing tracks right within the DAW, without having to plug in external digital or MIDI instruments. In addition, even at this level, most will provide a wealth of hidden bonus features and recording tools that truly will boggle the mind if you are new to the computer-based recording environment.

Several free, or nearly free, DAW downloads are also available out there, and one or another of these might be worth a try. Software such as this is coming and going all the time, and I can't vouch for its compatibility with different systems—or that it will come bug-free, for that matter—but a lot of home recordists have gotten a lot of use out of these things, and it never hurts to do a Google search and see what's out there. Such DAWs are likely to have limitations, of course, at least if they are truly free and not just rip-offs of more expensive software, but you might find that you don't need much more to accomplish

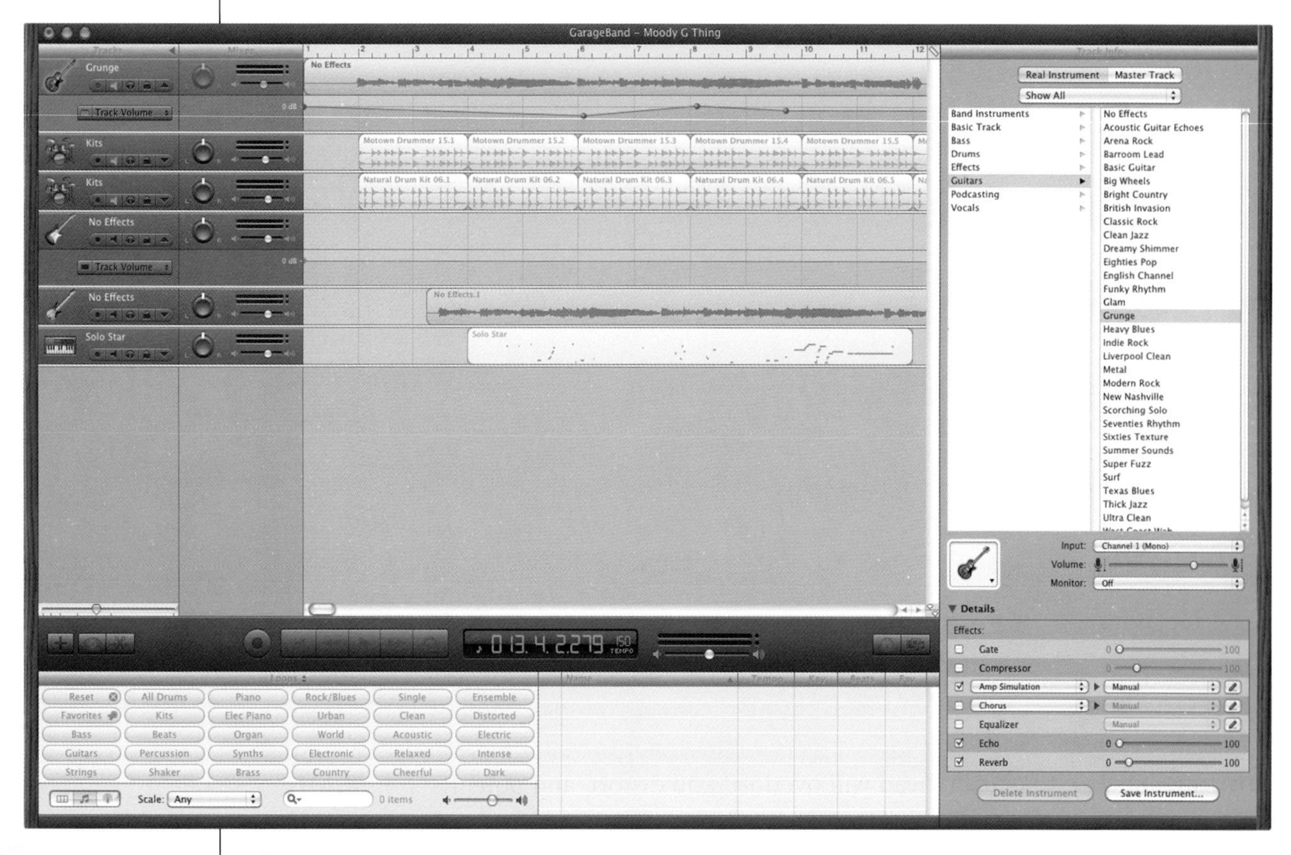

GarageBand provides all the facilities you need to record, and is simple to use too.

basic recording. On the other hand, given the sub-$100 price tag of several basic DAWs, you might want to go the safe route and just purchase the thing, and get the full support and glitch-free performance that usually comes with these tried-and-tested products.

One of the most popular and successful of the "nearly free" DAWs is Apple's GarageBand, which has been included with new Mac computers for several years and is available as part of Apple's very affordable iLife software bundle. GarageBand is extremely simple to use, yet offers surprising layers of functionality the more you get into it. It comes with a selection of user-friendly virtual instruments, and can be used with your Mac's internal sound card without need of an external interface, if you are happy with recording a maximum of two tracks at a time. All this has helped to make it a virtual revolution in basic home recording ... but the catch is that you can only use it on a Macintosh computer.

If any of these look like they will prove adequate for your needs, that leaves you more cash to put into microphones, preamps, and so forth. Any system that works directly with your computer's built-in sound card will be limited to two simultaneous tracks of recording at a time, as provided by the left and right signals at your computer's 1/8" TRS (tip-ring-sleeve) stereo input jack, but the majority of starter interfaces only allow two simultaneous record tracks anyway. You will, however, need some form of basic preamp to bring a microphone up to a line-level signal to inject into that computer input, so this route doesn't entirely obliterate your hardware requirements.

YOUR STARTER MICROPHONE Since there shouldn't be any major differences in the sonic quality of different interfaces in this price range (other than in the ultra cheapos, perhaps), your microphone, if you are starting with only one, will be the first ingredient in the sound chain that stamps its own sonic signature on your work, and should be considered carefully with this in mind. I'll discuss the characteristics of different types of microphones in detail in the Hardware chapter that follows, but for our purposes here, your choice for that one and only starter mic will depend on what you want, and need, to do with it.

If you are using a lot of virtual instruments and DI'ing real instruments such as electric guitar and keyboards, perhaps occasionally using a mic on an acoustic guitar, on other stringed instruments if you are that way inclined, and/or mainly for vocals, you might want to explore one of the more affordable condenser mics that are available today for under $100/£60. These offer the sensitivity and fidelity to produce at least an approximation of what expensive condenser mics do for vocals and acoustic instruments in professional studios.

Condenser mics can also be used to record drums if they are used at some distance (anything up close to a drum head will overload and distort, and potentially damage the mic's diaphragm in the process, unless the mic is specifically built for such applications), and guitar amps if they're not too cranked and too close (check each individual mic's ratings for SPL-handling in this regard). But if you plan to record a lot of loud live instruments right from the start, a better choice for your one mic might be a rugged dynamic microphone. Shure's SM58 is one of the standards in this category (there are several cheaper SM58 wannabes to choose from too), and can be used for a little of nearly everything. It won't offer the same sensitivity as a condenser on vocals and softer acoustic instruments, but you might actually prefer its solid, balanced sound to the potentially brittle sound of cheaper condensers. Its sister, the SM57, is a classic for close-miking guitar amps, and even snare drums, and might be another good choice. Some people don't favor its midrange-forward response on vocals. Others, though, really dig it.

STARTER MONITORS You might already have access to a home stereo (hi-fi) system that you can connect to your computer or interface's audio output for monitoring your recording work. If so, and if it's a decent set-up, this might actually sound better than many of the cheaper powered speakers that you would purchase on a low-level start-up budget. Powered computer speakers will work, of course, but won't offer the kind of fidelity that enables any real fine-tuning of EQ, or any great impression of overall low-end content, unless they are pretty expensive and high-quality units in the first place. Even the cheaper ones will, however, get you by in a pinch. If you spend about twice as much on powered studio speakers as the cost of the upper range of starter interfaces discussed above, you will land something that will do you proud at this level. And remember to pick up the correct line-signal cables to go from computer or interface outputs to speaker inputs.

If you need to do a lot of noiseless monitoring of your work (a state of affairs that often goes hand-in-hand with the starter studio), you might get by just as well with a decent set of headphones. Read a few discussions on "best headphones for under $100," and the popular choices in this category are likely to sound better than speakers in the same price range. It is notoriously difficult to gauge low-end content on headphones, but as cheapo speakers won't do much better for you, you really aren't losing much ground there. Plus, by monitoring with headphones, you eliminate a lot of the monitor-positioning issues that will be discussed later in the chapter.

In any case, if you are ever going to overdub "live" instruments in your recordings, such as an acoustic or miked electric guitar or real piano, or record vocals, you will need a set of enclosed headphones for this purpose, so account for at least a little expenditure in this area, even if you are buying some monitor speakers, too. If you plan to have another musician recording while you monitor the input, you will need two sets of headphones.

STARTER ACCESSORIES Although you might get by for a while by duct-taping your mic to an old coat stand, do yourself a favor and purchase a decent mic stand with a boom right from the start. You will, of course, need a mic cable, too. If you are using a condenser mic you will also want to purchase a pop shield to place in front of it to absorb vocal plosives—although, yes, we all got started with a pair of (clean) tights stretched across a loop made from an old wire coat hanger.

Mid-level set-up: a little more of it

You could also call this one "the studio that most home-recordists need to aspire to if they actually want to lay down some high-quality tracks." This is still a pretty sparse collection of gear as far as studios in general go, but it will give you what's needed to record several tracks simultaneously, which brings live drums and full-band recordings into the picture. Live drums are really your step up into the big leagues for many genres of music, and a move away from virtual and loop-based drum tracks that really aren't fooling anyone in the real world, at least if you're trying to produce old-school rock, blues, jazz, or roots-rock. We have already looked at the basics of each category, so this time out I will tell you what extras you are likely to get for your money by jumping up to this level, rather than re-describing each piece of gear from top to bottom.

MID-LEVEL INTERFACE Rather than the compact desktop units at our start-up price level, mid-level interfaces (roughly $500 to $1,500/£300 to £900) are more likely to be full-width rack-mounting devices. Which isn't to say that you can't also sit them on the desk next to your computer keyboard, but it will look a lot more professional if you rack them up along with some of the other up-market gear you are likely to be acquiring. Stepping up to this level should at least allow you to record eight analog tracks simultaneously, with input gain controls over all inputs, which might include mic pres (with associated XLR inputs) on two of these, or even all of them. Such units also offer further simultaneous digital recording from S/PDIF or ADAT lightpipe connections, and more.

A slight improvement in sound quality might come with some of these models, although you are paying more for the multi-tracking capabilities, so the AD/DA converters aren't necessarily going to be any better than those in the two-channel starter interfaces. Most of these larger units do, however, give you a step up in resolution to a maximum 24-bit/192kHz audio, if desired. In addition, though, most units available at this price range offer a wealth of added features—some of them truly impressive—to lure you into the step up. MOTU's 828 MkIII, for example, offers built-in effects and its CueMix monitor routing, among other things, which can be used independently even when the unit isn't feeding your computer and DAW. Avid's Pro Tools Mbox Pro and 003 Rack Factory (which includes a copy of Pro Tools 8 at the time of writing), also carry similarly enticing feature bundles. Other popular interfaces include Echo's Audiofire Pre8, Focusrite's Saffire Pro 40, and Steinberg MR816X, each of which boasts eight full mic preamps and several other useful features.

MID-LEVEL DAW Some of the upmarket DAWs that come bundled with an equally upmarket interface will give you improved service over the average starter DAW. But if you're able to purchase your software independently you can expect an astounding depth of features and performance (costs here are likely in the $250 to $600/£150 to £450 range). In sonic terms, these DAW's should enable the processing power to allow you to work with the higher resolutions made possible by the improved interfaces discussed above. What you are more likely to notice, though, is the wealth of production and editing features such software is likely to include, tools that bring unprecedented power to your ability to craft, mix, and reshape your music.

To name but a few, such tools might include beat detection to analyze and, if necessary, tidy up the rhythms of different tracks in a recording; pitch correction; far more intricate control over the parameters of the effects and processor plug-ins included; improved mix automation, and more. Plus, these should offer things that you *aren't* likely to notice, except when they are working against you in lesser systems, such as automatic latency compensation, which allows different plug-ins to cooperate with your system simultaneously, without causing delays in the tracks on which they are applied.

Popular DAWs in this range include, at the time of writing, Avid's Pro Tools 9, MOTU's Digital Performer 7, Cakewalk's Sonar X1 Producer, Propellerhead's Reason 6, Apple Logic Studio 9, and several others. Note: You will need a faster, more powerful computer and more storage to make use of the full power and highest resolutions offered by these more

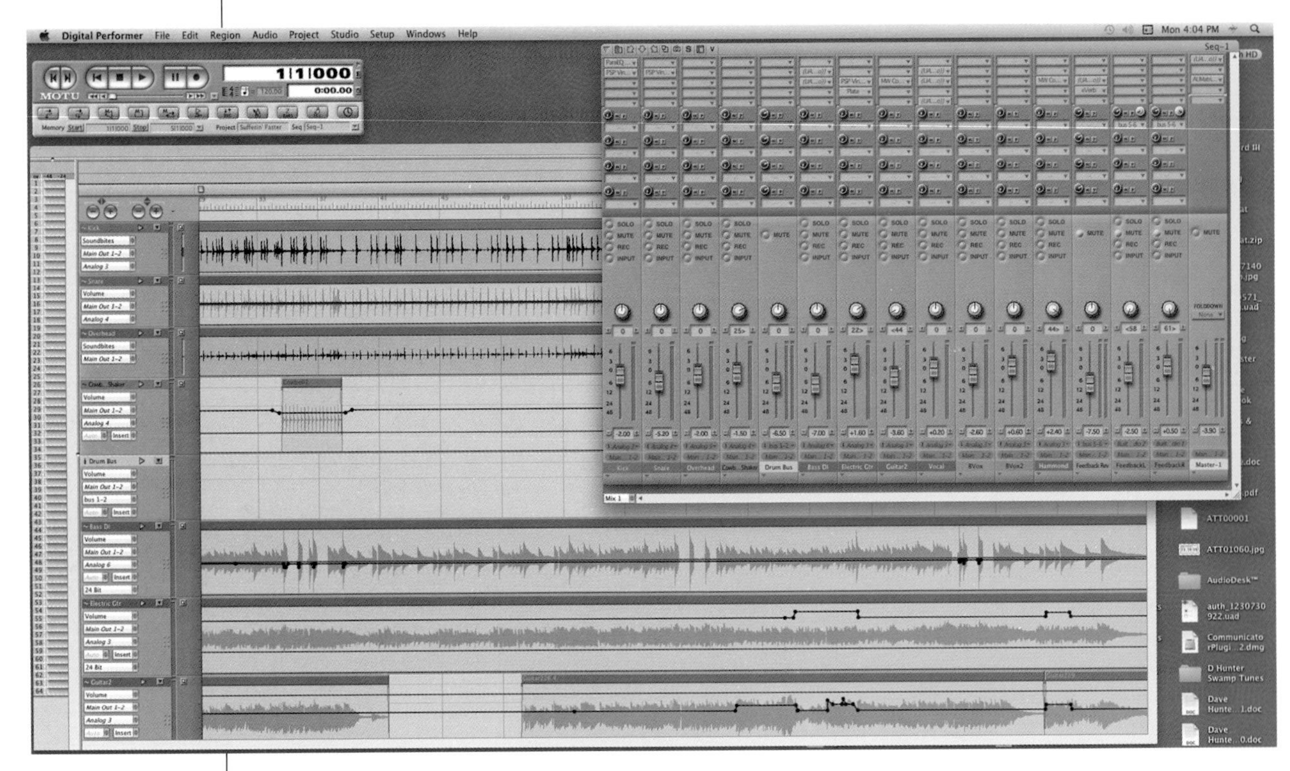

More advanced systems, such as MOTU's Digital Performer, provide enough recording and editing features to enable you to produce truly professional results.

advanced systems, so that is another expense to consider, if you don't own such hardware already. A standard step-up computer might be a dual-core MacPro tower or similar, a jump up that will cost you another couple of grand, if you need to make such a move to get the most out of an upmarket DAW and/or interface.

ADDITIONAL SOFTWARE/PLUG-INS As noted, most DAWs in this range will come with a pretty impressive bundle of plug-in effects and processors (meaning reverbs, delays, compressor/limiters, EQs, guitar and vocal effects units, and more). The more advanced your set-up gets, however, the more likely it is that you will want to track down additional plug-ins that are of particular use in the kind of music you are making.

There are many, many options available these days, and the more you investigate the world of digital recording the more you will learn about them. Several of them—from PSP's affordable Vintage Warmer to iZotope's very useful Ozone mastering software—are available as relatively inexpensive software downloads or boxed packages. Others can be found as freeware and shareware, offering free trials before you buy, or even free lifetime usage (check the veracity of any such offers as best you can, and check recording chat rooms to find if any such offers are known to come with bugs attached). Others still, such as UAD's Powered Plug-Ins or TC Electronics' Finalizer (mainly a mastering tool), require

PSP's Vintage Warmer is a popular compressor and sound-enhancing plug-in.

additional hardware that is installed in, or linked to, your host computer, but offer more powerful tools as a result.

MID-LEVEL MIC COLLECTION That's right, in order to make any use of your ability to record more than two tracks simultaneously, you will often need to make use of a handful of mics, so our mid-level mic option is a collection rather than a mere upgrade. The characteristics, and broader functions, of each of these mics will be covered in more detail in the microphone section in the Hardware chapter, but ideally I would suggest stretching your budget to at least five microphones at this point:

- a sturdy dynamic mic for recording snare drums and close-miked guitar amps (Shure SM57 or Beyer-Dynamic M201 or similar)

- a sturdy low-frequency specialized dynamic mic for recording kick drums and bass amps (Shure Beta 52A, AKG D112 or similar

- a pair of small-diaphragm condenser mics to use as stereo drum overheads and for stereo acoustic guitar (AKG C451 if you have the money, or a Rode NT5 or AKG Perception 170 or similar for a lot less), and...

- a large-diaphragm condenser mic to use on vocals, drum and amp room miking, acoustic instruments, and more (Audio Technica AT3035, AKG Perception 220, CAD M179, Studio Projects B3, Rode NT1 or NT2, or similar).

Alternatively, and this is a collection that I like for several applications, in place of the latter two entries (comprising three mics), buy either a pair of ribbon mics that can be used as stereo drum overheads and more, and one large-diaphragm condenser; or two large-diaphragm condensers and one ribbon mic. Don't stress over the mix for now—the uses of these mics will become more clear in the following chapters as we begin to put them to work.

Either way, the aim here is to acquire a range of mics that are suitable for different applications—some for rugged close-miking, some for more sensitive high-fidelity applications, and at least one that is the best vocal mic you can afford, if you are recording any vocals (as it happens, a lot of good vocal mics in this price range also double up beautifully on acoustic instruments, and some make good drum overheads, too). If you simply aren't recording any real drums, ever, you can adjust your requirements accordingly. If you won't ever record kick drum or a bass amp, you can do away with the low-frequency-specialized dynamic mic. Assess your needs, and tweak the collection as necessary; but the above set is a pretty good starting place for the average mid-level studio.

Twenty years ago, the effort to fulfill this five-mic shopping list would have cost you upwards of a couple of grand in itself. The influx of cheap but functional Asian-made mics in recent years, however, which are available in a far wider variety of types than ever before, means you can kit out your mic cupboard in impressive variety for between $500 and $600 (£300-£400). If you are working on a tight budget like this, search out reviews that point you toward the best affordable reproductions of classic mic types, shop carefully, and spend wisely. You might tip the balance of your spending toward your main vocal mic, which also gives you a higher-quality mic to use on acoustic instruments and in the room with drums and amps. Or if you can push the boat out a little, stagger the selection accordingly, and you can still use great, so-so, and cheapo mics together to track a full drum kit, or in various combinations on other instruments. Note: Either of these collections gives you great options for tracking a live drum kit; of course, to do that successfully, you will ideally want to play some guitar and bass, for example, along with your drummer, and provide a guide vocal so he or she knows where they are in the song. You can DI the instruments at this stage and replace them with miked-up takes later (such techniques will be discussed later), but you will need another mic of some sort for vocals, so you might need to extend your collection to something else beyond these two five-mic selections to get any serious real-world recording done. That said, see my suggestions in the Recording Drums chapter for more minimalist drum-miking set ups, too.

MID-LEVEL MONITORS As mentioned regarding start-up monitors, if you are any sort of an audiophile to begin with and happen to have a good home hi-fi set up already, the quality you get out of that system just might be better than that offered by cheaper studio monitors. That said, even if you own such gear it might not be convenient to set it up in the room you will use for your home studio, or to position it precisely where needed for studio monitoring (as discussed later in this chapter).

Fortunately, a broad range of options exists at this level, which I would roughly call the under-$500/£300 price range (note that we could categorize the monitor options in the Start-Up selection above as "just barely getting by in a pinch." This selection is a more realistic starting point for lower-priced monitors, whereas those in the following paragraph are more "mid-priced"). These days, powered monitors are often the most convenient; several makes offer excellent sound reproduction, they eliminate the need for a separate stereo amplifier, and can be connected directly to—and controlled from—your interface or computer. For studios of this size we will mostly be talking about speakers that are used as "nearfield monitors." That will be explained later in the chapter, but in short, they are speakers that are used fairly close to the listener's ears, rather than further back in the room. As such, most of these will have woofers that are around five to six inches (120-150mm) in diameter. If you have a large room to work in, you can probably get away with some midfield monitors, set a bit further back, and jump to eight-inch (200mm) woofers, but unless you can spend more money to get them, you will probably still get better performance out of speakers designed more for nearfield use.

Among the popular choices at the time of writing are speakers such as Yamaha's HS50M, Mackie's MR5, Tannoy's Reveal 501a, and KRK's RP6 G2. Some better-quality powered hi-fi speakers that are hitting the market these days, as differentiated from speakers designed solely for studio use, might also do the job, such as the Audioengine 5 system. If you can bump up your spending into the $500-$1,000 (£300-£600) range, quality advances accordingly. Mackie's HR624s are a popular choice at that level (with six-inch/150mm woofers, or the HR824s if you can spend even more, and need a powerful midfield monitor with an eight-inch/200mm woofer). Likewise, you can move up to Yamaha's HS80Ms and their bigger woofers, or KRK's V6 or V8 (six-inch/150mm and eight-inch/200mm respectively). With many of the smaller of these monitors you might also want, or need, a powered subwoofer if you work with kicking low end, and want to hear and feel what it's really doing. Many of the models with eight-inch/200mm woofers will do fine without an additional sub if you keep your bass at realistic levels (more of which in the chapter on mixing, later), and even plenty of the six-inch/150mm models will suffice on their own, too, if you aren't trying to mix hip-hop or drum and bass.

Ideally, you will want some "cheapo" speakers to check your mixes on, in addition to the higher-quality monitors that you do most of your listening on. If you can route your interface's outs through the average "boom box," that can make a great safety check system. You can find these cheap all over the place, in thrift stores and pawn shops, and some of the better units have Aux inputs that will work for this purpose. Otherwise, you might have to splice into the speaker wires and run them off of an external stereo amp of some sort. A pair of lower-quality domestic bookshelf speakers will also give reasonable service here. In any case, the cheapo-speaker requirement shouldn't add much to your studio budget, but is an important tool for hearing your mixes on something close to what the average listener is likely to hear your work on.

HEADPHONES With most mid-level studio set-ups you will also need several sets of enclosed headphones for tracking live instruments. For example, to track live drums in a room you will usually want a guitarist and bassist to play along, so all three musicians will need enclosed headphones in order to hear each other *and* prevent their monitor mix from bleeding into the drum mics. Most of these can be affordable options, as long as they have enclosed earpads to prevent sound getting out, and are fairly rugged (headphones used for tracking in the live room tend to take some abuse). It's still worth having at least one set of good quality headphones, though, to use for rough mixing when you aren't in a position to make noise through your monitor speakers, so consider doing your research and putting a little more money into one set out of the bunch.

While we're here, let's consider that you will also very likely need a multi-channel headphone mixer/amp, too, if you are going to have more than one person at a time monitoring sound while recording. Better quality comes with higher prices, as ever. But the basic units from makers such as Nady, Art, PreSonus, Behringer, and a handful of others should provide adequate performance and enough volume to let you hear yourselves, with individual level controls, if a little lack of fidelity too, with the cheaper units in particular.

MID-LEVEL MIXER Unless you have purchased one of the interfaces with eight XLR inputs with related microphone preamps that can be used simultaneously, you will need an external mixer to record anything but the simplest of live drum tracks. Even *with* such an interface, you might get better performance with an external mic pre of some sort (see below for more of this), and an external mixer will almost certainly give you more versatility, and perhaps prove useful in other ways, too. There are a lot of mixer options out there so I won't try to make specific suggestions here. This is a category of gear that is well-supplied in the used market, too, and a second-hand mixer might offer great savings, provided you check thoroughly to ensure it is entirely functional, and get a return guarantee if you are buying online.

Given our purposes here, you will want a mixer with at least eight channels, or you are back to not having enough preamp channels for each of your interface's inputs (although you could get by with an eight-channel mixer, plus the two mic pres on the average mid-level mixer). Note that this is a studio mixer, and not one made primarily as a live PA desk, so you don't need a powered unit (though, again, if you already have one as part of your band's PA rig, you can use it here if it offers the right features). You can, however, double-duty your studio mixer for live use by adding a power amp, or using powered PA speakers. In any case, whatever you work with, you need a mixer with independent direct sends on each of the channels used for preamping mics. If a mixer lacks these, but does have independent sends/returns on the channels you are using, you can use the send jacks only to send the preamplified signal to your interface (or, if it is a send/return by way of a TRS stereo jack designed to be used with a "Y" cable, most of these allow use as a send-only output with a standard mono cable). The key point here is that you want a mixer that lets you send individual channel feeds to your interface before they are mixed together at the stereo "main output," at which point you're back to having two channels of mixed-together sound.

If you want to experiment with mixing externally, or feeding some of your in-the-box mix out for external processing, a mixer can also be handy in this regard. On top of this, a mixer can be extremely useful for routing and/or monitoring signals while overdubbing, so you can monitor what you are playing—and playing along to—outside of the DAW, to avoid any latency issues that might come with higher track counts, plug-in usage, or bigger files.

MID-LEVEL MIC PREAMPS AND PROCESSORS Once all of the basics are in place and sounding good, the next "step-up" accessory that many home studios need is a better microphone preamp. As already discussed, most interfaces in this range will have two or more mic preamps, and if you're going the mixer route, as above, you will be able to boost your mic signals to send to line-level interface inputs, too. However, the fidelity of these preamps in more affordable and mid-priced mixers is still just middling when compared to the high-quality mic preamps that any professional studio would use. If you've got a little more cash to spend, therefore, you might want to put it into a good one or two-channel microphone pre that you can use on your most important mic signals: vocals, acoustic instruments, an important guitar overdub, maybe kick or snare drum (both, if you have an outboard two-channel mic pre) or drum overheads.

Many of the super-budget mic preamps available today won't offer any better sound than a serviceable interface or mixer will give you, so don't spend your money on the cheapest new pre available just for the sake of it. Also, be wary of starter-priced mic pres carrying tubes/valves that are powered from wall-wart AC mains adaptors and promise to fatten up your sound with "real-tube warmth." For one thing, the tubes in better quality tube preamps run on much higher voltages than standard adaptors can provide (and need to do so to sound their best); for another, the desirable qualities of tube signal paths don't always have as much to do with "tube warmth" as the lower-end audio manufacturers' marketing departments would like us to think.

That said, a lot of respectable-sounding mic pres selling for a notch or two above the entry level price range are throwing in a tube or two these days because it has become a marketing essential, and some of the largely solid-state signal paths in these actually sound pretty good, tube or no tube (I recall my friend Huw Price, a writer and studio engineer, pulling the tube from one of these during a review and declaring that the unit not only continued to function, but sounded virtually the same as it did with the tube in its socket). Better mic pres at this level are likely to cost around $500/£300 for "decent" two-channel units, or closer to $500/$300-per channel for "pretty darn good" units. Check the reviews in the studio mags, and users' reviews online, assess all available units in your price range—with full consideration of the microphones and applications with which you intent to use an external mic pre—and shop accordingly. Be sure to consider whether you will need phantom power to run condenser mics, or other handy features such as phase-reverse switches, low-frequency shelving switches, pads, and so forth.

These days, many home recordists, and those in pro studios too, are making use of repackaged vintage mic pres. Many old and esoteric audio preamps, tube and solid-state alike, can be repurposed for use as microphone preamps, and plenty of them have a lot of character. With the demise of so many of the big old studios, large mixing desks that carried several preamps are often split up and reboxed individually or in pairs or quartets, with power supplies added, and can make great mic pres—although often these aren't cheap options either, as the better of them remain highly desirable. Any of these should be approached with full awareness of the "buyer beware" principle, and I would

FMR Audio's Really Nice Compressor (RNC1773) is a standby of affordable, compact hardware compressors, while AEA's TRP ("The Ribbon Preamp") is a clean, high-gain dual-channel mic-pre designed especially for use with ribbon mics.

recommend only buying something from a reputable seller who offers the unit on a trial-and-return basis, and with some form of guarantee, unless you are adept at repairing old and busted-down audio electronics yourself.

The next piece of external processing gear that any mid-level studio is likely to chase down is a compressor/limiter. If you are doing everything "in the box" you will use digital plug-ins to achieve such processing after the signal has been recorded. Even so, it's still worth considering a hardware compressor unit to apply compression to instruments that can benefit from a little of this treatment on their way *into* the box, even if you are going to give them another dose in mixing. Drum overheads, bass, louder and rockier guitars, and vocals are some of these, as we will discuss in more detail in the relevant chapters of this book.

The better mid-level compressors sell for similar prices to the mic pres discussed above. FMR's Really Nice Compressor is a compact and good sounding two-channel unit that knocks many of these out of water price-wise, though, at a street price of around $175 at the time of writing. Other units from longer-established makers, such as dbx's 160 and Art's Pro VLA continue to be popular, and fun new options hit the market all the time. Again as with mic pres, vintage units can add flavor and character to your tracks. Some are more likely to be used as semi-special effects (for serious squash or fuzzy thickening) than as the transparent dynamics processor for which compression, in theory, is intended—and that can be a cool thing in and of itself.

Other outboard gear that would have been essential in an analog or outboard-and-tape-based digital studio ten or 20 years ago can largely be dispensed with today, such as rack-mounted reverb and delay and EQ units and the like. If your budget allows, though, and you are tempted to mix by running your signals out through your interface's digital/analog converters into the analog world, some funky old analog reverbs, delays and EQs can add a cool vibe to that process, and to your final results, while perhaps bringing a little extra noise along for the process. Outboard digital reverbs and delays really aren't worth spending your money on for this use, unless you really do love the sound of one of them, because the power, versatility and overall sound quality of even the more basic plug-in digital processors are likely to blast any of the affordable or older outboard digital units out of the water.

MID-LEVEL ACCESSORIES More mics and more input channels, and a bigger studio, obviously means more accessories. You won't necessarily need anything broadly different from the bits and pieces described in the Starter Accessories section, you just need more of it: a solid mic stand, clip, and cable for every mic you intend to use simultaneously.

The dream team

Hell, if you have the cash to go this route, fantastic. I'm not going to try to detail this one for you. In this scenario, there are a myriad options out there; do your research, consult reliable sales technicians, and kit out the studio of your dreams. Also, when you start getting into higher-end gear, a lot of choices will be more particular to specific function and what you need for the kind of music you are recording, and less generalist than the starter and mid-level choices for mics and processors and so forth, so these will be purchasing decisions that you need to discern for yourself.

I would say, though, that if you can throw just another couple grand at the overall expenditure represented by the mid-level studio, it would possibly be best to spend it in microphone and mic-pre upgrades. Improving the overall sound quality of the signal entering the system is likely to do more for your finished product than just heaping on extra features inside the box, or extra gizmos outside it that you only use on rare occasions.

A few more nifty plug-ins never hurt, of course, and a high-end compressor (hardware, rather than digital plug in) can do wonders for your tracks, too. Come to think of it, stepping up the quality of your monitors (and amp, if they aren't powered) will have you hearing your work more accurately and make an impact on your mixes as a result, as will some more professional room treatment, and ... well, you see how it starts to add up.

A Room of One's Own: your recording space

In a 1929 essay that carried this title, the English writer Virginia Woolf famously declared the need for "a room of one's own," in an age when women were unlikely to have a private space in which to gestate creative thought. These days we're more likely to say

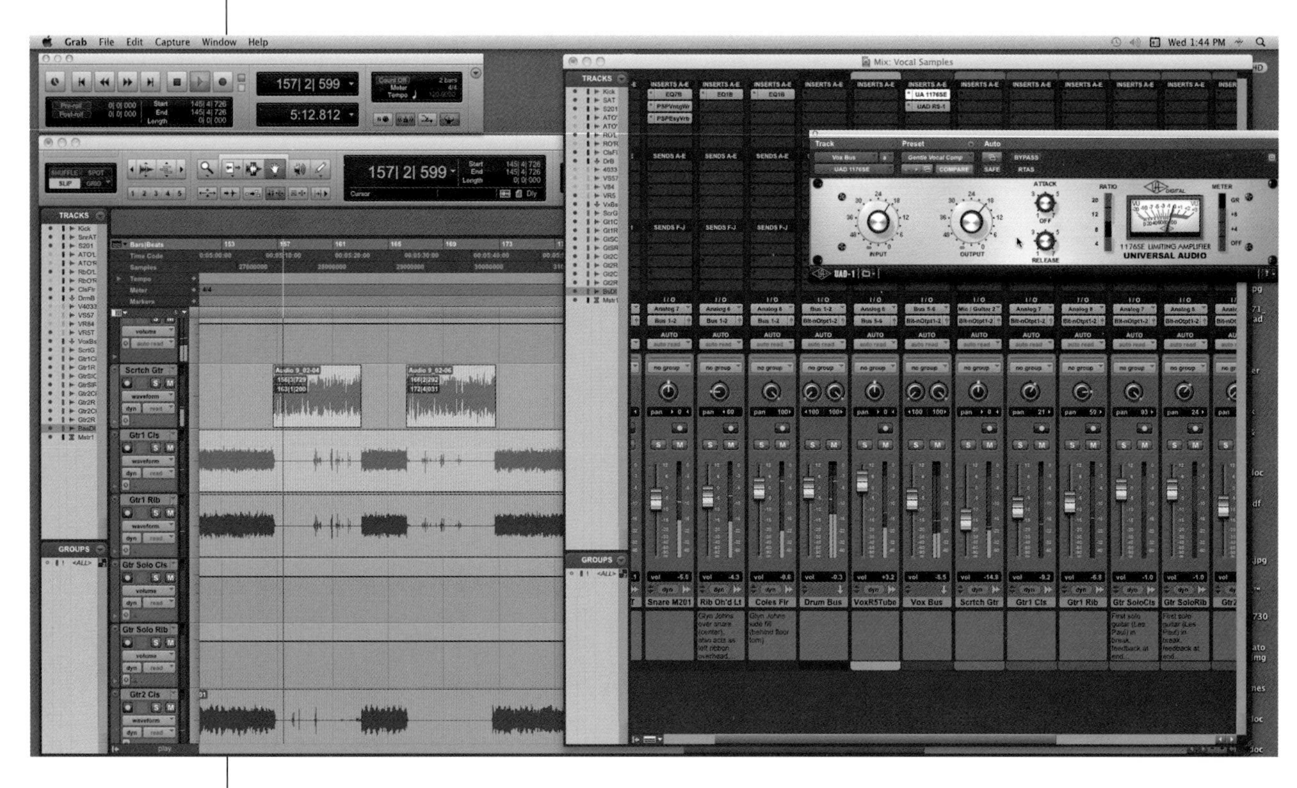

Avid's Pro Tools (Pro Tools 9 seen here) has long set the standard for professional recording DAWs.

"you need your own space," but the same principle applies to recordists today as it did to would-be female writers of the early part of the 20th century. This space might, of necessity, be shared family or communal space, and if that can't be helped then that's just the way it is. Even so, you will—with your cohabitees' permission—want to make it "your own" as much as possible in order to get it working for you as a recording venue. Whether large or small, the room that will henceforth be known as "your studio" will need to fulfill certain requirements.

First among these, I would venture, is the ability to have at least the core essentials of your recording system permanently set up. That means a desk or table on which your computer or laptop (or other recording workstation) sits, monitor speakers set up either side of it, any mic/instrument preamp or recording interface within reach to the right or left of your mixer, and your mic and its stand and cable easily accessible. And, of course, you also want whatever instrument(s) are your main stock in trade to be readily to hand, too. Insist on this kind of accessibility, and you are making it easy to get something done in whatever spare time your life affords. Create a workspace that needs to be set up and packed away each time you use it, however, and you will not only get less done because of the set-up/break-down time required, you will get down to recording less often in general, because of the frustration caused by this extra effort. Even if your recording station is a shared computer in a home office or some such space, you can keep the basics ready to go, and, hopefully, convince anyone else who shares the space and the computer itself that those extra few pieces of hardware on the desk really are important to you.

Aside from this, the three main requirements from this room have to do with sound. Namely, that the space works to:

- keep internal sound in
- keep unwanted external sound out
- allow music produced or monitored within to sound as natural as possible.

In truth, the first two of these are virtually impossible to achieve in any total sense in the home studio. I have maintained three different home studios in the three different houses I have called home for the past 15 years, and have devoted a lot of thought to my studio space in each instance—and a lot of time to using it—without ever having had anything you could truly call a "soundproof room." In fact, the home recordist who doesn't struggle with the issue of noise getting out and bothering cohabitees and neighbors, and/or noise getting in and interrupting recording, is far more likely to live out in the sticks with no neighbors to bother in the first place than to have achieved any genuine "soundproofing" of an existing space.

Real soundproofing involves a lot of construction work, and a lot of expense, rather than just putting soft foamy stuff or egg cartons on the inside of any room that already exists. To achieve even considerable noise retention you need to add layers of solid material to a space, ideally with some insulation in between—essentially building a room within a room—*and* to seal any gaps, cracks, joints and fissures between walls and floors and ceilings, windows, and doors.

This might sound simple enough, but consider the real work required and you will realize that it's a major undertaking. You can add internal framing to your room and hang up another layer of sheetrock (aka plasterboard or wallboard), but you also need to wrap the points where the walls join the floor and the ceiling. Oh, and for that matter you need to build another floor on top of your existing floor, and to insulate the studs beneath the new floor from vibration so they don't resonate into the old floor. Of course, you need to bring all light switches and electrical outlets into your new interior walls (without creating gaps through which sound will leak out) ... and, ah, all doors and windows will need to be doubled up—although you will still want some natural light and fresh air. Beginning to get the picture?

There are books and web sites that will walk you through the intricacies of genuine soundproofing, but it isn't something I will get into here because, realistically, it isn't something that most home-studio users are likely to achieve. Consider the cost of hiring a qualified builder to add an entirely new room to your house, and that's roughly what you would be looking at paying to truly soundproof an existing room.

If you have the resources to do this, fantastic; you are a fortunate person, and in a great position to achieve hassle-free recording. If not, you will be constantly seeking workarounds, like the rest of us. But don't sweat it, that's just the way it is. All the stuff you see on the walls of your pal's home studio—the geometrically-shaped foam squares on the walls, and the thick foam wedges in the corners—in short, all the stuff you used to refer to as "sound proofing"—really doesn't keep any sound in or out, it's just to minimize undesirable reflections and tame low-end resonance. These are the kinds of beneficial acoustic treatments that we can usefully examine, and work with ourselves. They can be bought as commercial products or achieved through repurposed elements that already exist in the domestic environment.

As for keeping noise from escaping from our workspace and annoying the neighbors, well, the simple answer is that we really can't. We need to make less noise, I'm afraid, or make it at times that won't bother others. If you are recording live drums, talk to neighbors and housemates to find when the big noise can be made without constituting a nuisance. If no such time exists, explore recording drum tracks elsewhere; if you're in a band with a drummer, he or she might have a practice space where you can set up the basics for recording their tracks along with your basic guide tracks (any experienced drummer will have dealt with noise issues their entire life). Or seek out community centers, paid-for rehearsal spaces, or, if you really have to, a professional recording studio that will let you lay down drum tracks and take them away in a format that you can continue to work with at home.

I will further address the approach to these issues in the chapter on Studio Approach later in this book, and I'll also put forward a number of methods for lowering the nuisance factor posed by recording guitar amps, a pet subject of mine. If you're not averse to recording guitars direct (DI) with or without any of a number of digital amp and effects simulators that are available—more of which later in Recording Guitars—this will instantly reduce the noise factor of these instruments (especially if you do so while monitoring yourself in headphones).

Vocals are likely to be less of a nuisance. While they might be heard outside the room, they aren't likely to be a concern in that regard, unless you are (or the vocalist in question is) a particularly bashful singer. More likely you will struggle to keep external noises out of your more sensitive vocal mic—the barking dog, car alarms, or the tinny jingle broadcast by the passing ice cream truck. Again, assuming the inability to truly soundproof a space, getting satisfactory takes will be more a matter of picking your time right, and going back for another pass when the occasional police siren invades your big chorus.

So, we have established certain likely compromises, and it is best to accept them sooner rather than later—or at least before spending a lot of money (but not quite enough) on what you think of as "soundproofing" only to achieve a minimal, if any, reduction in escaped decibels. Having accepted this state of affairs, our main efforts in shaping the acoustic response of our studio space will be toward neutralizing its sound, that is, ensuring as much as possible that live instruments recorded within it sound real and natural.

ROOM TREATMENT

All that chunky geometrical foam stuff you see on studio walls, and until now referred to as "soundproofing," actually does little or nothing to keep sound in, but it does help immensely to deaden undesirable reflections and resonant frequencies within the room itself. In most cases, you will want to record the sound coming from the instrument or amplifier itself without any interference from reflected sound within the room you are recording in, unless you are fortunate enough to have a great sounding room. Whatever room you use as your "live room" to record in, you really ought to give some thought to treating it to dampen reflective sound; and the room you monitor in should be treated similarly (they will very likely, for most of us, be one and the same room). Professional sound treatment requires professional acoustic analysis of the room to determine which frequencies and reflection points need to be tamed. Again, you aren't likely to have the money to spend on such services. But some educated guesses, and a little hit-and-miss treatment here and there with the usual culprits in mind, should at least help to improve your sonic environment.

Let me make it clear that I am no expert in room treatment, and have no training in acoustical engineering or studio design. To treat my own home-studio spaces over the years I have simply absorbed what I could from others who were experts, copied what I have seen in professional studio spaces, and hoped for the best. And, fortunately, this has always seemed to work—or work well enough that there were no howlingly detrimental acoustic problems in my rooms after the foam was stuck up and the recording begun. So let's put that down as our own goal here: dampen things down a little without smothering the room entirely, restrain bass frequencies in particular, and vow to avoid obsessing over the limitations of whatever space you are stuck with. Unless you can afford to get a professional in to read your acoustic space and advise accordingly, this should allow you to get satisfactory results, and get on with the job of recording some music.

There's a broad range of acoustical treatment products available. If you can afford to invest in a little professionally-made studio foam—and this doesn't have to be all that huge an investment if you plan things carefully—these products are likely to pay off in the long run. Such products fall into three main categories: wall-mounted foam products designed to absorb sound, slightly more dense and rigid wall-mounted treatments designed to diffuse sound, and foam bass traps designed to be mounted where walls meet (and where walls meet ceilings) to prevent these corners from amplifying low frequencies. Since diffusers usually require serious analysis of the room's characteristics, and thoughtful design and construction, you are more likely to work with the two types of absorption and trapping products. Each of these comes in different sizes and thicknesses, and with surfaces textured to different geometrical shapes and patterns, which are designed to handle their sound-dampening jobs in different ways, and to work on different frequency bands. Whatever manufacturer of sound foam you seek out, however, and whatever product you use, also check that the stuff is adequately fire resistant, and meets applicable codes for such.

The amount of foam you need will depend upon the size of your room, but you don't need to create the entirely foam-lined "padded room" that you might see in some vocal and isolation booths. In most cases, strategically treating 25 to 35 per cent of your wall space will work wonders, and sometimes you can get away with less (people selling treatment foam will usually advise you cover 25 to 75 per cent of your wall and ceiling space, which might be great if you can afford it, but might also be unnecessarily excessive). To use your treatment effectively, create a larger non-reflective area in the center of each wall, and smaller squares used in other positions will work with it to tame harsh reflections, in most instances. If you can mix and match the thicknesses and patterns of wall squares used, so much the better, as this will usually afford a more complex absorption and diffusion of unwanted reflections.

While wall treatments should keep sounds from bouncing back and forth between parallel surfaces and wreaking havoc with your recording efforts, you also really need to dampen down your corners and wall/ceiling joints some to keep from amplifying bass frequencies in certain parts of the room. Bass traps generally come in the form of large wedges that might be about a foot (300mm) across, two feet (600mm) in length, and 10 to 12 inches (250 to 300mm) deep from the apex of the "wedge" at the back to the center of the front. This kind of thickness is needed to adequately absorb low frequencies, and standard two, three, or four-inch (50mm, 75mm, or 100mm) absorption squares bent into corners simply won't do the same job. If you can treat all corners of the room, great; a wedge mounted in the vertical wall/wall joint and two more—one either side of it—in the wall/ceiling joint, repeated in each corner of the room, would do wonders.

Bass traps can be expensive items, though, and the cost will add up fast if you click that button to send 12 of them into your shopping cart. If you need to treat all corners equally, four wedges, one placed high in each vertical joint, should at least help matters. Or, in many cases you can make do with treating two adjacent corners of a room where bass frequencies from instruments are more likely to be produced, and therefore reflected (or at which you monitors will be aimed during mixing) and do the job more efficiently, but still satisfactorily.

In many cases, the best way to go about treating your room will be to approach the job bit by bit. Purchase what you feel might be the least amount of foam needed, position it strategically, and see how the results come out in your recordings. If you are haunted by low-frequency woof and slappy, sloppy reflections, add more.

If you can't afford to purchase any factory-made acoustic treatments, there are still several things you can do to dampen a room down significantly. And even if you can afford to purchase some absorption squares and bass traps, you are still very likely to do the best job of treating a home studio by mixing improvised and purchased elements. Sound can be absorbed and diffused by bookshelves loaded with books, heavy drapes or curtains, even a thick old quilt or duvet, or a mattress leaned against a bare wall or window. Anything and everything you can use to "deaden" the recording space slightly—and you will hear it when you achieve it—will help to give you better control over the

A thick, wedge-shaped bass trap (above left) is designed to reduce low-frequency reflections in corners. A variety of treatments, as seen above right, might be needed to dampen different frequencies and achieve a neutral-sounding room.

sound of your recordings, so they sound the way you want them to, and not the way the room would otherwise dictate.

Treating a room goes toward creating a neutral monitoring and mixing environment as well as a neutral recording environment, and if you will be recording and mixing in the same one room, all of your efforts should go towards both ends. If you are fortunate enough to have a second adjacent "control room" to mix and monitor in, then … well, you will be unfortunate enough to have to treat that one too. In addition to dampening unwanted sound reflections that will be picked up by the mics while tracking, wall and corner treatments will perform similar duties when you are playing back the material on your studio monitors to check the veracity of recorded sounds, or to create your final mix.

DESK POSITIONING

In addition to the neutral room you have ideally created, the position of your mixing station and the placement of your monitors will have a major effect on your accurate perception of recorded sound while seated at your workstation. If your room is extremely small, your options for positioning might be fairly limited. The basic rules to follow here, as far as possible, are to:

- Position your monitor speakers some distance from the wall behind them
- Position your work station as symmetrically as possible within the room, or the portion of the room you are working in
- Place your seat at a symmetrical position between and in front of the speakers.

If you get all of these "as right as possible" within the parameters that you have to work with, you will achieve two important functions in your listening environment: you will minimize reflections of your monitored sound, and achieve an accurate stereo field.

If you are working in an extremely small room and can't achieve one or both of these objectives, you can partly overcome this handicap by adding extra sound absorption to the walls and corners behind the monitors, and also those behind and to the side of you if reflected sound is likely to bounce back from behind you and skew your perceptions of frequency and the stereo spectrum. In a medium-sized room, however, if you can place your speakers at a distance from the wall behind them that's about half the distance from the front of the speakers to the wall behind you, you won't usually need to totally deaden things down, and ideally you do not want to do so. Also, avoid placing monitors in corners at the end of a narrow room (well, any room really), as this will accentuate bass frequencies and make it impossible to know how the low end in your mix will sound in the average listening environment.

The standard control room in a professional studio isn't usually an enormous space, and isn't totally swaddled in absorption foam, either. Retaining a certain amount of liveliness in the listening room yields a more natural feel, and will usually give you better results, provided there aren't any conflicting or misleading room tones or reflections. But if you're working in a glorified closet you might need to give a little extra thought to acoustic treatment to overcome standing waves and early reflections—or do a lot of your monitoring in high-quality headphones, and test your mixes' low-end content elsewhere, on other reliable audio systems, before committing them to a final master.

To get your monitors-to-listener positioning right, place the speakers on stands or a firm, non-resonant surface at a height adjacent to the listener's ears, and at the same distance from each other as they are from the listener's ears. Place them head high, and at the points of an equilateral triangle that includes the engineer's head as the third point. This sounds simple enough, perhaps, but you also need to make that spacing happen without putting the monitors in a position that has the sound that's coming from them bouncing off the back of, or obstructed by, your computer monitor, or any other gear on the desk such as a mixer or processing equipment. Work with the geometry to get your spacing right, but also to keep your stereo field clear of obstacles that might skew your perception of what's actually coming from the speakers.

FOLLOWING PAGE: The familiar clutter of the home-studio work station. The home recordist rarely has an ideal space to work in, but with care, planning, and a little trial and error, he or she can usually achieve an efficient environment and a good sounding position.

You can place monitors upright in the standard position, but many people like to lay them on their sides instead. If upright, aim the tweeters at your ears, with the woofers just a little bit below that plane. If on their sides, put both monitors with woofers to the center (that is, toward each other), so that low-frequency sounds that are traditionally mixed in the center of the stereo spectrum (what you might think of as "mono"), such as bass and kick drum, are accurately heard in that position. If you are using a sub-woofer, ensure that that is also accurately centered, and in front of you. Sub woofers used with home audio and surround-sound systems might instruct that they can be positioned almost anywhere in the room and still provide full and realistic low end, but for monitoring in the studio, you want that low end coming at you from front and center.

Depending on the stands or the solid surface on which you mount your monitors, you might also want to place them on some form of isolation pad to decouple the speaker vibration from the stand, shelf, or desk top, and thereby prevent resonance in that structure that can throw out its own misleading sound waves. These come in the form of Auralex's rather expensive MoPADs, and Primacoustic's even more expensive RX7 Recoil

To get your monitors-to-listener positioning right, place the speakers on stands or a firm, non-resonant surface at a height adjacent to the listener's ears, and at the same distance from each other as they are from the listener's ears. Place them head high, and at the points of an equilateral triangle that includes the engineer's head as the third point. This sounds simple enough, perhaps, but you also need to make that spacing happen without putting the monitors in a position that has the sound that's coming from them bouncing off the back of, or obstructed by, your computer monitor, or any other gear on the desk such as a mixer or processing equipment. Work with the geometry to get your spacing right, but also to keep your stereo field clear of obstacles that might skew your perception of what's actually coming from the speakers.

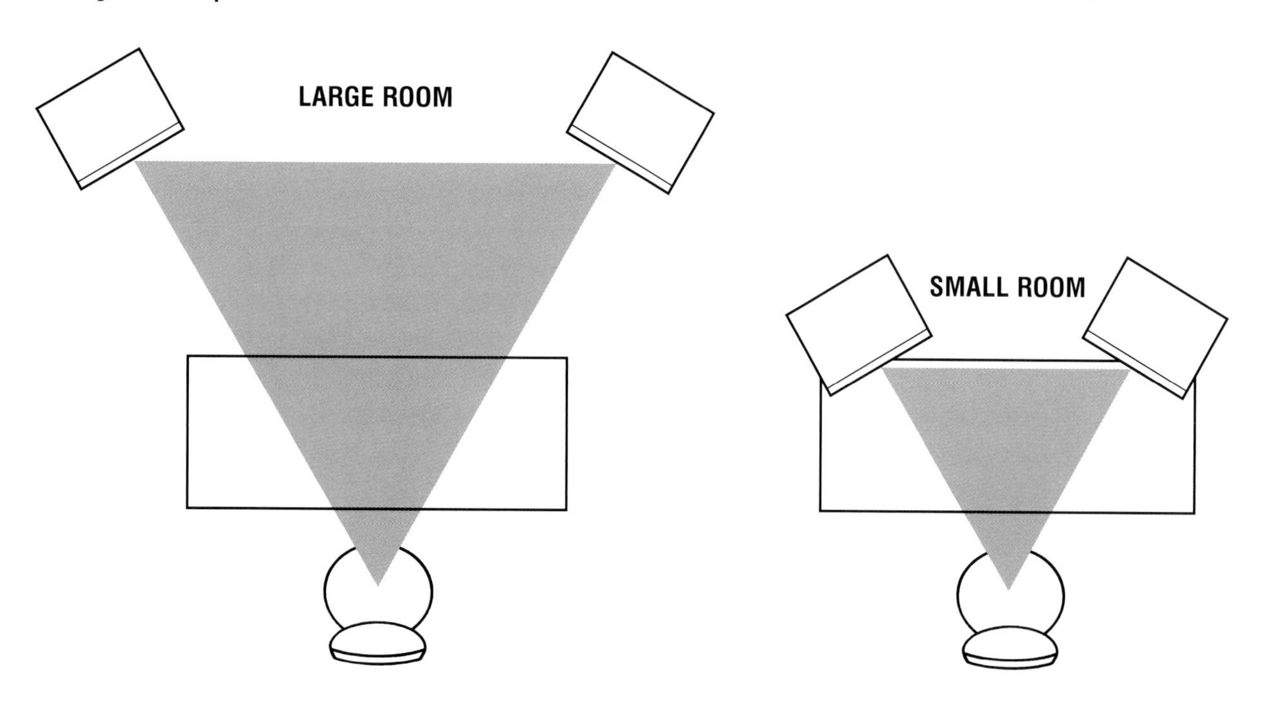

STAR GUITARS

Stabilizer. Or, to achieve at least a partial isolation, try laying your monitors on slices of inch-thick foam carpet underlay or other dense foam padding, and see if that seems to produce a more uncolored and resonance-free listening experience than that of speakers directly on stands.

With monitors adequately spaced and placed, you still need to angle them in the optimum firing lines from speakers to ears, and for a tip on that I'm going to turn once again to Huw Price, who also recounts this advice in his book *Recording Guitar And Bass* (Backbeat Books, 2002). While sitting precisely in the middle of the stereo field that you have created, listen to a good commercial recording of a type of music similar to what you are likely to produce yourself, and ideally one with which you are fairly familiar already. As Price puts it, if the vocals sound "thin and unfocused," try turning the speakers in slightly toward the center (that is, angle them so the imaginary direct lines shooting straight out from each tweeter cone are likely to meet more in front of you than behind you). If the vocal sounds too "up front" and the stereo field sounds too narrow, angle the speakers outward slightly in equal amounts. Work slowly and gradually, and tweak back and forth as necessary to get your listening position sounding as good as possible. When you are done, you should still hear some air and space and dimension in the stereo mix, while experiencing a solid center with firm lows, and no sense of "hollowness" up the middle.

Digital recording basics

The users manuals included with any interface or DAW you purchase in the course of setting up your home studio should offer some tips on the basics of digital recording, but it's worth covering a few essential terms and reference points here. As compared with old analog tape recording, digital systems will do a lot of the technical work for you, but you do need to understand a little something about digital "resolution" and digital distortion in order to get the most out of recording with these new wonders.

RESOLUTION (ie, BIT RATE AND SAMPLE FREQUENCY)

Thanks to the proliferation of digital cameras and HD TV, most of us are familiar with the concept of "resolution" as it applies to visual media these days. Just as the higher the number of elements composing your picture the finer the quality of that picture, increased audio quality is defined by increasing bit rates (also "bit depth") and sample frequencies (also "sample rates"). Bit rate determines the number of decimals in each sample of audio taken in the recording process, and sample frequency determines the rate at which at which samples are taken (as a per-second figure).

You don't really need to understand the science behind all of this in order to record great-sounding audio, although a little knowledge can at least help you to sound like you know what you're talking about. What you really *should* understand, though, is how to use the best resolution for your final product, or for the recording project as a whole. It's also essential to know what rates you might need to convert to for your final release, depending on media used.

CDs are manufactured to a standard of 16 bits at 44.1kHz, which means a 16-decimal sample is taken 44,100 times per second. These are the rates that any standard CD player will be able to read, and CDs burned at different rates will be unreadable. Today, the ability of good digital recording equipment to work to higher standards means that most project are recorded at bit rates of 24, with sample frequencies of 48kHz, 88.2kHz, 96kHz, or even 192kHz, and the result is converted down to 16/44.1 in the mastering process for final release on CD in a process called "dithering." MP3s are even lower resolution, since they are also further compressed into smaller files.

So, if 16/44.1 is the best resolution that your end listener is likely to experience, shouldn't you just record at this rate in the first place? In a word, no, and for a few good reasons. Recording audio at higher rates produces a better raw product in the first place, giving you more headroom and better dynamic range. It also lets you process tracks more effectively through plug-ins that are capable of working to much higher standards, and do their best when working with higher-resolution files. If you record at higher rates, at least you have that fidelity for posterity, rather than losing a lot of your sound quality at the very start—and it's possible you will want to make higher-than-CD-quality releases available at a future date, too. Even most basic DAWs and interfaces made today are capable of recording at higher-than-CD quality, so clearly you should you use your highest recording setting as a rule, right? Well, not necessarily. Higher rates use more processing speed and more memory, and these factors might put a strain on computers that are less than optimum for the job.

Also, unless you have a high-quality dithering machine, your DAW might not do the best job of converting some of the highest frequency rates available down to 44.1kHz, and crucial elements of your sound might be lost in the process. For this reason, a lot of people find they ultimately get better results recording at 24-bit/88.2kHz than at 96kHz or higher. Even if the higher frequencies sound impressive when listening back on the studio monitors pre-mastering, you will lose a lot more when it is dithered down to 44.1kHz on anything less than a truly professional-grade machine. On the other hand, 88.2kHz—being an obvious doubling of 44.1kHz—will still sound great, and is easy for many more affordable DAWs to convert to CD standard. For the time being (that is, until new technology makes this advice redundant), 24-bit/88.2kHz is likely to be the optimum standard for the home recordist.

DIGITAL DISTORTION

Unlike analog sounds such as tube distortion or tape compression, digital distortion is *never* desirable, and sounds entirely nasty when it does occur. No soft, warm, fuzzy blurring of the audio along the lines of gentle tube clipping, digital clipping is a harsh *"Kkktchhhk"* that sounds like the overload it is, and indicates "technical failure" in any recording in which it occurs. For that reason, you will want to do your best to avoid digital clipping throughout the recording process. This is not to say that you can't record, for example, a distorted electric guitar amp into a digital system, but that you want to avoid letting the signal from the mic or DI'd instrument distort at the point of input into your interface, computer, or DAW. Once digital clipping occurs in the recording process, you can't do anything to clean it up, and are really stuck with it unless you edit that segment out, or re-record it.

To keep all digital signals safely distortion free, ensure that both your interface and DAW meters stay well short of the red overload zone at all times. As a rule, that means keeping peaks at around –3 dB and below, and average levels somewhere in the –10 dB to –14 dB zone. Coordinate any gain controls on external preamps and the interface's input levels to present a clean, safe level to the analog-to-digital converter, and keep already recorded tracks well below the red zone in the DAW when mixing. Recordists who worked in the analog realm in the good old days might recall the advice that you push levels recorded to tape so that they are just touching on the meters' overload zone, in order to get the best signal-to-noise ratio. The inherently low noise of digital recording means that that standard no longer applies, and you should in fact do something close to the opposite: keep recording levels well down into the safe zone—not even in the yellow warning track—and you can always bump up the volume later without increasing your background noise.

When mixing several recorded tracks together, even just to monitor existing tracks while overdubbing new instruments, you also need to rein in signal levels to avoid digital clipping in the DAW. If you need more volume, but pushing up all the individual track faders is putting you in the red, try pulling down individual tracks then pushing up the master just short of the red, and if you still need more volume in the monitors, turn up your monitoring system itself. For tips on optimum levels for mixing your final product, see Chapter Nine: Mixing And Mastering.

CHAPTER 2
THE HARDWARE

Whatever DAW you work in, and with whatever interface and computer system, the primary recording skills you will want to master still revolve around your use of the *hardware* components of your home studio. And since we are primarily focusing on computer-based digital recording in this book, "hardware" mostly means microphones, along with the gear you plug them into and process them through. Different interfaces from different manufacturers might all function a little differently, but will do much the same things in broad terms. The same applies to the majority of DAWs; some might have specific advantages or disadvantages, and their tools and features might differ, but the better packages available today will all perform broadly the same functions needed to get the job done. The biggest differences, therefore, in the sound of one home engineer's recordings over that of another are likely to come from their use of different types of microphones, and where they are placed in relation to the sound source. Or, for short, their "mic technique." Other hardware components that you are likely to use, such as mic pres, compressors and limiters, and possibly mixers, also deserve a little look, but can be addressed in more of a general overview.

Studio microphones

The basic microphone types and their uses warrant a detailed look, because each different type performs quite differently and has a job it is likely to excel at, even if there is some overlap. This knowledge base will be added to in each following chapter as techniques for recording specific instrument groups are discussed—and that's where real "microphone technique" will come into play—but let's dig in now and at least lay the groundwork for an understanding of the different types of microphones commonly used in studios, and what they do best. (A discussion of the pick-up patterns offered by different mics will be included in the following chapter, Studio Approach, and should be considered hand in hand with mic make and type when equipping your studio.)

DYNAMIC MICROPHONES

Also known as "moving coil" microphones—because that's how they operate—dynamic mics function similarly to a standard loudspeaker, but in reverse. Whereas the signal from some form of amplifier moves the voice coil mounted within a speaker's magnet, causing it in to move the speaker cone and produce sound, a dynamic microphone produces an audio signal when sound hitting the diaphragm moves a coil wound around a magnet and causes it to generate an electrical signal. There is no electrical circuit within a dynamic mic, and no electricity is applied to it to enable it to function: it is an entirely passive device containing just this diaphragm, moving coil, and magnet, and needs nothing else to produce the electrical signal that transmits your precious sound to the next stage in the signal chain.

The dynamic mic's simplicity and its lack of any active electronic components help

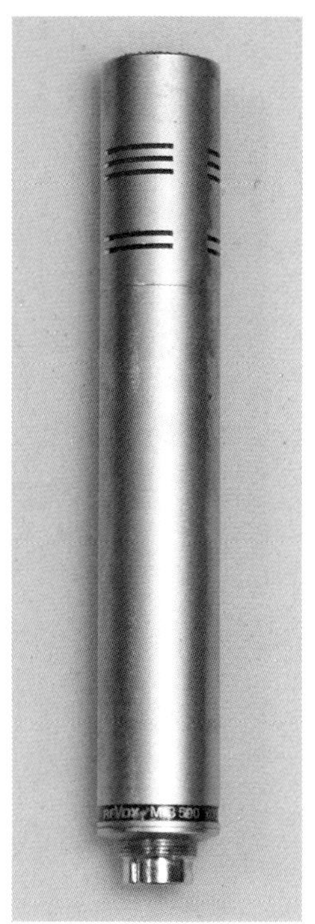

RIGHT: The rugged Shure SM57, a classic dynamic mic. FAR RIGHT: The Beyer-Dynamic M201 dynamic mic is particularly popular on snares and guitar cabs.

to make it the most rugged breed of microphone out there. These qualities also help to make it more affordable to produce, and therefore cheaper to buy. None of which is to say, of course, that you can't buy plenty of budget-grade condenser mics for far less cash than many high-end dynamic mics, but when you compare like with like—Asian-made dynamics vs Asian-made condensers, or western-made dynamics vs western-made condensers—the dynamic mic is likely to be far more affordable than the condenser from the same or similar manufacturer.

The dynamic mic's ruggedness of build also translates, in rough terms, to a certain ruggedness of sound. As a breed, it isn't as sensitive as the active condenser mic, either as regards fidelity or output level, and lacks high-end detail in particular. That said, many good dynamic mics can still capture more than enough high-end detail for plenty of applications (it all depends how much you want, right?) and their sturdiness means they can take more punishment from loud sound sources, too, without distorting or, even worse, blowing out entirely. Although there are a few exceptions, dynamic mics are therefore the common choice for loud guitar amps, snares and kick drums, relatively close miking of loud brass instruments like trumpets and trombones, and so forth. The other side of the coin is that dynamics often lack the sensitivity to handle quieter sound sources, and by the time you boost them enough to do so (through whatever form of mic pre) you might introduce too much noise to make them viable for the application.

Since they are designed to take this kind of punishment from close-miking applications, many dynamic mics lose even more detail when used at a distance from the sound source. Dynamic mics that are designed to be sung right on top of for live use, for example, might suffer dramatic decreases in output at just three or four inches from a singer's lips. Used on a loud enough sound source, however, most will still give you plenty of signal. And some dynamic mics can still be used, at a pinch, for drum overheads, guitar-amp room miking, and other more distant applications where the source is still pushing enough air to be heard, if you just don't have access to the condenser mics that usually excel at these jobs.

Another inherent "drawback" of many dynamic mics is that the traits described above

Shure's Beta 52A is a "low-end specialist" used on kick drums and bass amps.

convene to give them specific characters, or what is often called a "colored" response, as opposed to an even and balanced response across the frequency range. Once understood, these characters can be used to your advantage in some situations: a mic with pronounced midrange used to record punchy electric guitars, or one with a big low-end response used on bass or kick drum, for example.

Some of the most classic, and most popular, dynamic mics are made by Shure, AKG, Electrovoice, Sennheiser, and Beyer-Dynamic. Prices for these today, purchased new, will range anywhere from the $100/£90 street price of a Shure SM57 (a classic for close-miking guitar amps and snares), to the $400/£320 for a Sennheiser 421 (drums, bass, guitar amps) or the $430/£470 for an Electrovoice RE20 (kick drum, guitar amps). Fortunately, the robustness of these dynamic mics means they can be good buys on the used market; if your budget doesn't even stretch to that, several sturdy and decent sounding Asian-made mics based on many of these classic designs will give you reasonable service for a lot less money—even though, as with so many things in the recording realm, the old adage "you get what you pay for" still applies pretty consistently here.

CONDENSER MICROPHONES

Also known as "capacitor mics," that being another word for condenser, condenser mics include active electronic circuitry, and therefore need to have some kind of voltage applied to them in order to "hear" your sound source and produce a signal. The use of active circuitry allows a thinner, lighter diaphragm (part of an internal structure called a "capsule"), which moves more easily when hit by sound waves. A condenser mic is therefore significantly more sensitive than the average dynamic mic. All of this translates to greater fidelity, often a more balanced frequency response, and a strong output signal.

This sensitive performance also requires some sensitivity as regards handling and usage. Condenser mics aren't usually used very close to loud sound sources, other than those designed specifically to enable such use, and doing so can result in distortion (or even damage) when the diaphragm is moved too vigorously. Some condenser mics are designed to be used close to guitar amps and drums, but most will be placed at least a foot back from such sound sources, or even more. Condenser mics used as drum overheads, for example, are likely to be placed four feet or more above drum heads and cymbals (which is also to keep them out of the whacking distance of the drummer), and they can

RIGHT: Audio-Technica's AT4033, a versatile mid-level large-diaphragm condenser. BELOW RIGHT: The AKG C451 is a classic small-diaphragm condenser, great for acoustic guitars and other stringed instruments, drum overheads and hi-hats, and plenty of other applications.

even yield some useful and interesting results when placed several feet back from a guitar amp or other loud instrument to be used as room or "ambient" mics, often blended in with a second close mic.

The bonus of this increased sensitivity is, of course, that condensers are great for use on softer acoustic instruments and voice; they pick up nuances that most dynamic mics will miss, high-end detail in particular. Condensers are usually the mics of choice on acoustic guitars and other stringed instruments, piano, and vocals. Also, any effort to record a large ensemble—or even just a band in a room—in stereo in a "live" situation will usually involve a pair of condensers, rather than dynamic mics (using a range of techniques that will be discussed elsewhere in this book).

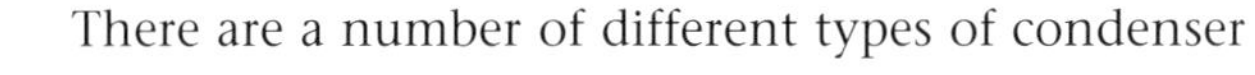

There are a number of different types of condenser mic. The two main categories are differentiated by those that contain a vacuum tube (valve), and those that use solid-state circuitry. Tube mics, which are less common but still plentiful, generally require an external power supply to deliver the higher voltage levels that the tube runs on. Solid-state mics are usually powered by the 48-volt "phantom power" that many mixers, mic preamps, and interfaces supply through a standard XLR cable. Tube mics used to be universally more expensive, although as with all mic types, prices have come down considerably in recent years, with Asian-made tube mics from companies such as MXL and Behringer bringing them in at street prices under $200/£120. The same trend has delivered solid-state condensers at the kinds of pocket-friendly prices that you would have paid for a budget dynamic mic 20 years ago,

Some of the most classic, and most popular, condenser mics have been made by Neumann, AKG, Sony, Shure, and Audio-Technica, although the field has been blown wide open in recent years thanks to affordable new options that emulate some of

these designs at a much lower cost. Again, however, you get what you pay for, and if your budget can stretch to one or two good "starter level" condensers from long-standing makers—an AKG C414, Neumann TLM 102, Audio-Technica AT4033 or similar, or even a lower-mid-priced option from Rode, Blue, Octava, Sennheiser and others—your recordings are likely to benefit from it.

Beyond the type of circuit they carry, condensers can vary in several other ways. They are also split broadly between "large diaphragm condenser" and "small-diaphragm condenser." The former group includes the large, and particularly broad, mics you see in front of vocalists in many studio photos, mics such as the Neumann U87 and U47 or AKG C414 and C12. In addition to voice, they are also popular on pianos, stringed instruments, as room/distant mics on louder instruments, and drum overheads. Small-diaphragm condensers, as their name would imply, are able to be made in smaller packages, and take the form of the "pencil mics" such as AKG's C451 or the more affordable Rode NT5 or Audio-Technica AT2021. These are also popular in stereo pairs as drum overheads, and are often used on acoustic guitars and other stringed instruments, though less often on vocals, unless they are simply the best-sounding mic you have in the cupboard for such an application.

RIBBON MICROPHONES

Limited for many years to high-end products—or to the fringe market of odd cheapo and off-brand types that turn up now and then, but often don't sound great—ribbon microphones have benefited from a huge resurgence in popularity since the early 2000s and the affordability of new Asian-made makes and models, too. Before the advent of condenser mics, several major ribbon mics were the big boys in town, and great vintage versions from RCA in particular were the go-to mics throughout much of the jazz age.

Although generally considered to be in a category of their own, ribbons really are dynamic mics by function, and are passive designs that produce their signal through a similar electronic interaction to the one that makes a good old SM58 tick. The difference with the ribbon mic, though, is that in place of the thicker, heavier circular diaphragm and coil of the SM58 and its kind, it uses a long, narrow, and extremely thin "ribbon" of aluminum clamped tightly between the poles of a magnet, or two magnets, with a transformer coupled to it. In a sense, the ribbon performs as both a diaphragm and a transducer in one. As such, ribbon mics are less sensitive than condenser mics in terms of output level (again, like the more common dynamic mics), although the topology of a good ribbon mic offers a certain depth, thickness and "air" that can make it a great sounding mic—one that many consider very "real" sounding—for many applications.

Their resurgence in popularity is perhaps due to many recordists' rediscovery of these benefits of good ribbon mics, especially in this age of digital recording, when any tool that inherently "thickens" and "warms up" a track can be useful. I personally find, and other engineers agree, that the right ribbon mic can often make a guitar amp or drum kit sound "more like it does in the room" than almost any other mic in the collection, when

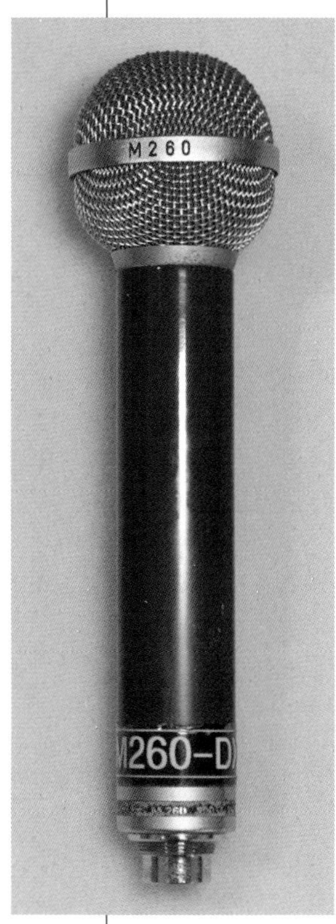

RIGHT: The BBC-designed Coles 4038, originally made in the UK by STC, is a justifiably legendary ribbon mic.
FAR RIGHT: A vintage M260 from Germany's Beyer-Dynamic, another maker of great ribbon mics.

a standard dynamic sounds too dull or a condenser sounds too tinny and detailed. One "bonus quirk" of many types of ribbon mics is that their design, when mounted in the right enclosure, allows them to detect sound waves from both the front and back of the ribbon. For this reason, many have a figure-eight pickup pattern, which is part of what helps them to produce the great live, airy, "in-the-room" response for which they have become famous. In addition, the figure-eight pattern makes many ribbon mics great choices as side mics in mid-side (MS) stereo recording pairs, as discussed in the next chapter, Studio Approach, and some of those that follow.

There are several downsides to ribbon mics, but they can be worked with, or around, for the most part. Many ribbons exhibit a characteristic known as "proximity effect," which puts a greater emphasis on low frequencies the closer you use the mic to the sound source (many mics of other types do this too, but it tends to be more pronounced in ribbons). This means you need to keep them 12 inches (300mm) or more from the sound source in many cases, which can compound the difficulties of "downside number two"—their low output—but is something you would want to do anyway in light of "downside number three"—their fragility. The low output of ribbon mics means you need to use them with a quiet, high-gain preamp in order to achieve acceptable input levels without ramping up the background noise. Such mic pres are out there, but are often not found in the built-in preamps in the average mid-level interface.

The other issue that might limit some recordists' use of ribbon mics is their inherent fragility. Put an old-school ribbon mic too close to the speaker of a loud guitar amp, a snare drum, or certainly a kick drum, and you will stretch or damage it, and very likely blow out that thin aluminum ribbon entirely. Some are so delicate that you wouldn't risk them *anywhere* in front of an amp pushing more than 15 or 20 watts. Also, blow into it, or even carry it too fast across the room without shielding the ribbon from the air pressure, and the same is likely to occur. Likewise drop it, shout into it, hit it with a drumstick ... you get the picture. Many types do not like to have phantom power accidentally applied to them either (as happens when you forget to switch off your mixer or interface or mic preamp's phantom power switch when changing from a condenser mic to a ribbon mic), and this can blow out your ribbon too. Handled carefully, and with full awareness of their limitations, most good ribbon mics can last for decades (and most can be re-ribboned when they don't), but they do require more care than the average dynamic mic. Having said all that, several new ribbon-mic designs seek to address some, and occasionally all, of these limitations, so even these factors are changing as we speak.

What you call the "classic" ribbon mic depends on where in the world you are buying your mics. RCA's model 44 and model 77 are arguably the most legendary US-made ribbons, and are perhaps best known visually for appearing with singers Elvis Presley and Bing Crosby, as well as newsman Edward R. Murrow and talk-show host Johnny Carson. Their rich, full-bodied tone is heard on countless great jazz, crooner, and rock'n'roll recordings, whether you know it or not. And while RCA really rules the roost stateside, Shure also deserves a nod for the 330 (later the SM33), a minor classic, and Electro-Voice made some pretty cool ribbons too. In the UK, Coles has continued to manufacture the BBC-designed 4038 (originally made by STC), known for its use by everyone from The Beatles to Led Zeppelin, not to mention the big horn sections in the BBC orchestras. In Germany, great ribbons take the smaller forms of models like the Beyer-Dynamic M130, M160, M260, M500, and others, which can easily be mistaken for more common ball-end-style dynamic mics. Also worth mentioning is Denmark's Bang & Olufsen, which has produced several great ribbon mics over the years, including the BM5 and BM6.

The Beyers are, conveniently, somewhat more affordable than the major American and British classics, and you can snap up a great-sounding and versatile M160 for a few hundred bucks, while a refurbished RCA 44 or 77 will now cost you easily into the four figures, as will one of the admirable new reproductions from American company AEA, or for that matter, a new Coles 4038. As for vintage-cheapos in ribbonville, you can sometimes get some fun out of old British-made Reslo models, mics probably best known for their live use by The Beatles in their Cavern and Hamburg days. Often a little raw and fluffy sounding, low of output, and perhaps thicker and warmer than you might always like, these Reslos can occasionally be just the ticket for fat vintage-styled guitars or drums, and you can still land them in the $200-$300/£120-£200 ballpark now and then.

The resurgent popularity of the ribbon mic has, however, broadened the field in both pro-quality and budget-level options for purchase new in recent years. Royer arrived in the late 1990s as one of the first new high-quality ribbon-mic makers, and its range has expanded from the R-121, long considered a "modern classic" and a great guitar-amp mic in particular, to a diverse line up of models to suit all kinds of requirements. The R122 is an active ribbon mic that addresses its species's usual low output drawbacks (while the R122V does the same with a tube in the circuit), and several Royer models are capable of withstanding much higher sound pressure levels (SPLs) than traditional ribbon mics. The Russian company Oktava offers many mid-priced ribbon mics, and US maker AEA sells models such as the R84 and R92 that are big, bold sounding ribbons selling for significantly less than the company's RCA repros.

And, naturally, we can thank Asian production once again for an influx of really stunningly cheap new ribbon mics, which can display somewhat random and inconsistent quality, but can often sound surprisingly good. Shop for mics wearing the brands Nady, MXL, Cascade, Alctron, KAM, ART and several others—some of which (as their similar shapes might tell you) are actually made in the same factory—and you can land a stereo pair of ribbons for about a fifth of the price of a quality old-school ribbon mic. Frequently these can even turn out some really gutsy performances as drum overheads or guitar-amp mics in particular, and for relatively little money they can provide some great new colors in the home studio.

Several of these more affordable ribbon mics advertise surprisingly high specs for their SPL-handling capabilities, meaning you can use them up closer to, and with louder, guitar amps than you would normally risk a ribbon mic on. Plenty of engineers have discovered, though, that you can modify them for much greater sensitivity and depth of tone by removing the extra screen and foam padding that is packed into some to make them more robust, which at the same time deadens their response. Search online for "ribbon mic mods" or similar to find the precise procedure for this, and the makes and models to which they apply, but you can often liven up these mics considerably by making a few simple changes. These changes will also expose their delicate ribbons to greater hazards, of course, but handled right, as you would any old-school ribbon mic, the modified budget ribbons should still provide great service, and most recordists will welcome the trade-off for improved fidelity.

ODD MICROPHONES AND ALTERNATIVES

It would be remiss of me to leave our microphone section without mentioning some of the creative alternatives that can occasionally yield useful results. Many recordists have for years made use of the flat, surface-mounting mics known as PZM (pressure zone) or "boundary" mics. These are made by some of the more recognized mic companies, but the most popular, and best bang-for-buck, type was sold for several years by good old Radio Shack (Tandy in the UK), with an element purportedly designed and manufactured by Crown. The Radio Shack PZMs, which originally cost less than $50 new, are powered by a single AA 1.5-volt battery or two shorter 6-volt lithium batteries for a total of 12 volts, giving you improved headroom and fidelity. Several other mods can be found online to further improve them by wiring them to balanced XLR connections, replacing their poor transformers with better components, wiring them to use phantom power, and so on. They work best not as stand-alone mics, but mounted to a broad, flat surface, such as a well behind or ceiling above a drum kit, or a piece of plywood or Plexiglas suspended over a piano or in front of an amplifier. PZMs aren't for every application, but from drum overheads to stereo room mics, they can provide some surprisingly useful results. Other makes are still available for more money, and the preferred older Radio Shack examples can sometimes be found on the used market (often for more than they cost new, thanks to their reputation), but the more recent Radio Shack rendition is intended more for recording spoken voice in conference situations, and really doesn't cut it in the studio.

Following the "found junk" theory that would seem to be the origin of any Radio Shack microphone to have proved itself worthy in a professional studio, there's no harm in trying out other old, odd, or cheap mics that you find in pawn shops, junk yards, garage sales, and bargain bins. As is so often the case, you do tend to get what you pay for in the quality of any microphone's performance, but there are still some little-known items out there of surprising quality that just never caught fire price-wise. The Revox M3500 dynamic mic was, for a time, one such find, until it became common knowledge that this was essentially a Beyer M201 with a few alterations (which make it better for some applications, less desirable for others). Sniff around, and plug in whatever you find—let your ears decide whether it's junk, or a hidden gem.

A memory of a college friend plugging a set of headphones "in reverse" into a stereo cassette deck's mic input to spontaneously record an event also reminds me that you can use many sources that pump out sound to take in sound, too. Fidelity wasn't great in that case, but you can get interesting results by extrapolating this to other uses. Several engineers have achieved their killer punchy kick tracks by placing a 1x12-inch or 1x15-inch speaker cab in front of the kick drum—speaker facing outer drumhead—and running a cable from speaker (*not* amplifier) to a mic preamp and recording the results. Get creative, and you might find you've got a lot more tools to work with than you had previously realized.

Microphone preamps

Technically, a microphone preamp (which I will usually refer to as a "mic pre" or sometimes just "pre" when the "mic" part is obvious) is anything that takes the low-level signal input directly from a microphone and ramps it up to a line-level signal, adding an amount of gain according to where you set the "gain" or "level" knob. As discussed elsewhere, this can be done by a mixer and by many interfaces with built-in mic pres, but as discussed here I will be talking primarily about stand-alone units that specialize in this function.

The most basic mic pre might have nothing more than a knob that you turn up to add a certain number of decibels (dBs) of gain, as required to input a signal of an appropriate level into your interface and thereby your DAW. Most stand-alone mic pres will also include a few extra features, such as a phase-reverse switch, a low-frequency shelving switch to cut the response below a certain frequency point and reduce unwanted boom and rumble from vocals or instruments that don't need to be heard that low, a pad to cut the overall input level of particularly hot mics or loud instruments, a source for phantom power, and possibly more. Connectibility-wise, any useful pre really needs to have a low-impedance XLR mic input (some also have a high-impedance quarter-inch input that you can use to connect other instruments, to use the unit as a bass DI for example), and balanced line-level outputs on XLR and/or quarter-inch stereo TRS jacks, or possibly both of these, including perhaps an unbalanced quarter-inch option.

In the pure sense, the first spec attached to any mic pre that might catch your attention is the one that tells you how much gain it is capable of adding to the signal. Gain levels vary widely, from the 60dB maximum of something like M-Audio's Audio Buddy, to the 75dB max of Art's ProMPA II, to the whopping 84dB max of AEA's TRP. Just 40dB or 50dB might do fine for vocals through a condenser mic, but to use a ribbon mic on anything other than a very loud source, you will find yourself needing a lot more gain, and low noise levels at that—exactly the job the AEA TRP (for "The Ribbon Pre') is designed for, and one that a few others excel at too.

Although a mic pre's primary job is to add gain to the signal, most will inevitably color that signal sonically in one way or another, and that can be part of their charm. Old tube and solid-state classics from Telefunken, Ampex, Altec and others are known for certain "sounds," even though they are designed as gain-providing units and not "effects processors" in and of themselves, and re-boxed channel strips from the likes of Neve are treated like gold bullion by engineers who crave the warmth, depth, and clarity they can give a track. Usable mic pres can be had for much less than the hundreds to thousands of dollars that these command, and there are plenty of decent stand-alones available these days that will provide good service, decent sound, and some useful features. Read the reviews, shop thoroughly and carefully, and discern what might work for your studio.

Compressors and limiters

A compressor's job, on paper at least, is to balance out the levels at different points in any given performance, so that there is, on average, less of a difference between the peaks and the troughs. Compressors are used in many different ways, though, to help balance out the respective levels of different tracks within a mix as a whole, or to smooth out different sections of one track or performance, by pulling down the peaks and lifting the troughs. In actual fact, many compressors also add a little of their own sound while doing so—and occasionally a slight sprinkling of magic that can be difficult to define—so they are often used for these reasons as much as for their basic technical function. A limiter, similarly but somewhat differently, reduces peaks that hit or exceed a predetermined level, to keep tracks from running too hot. Several more complex units will do both: compress an overall signal to your selected parameters, then limit any peaks that threat to overload the signal above and beyond your compression limits.

These essential tools of the studio have been successfully replaced by plenty of great digital processors that are useful to those working entirely "in the box." The convenience of this allows you to record your tracks straight in—mic to pre to interface—then treat them with compression or limiting in the DAW, trying different levels and parameters to see what works, rather than gluing yourself to whatever amount of compression would be applied by an actual unit used inline after the mic pre or mixer during recording. Even if you never intend to own or use a real-life hardware compressor, however, it is worth reading and digesting this section, because the same techniques for using compressors apply whether you are working in the actual or virtual realm.

And having said all that, any reasonably well-equipped home studio should still have a few channels of real-life compression available. To reiterate, you can get by without it in this virtual and digitized world, but some instruments just love to have a little compression applied in the recording process itself—it's almost as if certain situations react *with* the comp, rather than being processed *by* it, and even if you apply more later during mixing, they remain all the better for having been tracked with comp applied. And having said all *that*, it's no good having hardware compressors and limiters unless you know how to use them … which will be covered in more detail at various points later in the book, where their use in tracking specific instruments is discussed.

Compressors do their job by controlling five basic parameters of the signal passing through them: the threshold, compression/expansion ratio, attack, release, and knee. Most will also have two other controls, for "gain" or "level" and "make-up gain"; the first determines how much signal enters the compressor circuitry, the second determines how much gain is added after the circuit to bring back what the compressor took away, in terms of volume (some might have only a single knob marked "gain" or similar, but that will usually function as gain make-up). Many of these parameters will need to be set manually by the user, while some, with certain units, can be achieved automatically.

- The **threshold** setting determines how loud a signal needs to be before the compressor jumps on it and reduces it. This is expressed in dB units. In use, this control can sometimes be confusing, though, since a "high" threshold setting means the compressor will work on less of the overall track and just act upon signal peaks that reach that level. A "low" threshold setting, conversely, means the compressor will jump on anything that reaches that lower dB level.

- The **ratio** determines how much the compressor lowers the upper-level signals, or raises the lower-level signals. This is expressed as exactly that, a ratio: 2:1 would be very gently compression, for example, for something like vocals or acoustic guitar; 6:1 or 10:1 would provide heavier squash for drums or bass, or maybe a heavily distorted electric guitar.

- The **attack** rate determines how quickly the compressor acts on a signal that exceeds the threshold setting. This really needs to be adjusted by ear according to the general "punchiness" or "smoothness" (in broad terms) of the track you are compressing. Most advice advocates starting with the fastest attack available, and slowing it down gradually until you hear the results you are looking for (which often means getting it to results you are *not* looking for, then backing it off a little).

- The **release** setting determines how quickly the compressor lets go of the signal after it has acted upon it. Here, a medium release setting is usually the best starting point, to avoid excessive "pumping" sounds in the track, and adjust from there according to the characteristics of what you are compressing.

- The **knee** setting is usually simply a switch that gives you "soft" or "hard," but is one of the parameters that is more likely to be automatic on many compressors. Easily confused with attack, this "knee" (imagine a line drawn to the angle of a sharply bent, or only slightly bent, knee) determines how gradually (soft) or quickly (hard) the compressor reduces the level of the signal. That is, attack time tells the compressor how quickly to grab a signal, while knee tells it whether that signal should be ramped down sharply or gradually once it has been grabbed. Setting here will depend on the feel and pulse of the track.

- **Gain** and **make-up gain** controls are there to let you achieve a suitable level going into and out of the compression circuitry. Some units have both, although many smaller compressors have only one, to make up the gain after it has been compressed, so you are still sending an adequate signal on to your recording device. These don't determine the compression parameters as such, but turning up a pre-gain control will sometimes get the compressor working harder, since it will show the circuit a hotter signal; simultaneously, however, it can also induce distortion in the circuit. On vintage-style compressors (and units that emulate those characteristics), the gain circuitry can often still be part of the "sound" and personality of a compressor, adding depth or warmth or richness to the signal, apart from the effects of the compression itself.

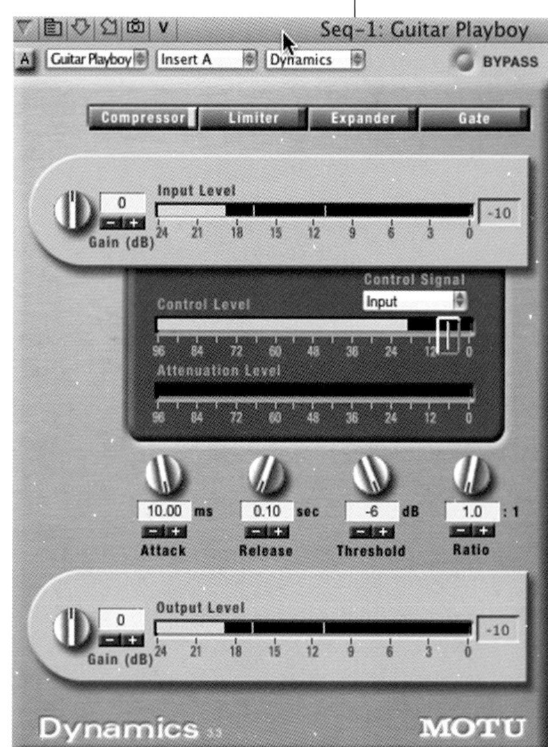

A standard compressor plug-in, this one the Dynamics unit included in the MOTU DAW bundle.

Using a compressor well can definitely be something of a black art, and you really need to spend some time with it, as applied to your music, to get the hang of it. The ideal is to find settings where the compressor is doing its job of smoothing out the peaks and troughs so it improves the overall sound of the track, without killing the dynamics, but isn't heard so much as a "pumping" or "breathing" effect that overtly alters the track as a whole… unless you want it to. A compressor definitely can kill the dynamics in a track when used poorly, and it can be surprisingly easy to get into this habit. Unless a track has some really extreme peaks that need taming, light compression is generally better than heavy compression, and no compression is almost always better than extreme compression.

Some engineers advocate starting with extreme settings, however—a high ratio, a fast release, and a fairly sensitive threshold—so you can hear these effects working on your music while you adjust the attack setting to suit, because the effect of attack adjustments can otherwise often be difficult to hear. Then, they say, when the attack is where you want it, put the other parameters back to more sensible, more musical settings.

Most new compressors will come with some useful instruction on how to use them (such manuals are worth reading, for a change), and there is plenty of good advice out there in that ethereal realm known as "online" too. Also, some hardware compressors, and almost all digital plug-in compressors, will have presets for use on specific program material: vocals, guitars, drums, bass, overall mix. These can be extremely handy, for the beginner especially, but ultimately you should try to listen to what each individual parameter is doing to the sound of your track, and work toward adjusting them manually for the best and most desirable sound. Or, use presets as a starting point, note where they set different parameters for different types of material, and then adjust each a little in each direction to hear what that does to the track. Most plug-in compressors will let you re-save your adjusted factory presets as "user presets" for instant recall on another occasion.

A limiter is much like a compressor, but typically has higher ratio levels, and is often ideally used with a high threshold setting so only the peaks are squashed severely. Heavy limiting of an entire track with a low threshold setting will usually result in a severe obliteration of your dynamic range, and is not usually desirable.

Reverbs, delays, and other outboard effects

From the 80s well into the 90s, studio racks were often dominated by nifty new digital reverbs and delays, while any longstanding professional facility would also have tended to retain its big, clunky analog outboard units from the 60s and 70s. Even when the digital recording age dawned, in the form of digital multi-track tape machines that operated in real time, and were mixed through traditional, physical, mixing desks, powerful outboard reverbs, delays, EQs, and the like remained essential tools of the trade. These days, whether you are mixing entirely in your DAW, or running some or all of your tracks out to a physical mixer and back again, you are likely to get better sounds, better fidelity, and more options from quality reverb and delay plug-ins than you are by running your tracks through analog into an outboard digital unit and then back into digital again. Unless you can afford the best professional-quality units, the bit rates of many outboard digital processors will be inferior to those of the software versions stored in your computer, and they will almost certainly induce more noise, too. If a rack-mounted unit has a sound that you happen to love, and which you can't achieve otherwise, sure, go for it, but chances are your life will be easier, and your tracks sound better, if you keep that stuff "in the box.".

For that reason, the outboard processors that today's home studio *is* likely to use are very often going to be old, possibly esoteric analog gear that provides a sound that really can't be achieved by a plug-in. Which is to say, if you are going out of the box and into the analog realm, you really might as well go all the way. To that end, plenty of recordists make great use of funky old effects units that would mostly have been left to gather dust in studios 25 years ago when everyone was obsessed with their fancy new digital toys (and when so many recordings came out sounding that way, too).

Analog spring and plate reverbs, analog delays based on bucket-brigade chips (common in the late 70s and early 80s) and both solid-state and tube tape echoes made before them, funky discrete EQs, and other such processors can add a lot of character to an otherwise wholly digital recording, and many of the bigger studios still tend to rely on several of these for character, even when they are recording to, and mixing from, digital hard drives and setting up most of their mix parameters in Pro Tools. If you plan to experiment with mixing out of the box, keep an eye out for such devices, or press into service such units that you might already be using as guitar effects. Or, if you want to keep your mixes entirely in your DAW but like the idea of printing some real-life analog effects into the final results, you can run individual channels out via your interface and through whatever reverb or delay you like, and back into the DAW to be recorded alongside the original track as "auxiliary" tracks. Then, in the final mix, blend in as much of the effected version of the track as is necessary to achieve your desired sound.

CHAPTER 3

STUDIO APPROACH

With your studio set-up and hardware covered, it's important to put some thought into basic studio approach before launching into recording. It's relatively easy to buy the gear—if you have the cash—and to follow instructions for laying it all out, but the real work comes when you get down to actually using it to record music.

Too often, newcomers to the craft will equip themselves well, and get their room ship-shape and ready to go, then be struck by a numbing sense of, "Okay, now how the hell do we begin this process?" The answer is, of course, that there are several different ways to approach a recording session. The one that is right for you will be determined by your circumstances, and it's very likely you will use a number of different approaches to recording in the course of any one project.

Techniques for placing mics to best capture each live instrument will be covered in detail in the following chapters, although we will lay the groundwork for some standard configurations later in this chapter. Our discussion of studio approach here, though, will mostly take the form of examining ways of working together in the studio to effectively and efficiently lay down the tracks that constitute a "song." This process is called "tracking," and it is done in a number of different ways.

Tracking rhythm instruments together

Perhaps the most common approach used in studios today involves tracking rhythm instruments together at the start of any session—guitar, bass, drums—primarily with the aim of capturing workable drum tracks. Along with these three, a "guide vocal" is usually laid down to help the musicians remember their way through the song and play with the right feel.

Often such sessions will be approached with the notion that you will also come away with usable bass and rhythm-guitar tracks (and perhaps some vocals, although that's a trickier proposition). But, while this might be possible in a professional studio, several factors can make it difficult to manage this with any practicality in the home studio. If you want rough'n'ready live studio recordings, with both the spontaneity and all the rough edges that these usually entail, you should approach your tracking as such, as described more precisely further along in this section. But if your goal is to achieve good, solid, professional-sounding studio tracks with decent isolation on each instrument, it's usually best to focus on the drums and not expect to walk away with much else from your first sessions, other than the guide tracks (or "scratch" tracks) that will enable you to find your way in the song when you get down to overdubbing later. Four times out of five when I have tried to get good "live" drum, bass and guitar tracks together in the initial tracking sessions, with the hopes of keeping them all, I ended up needing to overdub the bass and rhythm guitar later anyway, and was left working with less-than-ideal drum takes as a result. Several factors conspire against such efforts:

- Most home studios will have limited facilities for truly isolating instruments. Even if you can achieve decent isolation by putting your bassist and guitarist (and vocalist, if the person laying down the guide is another band member) in different rooms from the drummer, you aren't likely to have a means of maintaining visual contact during tracking, a detriment to successful recording, and to getting a "band" feel in your tracks.

- You're unlikely to have adequate facilities for monitoring yourselves in different, perhaps distant rooms.

- Few home studios have vast collections of mics, and the majority of the best mics in the cupboard will be used to get good drum tracks. Sacrificing one or two of these to capture good guitar tracks usually means compromising your drum tracks right out of the gate.

- Compromising your mic selection, when options are limited, also means getting an inferior guitar sound to that which you would ideally achieve in a separate, properly isolated tracking session.

Now, if you go into this with a full awareness of the limitations of the approach, and still want to track these instruments (and any others) together in what will be a "semi-live" session, with others overdubbed later, that's fine too. A lot of bands do enjoy such an approach for the lively, "playing as a band" feel that it can lend to a recording. I would argue that you can achieve these same qualities by tracking instruments separately, because you are at least playing together in the first place, even if you will re-take bass and guitar later, but whatever works for you works.

To make this process work as suggested, you use your best suitable mics on the drums, and DI both the bass and the guitar to avoid any spill from other instruments into the drum mics. Even if the main rhythm track for your song will ultimately be an acoustic guitar, use an electric for the scratch track, for this very reason. If possible, use a good DI-capable processor like a Line 6 POD or other digital amp and FX emulator to give your guitar sound a little oomph, which will help the drummer play better than a dry, thin, old-school DI'd guitar straight into the board. Set up whatever cheap mic you have left for a guide vocal, and place the singer at the far side of the room from the drums, facing the drummer so that he or she is more likely to be out of the drum mics' pick-up zone. If necessary, construct a little baffle of sorts out of some cardboard that you hang around the guide-vocal mic (if you're using a standard dynamic mic, which is fine for guide vocals, just punch a hole in a thick cardboard disc about a foot-and-a-half/450mm in diameter, and slip the mic through it before setting it on the clip). In any case, instruct your singer not to belt it out with full gusto, but to sing close in on the mic and tone it down a little volume-wise, providing vocals as a guide rather than a performance. You

RECORD, CHECK, TWEAK, RECORD ...

The processing of honing any mic set-up into something usable can be extremely labor-intensive, but this is where you do a lot of your hand-on learning, too. Record, listen, adjust, record again, listen again ... it can go on and on, but by trial and error—the only way to really build your miking experience—you will narrow it all down to the positions that work best for you for different instruments and different situations. Far more often than not there is no "best" way of doing a thing, but you still need to make choices about what sounds "better" to you. And, after making those choices, you eventually need to get on with the job of recording. It's important to get the best sound you can at the start of a session, but you can also go on tweaking and repositioning forever if you're not careful, and eventually nothing will sound good enough to be getting on with.

The compounding difficulty is that you really won't know if your fully tweaked-out drum mic set-up, for example, works for the song or songs in question until you put down some more instruments to hear it with; and you won't really know how your starting point succeeded until you have finished and mixed the entire tune. That's the Catch 22 of recording in general, sadly: you have to start somewhere, but it's impossible to know whether your starting point is the best first step in the road you eventually hope to go down until you have reached the end of that road, at which point it is too late to change it. Or, to correct that, perhaps it's only impossible to know this when you are starting out in the craft; over time, you build a repertoire of drum (or guitar, or vocal, or whatever) techniques that you know to work well in different situations, so you are more in the position of making educated guesses than stabs in the dark. As one studio engineer in London phrased it while I was mixing a project several years ago, "Recording is a game of infinite variables." That sums it up, and even when you have all the experience in the world you still have to make some difficult choices mid-process, and move on.

Before you have acquired the sort of empirical knowledge necessary to enable educated decisions (call them "half guesses" if you prefer), it's a good idea to work ahead somewhat—cheat ahead, if you will. Record a little guitar and bass in a more considered manner final form, ideally some vocals, too, and some keyboards or whatever other tracks the song requires to start sounding "complete," rather than just trying to judge the drums against the rough DI'd tracks that were used as guides for the drummer to play along with. This might mean breaking down a few of the drum mics and miking up an amp for a few takes, then setting up your best vocal mic, and so forth. Even if you know you will do all of this again later in its final and improved form, testing your drums alongside some good-quality tracks from other instruments will let you go back and tweak them now, before it's too late, if they really just aren't working.

want the feel of a band playing to the vocal, certainly, but you don't want to end up with scratch vocals audible in the drum overheads, which will inevitably be out of sync with the final vocal you lay down later.

As much as space allows, keep your bassist and guitarist as far as possible from the drummer, but within easy lines of sight, so the acoustic jangle and slap of electric and bass guitars don't rattle away at the back of the drum tracks. Musicians should sit or stand as preferred, whatever makes them the most comfortable and brings out the best performance. Remember, you are here to get the best drum takes that you can, for these initial sessions at least, so you want to favor your drums—and drum sounds—in all matters at this juncture. Ensure your drummer has the best possible mix in his headphones, and if your system only allows for one monitor mix, let it favor the drummer's requirements rather than those of others playing the scratch tracks at this time. Also, do what you can to keep the drummer from getting tired: it is usually worth plowing through the full length of a song in your first take, even if a few mistakes are made early on, so the drummer, and everyone else, can start getting a feel for it; once you get rolling and seem close to nailing "keepers," however, stop and go again if any major goofs are committed in the earlier sections of the track.

Having said that, though, if things are going well and a minor mistake or two are made a good way into an otherwise great take, push on—you can account for that through the convenience of digital editing (see "Tips and tricks for digital tracking," p62), and save everyone some time and effort. The key is to nail the best overall feel and performance for the song, and if the feel is right but there are a couple of glitches in an otherwise stellar performance, you can repair those after the fact.

Once you get the drum takes you're happy with, you will move on to overdubbing other instruments, as discussed below. Most likely that will occur in another session, unless you are only recording a song or two, and have time to move on to other stages in the process right away. Often, bands will record all their drum (and basic rhythm) tracks in a series of sessions over the course of a number of days, and start building them up with overdubs only after that is finished. The alternative approach, though, of tracking a day's worth of drums, then moving on to a few crucial overdubs, then back to drums for the next series of four or five songs, often works well. Doing things this way can sometimes help other band members maintain the feel and momentum for a set of songs, rather than waiting several days or even weeks before getting down to their own "keeper" parts, and can sometimes result in better energy and dynamics, and overall performances, in the final songs.

Building songs to a click track

Another way to build up your songs is to lay down master vocal and rhythm-guitar tracks to a click track, and overdub other instruments to that foundation in whatever order

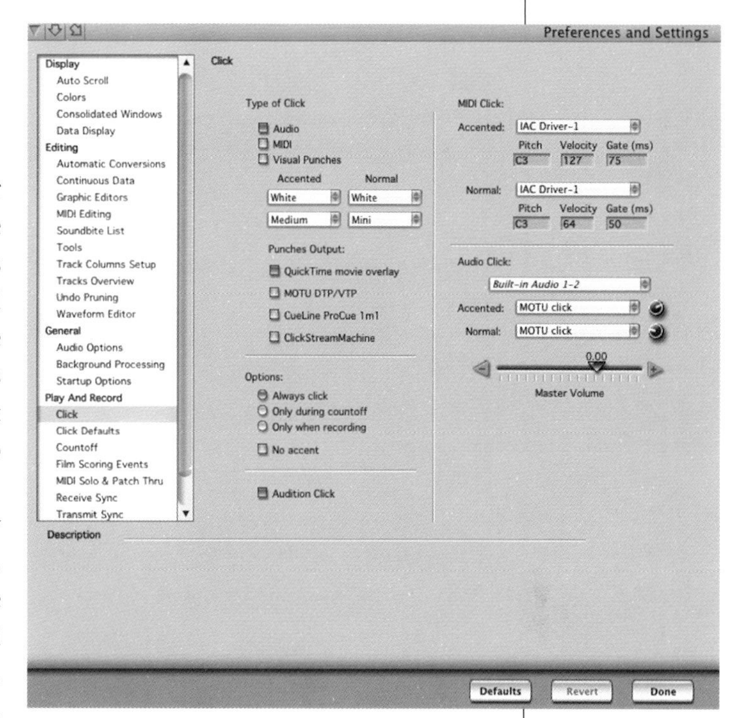

All DAWs these days should offer a click track function, usually with a range of parameters for sound and time signature, as seen in Digital Performer's click window.

proves most conducive to a good end result, or simply most convenient. Producers have worked this way for years, and this process is sometimes used because an artist wants to nail down the main gist of a song while the creative juices are flowing, or sometimes simply because it isn't possible to get the right session drummers and others into the studio to do things differently.

In the past, an engineer would simply record a click to a track of multi-track tape, and everyone else would work to that as the overdubbing process proceeded. Digital recording makes this process even easier today, since you can set a steady tempo in your DAW, bring the audible click in and out as desired (using different click tones, too, from cowbells to blocks to sticks to hi-hats), and even edit the final results in precise blocks that are locked to that embedded click tempo.

Opponents of "playing to a click" will argue that this process can hurt the dynamics and overall feel of a song, and sometimes that might be true, but when it's done well, no one ever needs to know that you built the song up from a click. The benefit to the home recordist, who is also frequently the singer/songwriter and principal musician of the project, is that you can get right down to recording master takes while the creative juices are flowing, rather than waiting until you can get your band together.

The user's guide to your DAW will tell you how to set and adjust a click for your session. Once you have the right tempo, and have played along some to ensure that fact, you might also want to add some other simple percussion or drum loops to fill out the rhythmic momentum a little further, rather than just playing to the thin mechanical click, which sometimes can easily be lost in the headphones when you start putting some gusto into your take. The order in which you build up your tracks from here, when working to a lead vocal laid down to a click, really depends on a number of factors. Ideally, though, you want to have the bass down before your drummer comes in, and the drums down before your bassist comes in. Huh? Well, that would be the ideal, although it is clearly impossible. But the point is that the bass and drums should work together in any recording—any performance, really—and ideally each needs a little of the other in order to attain the right feel for the song. If possible, you can have your bassist and drummer playing together, with the bass DI'd so there's no interference with the drum mics. You might come away with a bass part you can use, but aim to nail the drums first and foremost, and the bass can more easily be overdubbed at a later date if it needs improvement. You can also "re-amp" the bass later (which will be covered in the Recording Bass chapter) if you want some genuine amp sound, without the noise of using an amp while tracking drums.

When building tracks around a click, you can even take the whole theory of drum recording apart somewhat, too, if it helps you get where you're going. Consider laying down a kick part first, which can be played "live" to the click and backing tracks, or created in a loop, then you can overdub the rest of the kit after. This might be a fairly mechanical-seeming means of working, and as such might suit more mechanical music, but it's another way of getting things done, and of achieving a no-worries kick track that is utterly tight to the groove.

Tracking "live in the studio"

If you really want to go all out for the live-in-the-studio feel, and who cares about the bleed, there are some good ways to maximize your chances here. First up for consideration is whether you really want live lead vocals going down, too (and backing vocals?), and if so, you will have to get vocal mics and drum mics (and drums and vocals and guitar amps) all away from each other. That means achieving some form of isolation, by using different rooms of the house, and very likely resorting to audible cues through your monitor headphones, rather than visual cues, to count in, and signal any breaks or breakdowns, and so forth. Working this way makes the entire experience a little trickier, although it can be done.

If you have the luxury of a space that you have converted into something a little more like a professional studio of old, with windows between rooms to maintain visual contact, that's a great plus. Otherwise, move any singing band members out of the drum room, dampen down reflective sound as best you can—drums have a way of finding their way down halls and around corners and under doors and into hot vocal mics one way or another—and give it your best shot. You can also isolate guitar and bass and keyboard amps in separate rooms or closets, or at least build up little isolation enclosures with sound baffles and mattresses and blankets, to minimize their bleed as much as possible.

Experiment with your set-up before running any takes, and try to devise a system that lets everyone work comfortably. You don't want to be so constrained by the limitations of your chosen method of working that the mutual discomfort constrains the live and dynamic feel that you hoped to obtain by working this way in the first place. Get the entire band comfortable, and comfortably hearing each other, run a few partial takes with everyone in, and listen back—setting up a rough mix as you do so—to hear whether your system will work at all, before committing a lot of time and effort to tape.

If you want to go for the genuine all-in-one-room live recording, you will most likely need to forego a usable vocal, but you might achieve a sizzling, exciting band take. You will undoubtedly need to obtain, or construct, some solid sound baffles (or "gobos" in studio parlance) and position them carefully to block certain sounds from specific rival mics at least, and even then you won't come close to eliminating the guitars from popping up in the drum overheads and the snare from cracking in the guitar mic, and so forth. But, with everything set up optimally, and a great, dynamic performance besides (which, let's face it, is the key a great song, however you record it), you should get enough isolation in each instruments' close mics to put them where you want them in the final mix, and some happening room sound from other instruments that aren't supposed to be in those mics, but by doing so will contribute that live sound and feel that you are seeking.

When recording like this, you really need to be aware of the pick-up patterns of each of your mics, and use any sound-rejection capabilities therein to minimize bleed. For example, set a guitar combo at the far side of the room from the drums, behind a baffle if possible, and with its cardioid close mic positioned at an angle that rejects as much of the drums as possible, while the guitar cab is also rejected as much as possible by its angle relative to that of the respective drum mics. Proceed with these principles in mind while setting up anything and everything that either makes sound or captures sound, and you stand a chance of succeeding. And in the end, if you still get a little spill here and there—which, inevitably, you will—don't sweat it. If the feel and drive of the performances are right, you have won the game.

Recording this way also requires a larger selection of mics. If you only have enough to adequately record the drums in the first place, you will have to borrow or buy a few more, unless you want to DI all other instruments, which, I would argue, defeats the effort of recording live in the first place. Decide which of your better mics really need to be used where to achieve the results you require, and which instruments can make do with something a little less, and get down to it. Oh, and if you really need to record acoustic guitar or acoustic piano or any other softer acoustic instruments as part of this live-in-the-studio scenario, you might have to break with the one-room effort, and at least set this up through another doorway or around a corner, to stand any hopes of adequate isolation.

Overdubbing

The process of overdubbing might seem rather self-explanatory, but a little guidance will help you get it all done more efficiently. "Overdubbing" is the name applied to the process of recording a new track to tracks that were recorded previously, whether that was the day before, or last year. If you are building up your song by starting with a lead vocal and rhythm guitar part performed to a click track, your entire band will be pieced together by overdubbing. If you are starting with the most common method, the first detailed above, where drums, bass, and rhythm guitar are laid down first, you might

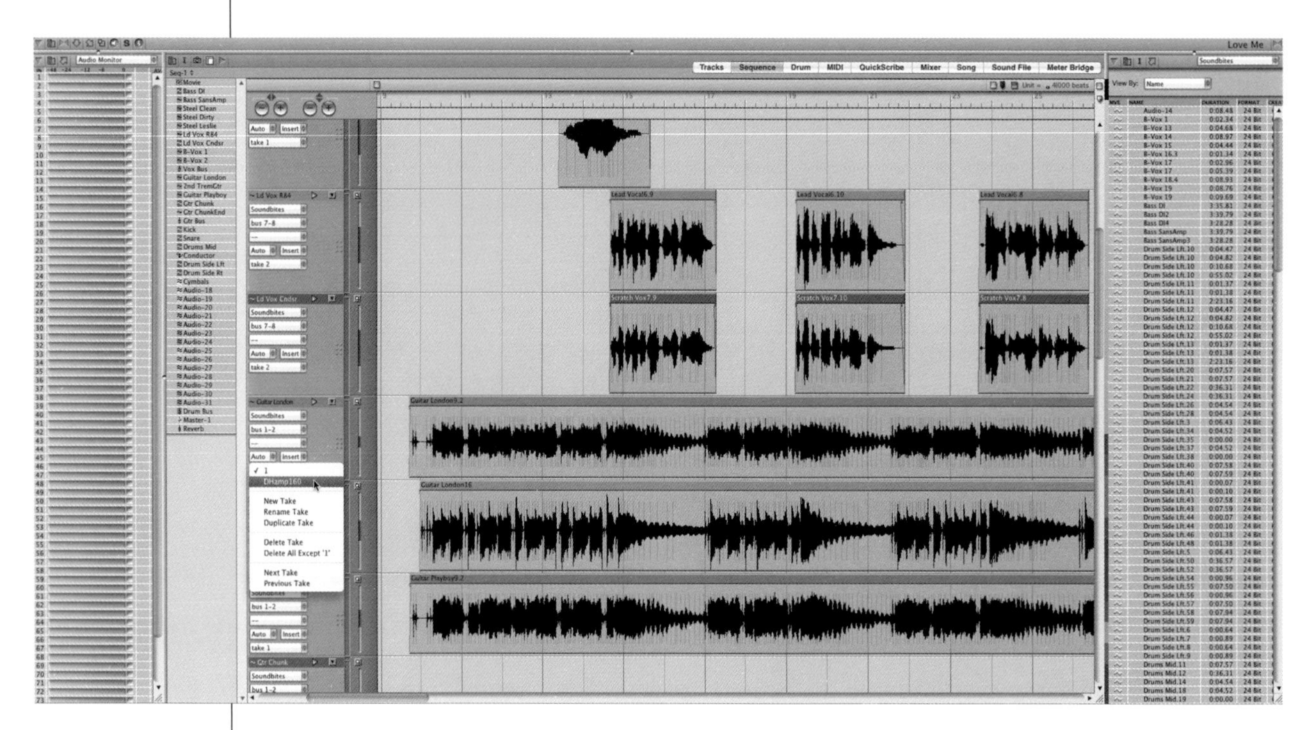

Selecting an alternate take lets you overdub a track without erasing what has already been recorded there.

overdub to replace the bass and guitar parts if you need to improve these, or if the originals are good enough, to add extra layers of rhythm guitar, lead guitar, lead and backing vocals, and keyboards and whatever else your song might require.

The current digital technology makes overdubbing a breeze, and gives you a lot more freedom to try different sounds and different approaches, too. Back in the day when the professional standard was 16 tracks of reel-to-reel tape, and then even 24 tracks, you could run out of space surprisingly quickly once you got down five to seven tracks of drums, a track or two of bass, a couple of rhythm guitars, keyboards, and needed to save a track for lead vocals and a couple for backing vocals. By the time you got around to overdubbing guitar solos, you were lucky to have even two tracks to alternate between, and had to start making creative decisions early on in the process. These days, most DAWs offer near-infinite "takes" within each track, which can be recorded with the same track settings without erasing your initial take. You can try and try again to perfect that part, and choose the best—or even best bits—of several and patch them together (a process called "comping") without ever destroying any of the tracks attempted before. The inherent restrictions of gear available in "the good old days" did impose, however, a degree of discipline that is worth retaining today, when possible. No doubt it can often require several takes to get a part right, particularly a lead vocal or a crucial solo, but the availability of infinite space in which to work at this can lead some people to put off crucial creative decisions that will need to be made eventually. It's great to have all those alternate takes available, sure, but if you need 10 or 20 or 30 to nail down your solo, it might be better just to take the track out of record, take a breather, and *play* for a while to figure out what you really want to do with it, rather than hoping to hit it lucky without putting in much thought or effort or making any difficult choices.

Another beauty of the power afforded by most DAWs today is that you can, for example, record all three mics of your great-sounding three-mic set up for the lead guitar track to different tracks and blend them together later in the mixing (or pre-mixing) process. Back in the day, you usually would have needed to mix these down to a single track to tape, making that creative choice early in the process. Again, there's something to be said for the way such a decision-making deadline was imposed on the process by the limitations of the equipment, but it's a great advantage to be able to tweak your final multi-track overdub parts later in the mixing process, when you can hear them in the full context of the completed song.

One potential stumbling block of the efficient new digital systems is that the speed with which you can scroll back and run your take again and again can potentially lead to a little more "red light fatigue" in the performer. Even though the contemporary DAW makes it possible to blast through take after take with virtually no pause between efforts, let your performer (or yourself, if you are playing and recording) take a breath between takes, if desired. Pause to stretch and refresh your thinking a bit, maybe even just listen back on the monitors without trying to play anything, to get a new perspective on whatever it is that's giving you difficulty.

As for the practicalities of overdubbing, the main requirement is a good set of fully enclosed headphones. These will let you hear the tracks you are playing, and hear your own performance mixed in accordingly, without too much of the external sound getting in the way. Enclosed headphones will also keep the monitor mix of the backing tracks inside your head, so it doesn't bleed into the mic that's recording your current takes. It's a good idea to pause and listen back to any take on the main monitors every so often, to make sure the sound you have set up, and the performance, sits right in the rough mix, but be sure to silence those monitors again before recording further takes, unless you have the luxury of a separate control room with good sound isolation from your live room. If, however, like most of us, you are recording and manning the controls in the same room, the person at the desk should also have a good set of enclosed headphones on and dialed in to the mix to monitor the process.

Alternatively, if you do have the benefit of a separate control room—or at least have a good closet in which to put an amp for an instrument overdub, or can easily run cables down the hall and under a closed door to a bathroom or bedroom—monitoring overdubs through the main speakers *while recording* can sometimes be a great way to work. Test it out, and see if you get much spill from the monitored tracks in the mic you are recording to. If your mic is at least one room away, chances are that any spill will be minimal, and so little, if any, that you can work with it without really hearing its presence in the final mix. Taking the headphones off and playing to a good rough mix in a decent set of speakers can sometimes prove a much more comfortable way of working and can help to ease the claustrophobia that some performers feel when they strap on the cans.

Tips and tricks for digital tracking

Many tips and tricks will be addressed in individual chapters dedicated to specific instruments, and many more still in the Mixing chapter. But I want to lay down a little of the philosophy of digital recording now, so you start getting your head around it even before you work through the entire book. If you first got your feet wet in recording back in the analog days, as I did, or have any preconceptions about recording that are grounded in "the way they used to do it," making the most of digital recording requires a major shift both in mindset and working practices. In short, you need to remember that almost anything can be fixed, and usually in a way that will be undetectable to the listener. There are so many aspects to this that it will be impossible to cover them all here, or even elsewhere in this book, but let me offer a few examples of what I'm talking about. Hopefully you can extrapolate from that to discover countless applications of your own.

The beauty of Pro Tools—or any other comprehensive modern DAW—is that you never have to scrap an otherwise smoking whole-band (or drum-tracking) take because your drummer fluffed just a single tom hit in the roll leading into the bridge. In the past, single-instrument overdubs were easily fixable by punching in and out for very short segments of a take, sure, but rarely would an engineer attempt to punch into five or more drum mics and a guitar, bass and guide vocals all at once. In any decent DAW, though, saving that "nearly perfect" take is a breeze. Here's what you do:

- If you aren't playing with a click in the first place, scroll back to a point shortly before the fluff and play it back to let your drummer get a precise tempo reading lodged in his head.

- Then, scroll all the way to the *end* of the entire song, fire up "record" for all relevant tracks, and tell the drummer to count it in from a relevant section before the one that you need to replace (any place that let's the performers get back into the groove—the previous chorus, verse, whatever precedes the re-take section).

- After successfully re-recording just that section, you select and copy all tracks of the replacement section, then select the fluffed section, and paste over it.

To make it all work seamlessly, ensure that you select precisely the same start and end points for your copied and replaced sections, and, because human tempo always fluctuates slightly, you might even want to select and remove the fluffed section first, and drag the original sections of the tracks after the mistake a little further back in the editing window, then select and copy the replacement tracks, paste them into the gap, and drag everything into place until it all buts up tightly. Zoom way, way in on your soundbites, and pull the crossfades of each so there's no "click" as the playhead rolls past the pasted-in section. Note: You can use a "select all" function to draw all crossfades at once, but sometimes you can make these pastes even more seamless by scrolling the cut points of different tracks to different places, and cross fading them individually. That is, when you're editing digitally, your "paste"—today's form of punch-in—doesn't have to form a straight line right down the editing window: it might be advantageous to a cymbal crash to cross fade the overheads at a different point than you do the kick and snare, for example, to take best advantage of the differing attack and decay of each instrument.

In the same way, you can try several different endings to a song and decide later which one best fits the feel of the track, without playing the entire thing again just to get the ending right. Or even alter the way the drums come in, run takes for a few alternatives to the drum pattern in the bridge or a breakdown, or whatever. The sky's the limit. Even when you're not recording to a click track, a good live read on the tempo and jumping back into the part while you've still got the feel in your head will almost always result in alternative parts and fixes that you can paste in later without any final listener ever hearing the difference.

Pasting in a new, corrected, drum ending in Pro Tools, and linking it all seamlessly by "drawing" crossfades at the joint between sections.

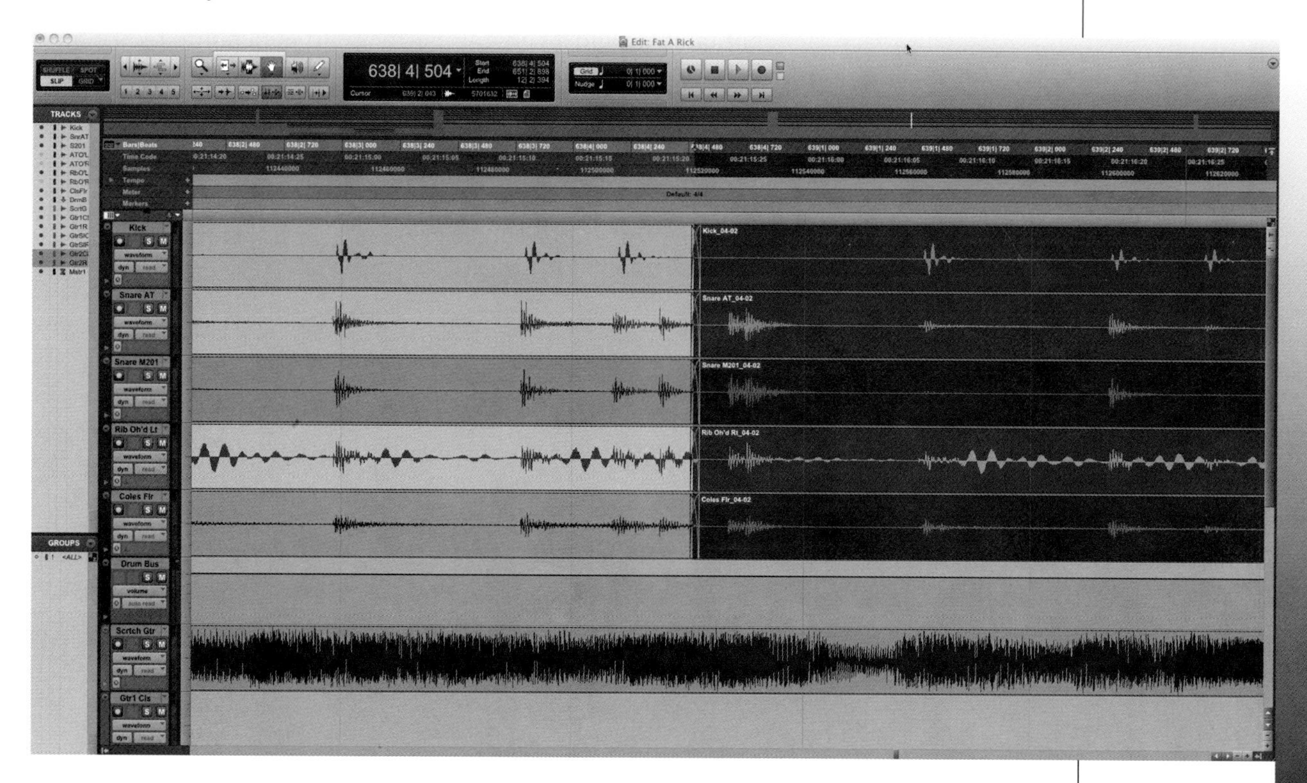

THE DIFFERENT "TRACKS" AVAILABLE IN THE DAW

The word "track" can have several meanings in the music world. We use it to refer to complete songs, or as a verb meaning "to record an instrument," or as the designation for one of many individual tracks on a multi-track tape or multi-track digital audio recording, and so forth. When referring to the tracks in a session in any conventional digital audio workstation, however, the term is attached to one of a handful of very specific meanings. Most DAWs offer five types of track, which can be loaded into the editing window (and, consequently, its mixer) according to the needs of your session. The main types, and their functions, are:

Audio track: a track to which audio is recorded in any manner, whether from DI or microphone, or a track into which previously recorded (or sometimes sampled) audio is pasted or imported. If you are recording directly to a track, its input should be set to the interface or soundcard input to which the microphone (or mic pre) or DI is connected for recording. Its output will go either to a bus that routes the signal to an auxiliary track (as below), often with a group of similar instruments, or to the main stereo outs of the mix. Audio tracks also have their own "inserts" for plug-ins. They usually also have "sends" that can route the signal elsewhere, usually to an effect on an auxiliary track, without removing it from the main output of the audio track itself.

Auxiliary track: a "secondary track," useful for a number of different functions, from carrying effects plug-ins to which several different audio tracks might be routed via their effects sends, to providing a "sub-master fader" of sorts (along with any desired plug-ins) for a group of similar tracks routed in a "bus." The input to an aux track will usually be designated as a mono or stereo bus track that receives the output or a "send" signal from one or more audio tracks, while its output will usually be the main stereo outs of your mix, unless it is routed to a further aux track for additional treatment.

MIDI track: used to carry MIDI information that is recorded or entered into it to trigger the sound of a MIDI instrument. A MIDI track has no "sound" of its own, but essentially just carries code that tells a MIDI hardware or plug-in instrument what notes to play. Its input can come from an external MIDI controller, and its output will go either to an instrument track in the DAW (see below) or an external MIDI instrument, to be triggered during 'play' mode.

Instrument track: somewhat misleadingly, an instrument track is used to carry a digital plug-in instrument in the DAW, such as a software keyboard or drum program, rather than an instrument that you have recorded to it. These tracks can be used in different ways: the input might come from a MIDI track intended to trigger it, or it might be "played" with

ABOVE LEFT: the five basic track types side by side in Pro Tools's mixer. RIGHT: selecting a plug-in from Digital Performer's insert menu.

the computer mouse and/or keystrokes of the computer keyboard. Its output will go either to an audio track for recording a "live" performance of the plug-in instrument during tracking, or to the main outputs if it is being triggered by pre-recorded MIDI information, or it might also go to an aux track for further processing.

Master track (fader): much as it sounds, a master track—sometimes called "master fader"—is a track that governs the overall level of all other tracks, and is a means of controlling the output of the mix as a whole. Frequently these also have inserts for master-bus plug-ins, processors that are used to treat the entire mix. A master track will usually have no input as such, and should always be the main stereo pair that constitutes the output of your mix; the main stereo outs are also the master fader's output.

Further information on the specific functions of these tracks should be available in the user's manual with your own particular DAW. More advanced products will usually offer more complex functions and routing facilities, but most should have tracks that resemble these basic templates, to some extent at least.

For individual tracks that need a little fix—what would have been the old school "punch in/punch out" as discussed above—you don't even need to drop in on the original track: just cue up another track (or flip to a virtual take beneath the original) and run that. This lets you play engineer and musician simultaneously without having to try to hit the "record" button then get back to your instrument in a split second, and out again at the end of the passage. Another benefit of doing your fixes on an entirely new track or take is that you can also play more than just the few bars that need re-doing, and possibly get a better overall take, or at least some sections elsewhere that you also prefer to the original. When you get it the way you want it, simply lock the two tracks to the same point in your time line, and copy and paste in the new section(s).

Even with all the power afforded by digital editing, however, it is still always worth trying to capture the best performance, rather than thinking you can fix everything during the editing and/or mixing process. I have spent hours working, for example, to move portions of drum tracks to line them up better with the feel of the song, when it would have been quicker to get the drummer back in for a few takes just to play the damned thing right—and you can bet the feel would ultimately be better than that of the heavily pieced-together take, too. Still, sometimes you have no choice but to fix it after the fact, and digital editing is a great tool when you need it.

Also, as handy as these fixes are, you are likely to retain the best drive and dynamic sense in a part when you use digital editing to comp together alternate parts that are played well in the first place, rather than to construct a passable take from otherwise sloppy performances. Having said all that, there is nothing wrong with editing together a series of great performances to construct a whole that is better than the sum of its parts. A lot of musicians still have a certain bias against "Pro Tools recording," and the "cheat" of editing together different stellar moments from a selection of takes. But hey, you played those stellar moments in the first place, right? If you had all the time in the world, and were being paid to record—as so few of us are these days—you would have learned those stellar moments and eventually nailed them in one take. In the real world, we rarely have that kind of time or resources available to us today as independent musicians, so there's nothing wrong with taking your moments of magic and creating a stunning track from them.

The truth is, musicians have long done it this way, and certainly did so back in the "good old days"; also, at least the track comped from the best parts of several takes is likely to retain some spontaneity in the whole, which is probably what resulted in those stellar moments in the first place. Work with that, accept it. Learning all the "best bits" and finally playing them in a one-take solo might have you so worn out by the time you nail it that you find you have lost the drive and dynamics in your performance, even if you have captured the riffs and melodic directions you were seeking. When constructing a track in this way, though, you still want it to have the flow and direction of a considered performance, rather than being a stitched-together string of somewhat random best bits. Unless that's what you're aiming for.

Microphone pick-up patterns

Many of the old-school skills that you need in your new-school studio involve correct microphone usage. Mics are designed to meet several different parameters, more than just those of basic sound and application that we have discussed already. An important aspect is the way in which they *reject* sound from certain angles—a factor determined by their pick-up pattern (also called "polar pattern"). To the inexperienced recordist, a mic's inability to adequately "hear" sounds coming from certain directions might seem a shortcoming, but this is actually an intentional aspect of any good microphone's design and one that an experienced engineer uses to his or her advantage in the studio.

The fact that a mic might be less sensitive to sounds coming from behind it, for example, means that you can position it so that unwanted sounds from other instruments are all happening in that region, and are less likely to bleed into the instrument that you are intending to record with it. Selecting mics according to pick-up patterns as well as sounds and applications will help you to record different instruments in the same room without excessive bleed between them, or even just to record an entire drum kit with a minimum of kick and hi-hat in the snare mic, and so forth. Of course, a mic that rejects sound from the rear of its capsule might still pick up reflected sound that bounces off a wall behind the thing you intend to record, and into the front of the capsule, but that's another matter. Check the spec sheets of your own mics to learn their pick up patterns, and use them to work for rather than against you.

CARDIOID Sometimes also called "unidirectional," which is a more self-explanatory name for them, cardioid mics primarily pick up sound coming from in front of the capsule. As the sound source moves from directly in front of the capsule, it will be detected to a lesser degree and usually with some change in frequency response, until it is far enough off axis and is dropped entirely. Sounds from directly behind a cardiod mic should not be heard

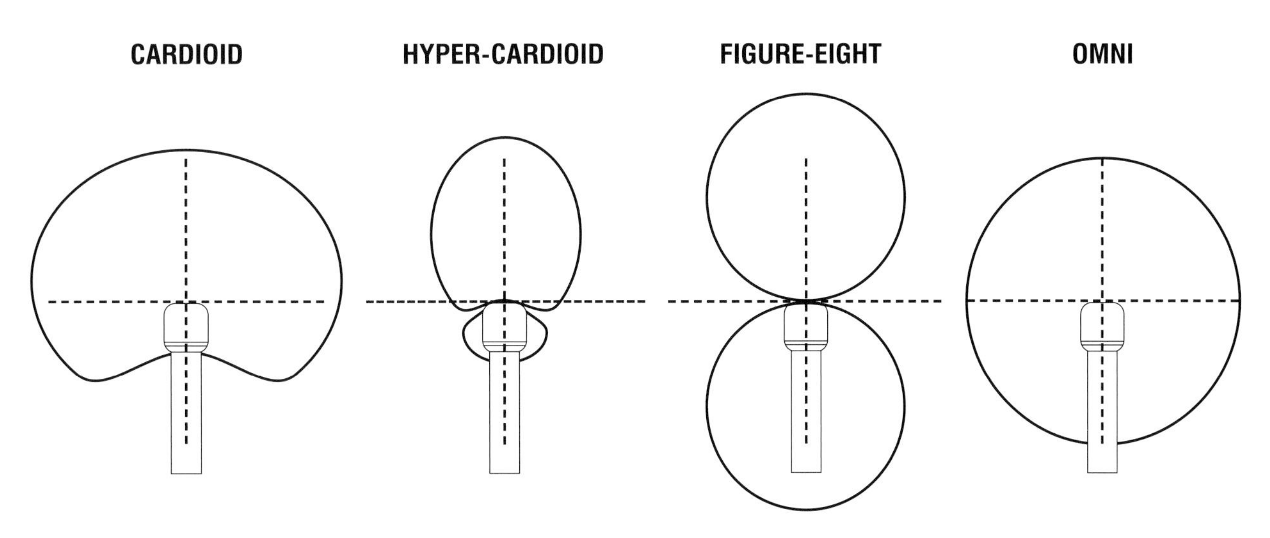

at all (other than via what is reflected off surfaces in front of the mic). In addition to providing a good recording tool, the cardioid pattern is popular for live sound, since its rejection pattern can help to minimize feedback. Examples of popular mics with this pattern are the Shure SM57, SM58, and Beta 52A; Electrovoice RE20; AKG C451 and D112, and several others. Many big condenser mics have switchable patterns that include a cardioid setting.

HYPER-CARDIOID Mics with this pattern have a slightly tighter pick-up zone in front of the capsule, with excellent side rejection, but also some detection of low-frequency sounds from directly behind the body of the mic. The relatively narrower pick-up pattern makes such mics less useful for singers, who might move off axis while performing and thereby change the output level of their vocal in the process, but good for fixed instruments like guitar amps and drums. The Beyer-Dynamic M160 and M201, Rode NT3, and Audix OM2 are all hyper-cardioid.

FIGURE-EIGHT As its name implies, the figure-eight mic (also called "bi-directional') hears sounds from two different and opposing directions. While this might at first seem undesirable, this pattern can be used to your advantage in several recording situations. Even when used as you would a cardioid mic, with the "front" of a figure-eight mic aimed at your sound source, this pick-up pattern can help to induce more "air" and room sound into the recording of many instruments. This can give a more natural feel, while offering good rejection of sounds coming from the side of the mic. It can also be used to record two sounds or singers at one time, or to capture a left-and-right image for a stereo recording when used in a mid-side (M-S) stereo configuration, as described in detail below. Although many figure-eight mics imply an equal pick-up of sounds from both sides of the capsule, many actually have slightly unequal pickup patterns, and it's best to check your mic's spec sheet to discern this. Figure-eight mics tend to be condenser or ribbon types, examples of which include the Royer R121, Coles 4038, and Schoeps CCM8. Some others, like AKG's hardworking C414 condenser, have switchable pick-up patterns that include a figure-eight setting.

OMNI Clearly self-explanatory, an omni mic picks up sound coming from all directions. Popular for some live-speech and broadcast applications, where it's useful to pick up speakers positioned in different parts of the soundstage, an omni mic's usage is more limited in the studio, and almost nil in live sound, where it might pose a feedback nightmare. In the studio, engineers have often used classic omni mics to record acoustic instruments in beneficial spaces, where the nuance of the room is captured, as well as to record drums (a great tool in a minimal drum-miking set-up), piano, or even electric guitar amps where you want a lot of room sound in the track. They are also used, as already implied, as a more distant, ambient "room mic," often in partnership with a close mic on the sound source itself. The AKG C414 includes an omni setting, as do the multi-

MINI-GOBOS: MAKING FIGURE-EIGHT PLAY LIKE CARDIOID

Figue-eight mics can be great at capturing airy, natural sounds with a good sense of room space. But what do you do if you don't want that room sound, or are recording in a room with unflattering reflections, but still want to use your figure-eight mic for the job? Block those reflections from the back of the mic with a "mini-gobo," that's what. A "gobo" (short for "go-between") is an acoustic baffle—which I usually just call a "baffle" in this book—used in the studio to create some separation between a mic and an instrument that you don't want it to pick up. A mini-gobo is a small version of this baffle, often just slightly larger than the surface of a large microphone, and is used close-up to a mic as more of a spot cure, to block unwanted sound coming from a specific place in the room, or entering a specific part of the mic. You can create your own mini-gobo from materials you are likely to find around the studio. To do this, cut two pieces of sound insulating foam and one piece of either thick cardboard or thin hardboard into squares a little larger than the back surface of your mic. Glue them together with the hardboard in the middle, in a "sandwich" sort of configuration. Attach this temporarily to the back of your ribbon mic with a large rubber band or two, and voila, you have converted your figure-eight mic into a pseudo-cardioid mic, and one that will capture a greater proportion of direct sound to room sound.

pattern Shure KSM44 and CAD GXL-3000, while a list of dedicated omni mics includes the Neumann M150 and Microtech Gefell M296.

Basic stereo microphone set-ups

We will learn several different mono mic set-ups too, of course, but those are easily covered individually as used for different instruments in the chapters that follow. These basic stereo configurations, however, make a good grounding for stereo recording of several different instruments, and are best discussed here. By doing so, I can refer back to them throughout the rest of the book, rather than re-hashing them in each subsequent chapter.

There are near countless ways to capture a stereo sonic image, and I am not going to consider all of them here. These are far and away the most popular basic set-ups, though, and others that you might use are likely to be variations of these. Note that most of these techniques are best achieved with a pair of mics of the same make and model (obsessive recordists even buy "matched" mics that are paired by the manufactured after having been tested to exhibit identical, or near-identical, characteristics). If you just don't have two of the same mic, though, and still want to record in stereo, try any of these with the two most closely matched mics you've got. What the hell—if it works for you, it works, and the end listener is unlikely to hit the stop button and shout, "Hey, those stereo mics aren't matched!"

A spaced stereo pair (these angled in slightly) used as drum overheads.

SPACED PAIR (AB PAIR)

Perhaps the simplest and most obvious stereo mic set up is the spaced stereo pair. Just as its name implies (though it's also called "AB pair" by some), this configuration involves using two identical microphones spaced some distance from each other but at the same height and distance from the sound source. These mics are usually placed away from the sound source, too, rather than close up, to enable the sound to bloom into the full stereo image you are seeking. When setting up a spaced stereo pair, engineers traditionally try to observe the "three-to-one rule," which says that these mics should be placed three times as far from each other as they are from the sound source, while each should be the exact same distance from the sound source. This configuration can work well for wide to semi-wide stereo panning, but even when the three-to-one rule is observed, you can get some sonic oddities from phase cancellation if you find you need to pan them to the center in mono. Also, when used super wide, this configuration can sometimes give the impression that there is a "hole" in the middle of the soundscape, a perception that other stereo techniques seek to cure. This is minimized with the use of omni mics where available, or some recordists simply put up a third mic equidistant between the two spaced mics to capture the center "mono" image.

The spaced stereo pair is best achieved with condenser mics, or ribbon mics in some cases, though you can use standard dynamic mics in a pinch if that's all you've got, provided they are fairly sensitive microphones. Cardioid, hyper-cardioid, figure-eight, and omni mics can all work well in this application, depending on what you are trying to record, and how much room sound you want to capture with it.

COINCIDENT OR XY PAIR

Another traditional configuration, the coincident pair (also known as XY pair) seeks to repair the "hole in the middle" that the spaced stereo pair can sometimes exhibit, while still capturing a full, broad stereo image. Slightly different versions of this set-up exist, with a few further variations in each. One common method says you mount two microphones at a 90-degree angle to each other, on the same plane, with their capsules positioned as if firing across each other. The other popular technique has the mics with the capsules one above the other, nearly touching. With either of these, you can vary the angle of the mics, tightening it down to 60 or 70 degrees for a narrow stereo field, or opening it up to 120 degrees for a broader soundscape. Note that, when setting up this pair, you need to track the mic that is *aimed* to the right of the sound source as the "right mic," and the mic aimed left as the "left mic," rather than confusing the fact that the bulk of the body of the right mic (if it's an end-fire mic, or a side-fire mic positioned horizontally) will lie to your left hand as you face the sound source.

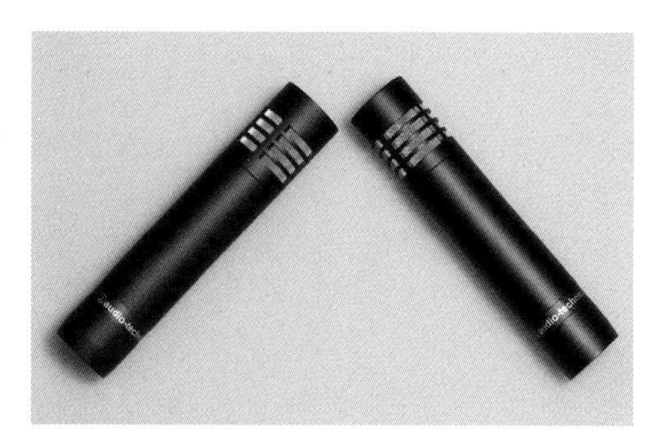

Small-diaphragm condenser mics (here, two Audio-Technica AT2021s) positioned as a coincident or XY pair.

Condenser mics are the traditional choice for the XY pair, although the right ribbon mics can also work well. Any of the common directional types will work fine, with differing results—cardioid, hyper-cardioid, or figure-eight—although omni mics don't really achieve the desired results here, for obvious reasons. When set up right, this configuration offers a realistic stereo image with a solid perception of the center of the field. Instruments in the center of your sound source (or the central resonating components, if you are recording a single instrument in stereo, such as acoustic guitar, drums, or piano) are captured equally by each mic, while the right and left mics each capture a stronger image of their respective parts of the field. The resultant two-channel recording can be panned somewhat as desired, to vary the width of the stereo image after the fact, but a panning that mirrors the angle at which the mics were originally placed one to the other will most accurately recreate the performance. This set-up also tends to work well when both mics are panned to mono, exhibiting minimal phase issues.

NEAR-COINCIDENT PAIR

Another method used to capture a broad, deep, and sharp stereo field is the "near-coincident pair." As with the coincident pair, this configuration uses two mics fairly close together, but in this case their capsules are spread some distance apart, usually from six to eight inches (150 to 200mm), and angled 110 degrees away from each other, at the left and right sides of he sound source.

Two small-diaphragm condenser mics positioned as a near-coincident pair.

Depending on the mics used, the width of the sound source, and the actual angle at which you position them, this technique can produce a very realistic and atmospherically diffuse stereo image, but can also sometimes result in a washy center, or a degree of that old "hole in the middle." Put another way, compared to its sibling the XY coincident pair, the near-coincident might give you broad and accurate stereo, but a softer center image. Similar mics work well for this as for the coincident pair, and of course yield slightly different results accordingly.

BAFFLED-OMNI PAIR (DUMMY HEAD PAIR)

This configuration and its variations result from the effort to record a stereo image that accurately replicates the perception of human hearing in the same listening environment. It involves positioning an omni mic each side of a round disc or spherical baffle that creates the sonic "shadow" of the human head. Some applications use an actual solid dummy head with mics positioned where the ears would be, while others use a disc-shaped baffle (called a Jeklin disc) or foam sphere. Omni mics are a critical part of this stereo configuration, since the human ear is essentially an omni listening device but for the head that gets in the way, but you can get interesting and often usable results with good cardioid and figure-eight mics, too.

This technique can produce an excellent and realistic stereo image, but does have a few drawbacks. It can, once again, suffer from a slight hole in the middle, and the accuracy of its stereo reproduction can end up being extremely dependent upon the end listener's position. Other techniques sometimes produce results that are more realistic.

MID-SIDE (M-S)

This clever and very effective set-up involves using two microphones to record a stereo image comprised of left, middle, and right tracks—yep, three tracks from two mics—to cure the "hole in the middle" issue. To make this work at all, the "side" mic has to conform to much more specific requirements than required by most techniques discussed thus far. It must be a figure-eight microphone, which means a condenser or ribbon type. Depending on the results you are looking for, the "mid" mic can be another identical figure-eight mic, or a different cardioid or hyper-cardioid mic with roughly similar sonic characteristics (you usually pair condenser with condenser, ribbon with ribbon). The figure-eight side mic's ability to capture sound from both sides of the capsule is what gives this configuration its broad stereo capabilities, while the mid mic fills in the middle.

To make the set-up work, the side mic's single output is recorded to *two* channels via a signal splitter (or recorded to one channel, then copied and pasted to a second track in the DAW), and the polarity of the second split or copied track is reversed. While the mid mic is panned dead center, the two copies of the side mic's signal—one the original, one the reverse-phase of it—are panned wide left and wide right. The original track reproduces the sound hitting the "front" of the ribbon, that is, one side of the mic, while the reverse-phase copy reproduces the sound from the "back" of the ribbon, the opposite side of the mic, so the two now represent the left and right in our stereo spectrum. Clever, eh!? The mid mic (think of it as a "center mic" if that's easier) is panned straight up the middle to give a full, solid center to the field.

In practice, these two mics are usually set as close to each other as possible in order to, like the coincident pair, capture the sound source from the same position in the room, and to minimize phase issues. The side mic is of course placed side-on to the center of the sound source and is thus often picking up much more reflected sound, too, while the mid mic aims straight at it. Done right, the M-S pair can produce an extremely full, realistic stereo image with a great balance of width and solidity. It does, however, offer the disadvantage of having a stereo image that is rigidly fixed: if you pan the + and – tracks from the split side mic toward the center, their precise positive/negative relationship finds them gradually canceling each other out, until they disappear entirely when you get them both dead center. Panning them in just a little does provide a means of lessening the stereo dimension, however, if that's what you seek (which simply pulling the +/– tracks down in the faders will also achieve), but you always retain the solid mid mic to keep a mono image in the mix even if the side mic's channels have depleted each other.

Large figure-eight ribbon mics, in this case a pair of affordable Alctron RM-8s, positioned for mid-side stereo recording.

PZM STEREO PAIR

If you have a pair of PZM boundary mics, such as the affordable model from Radio Shack mentioned in the Hardware chapter or more expensive types from Crown and others, you can use these for several different stereo configurations. To use them as designed, simply place them a good distance apart from each other on a wall across from the sound source. To minimize phase cancellation, try to observe the three-to-one rule as described in the Spaced Pair section above when setting these up. You can play with different positions on the wall relative to the ceiling and adjacent walls to find what works best for you. Or, mount your PZMs on a pair of square pieces of plywood or plexiglass (the bigger the piece, the greater the low-end reproduction) with sturdy clips or stand mounts attached to their backs or bottom edges, and position them wherever in the room you like.

You can also use a pair of PZMs in the manner of a coincident (XY) or near-coincident pair. Cut two plywood pieces of anywhere from a foot to two feet (300mm to 600mm) square, attach them together with a pair of hinges so that they swing through nearly 180 degrees, and mount your PZM mics in the centers of opposite sides of these boards. To recreate an approximate coincident pair, fold the boards so that your PZMs are on the surfaces within an angle of 90 to 110 degrees or so. To recreate that of a near-coincident pair, fold the boards outward so that the mics are on the outside surfaces of the angle formed.

CHAPTER 4

RECORDING DRUMS

We are tackling drums first because drums are often the first instrument tracked in a recording session, or the first "keeper" in the majority of traditional recording sessions. Even when a session starts with drums, bass, guitar, and vocals playing together, the goal is usually to get the best drum takes possible; the other instruments can be overdubbed at a later time. There are plenty of other ways to skin a drum track, of course, and often these days a home recordist will strum and sing to a click track embedded in his DAW to the correct tempo for a particular song, then come back and add drums—or just drum loops or samples—at a later time. This is valid, if you need to work this way to get the job done. But I would argue that you still want to lay the drums down first, if possible, to achieve a "live" and "real" feel to a song. If you just can't get your drummer in until a later date and don't want to stem your own creative tide, fine. But in the majority of cases, the blocks will all fit into place more tightly, organically, and fluidly when you lay down that essential beat first.

Of course, plenty of people seek to record the entire band together at the same time, or the rhythm tracks at least, as a way of achieving the ultimate "live" and "spontaneous" feel for a project, and that can work great in some circumstances. In such cases, the drums—given their size, dynamics, volume, and musical "weight"—will still be the center of your first recording efforts for any particular song, so you will very likely build your tracking plan around them.

Lots of musicians are intimidated, above all else, by the effort of recording drums. And this is totally understandable: all that noise, all those sound-producing surfaces and a broad multiplicity of frequencies bouncing around the room—and bouncing back, given the inherently percussive nature of the instrument. As a guitarist first and foremost—and neither a trained studio engineer *nor* a drummer—I was always similarly concerned about the challenge of capturing drums effectively. Then, when the occasion first arrived that I needed to do so for myself, I set up some mics and just went for it ... and it sounded pretty darn good. You can spend endless hours online reading recording chat boards that discuss complex compressor and limiter set-ups for capturing drums, intricate mic arrangements, convoluted systems for achieving punchy kick sounds, and so on. Undoubtedly some deep and extreme tricks can work, particularly if you are shooting for heavy rock sounds and a vast, spacious feel. But we're here to get creative and useful results from what we've got available to us, and I will tell you hands down that good drum tracks can be achieved with very little in the way of trickery or artifice, or for that matter, outboard processing pre-input. If you're sweating the process, and feel like you just aren't having success getting the big, powerful drum sounds you imagined, follow this piece of advice: don't abandon anything until you hear those drums in the track, after some other "keeper" tracks have been added. To do so accurately, you might need to press ahead and overdub a better bass line and some more accurate and involved guitar and/or keyboard tracks, to improve on whatever you played as guides during the drum tracking. They point is, you really don't know how your drums will sound in and of themselves, and whether they will work with the song, until you hear them in context.

Also, as with the prevailing emphasis throughout much of this book, my own primary focus is on recording real sounds, sounds with a little grit and presence and life. You might hear of engineers going to extremes of processing and technique to make drums (or any instrument) sound "real and present," and the good ones certainly know how to do it well; but as often as not our drive to simplify the effort, even out of necessity owing to a lack of gear and/or facilities, will get us there just as quickly. Often, doing things simply will also leave you with results that are easier to work with further along in the recording process—more of which later in this book. I still remember how fresh, live, and real the drums, and the snare in particular, on Lou Reed's *New York* album of 1989 sounded after a decade of over-processed "big rock drums" and lashings of reverb on everything. Often the way to get noticed is to go simple, go real, go natural, and the nifty thing is that it's often easier to get those drum sounds too, if you just put a little thought into your set-up and mic technique.

When I first started to try to record tracks that could stand as masters for release (after many years of home-demo recording), I had extremely limited resources for the venture. One notable session, and one that we had high hopes for, involved tracking a five-piece kit with three cymbals plus hats using only a pair of Radio Shack PZM boundary mics on the walls in the corner of the basement "live room" for stereo overheads, a battered Shure SM58 sitting right on top of the old pillow in the kick drum (a mic usage that's a "no-no" in itself for various reasons, as plenty of engineers will tell you), and a $30 pawn shop AKG D1000E dynamic mic on the snare. I had the drummer play, recorded a little, listened back, adjusted mics and settings, and recorded a little more ... then picked up the guitar, called the bass player in from his coffee break, and we hammered out the takes.

That project never came to fruition as a release in and of itself, but several years later, after forming a band that was playing some of the same material, I revisited those tracks, and liked what I heard. We re-tracked vocals and acoustic guitars and a few electric tracks on several of them, but kept the drums and bass because the feel was right. Of the 13 songs on the CD on which they eventually appeared, those three reconstituted tracks are among many people's favorite tunes. They have had radio play, several glowing reviews, and have been part of a disc that sold respectably well for an independent self-release. Which is to say, the cheap and nasty recording effort that constituted those drum takes was entirely successful in the sense that it contributed to viable songs; and no one ever said, "Man, what the hell did you record *that* with?"

Drum prep

As with everything in recording, the old adage "garbage in, garbage out" applies to drums. If you want good-sounding drum recordings, you need to record good-sounding drums in the first place. This is a point that you need to address in conjunction with your drummer. Perhaps he can't afford the new $5,000 kit with hand-made birch shells (if he can, great!), but his heads should at least be of good quality and in decent shape, his drums should be tuned, and his hardware should be free from squeaks and rattles. If you can afford the time, or even the money, and want to really make your drums pop in each track, ask the drummer to retune the kit for each song, or even change to more appropriate-sounding heads as required by the dynamics of the tune. Do this right, and the heads will resonate to frequencies that are sympathetic to the key of the song, rather than fighting it and creating subtle dissonances that might throw the listener off track, even if it isn't at all obvious what the aural conflict is.

Plenty of drummers might be reluctant to go to this kind of trouble, or even the effort of tuning up and putting their kit and hardware in good condition in the first place. For that reason, in addition to cultivating some skills in diplomacy—from subtle cajoling to gentle insistence—it is worth learning to do these things yourself if you plan to record a lot of live drums in your space. Ultimately, it can be extremely handy to invest in a decent kit of your own, too, and keep it set up, in good condition, and ready to go. A good house kit can help circumvent the downer of a drummer with an inferior kit, or one in poor condition, dragging down your otherwise successful recording efforts.

Very often you will need to apply some form of damping to some or all of the drum heads, to keep them from ringing excessively with overtones that might not be heard much in a live performance, but which can easily clutter recorded tracks. Many drums are built with internal dampers that can be tightened into place to mute the head slightly, or you can purchase clip-on dampers that do the same thing externally. Gentle use of these can do the trick in some instances, although you need to be careful to avoid applying too much pressure, or the damper will put the head back out of tune at its point of contact. Several other products are available to help with the job these days. Self-adhesive Moongel can work great, and can be used in different quantities and different positions to help you pinpoint any excessive ring or resonance. Evans, Remo, and others also make rings sized to the diameter of different heads, which can be laid atop any drum to help control overtones. Or, you can go with the old-school favorite of sticking loops of masking tape or duct tape—aided with a chunk of insulation foam in extreme cases—to strategic points on troublesome drumheads to rein them in a little. Or tape a square of cloth torn from an old sheet or t-shirt to the edge of the drum away from the point where the drummer habitually hits it, and lay it on the head as desired to create a cheap and easy on again/off again damper. Sometimes excessively rattling snares (that is, the actual metal snares on the underside of the snare drum itself) might need to be taped down or muted slightly, too. Be careful in all instances, however, to dampen drums only as much as necessary, or you can go too far and kill the natural tone of the instrument, take the "snare" sound out of the snare, and so on.

This book is very much about "use what you've got," though, and if you're just stuck with cheap, nasty sounding drums and can't beg, borrow, or steal something better, you might consider going with the flow and using techniques that emphasize treatment and artificiality. Dampen the room down even more than you might with good-sounding drums, find some plug-in compressors and EQs that will add body and weight, and in general emphasize the nurture rather than the nature of the situation. You don't want to go so far as to make your drums sound synthesized, unless that's what you're after, but with some clever mic placement and judicious treatment you might get your Craigslist special to sound okay in the track.

Also, before rolling tape—or spinning hard drive, at least—remove anything from the kit that won't be hit during that take. When you hit a drum or crash a cymbal, everything else in the kit resonates a little in sympathy. If you're tracking a song that just requires a kick, a shuffle rhythm on the snare, and the occasional light crash cymbal, get everything else out of there and you'll eliminate a host of potentially mix-cluttering frequencies. If the drummer has a tambourine or a cowbell mounted on a clamp on his cymbal stand but doesn't play the thing in the song, get it out of there to eliminate any unwanted rattles or sympathetic resonances. Same with any toms or cymbals he or she doesn't hit. Pack them away to minimize their sonic and physical interference, and you might find you've suddenly got space for a preferred mic positioning on the remaining parts of the kit, too.

This chapter will discuss several different set-ups that should help you to capture real, live drums, which vary from the simplicity of a single mic placed just right, to several mics. First, however, we'll investigate a range of techniques for miking kick and snare drums, since these are the building blocks of any punchy drum sound, and will usually be miked separately (and in a number of different possible ways) regardless of what else you do for the rest of the kit.

Miking the snare

The simplest, most common, and perhaps most obvious technique for close-miking a snare drum (sometimes called "spot miking") involves positioning your dynamic mic of choice just off the top rim of the snare (an inch or two or three above the rim, for example), firing approximately at the spot where the drummer hits the head (the "batter head"). There are several little refinements, however, that will help you to optimize even this simple technique, as well as several subtle but crucial variations on this placement.

The first addendum to this technique, if you will, is an entirely practical one: you need to place the mic where the drummer will not hit it, and it's up to you in your capacity as an engineer to find that position, rather than asking your drummer as a musician to alter his normal striking method or angle. The second is a more technical one: you want to aim the mic from a position where it will capture, as much as possible, snare only, and not the hi-hat or rack tom beside it, or the floor tom across to the other side of it. The third is that the "perfect position" you find with one mic on one drum, with one particular drummer, will not necessarily be the perfect placement for the next drummer or project, or even the next song. The sound coming off the drum head (and from the drum as a whole) and the response of the microphone to it will vary according to drum, drummer, and how he or she is playing it, with tempo, dynamics, and other factors all weighing in as variables. For this reason, that magic mic-and-position combination from one session just might not do the trick on the next. That said, a set-up that sounds good at the start of any one session should at least provide a good starting point for usable results through the day, even if you are going from thrasher to ballad and back again. But, if it occurs to you, reassess things when preparing to track a song that's dramatically different from what you started with, and you just might find some tweaks to perfect your set-up.

The second point from the above paragraph deserves a little more attention. Most mics used up close on snare—a Shure SM57, Beyer M201, or similar—will be somewhat directional, with cardioid or hyper-cardioid pickup patterns. Since you are using this mic to capture some extra "crack" and presence from the snare, which you will blend into the overall picture created by your overhead(s), you want to ensure as much as possible that it captures *only* the snare. Positioning this mic slightly under the edge or off to the side of the hi-hats, aiming toward the drummer more than the mounted toms or the floor tom across the snare from it, will help to use such mics' directionality to minimize spill from other drums and cymbals. Also, you don't want this mic level with the point where the hi-hat cymbals come together, or the gust of air from this might blow into the screen of the mic, even if the cymbals themselves are out of the meat of the mic's pick-up zone. In short, look up the pick-up pattern of the mic you are using, and aim it, if possible, so that no other noise-makers are within the main part of its field.

Close miking—or "spot miking"—the snare with a Shure SM57 aimed slightly downward at the batter head.

Engineers have traditionally enhanced this isolation in recording the snare by also running this mic through a gate (between preamp and interface, or as an insert in the mixer channel used as mic pre). Setting the gate's sensitivity to a point where it will open for the softest snare hit that you want to capture, but will stay closed for sounds coming from other drums, can help to maximize your isolation. Gates can be tricky to use, however, and a lot of factors can get in the way to mess up your efforts here. For one thing, setting the gate appropriately might sound simple in principle, but it is often extremely difficult to find the right cut-off point. For another, even when you get it right as regards the snare, a particularly fierce whack of a tom might open it up regardless, giving you a brief rush of non-snare information, and it's arguably worse to have mostly just snare but a few stray tom or kick whacks coming through and joining the snare track than it is to have a little bit of everything else coming through all the time, and being handled accordingly. These days, with digital recording systems, you can largely ignore the gate during the tracking process, and apply it later, and more precisely, if necessary. Otherwise, you can often forget gating entirely and just accept that a little kick, toms, hat and cymbals will spill into your snare mic, but that it will still capture mostly snare, thanks to your clever positioning of the mic in the first place.

While the positioning of a single snare mic as described above has long been the standard, I, and several others it seems, have found that a slight alteration of this can provide outstanding and surprisingly consistent results. By mounting a mic in the same place as just described, but aiming it straight across the snare's top head rather then down toward it, I have time and again captured a magical amount of "thwack" and presence that has blended beautifully with the overall drum mix. Imagine an invisible plane that hovers an inch and a half or two inches (40–50mm) above the surface of the snare and parallel to it, and fire your dynamic mic straight across it (a Beyer M201 has worked great for me). This positioning looks as if it's missing the drum entirely, but seems to have a knack, in many cases at least, for capturing most of the desirable characteristics of a close-miked snare, while rejecting much of the unwanted clutter that might otherwise come along with it. Give it a shot, and see if it works for you.

Firing a dynamic mic, in this case a Beyer-Dynamic M201, straight across the snare can sometimes capture a surprisingly punchy sound.

Plenty of people have achieved good results by miking snares from underneath, or by blending two mics, one set traditionally as above and another aimed at the bottom head (or "resonant head'). A mic placed underneath the snare should still capture plenty of "thwack', but will also add more metallic snare rattle to the brew, along with an entirely different set of overtones. Like any recording technique, you really just have to try it to find out what it does for you. The underneath mic is usually aimed at an upward angle that comes closer to approaching vertical, and can either shoot at the snares themselves, or at a spot on the resonant head that's somewhat clear of the snares, or a little of both. Note that if you are using both an over and under mic, you will most likely need to reverse the phase of one for them to blend correctly, although you will also need to test both against the rest of the mics used on the kit to ensure you are not blending the sum of two snare mics that are ultimately *both* in reverse of the rest of the drum mics.

In addition to, or instead of, an over and/or under mic, you can sometimes get good results by placing a condenser mic or ribbon mic off to the side of the snare drum. These mics are more sensitive than the dynamic mics usually used (the condenser more sensitive in terms of audio, the ribbon more fragile in terms of handling), so you need to take care with these placements, to ensure they are neither so close to the drum that they distort, nor that they drummer is likely to hit them (a good old SM57 can usually survive a serious stick bashing pretty well, but a condenser or ribbon mic is likely to crumble at the first blow). Consider starting with one of these mics about two inches (50mm) off to the side and three inches (75mm) above the top of the drum, aimed just slightly down toward the head. Whatever you do, ensure you do not have it directly across from the vent hole in the drum, as the gust of air emitted when the snare is hit could kill a ribbon quickly. With a condenser, you might also need to engage the pad on your mic pre, or insert one inline if such is available.

And after all this, remember that in most cases this spot miking of the snare will just be one part of the picture, and very likely the smaller part, with the overhead(s) ideally dialed up higher in the final mix, and this close mic or blend of mics used to produce as much snap and presence and immediacy as required.

BELOW: A mic positioned under the drum, aimed at the resonant head, will add a lot of snare rattle to the sound. BOTTOM: A condenser mic often gives good results, with a lot of clarity and fidelity in the "thwack" of the snare.

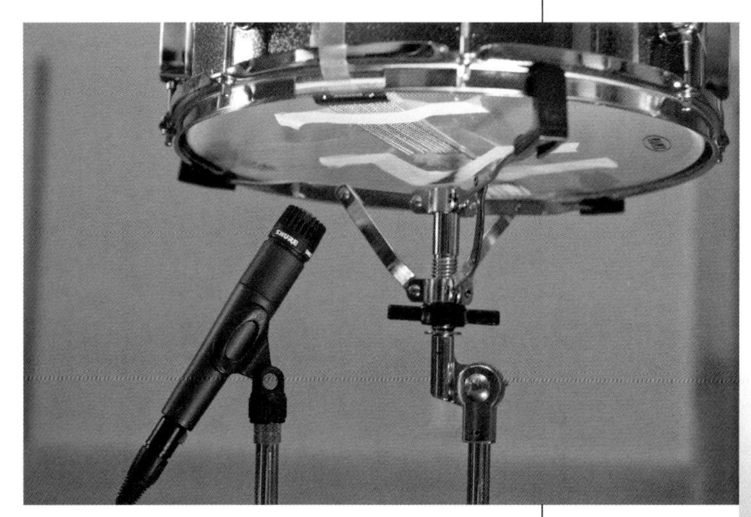

Miking the kick

Techniques for capturing effective kick sounds run through the same sort of simple-to-complex range as those used to record snares, and with a few odd and excessive endeavors above and beyond, too. Before you even select mic(s) and position(s), however, you need to consider other fundamental parameters that aren't addressed at all with the snare drum: do you (and your drummer) prefer the drum with the resonant head on or off, and if on, do you prefer that head to be uncut, or to have a mic-access port? Often the decision regarding these will be made simply because "that's the way drum was set up when the drummer arrived." Ideally, though, you should consider the different sounds offered by each of these alternatives, and make the effort to choose according to the right tone for the track, rather than for sheer expediency.

A kick with a fully intact front head has more "boom" and a greater presence of the fundamental note from the drum. A port hole lets some of the air escape when the beater hits the batter head, and gives you a punchier sound. Any hole cut in a resonant bass-drum head should be placed off center (right or left, but still at least two inches/50mm from the edge) and kept to a reasonable size, perhaps four or five inches (50–75mm). Any bigger—or placed dead center—and such a hole can negate the effect of having a resonant head in place at all. Seek further advice if cutting such a hole for the first time, or purchase a pre-cut head.

The four main positions for a mic up close on or in a kick drum are:

■ inside a hole in the front (resonant) head, aiming approximately at the point where the beater hits the other side of the back head (batter head), at a slight angle (off axis) rather than straight on

■ inside the drum itself with the front head removed, aiming fairly precisely at the point where the beater hits the other side of the back head, but from slightly off axis

■ just outside an uncut front head, aiming off axis at the front head, anywhere from three to 12 inches (75–300mm) away

■ aiming at the batter head (back head) near where the pedal beater strikes that head.

The overall sound of a kick drum might also come from other, more distant mic placements, whether room mics, overheads, or mics intended purely to capture a more ambient kick sound, but these are the main close-miking positions. Even with the same mic, each of these placements detailed above will capture a different kick sound, namely:

■ resonant with some solid attack from the beater
■ less resonant, heavy on the forward "click" edge of the beater attack
■ boomy and resonant—more "airy"—with less attack
■ less boomy than #3, with more attack (though often less than #1 and #2).

The logic in most of the placements, as you can see already, is fairly simple: aim the mic at the point where the beater strikes the back head, and you get more attack, more of that percussive front-edge "click" and "thump" in your kick sound; position it to capture the drum as a whole, and you get more resonant "boom" in the sound. Which isn't to say that the latter can't be punchy too. Plenty of engineers feel that something other than the mic-aimed-at-beater positioning produces a more natural kick sound, and some will go to great lengths to achieve that. Here are some more detail on how you achieve these four basic placements, then we'll get creative after that. With all of these, play with different positions and listen back, ideally with some other instruments in the mix (bass in particular), and tweak your position until it works for you.

Position #1 is perhaps the classic for general rock and pop, or "hyphen-roots" styles such as blues-rock and country-rock, where you want good punch but no extremes of beater click. Use a mic stand that will let you hold a robust dynamic mic such as a Shure Beta 52A, an AKG D112, or maybe an Electrovoice RE20 firmly in the hole in the front head (without touching the sides) and aiming approximately where the beater hits the batter head. The size of this hole in the front head usually limits your positioning somewhat, but you can still try a variety of different angles and move the mic a little further in or out to try to achieve the sound you are seeking. Ideally, this mic placement should give you good punch with a little click to it, along with a big, full, resonant thump from the internal space of the drum shell itself.

Aiming a dynamic mic, such as this Shure Beta 52A, directly into the hole, or "port," cut in the front head is probably the most common method of miking a kick drum.

Position #2, with a mic right inside the drum, involves placing a dynamic mic of a similar type to that described in #1 just a few inches back from the inside of the batter head, aiming directly at the point where the beater hits the other side. You mount this mic either on a boom stand capable of reaching far enough into the drum to position it correctly, or on a short desk stand that sits firmly atop some type of cushion placed inside the kick drum for damping (and to hold this stand without inducing rattles). If you don't have a stand that works, you can even try adding pillows and/or folded blankets inside the drum and propping the mic right on top of them in the correct position, but in doing so you want to make sure this damping doesn't contact the batter head to heavily (unless you seek a heavily deadened kick sound), and also that it won't shift during the take. Experiment with aiming this mic to different points, too; shooting it somewhere off the beater point will reduce your click slightly, but that might be entirely desirable, and shooting it at the joint between head and drum shell, for example, will offer more warmth and fullness, while remaining plenty punchy.

Also, note that you don't always have to remove the front head entirely to achieve such miking, and can often work through the cut-out in the front head that is used for mic placement #1 above. This can be a bit trickier to achieve, but some engineers prefer the sound of a kick drum with at least a partial head still in place on the front. While the theory says that you fire the mic right at the beater point, an inch or two back from the inside of the head, the reality is that you will usually move this mic around some and test-record different positions to find what works best. Sometimes you think you want a lot of beater slap and click—for heavy rock or hip-hop or other aggressive contemporary styles—but find that "a lot" is actually "too much" in the final product.

Position #4 is often used by engineers seeking elements of #1 and #2 when they don't want to remove an un-cut resonant head from the front of the kick drum, but is also simply another option for achieving an entirely different kick sound. You will usually place this mic on a short desk-top stand because it's too tight to get a boom in here, and position that stand to the right of the drummer's right foot (from the drummer's perspective, that is); in other words, between the drummers kick-pedal foot and his floor tom. While this one is different from what you usually observe in your typical photo or video footage of a pro studio drum recording set up, or that used for live performance, it's a pretty cool alternative in its own right, and it captures a good picture of the kick sound as heard from the drummer's perspective. The lack of availability of space back here limits your options, but you generally want to raise the mic to approximately the height of the beater and aim it at the point where the beater hits the head, from a couple inches away, and off axis (since "on axis" is the position of the kick pedal itself). This mic placement should give you some click and slap from the beater, with natural ring and boom from the batter head and a sense of some spaciousness, too. Difficulties with this one can occur, however, if you have a squeaky or clicky pedal—something you would want to work to eliminate in any case, but which will be accentuated by having a mic sitting mere inches from the pedal's moving parts.

Positioning a dynamic mic at the batter head, aimed at the beater, should give the sound a high proportion of "click" and thump.

I have taken these out of order because #3 is the most different of all of them. In some ways, it's the most natural, I suppose, if by "natural" you mean "as heard from a live listener's perspective." This is likely to be your choice for jazz or other rootsy, retro, or vintage genres where you do need some accentuation from a spot mic on the kick, but don't seek lots of percussive click in the sound. Mics of choice for this position will still often be those popular kick-drum dynamic types mentioned for use in the previous positions. But since you aren't dealing with any direct blasts of air here, you can also try a ribbon or condenser mic, provided you keep it a little further back from the front head than you would a dynamic mic. With an AKG D112 or the like, you will probably want to get right up to about an inch or so off the resonant head, and experiment with precise focal points to see what sound works for you: aiming the mic right at the center of the head will elicit the most "boom" from this mic placement, while going off-center will reduce boominess. With other types of mics and points further back, however, you often need to get into some clever tricks to help avoid excessive spill from other instruments, so before diving into that, let's talk about combining selections from our four basic kick mic positions.

Miking the front of a kick with the front head intact can capture plenty of resonance and low-end thump.

As with miking the snare, many engineers will mix two of the more popular positions to achieve the final picture (or, the pre-final picture, since the final picture will usually involve overheads and/or room mics). The permutations of the mix-and-match kick sound are many, so I won't try to detail them all, but you can pretty easily envision what you might get by blending the characteristics of the above options. Blending a mic aimed at the batter head plus one outside the front of the resonant head, or a mic inside the drum and further outside the front of it, can give you a best-of-both-worlds sound that might suit plenty of requirements. When combining signals from two mics on the kick, however, be sure to check phase relationships before committing any final takes to recording, and ensure that both mics are working together.

To maximize the sound of a mic placed out in front of the resonant head (that is, in front of the drum kit), while reducing the amount of the rest of the kit captured by this mic, many recordists build a "kick tunnel." Place your mic of choice two or three feet in front of the kick drum aiming toward the center of the head—further if you like, though the longer the tunnel the more difficult the process—and position a sound baffle, chair, speaker cab or some other chunky item on the far side of the mic. Gather together some heavy blankets or quilts, or possibly a couple more baffles or guitar cases or speaker cabs *plus* the blankets, and create an enclosed "tunnel" by draping them over the chair or

Creating a "kick tunnel" out of guitar cases and quilts (this one has the "roof off" to show the mic) or whatever you have handy can help to accentuate the boom and resonance of the kick in a condenser mic placed a few feet back.

baffle or whatever at one end, and the kick drum itself at the other, with the mic inside. Experiment with what you have at hand and with the size and length of the tunnel, and see what results. This technique can help to capture a full, resonant, realistic yet punchy kick sound, without too much spill from snare, toms, and cymbals getting in the way. The tunnel can also work great when blended with a mic inside the kick pointed at the back of the batter head, or with one used up close on the other side of the batter head.

One nifty trick alluded to in the Hardware chapter involves using a guitar or bass speaker cabinet as a "microphone" to record the kick drum. This can be hit or miss, but occasionally captures just what you are looking for. Put the speaker cab—a 1x12 or 1x15 works best—right up close to, but not touching, the front of the kick, so the front of the cab (ie the front of the speaker cone) is facing the front outside of the resonant head. Connect a guitar cable (not the usual speaker cable) to the cab's input, used as an output in this case, and wrap some blankets around the cab/kick set up to isolate them somewhat. The speaker you are using as a pseudo-microphone will be extremely lo-z, between 4 ohms and 16 ohms, but you should still be able to get a usable signal out of a decent mic preamp with a quarter-inch input. If your first efforts with this seem promising but not great, perhaps try a few different preamp options before abandoning the effort, since the speaker will have a far lower impedance than any traditional microphone, and therefore might be a little fussier about its interaction with the pre. When it works, this odd, improvised technique can capture a big, round kick sound with a lot of thump and punch.

Experiment with the traditional and not-so-traditional placements, mix and match a few, and try some original configurations of your own, and see what works best to produce the kick sound you are looking for in your final mix.

Basic whole-kit set-ups

Complex miking techniques might involve a mic on every drum in the kit plus the hi-hats, maybe even two each on the snare and kick (above and below, front and back respectively), two overheads, one or two room mics further away... and your track count really starts to add up, not to mention the outboard gear that is often employed to avoid spill and keep each mic separate. We will examine more intricate approaches later, but let's start with some simple, minimalist set ups that can get solid, real-world results. Some of these have even been used by stars of the studio world to capture classic drum tracks for major artists.

Given the large surface area of a guitar-speaker cone, an extension cab can make a surprisingly effective kick "mic" in some instances.

THREE-MIC MONO DRUMS

In most circumstances, three mics is the minimum number of ingredients you will need to capture a full and very usable drumset sound. Sure, you can even go whole-hog toward minimalism and work to achieve rockin' drum sounds with just one mic (and often succeed), but let's start from a more realistic position of three microphones. Employing three of the "basic essentials" mic types discussed in the Home Studio Set-Up chapter, this is a system that shouldn't strain even the most basic of studios too badly yet will produce very usable results.

There are several different ways to approach the three-mic drum set-up, but my favorite aims for punch and solidity more than space and depth—without necessarily lacking in depth. Use your low-frequency mic of choice—a Shure Beta 52A, AKG D112 or similar—on the kick drum, your snare mic of choice on the snare, and a condenser or ribbon mic above the kit as a single overhead (see "Miking the kick," p81, and "Miking the snare," p78, if you happened to skip over them, for a plethora of ways to set these mics). What, we're miking them in mono? You bet! For the beginning recordist in particular, mono drums have all kinds of advantages. Keep the drums straight up the middle, and you can make even a very simple kit tracked like this sound punchy and alive, and let it really thump with the bass, too, while spacing guitars, keyboards, vocals and any other tracks left-to-right for breadth and dimension in your mix.

This simple three-track mono drum set-up makes mixing a breeze, and can help to produce a final result that still feels extremely full and ambient and, well, stereo, since the drums aren't fighting the melodic instruments for space on either side of the stereo field. I recorded an entire album a couple years ago for release on CD using this technique, and everyone involved in the project was thrilled with the results (hear a sample from this on the CD, with alternative mixes for comparison). No one ever commented, "Hey, the

A single overhead, in this case a Coles 4038 ribbon mic, can be surprisingly effective at capturing a full, punchy kit sound, particularly when aided by close mics on snare and kick.

drums are in mono!" and everyone was just extremely pleased with the overall mix, the drummer in particular. The technique might not be for everyone, sure, and sometimes you do want wide, spacious stereo drums (which—aha!—can also be done with just three mics, as we shall see), but if the notion of recording workable drums intimidates you in the first place, I really do recommend you give this set-up a try for starters, and see what you end up with.

Although this is an extremely simple set-up, the results you achieve with it will still vary according to the nuances offered by slight changes in mic placement, so you still want to play around with that a lot at the start of your drum session. For that reason, by the way, this also makes a good one to start with here—and in your own recording efforts—because you will learn a lot about how raising or lowering the overhead mic a foot either way, or angling the snare mic differently, or putting the kick mic further into or out of the bass drum, and so on, can dramatically alter your results. For starters, try using your dynamic snare mic of choice firing straight across the snare aiming away from the cymbal to minimize spill, your dynamic kick mic of choice positioned a couple inches inside the front head and aiming at the beater's contact point, and an appropriate condenser or ribbon mic placed about five feet six inches (1.7m) high and firing down at the drummer's right knee (assuming a right-handed drummer). If you don't have either of these latter two mic types available to you, use the most sensitive and full-sounding dynamic mic you have for your overhead. Observe your drummer playing a typical passage, and if his sticks never come within a foot (300mm) of the overhead mic, you might even try lowering it six inches (150mm). If, however, they come perilously close on any occasion, keep raising the mic until it is in safe territory. A drummer hit my precious Coles 4038 overhead during a dramatic end crash in one session, necessitating a pricey re-ribboning of that mic; not his fault, either—you need to work around the performers with your mic arrangements, rather than expect them to constrain their natural movement.

Record some of the tune that you will be aiming to track with this set-up, then scroll back, listen-enable all the drum tracks, pan them all right up the middle, and listen back to your results. Then, scroll back again, pull the levels of your kick and snare all the way down, and listen to the overhead on its own. Is there a good balance of rack and floor toms in the mix, and are the cymbals represented fairly equally? If anything seems to drop out more than the others (ignoring snare and kick for now, though they will be in there too), make a mental note to consider aiming the overhead more toward that drum. Bring your kick and snare up so they are about half or three-quarters the level of the overhead, and listen again. While the overhead will also have plenty of kick and snare content, the individual tracks should give these drums a lot more presence. If you find yourself pushing the snare track up high and it still lacks the punch you are after, but the toms and cymbals sound plenty full, make a mental note to aim the overhead more toward the center of the snare. (Or if, ultimately, the kick and snare sounds just aren't happening for you, but the overhead seems pretty good on its own, try a different mic position, or a different mic, on whichever drum is ailing). Check it, move your mics, check it again, and ease your way toward a workable drum sound.

If you bring in the kick and snare faders and find that a drum track that was sounding pretty good with the overhead playing on its own suddenly sounds hollow and thin, you might have a mic that is reverse-phase of the others. Try reversing the phase of the overhead track in your DAW (the channel might have a button for this, or you might need to apply a plug-in). If that doesn't do it, put that track's phase back to its original position, and reverse the phase of kick and snare tracks one at a time and see if either of those makes a difference (if reversing the overhead doesn't cure things, you won't need to reverse *both* the kick and snare, because that achieves the same result). Once you find the culprit, you can cure the problem from the outset by reversing the phase of that mic at the preamp or mixer or interface channel, if it has such a facility, so you don't have to correct it later, but don't forget to put the phase back to its original position in the DAW after doing so.

If you are fortunate enough to have a control room that is separate from the room in which you will set up the drum kit, and at least a reasonable amount of isolation between the two, you can hone your set-up a little earlier in the process by listening to the sound of the miked drums through your monitors and adjusting the mics until it all sounds as good as possible in that way. You will still need, however, to record the drums and listen to them played back to get an accurate representation of how they will sound, so you haven't entirely eliminated the "try it, tweak it, try it again" process.

Also, alongside all of the above, you will inevitably apply some processing to the drums when mixing, and this will change their sound too (sometimes dramatically). In fact, most engineers and producers will start applying certain base standards of compression and EQ, and maybe a little reverb, early in the process of listening back, because these can be a big part of the overall sound of any drum track. One way you can do this in aid of your own recording efforts, without having to learn skills that we haven't yet covered, is by using presets for plug-ins in your DAW that give you a good starting point for how your treated drums might ultimately sound. For example, many EQ plug-ins will have something like "punchy kick" or "snare presence" presets that you can use on those individual drums, and you can send the entire kit to a bus group with a "rock drums" preset on your compressor plug-in of choice. Throw up a few quick and easy presets in your applicable genre, and listen to how dramatically the overall drum track changes when you click the "bypass" button on and off.

FRONT-OF-KICK MONO SET-UP

There's a variation of this three-mic mono set-up that can sometimes work great, too, and which gives you more room sound for a more spacious kit overall. There's no point trying this one if you have a room that sounds bad—either too small and cramped and reflective, or too large and washy and over-reverberant—but if you like the sound of the drums being played in the room when you stand about six feet in front of the kit, facing the drummer, this one might work for you too. Set the kick and snare mics to your preference, as before, but move the mic that you had as an overhead to that position I just described, about five or six feet (1.5-1.8m) from the front of the kick drum and five or six feet high, firing approximately at the drummer's face. For obvious enough reasons, this placement is often called a "front of kick" mic, and when positioned right, in the right room, it can produce a surprisingly full kit sound with somewhat retro leanings.

Go through the same processes that you followed to tweak our first three-mic set up—as regards precise mic placement, mic phase, pre-mix, and so forth—and get this one sounding as good as you can. The results should give you a thick, realistic kit sound, something that is appropriate to use in a session where you are looking for a very natural and slightly vintage feel from the drums. If the kit sounds too distant or "roomy" in the mix with the other instruments, this set-up might not work for you, and you might want to go back to the more traditional overhead. If you're digging it, though, and want it to sound even *more* retro, listen back to the drums in the mix with only the front-of-kick mic up, and the kick and snare mics dropped all the way down, or muted.

In fact, I was going to cover this one anyway as a possible solution for a great "crazy one mic drum set-up", for those who need to go as minimalist as that. And, well, it looks like I just have. This is also a great position to try your drum mic if you're looking to get a quick rough-and-ready live drum recording at a gig or rehearsal space, where you just don't have enough mics or preamp or recorder channels to sacrifice more than one mic to drums. If you're trying this one-mic set-up for a recording that you hope to do anything serious with, work with the front-of-kick placement until you hear a firm, solid kick in the blend, with a good balance of all other drums and cymbals, snare included—which is exactly what this mic position is intended to offer. Find the sweet spot in front of the kick, with the right mic, and this ultra-simple solution can sometimes replicate the sound of other three- and four-mic set-ups when you get it mixed right, with a little compression and perhaps some EQ if necessary.

In addition to any good condenser mic, I really like a big ribbon mic for this front-of-kick thing (whether alone or in a multi-mic group), especially if you're shooting for a fat, warm, vintage sound. I have had great results from a Coles 4038 and an AEA R84, each of which also gives you a big, spacious room sound thanks to its figure-of-eight pickup pattern. But you can get good results from any of the more affordable larger ribbon mics mentioned in the Hardware chapter. I would be less inclined to go with a smaller-dimension ribbon such as a Beyer M160, for example, or a small-diaphragm condenser like an AKG C451 for that matter. Both these, and others of their type, are great mics, but they might be a little too narrow and focused to capture enough of the picture in this application. Still, if either sits king of the heap as the best mic you own, give it a shot.

Or, if you have two good overhead mics to use, and still like the idea of going mono rather than stereo, you can expand our first three-mic rig, the one with the traditional overhead, to include a fourth mic placed front-of-kick. You will most likely have to put in a little extra attention to phase relationship with this one, and work carefully with the balance of all four mics in the mix. Done right, though, you should be able to get great punch from the single overhead above the drummer, and more room and space from the front-of-kick mic, even if you don't use a lot of it in the mix.

Simple stereo drum set-ups

Following the minimalist principle just employed for the "Crazy one-mic set-up," you can try capturing a full stereo field with just two mics, but I'm going to look at more likely scenarios that should give you very professional results, using what would still be considered a small number of mics in a professional recording situation. All of these expand on our foundation of a solid kick and snare mic set-up to bring two more mics into the equation, for a total of four, to produce a stereo kit mix that can be as broad or as subtle as you like.

Note that while many of the following set ups begin with what would appear a symmetrical placement of the two stereo "overhead" or "room" mics, geometric symmetry means nothing compared to balanced stereo weight and aural symmetry. Or, put another way, a pretty set-up means far less than a deep, powerful sound in the mix, so don't be afraid to play around with any of these if the resultant changes achieve the drum sounds you're looking for. Also, while stereo recording usually calls for matched pairs of the same make and model of microphone, if you ain't got 'em... you ain't got 'em. You can often get good and usable "stereo" results from two different but vaguely similar mics, so don't let the paucity of your microphone collection stunt your growth in this department. To justify my "different mics work fine" theory of stereo drum recording, I point to the fact that, unlike a stereo recording of an acoustic guitar or a guitar amp from any distance of a couple of feet or more, the sounds of any drum kit that you seek to emulate in the stereo spectrum are a composite of several different percussive instruments being struck in widely different positions anyway. In other words, to reproduce the sound of a pair of human ears listening to a drum kit from a few feet away, you want two identical mics positioned appropriately; but if your right mic and left mic capture the drums and cymbals nearer them ever so slightly differently, it often isn't a deal breaker, since the drums and cymbals nearer them will sound slightly different anyway. I don't want you to feel bad about not being able to afford two big, shiny, matching large-diaphragm condenser mics ... so stop worrying, and get back to recording.

TRADITIONAL STEREO OVERHEADS

This is perhaps the most traditional stereo mic arrangement for drums, and is still very popular. Overheads used like this are sometimes thought of as cymbal mics, but in truth they capture a pretty good picture of the entire kit, and often can be the main ingredient in your final drum mix. The simple description of the traditional stereo overhead mics is that they are placed above the drummers head, slightly apart, to capture a realistic stereo kit sound, but of course the beauty, as ever, is in the details, and there are endless variables for fine-tuning this set-up.

The basic starting point for setting these mics usually involves putting them virtually above the drummer's head, position-wise, out of drum-stick reach, and both at the same height. As for spacing, you can start with these mics about three feet apart, each aiming down an imaginary line that connects to the outside edge of the left and right mounted tom respectively (or where they would be, if they don't exist). This set-up usually produces a stereo picture that is plenty spacious, but not so wide and diffuse as to make it sound like the drum kit wraps around the entire room. For a tighter, more focused stereo sound (and a sharper snare sound to boot), aim each mic at the center of the snare, and ensure each is the same distance from that point.

To tighten up this picture even further, you can bring the mics close together in the traditional "coincident pair" configuration, with their capsules nearly touching and the mics angled away from each other at approximately 90 degrees. This configuration is a standard for capturing a realistic stereo image without too much of a "hole" in the middle, as can sometimes result from a spaced stereo pair (of course, with drums, that hole is generally filled by the close-miked snare and kick anyway).

A pair of small-diaphragm condenser mics positioned as a "spaced pair" of stereo drum overheads.

For a broader stereo image you can resort to the old rule of thumb for the spaced stereo pair (which I ignored above, as is often the case) and position the overhead mics three times as far apart from each other as they are from the sound source, the upper cymbals in this case. By the time you get the mics three feet (900mm) or more above the cymbals—to avoid the drummer's sticks—you end up with mics nine feet (2.75m) apart, but this placement does usually work well to eliminate phase-cancellation issues that can result from closer (but not quite coincident) stereo mics. This is one to try in a big room where you are looking for a big, roomy stereo drum sound with a lot of air and some natural room reverb.

As with all of these, you can quickly see that the "traditional" is never entirely traditional, or not set in stone at least. Along with these variations, small or great adjustments of overhead positioning according to the needs of your drum kit, drummer, and room might help to optimize your results.

Mics of choice for all of these variations have traditionally (there it is again) been a matched pair of small-capsule condensers such as AKG C451s, or Neumann KM184s, or the more affordable Audio-Technica AT2021s or the like. These mics capture the crispness and high-frequency detail that many engineers look for from overheads, and give full play to your cymbals if you aren't close-miking those as well.

To fatten up the overall drum sound, plenty of people like to use large-diaphragm condensers like AKG C414s or C1000s, or Neumann U87s, or any decent variation you can lay your hands on. These will still offer plenty of detail and fidelity, but should tame excessive highs somewhat, while capturing thicker tom and snare sounds. These days, many recordists have rediscovered the beauty of ribbon mics used as overheads, too. The Coles 4038 is an absolute classic in this regard (as the drum sounds of everyone from Ringo Starr to John Bonham will attest), and can help to capture silky cymbals and chunky, bovine toms. If your budget doesn't stretch to the $2,000+/£1,300+ for a pair of these or other high-quality ribbon mics, though, even a couple of the more affordable options out there today from the likes of Nady, Alctron and Cascade can yield some pretty nifty results, and make a refreshing change from the standard condensers. With any ribbon mics, and the cheaper ones in particular, you might want to add a little to the highs with your EQ plug-in of choice, to accurately render all the cymbal detail you need. Dynamic mics are an unlikely choice for overheads ... unless that's all you've got.

FRONT-OF-KIT STEREO PAIRS

Much like the single front-of-kick mic used in variations of our mono drum set-up above, a pair of mics set up in front of the kit can often capture a big, natural stereo sound. Once again I would start with these as a spaced stereo pair, perhaps about six feet (1.8m) back and six feet (1.8m) high, and experiment with spacing and firing angle to find what precise set-up paints the best sonic picture for the session at hand. Precise parameters will need to be adjusted depending upon the tempo and dynamics of the song, the drummer and the drum kit, and the size of the room, as well as the height of the ceiling. Front-of-kit mics like these will often pick up a more reverberant drum sound, with more room sound in the brew, while still offering a stereo spectrum that is wide and full. Done right, these mics (the choices of which will be the same as most of the types above) can also capture one of the more realistic drum sounds, something close to the audience's perception of a "live drum kit" as heard in a good-sounding performance space.

Jazz and pop producers in the early days of stereophonic recording might also have been likely to use traditional coincident X and Y stereo pairs in front of the kit, and these set-ups can capture great stereo drum sounds too. These set ups—and all front-of-kit and closer room-miking set-ups really—are intended to capture more of a whole-kit sound than correctly described "over-head" overheads, with the close mics on kick and snare used, as originally intended in these situations, as spot mics to fill in added punch and crack as needed.

Essentially, front-of-kit mics could be called room mics, or close-room mics at least, and if you have enough mics can be added to a mono or stereo overhead to increase your depth and room sound.

THE "GLYN JOHNS" STEREO TECHNIQUE

Named for the British producer who has worked with The Eagles, The Who, Led Zeppelin, Clapton and The Rolling Stones, to name but a few—and who frequently used this drum-miking set-up in the process—the "Glyn Johns technique" is a deceptively simple means of placing two overhead mics to create a deep and realistic stereo drum sound without the wash, phase issues, or hole in the middle that some other overheads set-ups can produce. Close mics are also used on kick and snare as spot mics, as with most of the above set-ups, but this one really aims to paint the picture with the two overhead mics, using the spot mics to add any solidity and punch that might be lacking from those up-the-middle drums after that.

Having called these "overheads" and "stereo," you actually approach the Glyn Johns technique as if setting up a three-mic mono arrangement much like the first multi-mic set-up we explored in this chapter, with one overhead mic proper, and another that is more of a side-fill mic. This pair is far from the symmetrical ideal that stereo miking implies, but can work a certain magic to capture a fat, realistic kit sound with plenty of stereo breadth as desired. I won't go into the kick and snare part of this equation, since those elements have already been covered, and will instead focus on nailing down the most common approach to Johns's two-mic stereo picture of the entire kit. Ideally, you want your best set of matched (if possible) large-diaphragm condenser mics or quality ribbon mics for this one.

Begin by setting your first overhead mic as you might set a mono overhead, roughly in the center of the kit and about three and a half to four feet (1-1.2m) above the snare. Some engineers aim this mic at the center of the snare (probably the more common method), while others shoot it down at the drummer's right foot. Now, take a tape measure if you have one, or a length of rope or string at least, and measure the *precise* distance from the center of the top snare head to the capsule of this mic. Next, set your second mic precisely the same distance from the center of the snare but position it off to the right-hand side of the drummer above the right-rear (outside) edge of the floor tom, firing toward the center of the snare. The necessity of placing both mics exactly the same distance from the center of the snare, essential to reducing phasing issues, means that this second mic will be a lot lower to the floor than the first. You can adjust the height/distance of both mics to account for the drummer's habitual motion and stick height and so forth, but the crucial point is that you measure them each time to ensure the distance of each remains identical.

What this set-up gives you is a thick, solid overhead sound like that of our punchy, fat three-mic mono set-up near the top of this chapter, but the full benefit of realistic stereo and full-kit coverage. And to make that work, you also need to take the technique into the mixing process too. While some engineers simple pan these mics at around 9 o'clock/3 o'clock left and right or thereabouts, or even hard left and hard right, to make the Glyn Johns technique work as intended you want to start by panning the first mic that you placed straight above the snare *right* to about 3 o'clock, then pan the second mic (the lower one, near the floor tom) *hard left*. This should keep the snare centered, but with some stereo ambience, with the cymbals and toms sounding like they emanate from accurate left-right positions in the stereo spectrum.

A pair of Alctron RM-8 ribbon mics in position for the "Glyn Johns" technique, a quirky but surprisingly effective method of recording drums in stereo.

PZM OVERHEADS AND ROOM MICS

If the best you can afford for overheads or room mics is a pair of the Radio Shack PZM "boundary mics" discussed in the Hardware chapter, don't sweat it: these can often be made to perform better than many of the cheaper condenser mics available today. These mics work by being mounted to another flat surface (even though the microphone element comes mounted on a flat, square metal plate as it is), so when you put them on a wall or ceiling the pick-up surface of the mic effectively becomes as big as the surface you stick them to. You can use gaffer or duct tape to mount these mics, or even hang them, by the slot provided, from a nail or picture hook.

If you can set your drummer up with his or her back to, but not too close to, a corner of your live room, ideally one with a ceiling that isn't too low, try sticking two PZM mics on opposite points of the walls that meet in that corner, each about four to five feet (1.2–1.5m) out from the junction, and about six feet (1.8m) off the floor. As with any of our stereo set ups, you can play with these placements to get the best sound from your drum kit and room. The result should be a broad, accurate stereo image of the kit, with deep, rich lows thanks to the effects of "corner loading," a phenomenon by which low frequencies are accentuated where two flat surfaces meet. If your drum sound is just too boomy and woofy, you might have a corner that accentuates too much bass, and will probably need to try a different placement.

Alternatively, if your drummer is set up toward the center of a long wall in a large room with fairly high ceilings, try mounting your PZMs on the same plane of the wall directly behind him, from four to six or even seven feet high (1.2–2.1m), and spaced as desired. (You usually want to avoid mounting them too close to the joint between wall and ceiling, unless the resultant sound just happens to work for you.) Similarly, you can also mount PZMs right on the ceiling above the kit, spaced and positioned as desired.

To use PZMs more as room or distant-room mics, where another mic or mics might capture your closer overhead sounds, you can try mounting them nearer the corners at either end of a long wall with the drummer set up toward its center, or more distant ceiling positions, or even adjacent rooms or hallways. As such, these relatively affordable mics can be great for adding some nuanced space and room sound to a mix, when you need to use your better "proper" mics for other applications.

M-S stereo recording requires a specific technique in the mixing stage, too, as seen set up here in Pro Tools.

MID-SIDE STEREO

If you want a wide, deep stereo kit sound, yet one with good punch up the middle (aside from what your kick and snare spot mics are doing), the M-S stereo technique discussed in the Studio Approach chapter might be a good way to go. Before launching into this one be aware that, used in its textbook fashion, this configuration inherently produces a very wide drum sound. It's a very natural stereo sound, in one sense, and can sound great in and of itself, but if it will sound unnatural to have a super-wide drum kit in your final mix, you might not want to employ this one. There are, on the other hand, ways of employing elements of M-S recording to provide stereo ambience to an otherwise punchy, solidly centered kit mix, so let's look at M-S from both perspectives.

To mic a kit with a traditional M-S set-up, you would place your mid and side mics as close to each other as possible in the correct relationship, and place them where you would the mono overhead in our first three-mic set-up above, with the center mic aiming down toward the center of the kit and the side mic side on to it. You can also place the mics where you would position a mono front-of-kick mic, as discussed above. I have had great results from both of these configurations, using Coles 4038 ribbon mics in both the mid and side position, or using a 4038 as side and either a AEA R84 or Beyer M160 as mid. Follow the instructions in Studio Approach for splitting your side mic to two channels and reversing the phase of one, then panning them hard left-right, with your mid mic panned right up the middle (mono), and balancing the channels as desired.

Figure-eight ribbon mics set up over the drums for M-S stereo recording.

A fun variation on the M-S technique, however, involves splitting the two mics apart, rather than having them as close together as possible, and putting the "mid" mic above the kit as a mono overhead, with the "side" mic in the front-of-kick position to record a wide room sound. Combined with solid spot miking of the kick and snare, this configuration can give you all the advantages of our solid, punchy three-mic mono set-up detailed above, but with as little or as much deep, broad stereo sound mixed in as you like, by only adding a fourth mic to the array. Since you are panning the erstwhile "side" mic (your figure-eight mic split to two tracks) wide left-right, you don't usually have to worry about the phase cancellation issues that would normally plague many set-ups with two overhead or room mics set at different distances from the kit. Also, if you don't want a drum kit that sounds as wide as your house, just bring up a little of the side mic's left-right split for ambience, and you'll have a very realistic yet present sound. Give it a shot, and mess around with your positioning. There are a lot of creative possibilities in this one.

Mike it all up

If you want to go big-production 80s style (or do it the way many rock records are still made), you can also try putting a mic on each drum in the kit, along with a pair of stereo overheads for ride and crash cymbals, and a dedicated mic on the hi-hat, too. Sounds like a lot of work already? Well, it can be. But it's also certainly doable, if you have the mics to cover the spread (which is already seven mics on a simple four-piece kit, with another mic for each additional drum). I would argue that fewer home recordists are likely to go this route, simply because of the nature of the music that is recorded in such projects, or the paucity of gear and facilities available. But if you want a powerful, direct, and

ROOM MICS

Recordists use room mics to capture naturally reverberant room sound when recording many different instruments, but they might be most common for use with drums. Regardless of what you do with your main drum-mic set-up, if you have a decent mic or two left over—and interface channels to record them through—consider putting up either a mono or stereo room mic(s) in a strategic position to record some natural reverb, and you might be able to dispense with a digital plug-in altogether.

If you are recording the drums in a large live space, try placing your room mics near distant corners or walls at the far side of the room from the kit itself. Walk the room while the drummer is playing, and listen to the sound in different positions, both facing toward and away from the kit, and put the mic(s) where it sounds best to you. If your drum room is small and fairly dead, try positioning your mic(s) in an adjacent room with any connecting doors open, or in a hallway, or even in a room down the hall from your live room. Whether your room mics are in the same space or elsewhere, try to position them so there are no direct lines of sight from mic to drums if you want a more distant, diffuse sound. Also, experiment with facing cardioid mics toward walls or into corners rather than toward the kit, so they pick up only reflected sound.

Play with a few locations, record a little, and bring up the room sound in the mix to see if it works toward your sonic goals. Done right, a little room sound can make your drum mix sound far more "real," and can be a real boon to the overall tone of a track, especially if you are seeking authentic, un-processed sounds in the first place. Often you only need a slight touch of it in the mix to do the trick, unless you are looking for a more extreme reverb sound for your session.

extremely punchy sound from each individual tom that can be panned around the stereo spectrum for those dramatic Neil Peart-style rolls, this is the way to get it. To make that work, you ideally need to isolate each mic as much as possible (which means gating them, either while recording or after the fact in the DAW) and you must position them extremely carefully in the first place.

To record the toms individually, you will use mic placements that are much like one or the other of those we have already reviewed in "Miking the snare". A dynamic mic such as a Shure SM57, Sennheiser 421, or Beyer M201 is your most likely candidate here, although plenty of engineers will choose a robust condenser like the AKG C414. Your starting point is to position the mic up over the top of each tom—out of the way of anything the drummer might need to hit—and aiming down at the top head at a slight angle from two or three inches (30–45mm) away. In setting these mics, you also need to take on board all of the considerations we have discussed so far, regarding mic directionality and rejection patterns, in an effort to minimize each tom mic's pick up of other sounds from the kit, although they will certainly get in there one way or the other. If you have the outboard gear available, you can further aid this isolation by setting a gate for each tom mic so that only your drummers lightest likely hit of the drum will open its respective gate—or, you can apply a plug-in gate later in the DAW. For a more resonant tom sound and less direct "boom," you can mic these from underneath. Angle your dynamic mic off-axis at the resonant head from a couple of inches away, and again adjust positioning to minimize spill from other instruments.

Since you are setting a fat-sounding mic on each individual drum with this technique, small-diaphragm condensers (SDCs) are a more common choice for overheads, where they are all about cymbals and some high-end details of the stereo kit image. That said, plenty of engineers will still use large-diaphragm condensers here, too. The textbook application would be to set up a pair of AKG C451s or Audio-Technica AT2021s, or whatever you've got, as a spaced pair, usually toed in toward the center of the kit just slightly, so they pick up a good stereo spread of cymbal sound with a realistic transition through the center of the space. The benefit of using SDCs here is that they will accentuate the cymbals' bountiful high-end content but, while they will definitely pick up the rest of the kit too, they won't over-accentuate the thump and punch of the other drums, which you are capturing with close mics.

With everything else close-miked, and the cymbals covered with overheads that are more precisely dedicated to their needs, you need to put a mic on your hi-hats too. A good old SM57 or SM58 similar will work in a pinch if that's all you've got left, but this application really calls for a small-diaphragm condenser with a cardioid pattern like an AKG C451 or something of that ilk, if you have one handy, to capture the high-end detail. Don't aim the mic in where the cymbals come together or the gust of air will wreak havoc with your sound, and very possibly the mic's diaphragm, too. As with all spot mics, you want to find a position that will use your mic's cardioid polarity pattern to pick up hi-hat, and reject other drums as much as possible. Also, when you are miking everything in this way, you want to be extra careful that the snare mic only picks up snare, as far as possible, or you risk trying to blend a rattier-sounding hi-hat sound from the dynamic mic on the snare with a more high-fidelity hi-hat sound coming from its own SDC mic, with inevitably dubious results.

Once you get all of this set up, record plenty of test runs into the system, and set up your DAW's virtual mixer to give you a dynamic, moving stereo picture as your drummer rolls around the kit. If you're going to all this trouble, it is usually because you want to really accentuate the placement of individual drums in the left-to-right spectrum, so you want to hear one crash cymbal on the right, the ride and a second crash on the left, and the toms move from hard right to hard left as your drummer goes at it. Making this kind of set up work also relies a lot on processing, at least more than other drum set-ups, so the following tips on outboard or plug-in dynamics will be important to you, too.

Compression and EQ for drums

A lot of engineers will tell you that you need to compress drums during recording in order to capture the punchy, driving sound that we all know from classic rock records. Traditionally, some strategic EQ was also applied at this time, to put the optimum sound down on tape. There's some truth in that, but with digital recording you can also record everything just as it is, using the correct mic and preamp selections for the job, and add compression, and EQ if necessary, later in the DAW, during mixing or pre-mix preparation. If you are keeping your budget down and can't afford a lot of outboard (or have chosen to invest what you have in mics and preamps rather than external hardware processors, which are arguably less essential in the contemporary digital home studio), no sweat, you can add individual plug-in processors to each drum track in your DAW, and easily taste-test the affects of different levels and types of compression without being married to it in the recording process.

Some experienced recordists will still tell you that it's best to add at least a little subtle compression during recording, and then to add more as required during the mix. This can be a good way to go sometimes, sure, but if you can't practically work this way, don't worry about it. Many engineers will swear by recording kick and snare with some comp, but I do know at least a couple of reputable professional producers who say they never record kick and snare with compression, because it can tend to "suck in" sounds from other drums that you are trying to keep out of these mics. For this reason, they only ever add it afterward, in the mix. Also, don't automatically assume you need any compression at all, if you have recorded great drum sounds in the first place. When you drop that comp plug-in in on a few drum tracks, or a good stereo comp package on a bus to treat the entire kit, chances are it will all instantly sound bigger, juicier, and punchier—but if not, or if you can make it work for your purposes in the mix without comp, or with a different treatment entirely, go with what your ears tell you.

The following are some classic recommended starter settings for compressing different drums, as used in inserts in individual tracks. And they should give you subtle starting points rather than anything drastic. Better compressor plug-ins should have some useful preset drum settings, too. Use any of these to get started, and experiment with lesser and greater degrees of each parameter to discover what they do to your drum sounds. Also, some notes on EQ are included, but these should mainly be considered corrective: if you find the ideal mic placement in the first place, you can hopefully entirely dispense with the need to add any EQ later. Note that, while a lot of engineers will check the audible effects of compressor or EQ settings by soloing individual tracks, listening to kick, snare, or overheads in isolation, for example, I find it's best to do most of your checking of these tweaks with the respective drum still in the mix with everything else. After all, you are aiming to achieve an optimal sound of any drum—or instrument, for that matter—relative to everything else in the mix, and listening over and over again in isolation as you adjust parameters will tell you little or nothing about how the sound will benefit your track as a whole.

KICK DRUM COMP

RATIO: **4:1**
THRESHOLD: **–6dB**
ATTACK: **40ms or auto**
RELEASE: **200ms or auto**
KNEE: **Hard**

This is a gentle starting point for kick, but will give you just enough for transparent but functional compression if you aren't looking for an "effect" from your kick drum processing. For a punchier kick sound, reduce the attack time first, before playing with other parameters. For a bassier "boom" from the kick, increase the attack time gradually. For more severe squash, you might push the ratio right up to 10:1, and the threshold up to –15dB or so. As far as gain make-up (output gain) settings go, the textbook usage says you should really just bring the level back up so the signal going out is equal to what was coming in, before any compression reduced it. You can check that you have done this accurately by taking the comp in and out (using the bypass button on your plug-in or hardware compressor). Some compressors do have their own sonic character, though, and add a desirable something extra to the signal aside from sheer dynamics processing. Engineers occasionally choose to "push" the gain controls of these in order to get a little more juice out of them, then reduce the overall level of the drum in the track itself at the fader.

KICK DRUM EQ

If your best mic-placement efforts still result in a kick that is boxy and flat-sounding, you can try pulling down different EQ points somewhere between 200Hz to 500Hz by just a couple dBs and see if you can zone in on the annoying frequency. As with this tweak, you are more often going to correct any issues by reducing certain frequencies in this drum's range, rather than increasing them. The kick is primarily a low-frequency instrument anyway, so doing what might seem the obvious—giving it a low-frequency EQ boost—is only likely to make the track sound muddy and boomy. If the low end feels cluttered, you can try a shelving EQ setting that drops off all the subsonic audio below 20Hz, or try a gentler peak reduction of a few dB at around 60Hz. Higher frequencies do, however, impact the punch and presence and immediacy of the kick, so some additive EQ fixes you might try include a little nudge upward at 1.5kHz if you want to hear more click from the beater, and a few more dB around 5kHz (give or take a "k" or two) to make the overall kick sound punchier.

SNARE COMP

RATIO: **4:1**
THRESHOLD: **–8dB**
ATTACK: **10ms or auto**
RELEASE: **150ms or auto**
KNEE: **Hard**

Note that our first two parameters are pretty similar to the starting points for kick above. Attack, however, starts at a fast 10ms because you are always going to want a pretty sharp, punchy attack from the snare, and you can reduce it even further if you feel it isn't quite present enough at this setting. As with the kick, you can get more resonance and body out of the snare by increasing the ratio right up to 10:1, and the threshold up to –15dB or so. Again, gain should really be used to get the signal going out post-compression to the same level as it was going into the box, but you can play with this to drive the channel harder, if you like.

SNARE EQ

As with the kick drum, the snare might benefit from reductive EQ as much as, or more than, from additive. There are no hard and fast rules here, because precise EQ points will vary according to the natural sound and the set of overtones that your snare produces, and should ideally be adjusted between songs anyway. Also, if you have a great sounding snare, and have miked it well, you might find you need little or no EQ anyway. Part of the logic of reductive EQ is that it will let other instruments find their place in the mix alongside that which you are EQ-ing, and avoid the "mud" of everything fighting for the same frequency space. Reducing the snare's midrange frequencies a little will let other instruments that live in that space—guitars, vocals, keyboards, horns—punch through better, and won't hurt the snare's impact one bit. Try pulling down a band in the 350Hz to 800Hz range by a few dB (the exact point will depend on your snare, and the song) and see if that brings it all into better focus. To fatten up the snare you might try boosting it by a few dB in the 100Hz range, while cutting by 4 to 6 dB at around 2kHz. And to bring out a crispy snare sound (that is, emphasize the sound of the snares on the resonant head) play with boosting it a little in the 8kHz range.

OVERHEADS COMP

RATIO: **2:1 to 4:1 (maybe up to 6:1 for more distant room mics)**
THRESHOLD: **–4 to –8dB**
ATTACK: **1.0ms or auto**
RELEASE: **100ms or auto**
KNEE: **Hard**

As we have seen, there are several different ways of placing overheads, from genuine overheads in a spaced or coincident pair, to front-of-kick placements, to room mics, and compression techniques will vary for all of these. Some recordists don't compress their overheads at all, if they are capturing a good, live drum sound in the first place, but many find that compression helps to add air and dimension to these mics. I would advise avoiding compressing these mics during recording, but trying out different settings in your pre-mix preparation to see what might work.

OVERHEADS EQ

Of all drum mics, I would argue that your overheads, if placed right, are least likely to need any severe EQ'ing. They are there to capture a broad range of frequencies from the entire kit, and emphasizing any particular frequency bands can just produce an odd, unbalanced sound. If you are getting too much of anything in the overheads, however, like a snare that rings differently than in its spot mic, or boomy resonances from the kick, you will want to locate that frequency band on a graphic EQ plug-in and pull it down by a few dB. Also, if you are setting overheads primarily to capture cymbals, while miking up all individual drums, you might find that you want some low shelving, or to reduce certain low frequency bands, if other drums in the overheads are messing up your efforts to isolate the spot mics. In this case, you might also perhaps benefit from rolling off some mids in the 250Hz to 800Hz range. Mostly, though, you will want your overheads to present a good, solid, and balanced picture of the entire kit, with the spot mics filling in crack and punch on snare and kick respectively as already discussed, so you won't want to create any holes or peaks in that broad sonic image.

TOM-TOM COMP

If you are miking toms independently, start with comp settings that are similar to those used on snare, and adjust as necessary.
RATIO: **4:1**
THRESHOLD: **–8dB**
ATTACK: **20ms or auto**

RELEASE: **150ms or auto**
KNEE: **Hard**

TOM-TOM EQ

As with the snare, you might benefit most from cutting some of the mids out of the toms to let the other instruments breathe. Try dropping a few dBs in the 350Hz to 800Hz range. If you want to make the overtones pop some to make them sound more "tommy" than "snarey," you can try bosting a few dB in the 6kHz to 8kHz range. Other EQ efforts for toms might be corrective—isolating and reducing any odd ring or resonance—and you will need to find and apply this according to the problem at hand (and if you can eliminate such things *before* recording with a little effective damping, so much the better).

Recording percussion

Clearly this chapter has already covered several techniques for recording percussion during the course of discussing microphone placements for the drum kit in general, and the individual parts thereof, but it is worth giving some thought to how all of this might apply to hand percussion. Even if mic choices reflect those used on some part of the drum kit already, the job of recording individual percussion instruments allows you to focus on that process a little more carefully, and to hone your technique. There are many potential instruments in this category, but for the sake of economy let's touch on a few likely candidates, and you can extrapolate these techniques to others you might encounter.

CONGA DRUMS

One of the big boys of Latin percussion, the congas can be miked in a manner similar to what might be used on toms (and you can adapt any of these techniques to the smaller bongo drums, too). Usually a pair of congas are played together, each tuned slightly differently, so a pair of similar mics is ideal if you have them, and the interface and DAW channels to spare. Even a pair of SM57s will do a pretty good job here, capturing both the attack and the tone of the instrument pretty well, as will other dynamics like the Beyer-Dynamic M201 or the Sennheiser 421. The tone and response of the congas asks us to adapt our snare and tom techniques slightly, though, so ideally you would mount dynamic mics between four and 12 inches (100mm and 300mm) away from the heads, spread somewhat apart for some isolation, and aimed down at the conga heads at a slight angle. Simultaneously aiming the mics slightly outward toward the outer edge of each drum can also help you obtain a little more separation in them.

For greater fidelity, a pair of sturdy large-diaphragm condensers such as AKG 414s or Audio-Technica AT2050s will do the trick, but they will want to be placed more like one to two feet (300–600mm) from the heads, above and slightly away from the drums, aiming down at an angle again. The Coles 4038 can also be a great percussion mic, and a pair of these mounted a foot or two from the heads of your congas can sound great, or try whatever other larger ribbon mic you can get your hands on. You're unlikely to want to mix your two mics full left and right, unless you want that dramatic a spread from them. But having a mic on each drum does work great at giving you some separation in the mix so you can hear the player's movement from one to the other. If you can only spare one mic, or one channel, you can still record very effective conga tracks even so. Use any of the above mic selections solo, and place the mic as described, but between the two drums, above and slightly away, aiming down at an angle at a point between the heads.

TIMBALES

Another Latin staple, timbales are less often encountered, unless you are recording a dedicated Latin percussion outfit. You can use techniques similar to those applied to the congas, although the timbales have a lot more ring and sustain than the conga drums, and can be a lot louder, too, and their tone is generated from different parts of the drum. A better technique might be to use a pair of dynamic mics mounted beneath the open shells (timbales don't have resonant heads like many mounted kit toms or snares do). Position each mic at around the center of each of the two drums in the kit, from four to six inches (100–150mm) down from the opening, but angled slightly outward toward the outer edge of each drum. If you want a really big, high-fidelity stereo timbale sound, you can add a pair of small-diaphragm condensers as overheads three or four feet (1–1.2m) above the drums. These will also improve the sound of any added percussion such as cowbells or wood blocks that are frequently mounted to timbales, and will also augment the sound of the drums themselves, especially when the percussionist plays the rims and sides of the timbales, which is traditionally part of the technique. If the timbales are a featured instrument, you might even add another SM57 or similar to the wood block/cowbell region to pick up the required thump and ring from those.

COWBELL

As in the discussion of the timbales, a good old SM57 or similar (or Sennheiser 241 if you have one) will do a pretty good job on the cowbell. It's a loud, strident instrument with a major attack, and many sensitive condenser mics will give you a little "*ktchck*" of clipping when faced with a cowbell. Certainly engage the pad, if one exists, if you are even considering such a mic choice for your 'bell moments. A big ribbon mic can do a great job of cowbell, however; position it above and a good 12 to 18 inches (300–450mm) away, even as much as two feet (600mm), aiming slightly down toward the bell (you can play with your angles some, as regards bell opening and stick attack, to decide what produces the most desirable sound). Slightly smaller and less aggressive than the cowbell *per se* are agogo bells (often just "bells" for short). They can sound great into a large-diaphragm condenser mic from a couple of feet away, which will help to make the most of their more musical, chime-like tone. Alternatively, you can often get good results from a standard cowbell played a long way away from a large-diaphragm condenser in a large and well-dampened room. Try anywhere from six to ten feet (2-3m) and see what you get.

TAMBOURINE

Sometimes thought of the instrument of Davy Jones of The Monkees, or any singer who really can't do much else but wants to have their hand on something, the tambourine is actually one of the most-heard percussion instruments in pop and rock music after the drum kit itself, and a well-recorded tambourine track can really lift an arrangement. I have always liked the way big ribbon mics like the Coles 4038 handle the transients of the tambourine—which can be surprisingly sharp and aggressive—and give it a smooth, silky feel, but still with plenty of jangle and cut. A lot of people might want a more detailed fidelity and a greater sense of cut in their tambourine sound, though, in which case a small-diaphragm condenser is often the choice, while an LDC will also work great. A standard dynamic mic often yields disappointing results, however, with too much of a dull *thunk* or *clack* from the little cymbals.

Any such mic should be placed above and a foot or two out from the apex of the swing of the tambourine. The instrument should be played so that it is swung back and forth in from of the mic, rather than towards and away from it, unless intentionally want to emphasize that "coming and going" sound with the volume naturally rising and fall with each sweep of the tambourine.

SHAKER, MARACAS, CABASA, FISH, TRIANGLE, ETC.

Techniques for any of these are likely to be most similar to that used for tambourine, above, and similarly intuitive, too. A good small-diaphragm or large-diaphragm condenser mic is the obvious choice, but again, a good ribbon mic can work some silky magic as desired here, too. The smaller and less noisy of these—modern plastic "egg" shakers, for example—might need to be played much closer to the mic than any of the above instruments, within three to five inches (75–125mm) depending on the mic itself and the aggression of your playing. Otherwise, if you adapt playing position as necessary according to the style of the instrument, and experiment with your angle to the mic before rolling, you should achieve satisfactory results.

Working with drum samples and loops

If you don't have access to a full band, or even a live drummer, you are likely to build your tracks from drum samples using loops or programmed patterns. Many, many musicians work this way today, and for several genres of music this is the norm rather than the exception. Anything in the broad range of dance, techno, hip-hop or electronic music is likely to be loop-based, but the availability and flexibility of loops also makes it easy for a solo performer or songwriter in any other genre to use them to create professional-sounding recordings.

A drum "sample" can be any sound taken from an external or synthesized or pre-recorded source and repeated in a sequence that creates a drum beat. Recordists have used mechanized drum sounds for several decades—programmed into drum machines or sequencers—but the power and convenience of digital recording makes it easier than ever today. They come from several sources these days, too, and might still originate from hardware or software samplers and sequencers or drum machines, but are often acquired as sample CDs or downloads, many of which include live drum kits played by session drummers, professionally recorded and mixed. As such, there isn't just one method of using automated or pre-recorded drum sounds in the DAW, but several; naturally we can't cover the from-the-ground-up procedures for each in detail here, but we can at least set the course for incorporating them into your recordings.

The drum patterns used in these situations generally come from two major sources: looped drums, and MIDI-controlled drums. Looped drums use brief sections of beats that are repeated a pre-determined number of measures (hence "looped") to extend the length of a drum passage as desired, often with different intros and fills pasted in for variety. MIDI drums, on the other hand, don't necessarily have to have the same degree of repetition as looped drums. You can record a MIDI program for drums that varies the pattern every measure if you like, but often, in use, they do involve some measure of repetition. Most comprehensive DAWs available these days will have convenient facilities for programming MIDI drums and creating drum loops, although the procedure for each might vary some depending on the software you are using.

MIDI drums (or any MIDI-triggered instruments) are generally created in one of two ways: the part can be played on a MIDI input device such as a keyboard or a guitar with MIDI capabilities, and recorded into a MIDI track in the DAW, not as audio notes, but as MIDI notes that will then trigger a specific MIDI instrument linked to the track, or trigger the sounds on an external MIDI instrument. Alternatively, many DAWs allow you to write MIDI notes directly into a designated MIDI track with your computer, putting them in measure by measure according to your selected tempo and time signature, somewhat in the way you would program an old-style hardware drum machine. These notes would then be linked to the software MIDI instrument of your choice that represents the drum sound that you want them to trigger. Some DAWs come with a selection of free MIDI instruments, which usually includes several basic drum sounds, but others can be purchased as downloads, and some good free sounds are usually available online, too. Or, you can cut up existing drum recordings to isolate individual drum hits and load these into a MIDI-triggered software sequencer. Check your own DAW's instructions for setting up MIDI tracks and instruments, and you will find that these things are usually pretty easy to work with, once you get the hang of the basic procedures.

Drum loops, as distinct from MIDI drum tracks, can just as easily be constructed from a section of live-recorded drums as from a mechanized drum part. In the early days of looping, the procedure required splicing a loop of recording tape to the precise length to represent your repeated section. Then, as analog delay technology progressed, artists often used a delay unit with a long enough delay time (or a "loop recorder") to record a section of rhythm and repeat it infinitely, as desired. These days it is infinitely simpler to create and edit a loop in the DAW. With most systems, you simply load in the drum tracks that you want to loop, or record a section of live drums, if you have the facilities, select your looping tool from the tool bar, click the start of the section that you want to loop, drag to the end of the desired drum part, and click off. Usually the DAW's looping facility will then provide a window in which you can enter the number of times you want that selected part to loop. Easy—and done!

Getting loops just right, though, often takes a little more craft than this. One consideration is avoiding any pops or clicks heard when the loop cycles between sections, something that usually occurs as a "glitch" of sorts when an audio segment starts or stops in an odd place. Ideally, you want your cuts to occur during brief gaps between audio, where the signal level dips to zero. Many DAWs offer an editing facility called "zero crossing," "snap to zero," or something similar, which locks your edit cuts to zero points in the audio wave length, and thus minimizes pops and clicks as the play head rolls past these points. Check your own system's instructions for the existence of any such setting.

You also need to ensure that you select the beginning of your looped section right at the very start of the first beat (or the rest that represents the first beat, if you are looping a syncopated beat that opens with a silent downbeat) and end it precisely at the very end of the last beat in the final measure of the loop section, immediately before the next downbeat begins. Starting or ending either early or late will create a "lopsided" loop that cycles an imprecise number of measures, and produces an unusable drum track as a result. This precision can be achieved more easily than you might think, however, by using the ability of most good DAWs to lock their editing grids to the selected tempo. Ensure that you have set the song's tempo precisely to that of the drum sample that you wish to loop, and have that drum sample loaded to start precisely at the beginning of a measure. With the editing window locked to grid, your looping tool should now begin its selection at the very start of the beat (even if your mouse click is a little less than precise) and end at an equally precise point, too.

Another consideration when creating loops is that you don't want any unnatural starts or ends to your looped section (unless intentionally so, for creative reasons), such as the sound produced when a cymbal crash toward the end of the section cuts off abruptly because the start of the section cycles from a downbeat that wasn't preceded by a similar cymbal crash, and so forth. It can sometimes be a little tricky to get around these things, because you probably don't want your first looped measure to start with the decay of a cymbal crash that seems to have come out of nowhere, either, but perhaps that crash sounds great at the end of the section (which is to say, between looped sections).

One way to work around this is to start your drum track with a selection of measures from the start of the drum sample, so there's no pre-start crash there in the first place. Then, rather than looping that section, loop a following section that begins and ends naturally with a crash cymbal (the crash is just an example: your own difficulty might

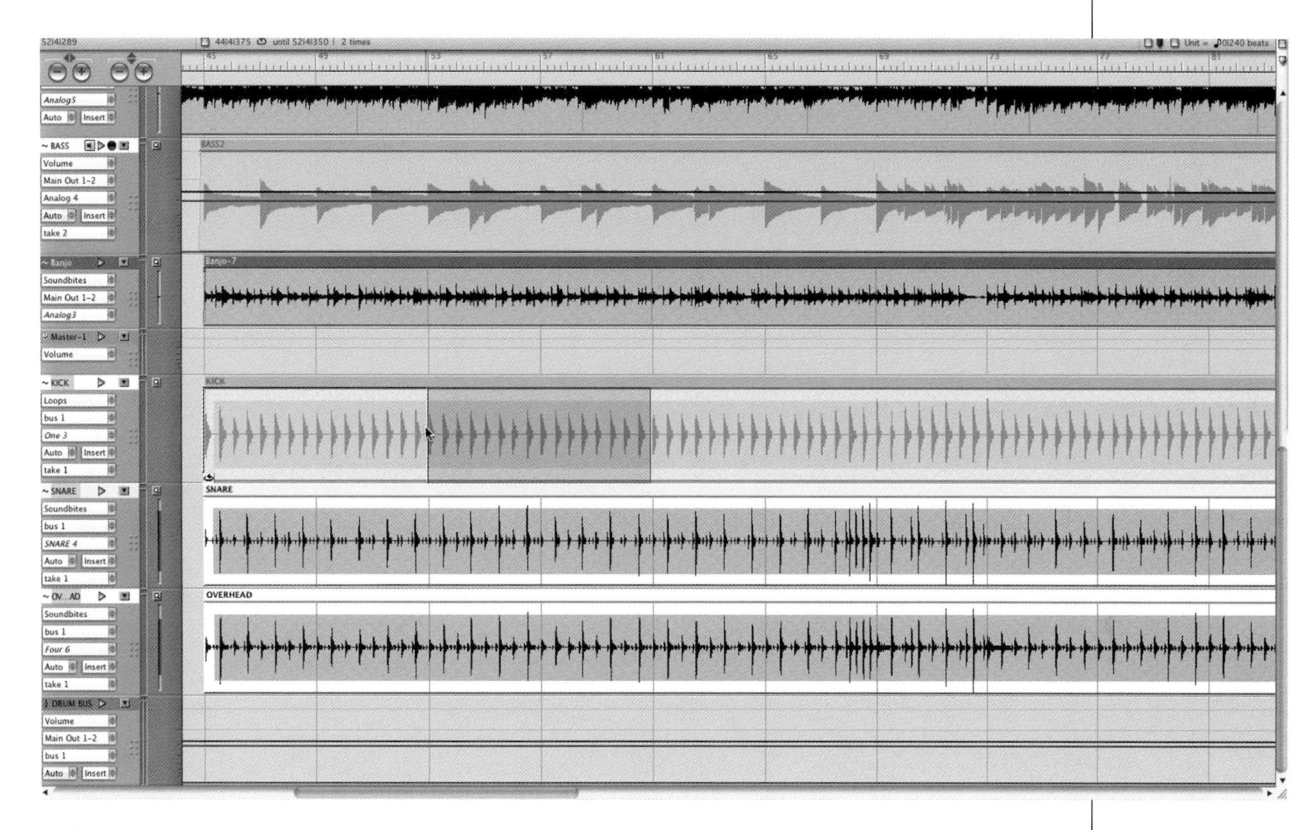

Defining a region of the kick drum waveform to be looped in Digital Performer.

come from any of a number of sounds with a longer decay that extends across the start and end of a measure). Also, consider looping several measures rather than just one or two, so that you include accents and varied beats from the original drum sample that can occur naturally within the course of, say, a four or eight-measure loop, rather than having to be "joined up" at the ends and starts of the cycled part. But what do you do when you want to end the entire song on a cymbal crash, and one that decays naturally rather than chops off oddly to silence as your last cycled drum section ends? One trick I have frequently used is to end the loop a certain number of measures short of the actual end of the song, then paste in after it the natural ending of the drum part that you have sampled, complete with the ending crash, or tom or snare decay, or whatever it is that concludes the performance. Mixing looped segments with different segments from the same sampled performance can also be a natural way of including drum fills and breaks, and ultimately making your drum tracks sound more "real." Simply loop the main drum section the required number of times to reach the point of a fill or a major change in the part, paste in that fill (which you can also loop if it's longer than the sampled segment available to you), then paste your main drum part in again after the fill, and loop it for the number of cycles necessary to take you to the next change.

If your DAW is a basic one that doesn't have a looping tool, you can, in most cases, still create 'looped' drum parts fairly easily by simply copying the desired section of the drum sample, and pasting in as many of them, back to back, as you need to create your full drum track. When doing this, you might need to draw some careful cross-fades between sections so you don't get any unnatural clicks or pops or odd transitions, but the result should work just the same as a drum part created with a looping tool.

MIXING LIVE DRUMS AND SAMPLES OR LOOPS

Clearly you can also play live drums over sampled and looped drums to create multifaceted drum parts, but a different approach worth considering is one that creates a single, integrated drum part from a combination of live and automated elements. For example, maybe you're not a bad drummer yourself, but it isn't your main instrument, and when you do try to record a full drum part on the kit in your studio your main weakness is revealed (as is often the case) in a slightly inconsistent right foot on the kick drum. You can get around this by either recording just a few kick beats on their own, working to get at least those few beats right, or by loading in a good-sounding kick sample. Then you copy or loop those throughout the song (with lock-to-grid enabled, and a click track enabled to the correct tempo) to created a kick part that is tight to the groove throughout the track. After that, chances are you can manage a pretty good job of recording the rest of the kit live without worrying about playing the kick at all. The result, when it's all mixed as desired, is usually heard as a very real drum track that has a live, human feel to it, but is still very tight and totally on the groove.

You can use variations of this kind of mix'n'match drum part in your work, too, even if you don't have a full kit to work with. Program or loop elements that need to be tight and precise to form the backbone of your drum track, then add bits and pieces of whatever live percussion you can get your hands on, and can play adequately yourself. Of course, you can also loop your own live parts if you can manage to stay on the beat for at least a few measures, but have trouble playing them steadily throughout the length of an entire song.

CHAPTER 5

RECORDING BASS

Bass comes second in our order of coverage here because it is often a partner to recording drums, although often that means recording a scratch bass along with the drummer and overdubbing a "keeper" at a later date. Even so, despite the importance of a solid bass part to any song, the sound of the bass is often given the least attention of any instrument in the recording process. I suppose that degree of neglect will be repeated here, in the relative sense, since there are perhaps more nuances to recording drums, guitars, and vocals—but let's aim to give the bass more respect and attention than it usually gets, at least, and dig into several different means of landing solid, lively bass tracks.

Recording electric bass

The old standby used to be to simply DI the bass into the board, perhaps with some compression and EQ going down while tracking, and leave it at that. Otherwise, if an amp came into play, an engineer would plonk a robust dynamic mic down in front of an Ampeg Portaflex, run that through some standard light comp and EQ, and never give it a second thought. Both of these results can yield outstanding results, and they have been responsible for countless classic bass tracks over the years. I would say our first step beyond one or the other of these simple approaches would be to aim to use *both* of them together whenever you can, so that you always have the option of picking the best of them, or of blending the two together to expand your low-end horizons. Beyond that, there are several nuances to both DI-ed and amped-up bass recording that can help you get better results and create better-sounding songs as a whole.

As ever, a good bass track really starts with a good-sounding bass guitar played well. But you can at least get acceptable results out of an "OK sounding" bass played well and recorded well. Also, since the majority of bass tracks are recorded clean and natural, things like playing method and string type and condition are likely to shine through. In most cases, you will want your bassist to be using fresh but slightly played-in strings, so they have plenty of punch, but not too many zingy, squeaky high frequency artifacts. Discuss the types of strings he or she is using, too, and ensure they are the best for the genre of music: if round-wounds are too punchy for mellower, more retro-influenced styles, perhaps flat-wound nickel or even tape-wound strings should be considered; if the tone is too mellow, go in the other direction. However your bassist might play the part live, he or she might need to reconsider the approach in the studio to make the track work within the song. Better players will easily move between pick and fingers to give a part more or less punch and presence and to fine-tune the feel of the performance.

With all of this in mind, let's examine several ways to get the low end down, both traditional and more creative, along with several means of processing and editing bass tracks to maximum effect.

DI-ED BASS RECORDING

The process of DI-ing (for "direct injection") a bass, or any instrument, really just involves running the instrument's high-impedance signal through a transformer to convert it to the low-impedance signal that a mixer or interface input likes to see, and giving it enough gain (via that mixer or interface) to provide an adequate signal for recording. Some basses with active pickups or onboard active EQ or preamps (those carrying a battery, in other words) can be plugged straight into a mixer for direct recording, but the process otherwise involves the use of some sort of DI box. These days, DI boxes fall into four main categories:

- **Passive DIs.** These use a transformer to convert an unbalanced hi-z signal to a lo-z balanced signal, provide an XLR output, and usually offer a parallel output (aka "input link") to send the original hi-z signal out to an amp at the same time, if desired. Many also offer an attenuation switch to cut the lo-z output by a fixed amount, and some offer a phase-reverse switch.

- **Basic active DIs.** These provide much the same as #1 above, but use a battery and an active circuit to provide a little more fidelity and headroom. Some of these might offer one or two more features, such as a high-pass filter (low frequency attenuation) and a ground lift switch.

- **Active DIs with gain.** These do all of the above jobs, but also carry a built-in preamp to add gain to the signal. You can run them through a line input on your interface, rather than using one of its built-in preamps.

- **Amp and speaker-simulating DIs.** Both digital and analog units—like the Line 6 Bass POD or SansAmp Bass Driver respectively—are plentiful, and are designed for DI recording as well as live use. These seek to give you an "amp in a box" sound, with speaker emulation too, to simulate the sound of a miked bass amp.

I know many bassists can feel underappreciated, or underserved at least, by an engineer's propensity to go straight to DI for recording bass tracks, but there are a lot of positives with this approach. While you might want a specific "character" or "voice" on some bass tracks, very often you simply want a firm, solid, clear, and dynamic "bass guitar sound," rather than an amped or effected sound, that will sit tightly in the mix and propel the song as a good bass part should.

The ever-handy passive DI box, your gateway to a world of bass recordings.

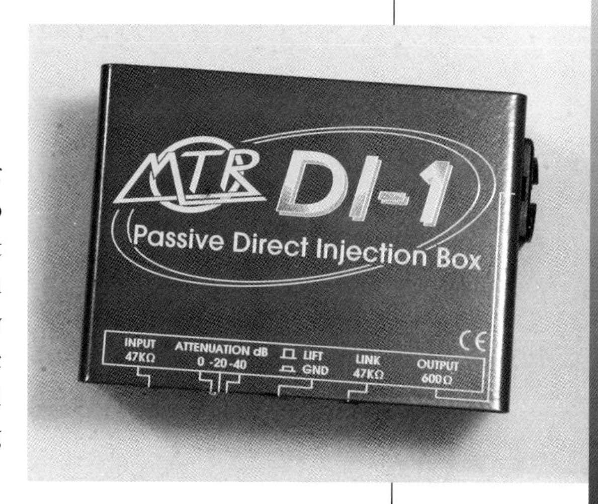

Recording through either of the first two types of DI, or the third if it has a clean, linear, and uncolored preamp, at least captures an accurate picture of the bass guitar signal as it sounds coming out the other end of its quarter-inch lead, before anything else gets in between. As such, you can always do what you want with it further down the road (more of which later under Post Recording Treatments), or just give it a little compression and EQ, if that's even necessary, and pop it into the track. As I'm likely to mention several times in the course of this chapter, even if you are miking a bass amp to obtain what you feel will be your go-to bass sound, splitting to a parallel DI-ed track as a "safety" is always a good idea, if you can spare the interface channels or recorder tracks to do so.

Another bonus of DI-ing, when overdubbing at least, is that you can crank up the backing tracks along with the current live take in the monitor speakers and let the bassist record in the control room, which can often help the feel of a performance. If you have the benefit of a separate control room from your live room, with at least decent isolation between them, you can also often get away with this while tracking live drums, without risking too much spill into the drum mics.

The availability of so many good-sounding amp and cab simulators these days, as discussed in #4 above, finds a lot of players using these for their primary bass tracks. They can definitely be great for dialing in miked-amp tones without the noise issues of a live amp, and let you track to the monitor speakers when overdubbing like other DI techniques. These units do marry you to a particular sound, though, just as a real amplifier does, and you might not want to get stuck with that fixed option this early in the process. So again, when tracking through a digital modeler or SansAmp or the like, it's a great idea to split out a paralleled DI signal pre-circuit and get that down too.

Be aware that different makes and models of DIs—passive and active, as well as DI-capable amp simulators—can and will sound a little different, too, and like anything, you get what you pay for. Plenty of basic passive DI boxes out there will translate your hi-z passive bass signal to lo-z just fine, and sound perfectly good enough for you to get something to work with. But others might deplete your tonal integrity along the way, and leave you with a thin, ratty bass sound that is harder to get good results out of when it comes time to mix. Be aware that you want to achieve your bass's full fidelity and dynamics in the signal you record, and prepare to find a better option if your cheapo DI doesn't seem to be cutting it. Also, while your decent but basic passive DI box might cut the mustard just fine when used right, you will want to keep cable lengths short to avoid depleting the signal and losing fidelity from bass to recorder. If you have to run long cable lengths, an active DI will present the best balanced, lo-z signal to make the run unadulterated.

MIKING BASS AMPS

Although I have just sung the praises of DI recording, there are many circumstances that really scream for a miked bass amplifier, and certain classic tones will be difficult to achieve any other way. As discussed above, recording two tracks simultaneously—one DI,

When possible, recording the bass to two tracks—one DI-ed, one from a miked amp—will provide far more flexibility in the mix.

one from a miked amp—really is the best way to go whenever possible, so all of the following techniques apply to that technique, as well as situations where you are only able to record one bass track and want it to be of the miked-amp variety.

Some of the more obvious amp-miking techniques might repeat themselves in the following chapter on Recording Guitars, but bass frequencies, and the types of microphones commonly used to record them, have slightly different requirements and often necessitate a different approach. First off—and let's say it out loud, as obvious as it might seem—you will be usually want to use a bass amp to record your bass tracks, one that is designed to reproduce low frequencies firmly and authoritatively. Ideally, though, you are likely to want to use a smaller bass amp than you would normally turn to for a live performance on a large stage, unless you are fortunate enough to have a recording space that's big enough to let a large amp move some air and sound its best and neighbors who won't complain when you do so. Also, since the bass is such a major part of the foundation of any song, you will need to think through your amp settings and overall tonal choices before committing any takes to tape. A little fuzz and natural amp distortion can sometimes give a bass track character in the right setting, but just because your big rock song will have crunchy cranked electric guitars doesn't mean you want lots of overdrive on the bass, too. Often, and especially when other instruments are sliding into sonic extremes, a tight, firm, focused bass will be needed to anchor the track and provide solidity. In many circumstances you will get the best results from a recording situation by using a smaller bass amp and/or cab, and keeping the gain down to maintain a clean, precise tone. Listen carefully to the amp in the room even before you place the mic, and if you notice any unwanted boominess or woofiness or wooliness, or any undesirable resonances, try moving the amp to a different position, or augmenting your acoustic treatment of the space, or both.

Learn to think several steps ahead, in sonic terms, and don't get stuck with a sound that will be detrimental to your overall mix further down the road. And if you're unsure of whether that cool bass amp sound you have dialed in will still be so cool when you get everything else tracked around it, record a parallel signal path via DI. Have I already said that?

CLOSE MIKING

Often a recordist will close-mike a bass amp with a sturdy dynamic like an AKG D112 or a Shure Beta 52A placed almost touching the grille cloth, aiming dead-on at the center of

RAISED OR ON THE FLOOR?

Even before you determine mic placement, one of the first considerations in setting up a bass amp for recording is whether you leave the speaker cab on the floor or raise it up with a stand, chair, milk crate or other form of lifting device. Any speaker cab placed directly on the floor will couple with that floor and resonate accordingly, amplifying the low frequencies through the structure. In some instances, this can add depth and fullness to the bass and be exactly what you are looking for. In perhaps the majority of recording scenarios, though, you are likely to prefer the punch and clarity of the amp when the speaker cab is decoupled from the floor. As such, you will still hear the full depth of low frequencies that the amp is capable of producing, without added resonances that might create mud and clutter the mix. What sounds deep, full, fat, and impressive in the room—and might work great on a live stage—can often just get in the way in the context of a recorded track, and produce more sub-sonic garbage that you have to try to remove with reductive EQ later in the process.

If you are lifting the amp by placing it on another hard object, you might also consider using a slice of carpet underlay foam, a folded wool blanket, or some other dampening material between the bottom of the speaker cab and the makeshift stand. Otherwise, vibrations from the speaker cab might be transferred through the stand and into the floor, retaining part of the problem that you are trying to cure by lifting the amp in the first place.

the speaker, just the way most live engineers will do in a gig situation, for a lively, punchy sound. For a rounder, warmer sound, you can also try moving the mic away from center, and aiming it slightly off-axis. Move it around and experiment as much as time allows, and you'll discover that every slight shift in position brings a slightly new sound with it.

Close miking is obviously a necessity in a live setting to avoid the spill that might occur with more distant mic placements, but this position can bring unwanted artifacts with it, too, and doesn't need to be your standard mic placement for all bass recording, especially when overdubbing, when you really do have plenty of other options to choose from. If you are recording more than one instrument together, though, in a semi-live situation, and using a bass amp rather than DI-ing, close-miking is likely to be your only practical choice.

When used close in, many microphones exhibit a sonic phenomenon known as "proximity effect," which accentuates the low frequencies of the sound source. Many mics used to close-mike six-string guitar amps will do this too, but the effect can give regular guitars more body and weight, since they are operating primarily in the midrange (note that many dynamic mics intended for use on live vocals have low-frequency roll-off built in to cut lows below a certain level and minimize proximity effect, so they aren't suitable for recording bass in the first place). Proximity effect as experienced when

A small Ampeg bass combo close-miked, slightly off-axis, with a Shure Beta 52A dynamic mic.

recording low-frequency sound sources, on the other hand, can make a bass track boomy and unbalanced, and might inhibit your Ability to capture a great sound. Often, the existence of this effect, or lack thereof, is rather hit and miss. Try moving the mic around, and aiming it at slightly different parts of the speaker cone, and you should find a position that works well for you. Before committing to any "keeper" takes, record your bassist playing a little something from everywhere up and down the neck, or at least the full range of what will be played in the track, to make sure no frequencies are unduly accentuated.

If you are overdubbing bass parts and don't have to worry about spill from other instruments being played at the same time, you have plenty of other techniques to choose from.

SEMI-DISTANT MIKING

Moving the microphone back from the front of the bass amp can often capture a much more realistic and better-balanced sound than close miking. When you consider the fact that the length of a sound wave increases, literally, as frequency decreases, it makes sense that a mic placed further from the speaker cabinet will obtain a fuller picture of your bass tone. That's not to say that low frequencies can't be heard at extremely short distances, of course, as anyone who puts their ear up to the front of an Ampeg SVT cab will tell you (Note: don't try it), and it's the *frequency* of the vibrations of a note (that is, their rapidity) that determines its pitch, rather than the mere size of any wave you could chart. So, for example, a note at the pitch of 50Hz with a sound wave that's around 25 feet (8m) long will still sound like the low-E on your bass guitar when heard from just a few inches away. But a little space can still help bass frequencies to develop more fully, as you can imagine, and giving the mic a little distance can often help to produce a fuller, more natural recording (just as it can with the guitar, as we shall see in the next chapter).

That said, it's not practical to record bass at a great distance—that of the length of the sound wave of the average note on the instrument, for example—because pulling the mic back that far will also open it up to more reflected sound and room reverberation than you will usually want in a bass track. When tracking bass, you want some depth and fullness, but you also want to minimize reflected sound even more than you would with most other instruments, and for two reasons. First, low frequencies are even more problematic when reflected in corners and against walls than midrange or high

Multi-miking a bass combo with a semi-distant Audio-Technica AT4033 condenser mic, and a Shure Beta 52A in close.

frequencies; second, you don't usually want much reverb in your bass sound anyway, other than perhaps the touch of room sound it gets with everything else in the final mix for some musical styles.

The first method of distant miking really just follows the same procedures used for close miking above, but you pull the mic back. Try distances of from six to 18 inches (150–450mm) to start with. Going further, you might experiment with placements of up to four feet (1.2m) or so if your room isn't overly reflective. See what works for the track. The results are likely to depend somewhat on the size and relative aliveness/deadness of the room, the amp you are using, and the type of music you are recording. Height and orientation-wise, start by positioning the mic dead center, aiming at the dust cap in the center of the speaker. Listen to the sound through the monitors or headphones, and ideally record a little and listen back to check the results. Move the mic up, down, and side to side to test other positions, and go with what sounds best for the project at hand.

For this semi-distant position you can use the same dynamic low-end specialists discussed above, but that safety zone of air between speaker and mic also opens up plenty of other possibilities. Provided you aren't cranking a large bass amp to the max, you can try any large-capsule condenser mic with adequate specs to record low frequencies. Most should handle the job just fine. If your condenser has a bass roll-off switch, be sure to switch it out before recording. You can also frequently get great results with one of the more robust ribbon mics. A flat-out rock or metal track looking for grind, meat and muscle might still prefer a dynamic such as an AKG D112 or Shure Beta 52A, but for a wide range of other genres you will get more depth, breadth, air, and fidelity from a good condenser or ribbon mic. When trying a ribbon mic with a figure-eight polarity pattern, you might consider placing a mini "gobo" (discussed in detail in the Studio Approach chapter) on the back of the mic to reduce the reflections that it will pick up otherwise.

In addition to any straightforward semi-distant miking placements, you can also enhance the interaction of bass amp and microphone with the following techniques:

CORNER LOADING Any corner formed where two walls meet will serve as a natural amplifier of low frequencies. You can use this phenomenon to your advantage when recording bass with a technique called "corner loading," achieved by placing the speaker cab with its back centered in a corner (though not touching the walls) firing outward. If the walls that form this corner are bare and hard, they are likely to be more reflective than you want, inducing undesirable phase-canceling reflections. The effect is usually at its best with a little damping of the walls, a set-up that still helps to throw the low frequencies forward, while minimizing phase issues. If you don't have a suitable corner to place the amp in, you can construct one with a pair of baffles arranged at an appropriate angle.

FLOOR FLOATER I don't know if there's a correct technical name for this position, and I suppose it's a form of boundary miking really, but floating a dynamic or ribbon mic just above the floor a short distance in front of the bass cab, with its capsule firing toward the ceiling, can often capture a full and realistic bass sound. Mount the mic on a sturdy stand so it hovers just an inch or so off the floor without touching it; if you are using a figure-eight mic, you might consider attaching a mini gobo to the back-side capsule, or at least placing some insulating material under it to avoid capturing unwanted reflections there. Of course, you can also apply this miking technique using a good old Radio Shack PZM mic laid flat on a solid floor at an appropriate distance from the bass cab or, on a carpeted floor, mounted to a sheet of plywood laid in front of the cab.

ISO TUNNEL Just as with one of our techniques for recording kick drum, a tunnel of semi-isolating material can help you record a sharper, punchier distant-miked bass sound if room reflections are getting in the way. As described in detail in Recording Drums, gather together whatever loose sound-damping and absorbing material you can find around the house, and form it into a tunnel that extends from the front of the speaker cab. Place the mic in the far end at your chosen distance, firing toward the speaker, and close up the back end of the tunnel as best you can.

RECORDING BASS WITH A GUITAR AMP

If you expect to get most of the solidity and fullness of your bass sound from a DI, but want some grit and grind from a tube amp, you can also mic up a smaller guitar amplifier to do the job. Be aware that such amps aren't made to optimally reproduce the lowest frequencies of the bass guitar, and shouldn't be used on their own for bass tracking, but if you are getting your firm low end from a paralleled DI track anyway, a smaller guitar combo might give you a little something that enhances your overall tone.

To avoid potential damage to the speaker, or at least to prevent loosening the cone up more than your donor-guitarist might prefer, you will want to run the guitar amp through a robust speaker rather than anything vintage or low-wattage, or ideally through a small bass cab if you have one handy (otherwise, keep volume within reason). Chances are you won't want too much distortion in your sound, and just a little will add plenty of fur and warmth to the overall tone when you blend it with your DI'd sound in the mix. So proceed judiciously with your gain and output settings before hitting record.

To make the "guitar amp as bass tone tool" thing work, listen carefully to what you are getting from your DI'd track, and consider what you might want to add to that. Whether it's more midrange grind, a little hair around the edges, or just a general perception of warmth and that oft-abused concept of "more tubeyness," you can usually dial it in pretty successfully with a 15- or 20-watt guitar amp. As a rule, I find that amps with 6V6 output tubes stand up to a little bass action better than those with EL84 output tubes, and 6L6s are great, too, but most amps carrying them will be louder than you want for this recording scenario. That said, whatever amp works to fill in the tonal cracks around your big, punchy DI'd sound is the one to go with.

RE-AMPING THE BASS

If you are tracking the bass with only a DI for whatever reason—either because you don't have an amp or the right mic available, can't get away with making the noise while tracking, or your bassist and drummer are tracking together and you don't want any spill in the drum mics—you can still get some real, live amp sound into your bass parts by "re-amping" the tracks at a later date. Re-amping is the process of running a pre-recorded signal back out from your DAW via one of your interface's analog outputs and into a real live amplifier, to record the track anew via a microphone. Sounds simple enough, and for the most part it is, but to make it work you need to convert the balanced low-impedance line-level signal into the high-impedance signal that your quarter-inch amplifier input wants to see.

A few products exist that are designed to do this job, such as Radial Engineering's X-Amp and the self-explanatory Reamp box. Both of these active units undertake the process as well as adding useful features such as level controls and ground-lift switching (along with two parallel hi-z outputs on the X-Amp). Keen-eyed and sharp-minded readers might already have figured out, however, that you can create your own re-amping device by reversing the signal through a passive DI box, which, as we have already learned, has a high-impedance input and low-impedance output. To make this work, you need to acquire—or create—a balanced cable with a quarter-inch TRS (stereo) male plug on one end and a female (output-end) XLR connector on the other, which is easily done by sacrificing a spare XLR to XLR mic cable (a conversion that will also be useful to connect any XLR-out devices to quarter-inch TRS-in devices).

With that in hand, the process is simple: route your DI-recorded bass track to your interface output of choice, connect the quarter-inch phone plug end of your nifty cable to that balanced output, the XLR end to the output of your passive DI box, and a standard quarter-inch guitar cable from the input of the DI box to the input of your amp of choice. Be sure you have made the connections and powered up your DAW and interface before switching the amp on, or out of standby at least, and proceed with a low amp volume, and a very low output volume from the recorded bass track to avoid overloading the input of the amp. Adjust both gradually as necessary to achieve the amp tone you are

Using correctly wired adaptor cables, you can use a standard DI box "in reverse" to re-amp a pre-recorded bass track.

looking for, and move on to miking and recording the amp as you would in any of the Miking Bass Amps scenarios above.

Many of the pros of re-amping have already been defined above, but there are a few cons, too. Chief among these is the fact that a bassist's playing feel will be different through a DI than through an amp, and that might change his or her performance slightly. The many advantages of re-amping are enough to make it a handy tool, though, and one worth having in your arsenal.

Recording acoustic bass

If you dabble in jazz, authentic rockabilly, bluegrass, vintage country, or even acoustic pop, you might encounter an acoustic bass now and then. These come in two flavors: the classical-styled archtop "double" bass with f-holes and fretless fingerboard, often referred to as a "stand-up" or "upright" bass in less classically minded circles; and the smaller flat-top acoustic bass that's designed more like a standard flat-top acoustic guitar, with a round soundhole and fretted fingerboard. They have to be recorded somewhat differently, and both are handled differently to recording an electric bass. Let's take each individually, and look at several ways of handling these beasts.

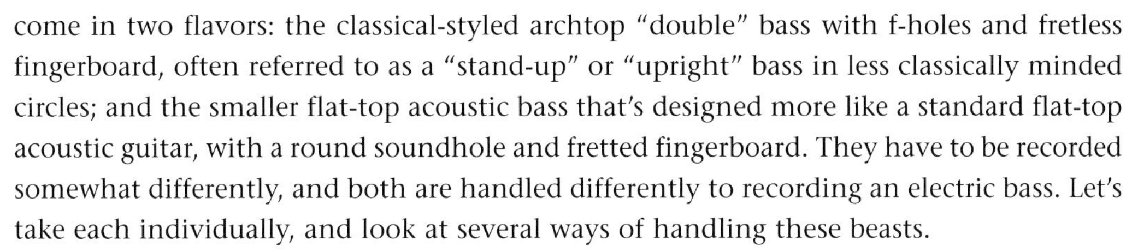

UPRIGHT "DOUBLE" BASS

These big throwbacks to the orchestra pit can be intimidating to deal with, but a double bass can sound great in the correct musical context when you find right way to record the thing. Although these instruments have f-shaped holes (f-holes) that are commonly referred to as "sound holes," you really don't want to be messing with the sound that comes out of them. Put a mic right in front of the scrolled "f" and you'll get something dark, murky, and not at all conducive to good bass tone.

Like archtop guitars, or any acoustic guitar really, an upright bass will throw out a surprisingly broad range of subtly different sounds from different parts and positions of its body, and you can often adjust your recorded tone dramatically simply by moving the mic around and listening. Before doing even that, though, move your ear around and listen for what you feel is the "sweet spot." A good starting point is a position in front of the strings of the instrument about half way between bridge and fingerboard and some six to eight inches (150–200mm) out. If you had the choice, you'd stick a great Neumann U47 mic there and be done with it. Not many of us have a U47 of course, but your best condenser mic, with high-pass or low-frequency roll-off switch disengaged, should do a pretty good job.

If you want an even warmer vintage-jazz type of sound, a good large-geometry ribbon mic like an AEA R84, Coles 4038, or even one of the (much) more affordable Chinese-made ribbons can do a great job in this position, too. You will probably want your ribbon to sit just a little further out to avoid too much proximity effect, which will emphasize the lows in an instrument that is already lows-heavy and possibly make it boomy and muddy. Or, if used closer in, be prepared to roll off some low end with the EQ further down the road, unless you've got a mic that avoids this phenomenon in the first place. Using a ribbon, and positioning it further away, also necessitates a good low-noise preamp with plenty of gain, since this isn't the loudest or punchiest of instruments, so that's another consideration.

If you want to add some sharpness and edge to the warmth and depth of this main mic, try adding a second mic—which can be a small-diaphragm condenser this time, or a smaller ribbon like a Beyer M160—positioned to fire at the lower bout of the bass, between the bridge and the endpin, either side of the front of the instrument. For more string noise, which will also boost your sense of attack, move this second mic (or your single larger mic, if you're still going with just one) closer to the fingerboard, or even a good distance up the neck, aimed at the performer's left hand, some eight to 12 inches (200–300mm) out from the fingerboard.

Most professional players are likely to have an acoustic pickup mounted to their upright bass, because these are rarely miked for live performance, and are usually jacked through a small bass amp. Such pickups will usually yield a tone that's far inferior to that of even a mediocre condenser mic placed in the right position in front of the instrument, but you can DI this signal nevertheless to see what you get from it, or run it through a bass amp and mic for another flavor. Either or both can be blended with your miked acoustic track(s) during mixing to craft your ideal tone for the project.

FLAT-TOP ACOUSTIC BASS

Acoustic basses of this variety seemed to come into their own during the same *MTV Unplugged* era that brought a renaissance for the acoustic six-string guitar. But most of these really aren't designed to be heard "acoustically," at least not in any venue larger than a living room, and rely on built-in piezo pickups to be heard in almost any live context. For this reason, the sound we have come to associate with the flat-top acoustic fretted bass is really a combination of the electric sound of the piezo pickup and the acoustic sound of the instrument, so you might want to consider blending these in your recordings, or at least having the tracks available to give you the option of doing so in the mix. Most such basses also have active preamps built right in, so you can usually plug these straight into a quarter-inch input on your desk or preamp without having to go through a DI box on the way. Have the bassist set this preamp's onboard gain control, if it has one, so it isn't clipping the input of the pre. Also, since a direct signal such as this usually has more extreme transients than you get from a miked acoustic instrument, set the input levels on your interface carefully so that even the most aggressive playing passages stay well short of clipping in the DAW's input meter. (It's a good idea to ask your bassist to play you something "harder than anything you play in the song" to test these levels; inevitably, musicians play more aggressively than they think they do once the song gets rolling for real.)

There are a lot of choices available for miking these instruments. As with the double bass addressed above, you want to steer clear of the soundhole in any flat-top acoustic bass if you hope to get anything other than woofy mud, and since that soundhole is big and round and right in the middle of the instrument, there's a lot of real estate to avoid. I have two favorite positions for recording a flat-top acoustic bass with just one mic. For the first, place the mic at around the 12th fret on the neck, some six to eight inches (150–200mm) away from the strings, firing toward the point where the neck and body meet. For the second, position the mic about the same distance away, but down at the body end, aimed at the region of the top just below and behind the bridge. As with recording the double bass, have your bassist play while you move your ear around in front of the instrument, and you will hear many different shades emanating from different positions. Try the mic in what seem to be the best of these to see what you get. The ideal mic is again a large-diaphragm condenser with no low-end roll-off present, or a big ribbon mic for a warmer sound, but a dynamic mic will do in a pinch, positioned closer to the bass.

If you're looking for more of an authentically *acoustic* acoustic bass sound, you might consider dispensing with the direct input (unless you've got enough input tracks to take it anyway, just for the heck of it) and putting two mics on the instrument. You can go with both of the two starter positions above—one mic on the lower part of the body, one on the fingerboard (which can be a small-diaphragm condenser if that's all you have left), or play around with other two-mic options. Acoustic or not, this is still your bass instrument, and is likely to be mixed right up the middle. For that reason, you aren't looking for a stereo sound from these two mics, but a solid representation of the instrument's best tones, which you can blend together for a good end result. For more single and multi-mic techniques, check the more in-depth discussion of miking acoustic guitars in the next chapter, and try adapting some of these to the bass.

Compression and EQ for bass

Bass is an instrument that traditionally is treated with a lot of compression during recording, and often some creative EQ-ing too. The peaks and troughs of the bass's dynamic range can vary dramatically, whether a player is using a pick or fingers, or thumb-slapping certainly, and compression is often essential to help smooth out the levels and keep the extremes from overloading your track, forcing you to pull down quieter moments more than would be ideal.

As with most of our in-the-box techniques, however, the DAW and the plug-ins available to it make it easy to record your bass straight, and compress and EQ the track or tracks later, in the mixing process. If you have a decent hardware compressor handy, and the wherewithal to use it correctly, you might still want to try recording the bass via some comp to apply this same levels-smoothing thinking to the signal entering the interface, and also to make use of a little of the juicy goodness that many analog compressors can add to a bass tone. Beware of over-compressing your bass tracks too, though, and squashing the life and dynamics out of them. If you are tracking through an analog comp, you might want to use slightly lower ratio and threshold settings than these starting points for plug-in comp settings. And of course some bass tracks—as with any other recorded instrument—might sound great and sit perfectly in the mix without any comp (and/or EQ) at all, so don't assume that you need to go straight to that 1176 plug-in on every occasion.

Try these settings for starters, but be prepared to tweak as necessary, depending on the material and the performance.

BASS COMP SETTINGS

RATIO: **3:1**
THRESHOLD: **–6dB**
ATTACK: **20 to 50ms or auto**
RELEASE: **150ms to 250ms or auto**
KNEE: **Hard**

The threshold level is particularly flexible, and you want to roll the knob up until you see your meter start to indicate some gain reduction, but not too much. You might start with a threshold of as little as –4dB for a less dynamically extreme performance, with a ratio of 2:1. For more serious squash, your threshold might go as high as –10dB or even –15dB, with a ratio of 4:1 proving useful on many more aggressive tracks, or even anything up to 10:1 if you really want to pummel it.

As far as EQ goes, you can often do right by the bass by carving a low frequency window out of other instruments that really don't need to play in that ballpark, as we will examine in more detail in the Mixing chapter. Bass and kick need to cooperate well, and a few nifty tricks for helping them do so will be examined later in the book, too. For the most part, though, the bass guitar is the only instrument that needs to be doing a lot in the sub-80Hz range, so you can help your bass track(s), even before you apply any EQ at all to them, by applying reductive EQ to other tracks in the form of a high-pass filter that dumps everything below 80Hz. Very often, reducing those low frequencies in other instruments will create the space the bass needs to punch through—often with the aid of a little compression, as above—without necessitating any boost in bass frequencies at 80Hz and below. If you still need more low-end boom than that provides, though, try boosting the bass below 80Hz just slightly. You can also usually give the bass presence a good goose by boosting its lower-mid and midrange elements somewhere within the 140Hz to 360Hz range.

These days, one major conundrum of bass recording and mixing revolves around the effort of maintaining any bass presence at all when the material is played back on the smaller speakers that abound today: earbuds, desktop PC speakers, iPod docks, and the like. These little jobbies just aren't going to thunder with your sub-80Hz goodness however hard you hit that band, but you can "trick" the bass track into maintaining its presence in the mix by giving it a judicious boost in the 900Hz range. This will help to make the overtones developed above many of the root notes to pop a little better, and give the impression of a deep, firm bass track.

Phase-aligning bass tracks

Any time you record two bass tracks, for example one that is DI-ed and one from a miked amp, as frequently advised in this chapter, you will need to consider phase-alignment issues in order to make those tracks sound their best together in the mix. I'm not talking about reverse-phase issues here, where one track is entirely the reverse of the other thanks to a mic or speaker or other link in the signal chain that flips the phase of one track relative to the other. This is an issue too, certainly, but a more obvious one, heard as a serious loss of low-end weight and a general "hollow" feeling in the track. To cure issues of 180-degree phase reversal between two tracks of the same instrument, bass in this case, you will ideally correct the problem before tracking, by punching the phase-reverse button on one channel of the mic preamp, DI, or mixer. Otherwise, you can always do it later in your DAW by using a plug-in with a phase-reverse switch.

Phase "alignment," however, as opposed to phase reversal, usually has a less dramatic but nevertheless deleterious effect on your tracks, and will be heard as more of a softening, furring, or muddying of the bass tone when the two tracks are combined in similar proportions. In this case, what you are hearing is the slight slurring effect of two sound waves that represent the same performance, but which aren't quite playing back as precisely parallel tracks—that is, one track is very slightly time delayed when compared to the other.

How does this "time slip" occur in the first place? When the signal from the bass is split at a DI box into two different signals—one recorded directly from that box, the other via a microphone positioned in front of a guitar amp—that second signal takes longer to get from the DI to the front of the amp, through the amp's circuit, out again through the speaker as sound waves in the air, into the mic's diaphragm and circuitry, down the mic cable into the preamp and finally into the interface and the DAW than the first signal

RIGHT: the waveforms of two bass tracks—one a DI, one a miked amp—before being phase-aligned. BELOW RIGHT: the same tracks after phase alignment: note how the peaks and troughs coincide more closely.

takes to get from DI to preamp to interface. The delay might constitute only a few milliseconds, nowhere near enough to be heard as an echo even, but when the two tracks are played back together the imprecise phase relationship of the two sound waves will cause slurs and cancellations of certain frequencies in the performance, and generally soften up your bass sound. If your combined amped and DI-ed bass tracks sound less happening than you had expected, try muting one and then the other in turn and listening to the song with just one or the other bass track in the mix. Does it sound tighter and more solid already? If so, you probably have phase-alignment issues to deal with.

While this might sound like a major pain in the ass, the DAW makes it a relatively simple problem to correct. Start by ensuring that your two bass tracks are next to each other in the editing window, then zoom in on them so that the transient peaks of the waveforms of each are clearly visible, something like the familiar *blip-blip-blip* image of a heart monitor on your favorite hospital drama. Find an easily identifiable peak in each track, most likely one at the start of a passage where it's clear that each represents the same sonic moment in the DI and mic tracks, then grab the mic track and slide it forward in the song (ie toward the left of the editing window) until you have aligned it precisely with the DI'd bass track. Play the song again with both bass tracks in the mix in near-equal proportions, and you should hear a much tighter, fuller, punchier bass this time. Now you can mix these two together in whatever proportion you desire to obtain the bass sound you are looking for in the tune, without the two softening up the punch and solidity of the part as a whole.

Make a habit, any time you record two bass tracks, of performing this phase-alignment at the very start of your mixing process, after you have edited (comped) together any alternative takes into your final bass performance. A lot of time can be wasted messing with compressor and EQ plug-ins in an effort to correct a soft, wooly bass tone which suddenly comes to life on its own once you have remembered to precisely line up the two tracks.

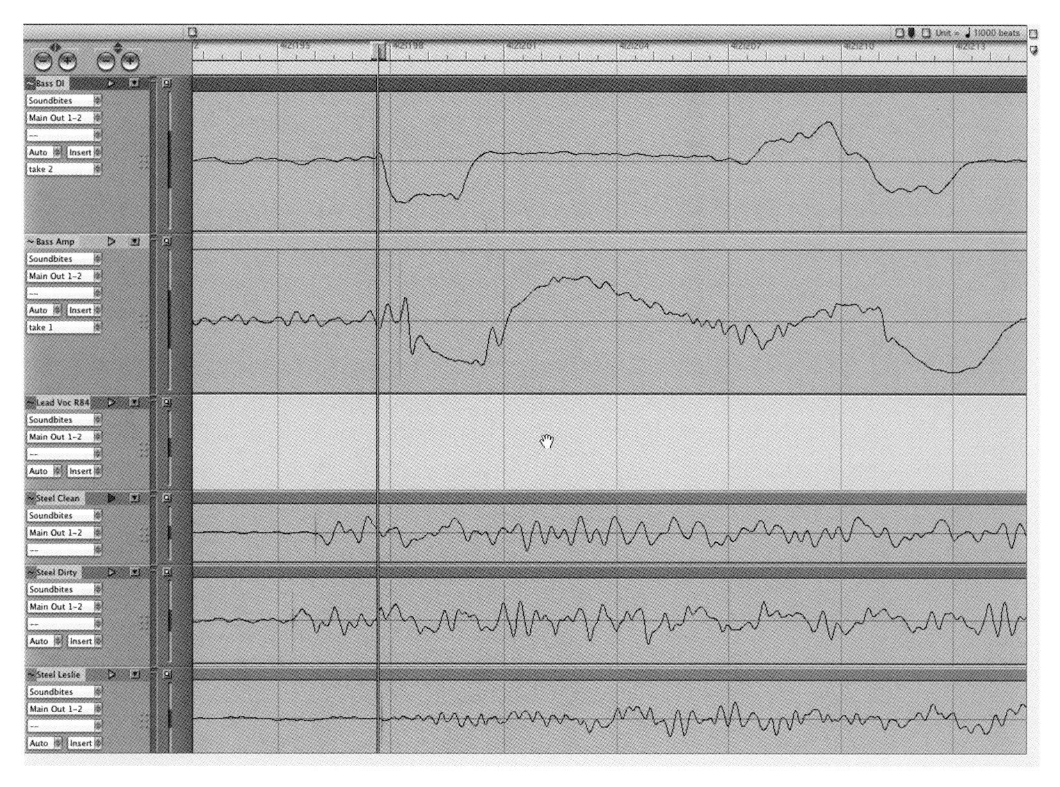
Bass DI
Soundbites
Main Out 1-2
Auto
Insert
take 2
Bass Amp
take 1
Lead Voc R84
Steel Clean
Steel Dirty
Steel Leslie

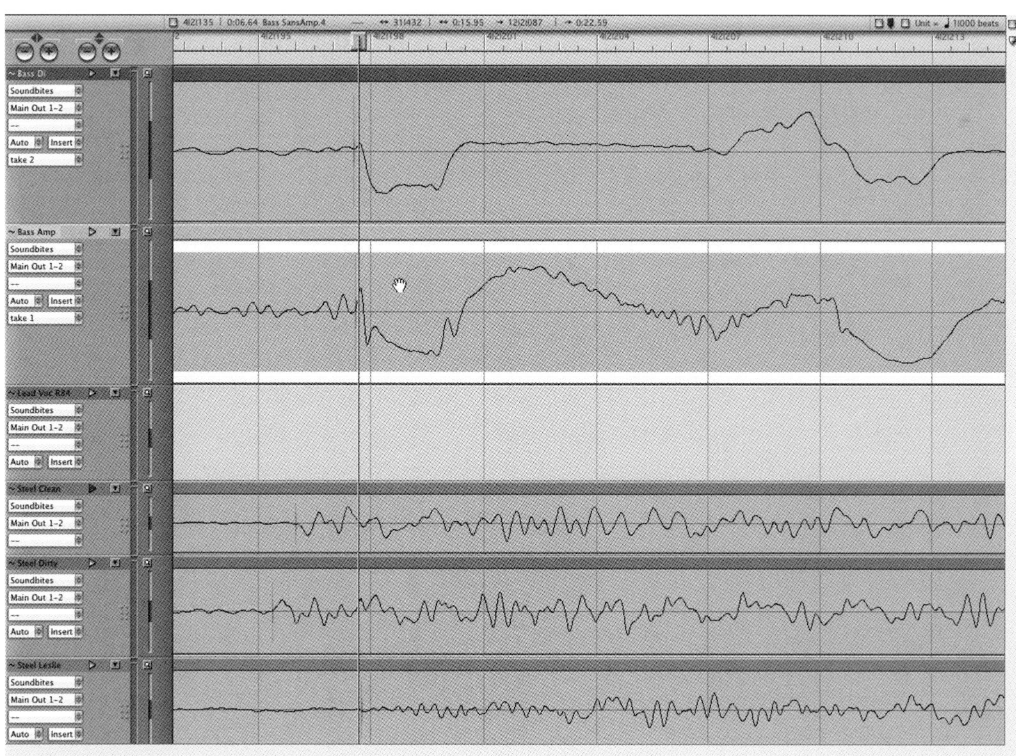
Bass DI
Soundbites
Main Out 1-2
Auto
Insert
take 2
Bass Amp
take 1
Lead Voc R84
Steel Clean
Steel Dirty
Steel Leslie

CHAPTER 6
RECORDING GUITARS

Speaking as a guitarist, this might just be my subjective slant on the subject, but it seems there's a greater multiplicity of techniques for recording guitars than for any other instrument. The extremely wide range of tones produced by the amplified electric guitar in particular, and the great many genres of music that it is used in today, necessitate a large number of methods for recording these diverse sounds; and capturing anything from the cleanest clean to the filthiest distortion—and everything in between—usually requires very different techniques. Even an acoustic guitar, an instrument that would seem to be married to its single inherent voice, presents a great many sonic nuances and subtleties depending on how you mike and record it, and can be made to sound quite different through different approaches. Let's go deep into recording techniques for both electric and acoustic guitars, as well as delving into the entire concept of creating guitar tones that are appropriate to the studio. Hopefully we will unveil a little something to capture the right sounds for just about any kind of music you might want to make.

Recording electric guitars

It is much more common to record electric guitars through digital amp and effects modelers these days than it was just a few years ago, whether via an outboard hardware unit such as the Line 6 POD or Johnson J-Station, or DI-ed and treated in your DAW with Amp Farm or any of the many plug-in guitar processors. These are indeed handy tools, and sometimes will work great for your projects, but I would argue that the real deal—a miked guitar amp—is still going to have more tonal veracity and dynamics in most recordings. If your music is at all guitar based, you should learn to work with the "old school" techniques if you want to produce recordings that stand out from among the herd, and that's what we'll concentrate on here.

In addition to a thorough exploration of mic techniques used for recording guitar amps, we need to get a grip on the amps themselves if we are to have success with electric guitars in the home studio. All too often that big rig that works for you on the live stage just won't hack it in any studio, much less a small and poorly isolated home studio. The recording guitarist needs to maintain the flexibility of attitude and performance to adjust his or her set-up to deal with the particular challenges posed by this very different environment. For this reason, you need to start your adventure in recording electric guitars by rethinking your idea of "the guitar rig" entirely, and re-shaping it into something more appropriate for the studio. That usually means either using a smaller amp, or constraining the volume of your big amp to make it manageable. I will discuss this in more depth in the Studio Amps and Crank It Down sections later in this chapter, but keep these principles in mind as the following mic techniques are discussed.

As with any instrument, the cornerstone to achieving good electric guitar tracks is recording a good guitar and amp in the first place. That doesn't have to mean expensive gear (though quality never hurts), but is really an impetus to keep whatever you have at your disposal in good shape, well set-up and maintained, with fresh strings and tubes (valves), and so on. Any guitar to be used should be professionally intonated before any session, if you can't do this work yourself, so that its overtones ring true and it fulfills its maximum potential in the harmonics department. It goes without saying that you want to tune the instrument, too, using a reliable electronic tuner, but remember to check and correct tuning frequently between takes, too, to keep it all happening.

During the tracking process, when layering up overdubs of two or more guitars to produce a big rhythm sound, or a rhythm-lead counterpoint, use two different guitars wherever possible (ideally, guitars with different types of pickup), and different amps as well, or at least different amp settings. The differences in timbre will help you achieve the size and depth that makes such efforts work, and avoid the muddiness incurred by too much of the same thing fighting for sonic space in the mix. Also, when layering multiple rhythm parts, consider changing chord positions on subsequent takes, or using a capo to play open chord shapes further up the neck. Anything you can do to keep from just piling on more of the same thing—whether tonally, or musically—will add to the depth and dimension of any multi-tracked part.

SINGLE CLOSE-MIC TECHNIQUES

Anyone who has played a gig in a venue large enough to have a full sound support system with all instruments miked is already aware of the most basic, and most obvious, means of recording a guitar amp. Position a Shure SM57 or similar dynamic mic so it's nearly kissing the grille cloth in front of your amp's speaker, and you're done. And this proves effective for many scenarios in the studio, too. If you're looking for pure punch and grind from your electric guitar parts, and seeking to minimize interference from reflected sound in the room, the close mic is often the way to go.

A Shure SM57 close to the grille cloth, aimed toward the center of the speaker cone.

Even when you're rolling with this technique in the broad sense, though, subtle variations of approach will reveal nuanced differences in the tones you can achieve. In the above "live sound" scenario, the more considerate engineer will have put some thought into precisely where on the face of the speaker cone he aimed the mic, or if you were playing a combo or extension cab with more than one speaker, might have asked you which was your best sounding speaker and miked that one. In the studio, we multiply these considerations exponentially, because the sound we capture will be more intensively "under the microscope."

Positioning your mic an inch (25mm) or less from the grille cloth and aiming it straight at the center of the speaker cone—pointing at the dust cap, in other words—yields a bright, punchy, detailed sound that suits many requirements, but can occasionally be too harsh for some. At the other extreme, aiming the mic at the edge of the cone, where the cone meets the suspension (the area just inside the speaker cutout in the mounting baffle) usually results in a looser, warmer, more raw and edgy tone. Between these two positions, there's a wealth of voices to be explore, and every inch of real estate that the mic covers between dust cap and cone edge will bring a noticeable sonic shift, without you even touching the amp's controls. Also, aiming the mic straight at the speaker, in other words, mounted at 90 degrees to the flat plane of the front of the amp, and aiming it off axis, at a slight angle to the speaker, will result in different sounds, too. With an assistant helping, or the guitarist if that's not you, try moving the mic around the surface of the speaker while listening through the monitors or headphones for the changes in tone. If you don't have enough isolation between live amp and monitors, record a little in each of several positions to listen back to. Pick the position you like for the track, and go with it.

Moving the mic (an M201 this time) toward the edge of the speaker cone, and aiming it off-axis, captures an entirely different sound.

Once again, though, you aren't likely to really know what works best until you get the song a little further along in the mix, when you can hear how the guitar sound sits with the vocals and other instrument tracks. Often, what sounds like the "best guitar tone" in the room isn't always the "most effective guitar tone" in the track, but as ever, at this point you can only take a stab at what you think will work—work ahead a little to verify that as much as possible, if you can—and build through experience a "tool kit" of mic positions that achieve what you are seeking.

Naturally, different mics will sound different too. An SM57, the classic, is typically thick and mid-forward; a Beyer M201 can be roughly similar, though with perhaps less of a midrange hump and slightly clearer high-end detail. Other more affordable dynamic mics of this ilk should be somewhere in the ballpark: anywhere from punchy to aggressive, with plenty of meat to the tone. Any decent condenser mic able to handle the sound pressure levels of close-miking will present greater fidelity and more high-end detail. A ribbon mic that can take the pounding—which a Royer R-121 is made for, and

TRACK WITH OR WITHOUT EFFECTS?

The traditional line about recording in a professional studio is that you should ideally track guitars "dry," or un-effected, so that more considered effects settings can be applied later, in the mix. While this maxim might make sense for vocals and some other instruments, or for bus or channel processors like compressors and EQs, guitar-specific effects pedals often play a big part in shaping a player's core tone. As such, his or her interaction with the instrument is likely to be very different with and without these units engaged. If the sound of a handful of pedals truly "makes" the guitar tone of a particular track, go ahead and record them live during the tracking takes. If you, as an engineer, feel that habitual effects selections (yours, if you are the guitarist too, or those of your performer) are likely to clutter the track and inhibit your efforts to maximize its sound later in the mixing process, consider altering the pedal selection. Or, if there's any doubt—or any heated debate—track from two amps split into different rooms, one with effects, one without, and you have the best of both worlds to work with.

a much cheaper unmodded Alctron ribbon can handle, or perhaps a Beyer M160 if you aren't setting amp volumes that can peel paint—will give you more sense of air and depth, and usually more warmth besides, along with a certain smoothness that is often very appealing on electric guitars.

Note that when using a single mic to close-mike a cab with more than one speaker, you will first have to decide which speaker to mic. Even if all speakers in a multi-speaker cab (a 2x12, 2x10, 4x12 or 4x10) are exactly the same, variables and imprecise tolerances in the manufacturing process often mean that different individual speakers in a selection will sound slightly different. Before choosing which one to mike, you will need to decide which sounds best for your particular needs; for the sake of your hearing, don't do this with the naked ear, but record a little of each and listen to it played back through your monitors. Or, if you have a way to isolate the wiring to one speaker at a time and listen to it in the room, that works too. Many speaker cabs have mixed pairs or quads of different types of speaker these days, too, and these will of course sound even more different from each other. We will cover other more complex methods of miking multi-speaker cabs later in our multi-mic techniques, but even when single-miking, you can give your tone a head start by selecting the best speaker for the job.

Of course, if you're looking for a greater sense of depth and air, and a little room sound in there with it, you will adapt your technique somewhat, namely setting up what we might call distant miking.

DISTANT-MIC TECHNIQUES

Some of the above-mentioned condenser and ribbon mics, and certainly their more delicate cousins, will be a lot happier positioned further out from the speaker. Aside from any considerations of mic safety, however, more distant mic techniques are usually undertaken for their sonic results, which are anywhere from slightly to considerably different to those in close-mic positions. Close miking is usually done at an inch or less from the front of the speaker cabinet, although you might pull some mics back a couple of inches further; distant miking, though, really begins ten to 12 inches (250–300mm) out, where many condenser and ribbon mics start to bloom. You can also get interesting results from dynamic mics moved back into this range (or placed somewhere in that "in between" zone too), but these techniques are primarily undertaken to let more sensitive mics breathe a little, and to capture a greater sense of depth and space in your guitar tone in the process.

With either your condenser or ribbon mic of choice, start about 12–18 inches (300–450mm) out from the speaker to record an electric guitar sound that is still pretty solid and direct, but which captures some sense of air and space and natural room reverberation. You can aim the mic straight at the center of the speaker for a direct and detailed tone, as described above, or move it around in the field, trying different direct and off-axis placements. Any position that achieves a desirable tone is valid, and you don't have to remain on the same plane as the speaker itself. Raising the mic up above the level of the speaker and aiming it down slightly to fire toward the upper edge of the cone can help to let the sound bloom as it reaches the mic. Or, in a room with a carpeted floor, you can try positioning the mic lower to the ground, even below the level of the speaker itself, to cut out some of that side of the reflected sound. Positioned as such, an end-fire mic can be shooting either toward the amp on a plane that hovers above the floor or at an angle toward the speaker, while a side-fire mic can be aimed in either of those ways, or positioned to fire straight at the ceiling with the amp sound washing over its capsule, as in our semi-distant "boundary miking" technique for bass guitar in the previous chapter.

Placing a mic at a distance from the guitar amp, as with this AEA R84 ribbon mic, brings more depth and overall room sound into the tone.

In most cases, mic placements of 12–18 inches (300–450mm) from a single-speaker cab shouldn't provide major phase issues (see the following section on ambient miking for considerations of this), but combos or extension cabs with more than one speaker might create phase issues in and of themselves. Some mic placements relative to, for example, a 2x12 speaker cab will induce time differences between the waves from one speaker hitting the mic relative to those of the other, and possibly create frequency cancellations that are deleterious to your guitar tone. Even when both speakers are of the same make and model, they are likely to perform slightly differently—thanks to subtle variables of the manufacturing process—and to present ever-so-slightly different resonant frequencies, efficiencies, core tonalities, and so forth. For all of these reasons, extra care is required when placing a microphone at a distance from any multi-speaker cab (by close miking one of the other of these speakers you all but eliminate such issues, but also eliminate your access to the great sounds available from distant miking). Cabs with two different types of speakers, popular these days, can also present phase issues, of course, but when the two are carefully selected to blend and complement each other well, a single semi-distant mic can often capture that successfully, if placed well. Use your ears, don't rush the process, and be prepared to tweak and tweak again to find that magic position.

AMP ON THE FLOOR, OR RAISED?

We investigated this issue in the previous chapter, Recording Bass, but I'm guessing many guitarists will head here first, so it's worth visiting separately in relation to the six-string guitar. One of the first considerations in preparing a guitar amp for recording is whether you leave the combo or speaker cab on the floor or raise it up with a stand, chair, milk crate, or other form of lifting device. Any speaker cab placed directly on the floor will couple with that floor and resonate accordingly, amplifying the low frequencies through the structure. Many players like this in their live sound, and enjoy the low-end boost that the amp-on-floor gives their tone—which is why some guitarists prefer to tip their combos back for better self-monitoring, rather than raising them entirely off the stage floor—but your considerations need to be different when recording. If leaving the amp on the floor increases the meat and body of your guitar tone in a way that will work toward achieving the optimum tone in the track, fine. If it only creates unwanted low-end resonances that will interfere with the bass and kick in the mix (or be cut by a high-pass EQ filter later in the process) it probably makes more sense to raise it up. Lifting an amp, or decoupling it from the floor with some sort of isolating pad, will often give you a clearer, punchier sound that works well in a recorded mix. The only way to know is to listen carefully to both options, and try some in your track, and to learn from experience.

If you are lifting the amp by placing it on another hard object, you might also consider using a slice of carpet underlay foam, a folded wool blanket, or some other damping material between the bottom of the speaker cab and the makeshift stand. Otherwise, vibrations from the speaker cab might be transferred through the stand and into the floor, retaining part of the problem that you are trying to cure by lifting the amp in the first place.

MORE-DISTANT OR "AMBIENT" MIC TECHNIQUES

To get more depth and room into your electric guitar tracks, particularly if you are fortunate enough to be able to record in a space with a "good sound" and some semblance of decent natural reverb, you will want to move the mic even further from the amp. The further from the speaker you place the mic, and the more into the center or far side of the room, the greater the proportion of reflected sound to direct sound in the blend of what the microphone picks up, and the greater the sense of "air" and "room" in the sound. Often you will want to combine this with a close mic to retain the option of blending in as much punch and directness as necessary, but if you only have one track, or mic, available, an ambient placement will sometimes do the trick on its own.

In discussing his recorded tone on 'Communication Breakdown' with *Guitar Player* magazine in 1977, Jimmy Page gave a major plug to distant miking techniques, and his words are worth considering here. "There's a very old recording maxim which goes, 'Distance makes depth,'" Page related. "I've used that a hell of a lot on recording techniques with the band generally, not just me. You're always used to them close-miking amps, just putting the microphone in front, but I'd have a mic right out the back, as well, and then balance the two, to get rid of all the phasing problems; because really, you shouldn't have to use an EQ in the studio if the instruments sound right. It should all be done with the microphones."

In addition to confirming the usefulness of an ambient mic, Page's words reaffirm that, if you want a particular sound in your guitar track, it's best to try to achieve it with the mics first, rather than fixing it in the mix with added effects, EQs, and processors.

Your ambient mic is most likely to be a good condenser, probably a large-diaphragm type although a small-diaphragm type will work too. Plenty of ribbon mics will give good service as ambient mics also, if you have a clean, high-gain mic preamp to track them through. And where do you put it? Well, three or four feet (1–1.2m) back from the speaker will start to get a significant amount of room sound into the mic, but for more ambient placements you might want to try six feet (1.8m) back or more, and experiment with different heights from the floor, too.

For a tip on finding the optimum ambient mic position, let's turn, funny enough, to Jimmy Page's former bandmate, John Paul Jones. Jones was not only the bassist for Led Zeppelin, but an outstanding engineer and producer in his own right. During an interview several years ago he told me that one great approach is to use your own ear like a mic, and stick the mic at the position in the room where the guitar tone sounds the best to you. This is ideally done with another person playing the guitar: cover one ear, and walk around the room listening to the sound in different positions. When you hear a sound that really nails what you're trying to capture, set up the mic right there. Done.

MULTI-MIC TECHNIQUES

Without specifically intending to, we have already stumbled into the fact that you will sometimes want more than one microphone on your guitar amp to achieve the ideal sound in your tracks. As discussed in the above section, many semi-distant and ambient mic techniques will be most useful when you track them along with a close mic, to retain the option of blending in a more direct tone to create your overall sonic picture. It almost goes without saying, therefore, that any single-mic positions discussed thus far can be combined into multi-mic sounds in the mix when recorded to different tracks. There are also several other approaches to multi-miking that might come in handy now and then, however, and which are worth some exploration.

To capture two speakers in a multi-speaker cab, or to record a bigger sound that delivers the response of two different microphones in similar positions on one speaker, you can try using two mics in a close or semi-close placement. If you're using two different mics on a single speaker, place their capsules as close together as possible, without touching, in order to minimize phase cancellation. This technique might seem redundant, but can often yield outstanding results, allowing you to blend the characteristics of two different microphones to capture one amp sound—a bright, detailed condenser and a punchy, midrange-heavy dynamic, for example. On guitar cabs carrying two or more different speakers, try miking each speaker separately, placing the two mics—of the same type, or different—the same distance away. Some amp makers use two different types of speakers in 2x12 and 4x12 cabs to fatten up the tone, and this miking technique will make the most of those. Even two speakers of exactly the same

Blending a close and a distant mic, such as this Beyer M201 and Audio-Technica AT2050, can achieve a sound that is tight and punchy but with plenty of depth and "air." Two Beyer-Dynamic mics used up close, an M201 dynamic and an M160 ribbon mic, are blended to capture the full sound of a 2x12 extension cab.

type, however, will often sound slightly different, and blending them might yield great results.

Interesting sounds can sometimes be captured by simultaneously miking the front and back of an open-backed speaker cab, too. Position a dynamic mic in the opening in the back of a combo or extension cab (I find the back-of-cab sound is usually a little more raw, fat, and boxy than the front-of-cab sound, and often it doesn't work on its own), and use your preferred close-mic technique on the front. Be aware that you will need to reverse the phase of one channel when using this technique (unless the different mics used are already reverse-phase of each other), since the sound produced by the back of any speaker is always 180 degrees out of phase with the sound produced by the front of the speaker. Used on an open-back 1x12 cab, this front-back blend can sometimes achieve much of the fat, boxy sound of a bigger closed-back cab—or can sometimes just sound terrible.

When you are also tracking a close mic at the same time, you might want to use any of our stereo mic techniques discussed in the Studio Approach chapter to capture some genuine stereo guitar sound in the room to blend in. Such techniques won't always be desirable, because you don't often want that much of the instrument present across the stereo spectrum; for punchier or more aggressive guitar tones, you are likely to want to blend mics into a single mono picture that you place somewhere in the L-R field, and chances are you will be overdubbing another electric guitar track to mix in elsewhere. But for more atmospheric or, well, ambient tracks, some stereo miking might go a long way. Or if you just want to bring in a little genuine stereo sound with your main guitar part (rather than creating it with a stereo reverb or delay plug-in) you might give this a shot. Any of the coincident or near-coincident, spaced pair, or M-S techniques will do a good job when used right. Or try a pair of PZM mics mounted on walls or ceiling points some distance from the amp.

Be aware that however hard you try, your two-mic effort—whether stereo or mono—just might not sound as good as one mic on its own. This might be curable with some attention to phase cancellation issues (as discussed below), but it might just be the way the sound is working for you that day. In that case, there's no shame in going with one mic. Do whatever sounds best in the track.

PHASE ISSUES

The more distance you put between mic and speaker, the more likely you will have to consider phase cancellation issues caused when waves reflected off walls and ceilings bounce sounds to the mic at slightly different times than they take to arrive directly from the speaker. The result of this is an effect called "comb filtering," which cancels out certain frequencies and emphasizes others, and creates an odd sound in general. Part of the reason for using distant-miking techniques is to obtain some "room sound" in the tone, which is created in part by such reflections, but at times these will have an adverse affect on the focus and solidity of your guitar sound. If a distant position with just one mic is sounding considerably more thin, loose, and washy than a close mic on the same amp, move it around, experiment with other locations, and see if you can eliminate these issues through mic placement alone. Otherwise, consider using a baffle or two to shield the mic from specific reflective surfaces. You can even go the whole hog and build a guitar-amp tunnel not unlike that recommended for semi-distant bass amp miking in the previous chapter.

The use of two or more mics is likely to result in other phase issues when these mics are combined in the mix, since they will almost certainly be capturing sound waves that reach the mic capsules (and ultimately, the DAW) at slightly different times. Whether such issues are bad enough to cause a problem, or even to be heard, depends on the situation. First, ensure you aren't trying to blend two mics in an entirely reverse-phase mix by flipping the phase of one of the two channels and listening again (many DAWs include "reverse phase" functions—often part of a "trim" plug-in—that you can use right on your virtual mixer). If your two-mic sound goes from hollow and bottomless sounding to fat and full, you had a reverse-phase issue. Once you know that both mics are at least in phase with each other, you can try moving the position of one around until any other phasing issues are less obtrusive, which is simply determined by finding a pair of positions that are really smoking tone-wise. Alternatively, you can often fix phase issues in the digital realm. Record your two-mic signal on two separate tracks, then zoom in on the sound waves (soundbites) in each of the two channels in your DAW's editing window, and drag or nudge the soundbite of the ambient mic forward a few milliseconds at a time until the soundwaves line up perfectly. Listen again, and you should hear a very different blend.

MULTI-AMP SET-UPS

Blending the sounds of two different amps can often achieve a deep, rich guitar tone, but it takes some thought and effort to get it right. Countless artists have crafted their larger-than-life recorded tone by blending two or more amps in the studio. Keith Richards and Stevie Ray Vaughan are among the more widely written-about examples, but the list goes on and on. Whether you want multi-dimensional clean, crunch with definition, or mega overdrive, give some consideration to the tone you hope to achieve with two amps that one amp just isn't getting you, and a blended pair might get you there.

Before you even set up the mics, though, you will need to address some basic issues that also come into play when two amps are used together live. There seems to be about a 50-50 chance that any time you connect to two amps simultaneously, one will be reverse-phase of the other. This will be heard as an odd "hollowness" in the tone when both amps are played together, and usually a lack of low end, too. It can also sound like an artificially enhanced stereo spread; I find it can almost make you feel a little seasick after prolonged listening. The problem can be cured by reversing the polarity of the wires going from the output jack to the speaker(s), or by using an A/B/Y "amp switcher" pedal with a phase-reverse switch on one channel. You will need the A/B/Y ("Y" means "both") pedal to connect the two amps in the first place. As well as the phase-reverse switch, it should have a ground-lift switch on one side to remove the hum that can result from a ground loop induced by connecting to two grounded amps at the same time. Suitable pedals are made by Lehle, Keeley Electronics, and Radial, among others.

Once you have two amps playing well together, there are a number of different ways to capture them. Obviously you can use any number of single-amp techniques to mic them, but you will need to consider the amount of spill between amps if you want some degree of separation in their sounds when mixing. Or, to simply blend the two-amp sound as heard in the room into a single mono track, you can use just one mic to record both. To best achieve this, set the two combos or cabs side by side, angled inward at a slight "V', and place your mic of choice anywhere from around 12 inches (300mm) to a few feet back, firing at a spot that captures a good blend of the sound from both amps. You can't use any truly direct-mic placements to do this, of course, but you can still vary your mic position to achieve a range of different tones. If this sound works for you, and you don't need multiple tracks to work with later, go with it. I have also had pretty cool results recording amps configured in this way with an M-S stereo mic placement a couple feet out from the speaker cabs. The mid mic captures a good, solid picture of the two-amp blend, while the far left-and-right stereo images offer each respective amp with more separation, along with a little reflected sound of the amp from the other side.

With two amps side by side, any good close-mic placement on each should work fine, and most cardioid or hyper-cardioid dynamic mics will minimize spill from one amp to the other's mic. If you want to use the mics slightly further away, or to combine a close mic with a semi-distant mic, you might need to create some form of baffle between the amps to shield each mic from the sound of the other. A rectangular hardshell guitar case

"DUAL MONO" GUITARS

While most mic techniques for guitar amps discussed so far, other than the dedicated stereo techniques, have been considered with a view toward blending multiple mics into a single mono guitar sound when mixing, you can also use different mics on the same guitar amp in an infinite array of "dual mono" configurations. That is, while true "stereo" is a balanced and ideally equal left-right sonic picture, there's nothing to stop you, for example, from mixing your close mic at 11 o'clock and your ambient mic at five o'clock, or two close mics on different speakers at ten and two o'clock, and so on. Placing your multiple mic tracks from the same guitar takes at different positions in the stereo field can help to create a bigger guitar sound, and give one guitar part much of the depth and dimension of two overdubbed parts, while retaining the tightness and precision of a single take. In some cases spreading multiple mics around the stereo field will just get in the way of other instruments competing for space in the mix, and ultimately clutter your efforts. Often, though, I have achieved great results by using guitar tracks in this way.

with a quilt draped over it can do a decent job of this in a pinch, or get creative and use what you've got to build a semi-absorptive barrier between the amps. If you want optimum isolation and have another room to work with, put the amps in entirely different rooms, run your cables to and from them, and shut the respective doors as much as possible. Degrees of isolation such as this are ideal when you want to treat each amp slightly differently, or to blend them in some manner other than pure mono.

MIKING THE STRINGS

If you want to add a little acoustic jangle to any electric guitar part, you can also put a mic on the strings of the instrument, with the amp in a different room. Although not a lot of volume is produced here, from a solidbody electric especially, you can still usually capture enough of a picky, percussive chime to add some attack and presence to your amped guitar sound. This technique can be great at livening up clean arpeggio parts, as well as some slightly grittier strummed rhythm parts. It is usually less useful when blended with heavily overdriven parts, or anything based around aggressive power chords.

DIRECT INJECTION GUITAR RECORDING

Direct injection, or DI-ing, does have its place in the recording of electric guitars, and might prove a useful tool in a number of circumstances. There are plenty of ways of achieving good results with DI-ed guitars, so let's examine a few of these here.

DI-ing just might provide the best means to the sound you are looking for, particularly when trying to achieve that funky, snappy Stax or Motown rhythm tone, retro Nashville guitar tones, or a super-clean electric-pop guitar sound. Namely, sounds that were and are desirable when you really want the guitar to tackle rhythmic duties, rather than taking up too much sonic space in the mix. Today, you will most likely DI a guitar with the intention of perfecting the tone later with judicious processing, although plenty of vintage guitar sounds on classic recordings of the past were achieved guitar-to-DI-to-board-to-tape. Voila! Sometimes a passive DI straight to your preamp of choice or direct to the interface's preamp channel, then some judicious compression applied in the DAW, is all you need to nail any of the above-mentioned tones.

Other applications for DI-ing will be used to achieve "in-the-box" tones that replicate a miked guitar amp, without the fuss and noise. Several digital and a few analog amp and effects emulators will work well for these purposes, or you can use a pure DI to record the track, then apply your amp tones as desired later in the process using Amp Farm or Eleven Rack or any of a number of other guitar-processor plug-ins after the fact, many of which are included with the DAW software you might purchase.

DI-ing is also a great solution when you want to track guitars alongside live-miked drums or other instruments and don't have the isolation available to do so without spilling guitar amps all over the live mics. This can be achieved by using an amp emulator to record through, or by using a straight DI with the intention of re-amping the sound later, as below.

Amp-simulator plug-ins, such as Digidesign's Eleven, provide a handy means of attaining miked-amp tone from a DI'd guitar track.

RE-AMPING GUITARS

We discussed re-amping guitars in the Recording Bass chapter, and you should revisit that section for the mechanics of achieving this. The basic process is similar, but there are also some other considerations that bear upon this tool as applied to guitars. Bassist friends will tell me this is just a biased guitarist speaking, but I would argue that the tone and feel of an amp is usually even more integral to a guitarist's performance than it is to a bassist's, and tracking without that amp is more likely to alter his or her performance, even if only slightly, as a result. You can cop some of that amp feel by having the guitarist monitor through plug-in guitar amp and effects emulators, or even by splitting the guitar to two tracks—a DI and a live amp—which retains the option of re-amping just the DI'd signal at a later time to more precisely hone your tone for the track.

In a pinch, I have even re-amped guitar tracks that were originally recorded through relatively clean amps in the first place, or on one occasion, even a semi-overdriven amp that wasn't quite overdriven enough. Re-amping is also a great means of bringing in in-amp or before-the-amp analog effects that you didn't use in your original tracking, or which weren't available to you at that time, such as a tube-driven spring reverb unit of the type that performs best pre-input, a vintage amp-based tremolo sound, or perhaps a tape delay that sounds more authentic when used into a particular amp. I have also found re-amping to be a great way of making the most of a Leslie guitar track. Part of the magic of running a guitar through any Leslie or Fender Vibratone or other rotary speaker cab is that dynamic sound you get as the rotor(s) speed up and slow down during changes between speed settings, but it can be difficult to achieve optimum timing for these changes on the fly while playing anything but the simplest guitar part. By DI-ing the guitar and then re-amping it through a rotary speaker cab with a live mic on it, you can hit the speed footswitch exactly where desired, without playing at the same time, and get that multi-dimensional movement happening where it creates the most magic in the track as a whole.

STUDIO AMPS

Put simply, a "studio amp" is usually smaller and significantly less powerful than an amp that might be used for live performance on a large stage, although more and more guitarists are turning to smaller amps for live use these days, too. In the course of this examination I will occasionally revisit some ground that I covered in my earlier book *The Guitar Amp Handbook* (Backbeat, 2005), although it should be even more apropos in its present context.

Plenty of players going into the studio for the first time imagine hauling in the big amp stack they use live on large stages, miking it up for enormous sounds, and just wailing away. The truth is that the recording environment and live environment are so far from each other in their requirements that they could exist in different galaxies. Forget the scenario of your favorite guitar hero slamming his or her Les Paul or SG through a pair of 100-watt full stacks the way he did it at the last major arena-rock show you attended: the chances are they didn't record those blistering lead sounds on the album that way, and trying to do it yourself might only result in disappointment, frustration, and a lot of wasted studio time. The solution? Enter the "studio amp'.

"But that's not the way they did it in the good old days!" you declare? Ah, think again, Captain Overdrive. Whatever fire-breathing monsters they used on stage, guitar greats such as Jimmy Page, Eric Clapton, Brian May, Keith Richards, Pete Townshend, Dave Davies and even sometimes Jimi Hendrix all crafted some of the most classic

The humble tweed Fender Champ, a classic among smaller studio amps.

tones of all time from diminutive, low-watt amps in the studio—amps that in many cases wouldn't even be loud enough for a small gig, but that sound phenomenal fired up with a good studio microphone in front of them. The fact is, there's a paradox when you get down to recording: in the very refined and often enclosed environment of the studio, small amps can easily be made to sound very big, whereas big amps often sound disappointingly small, because they descend into sonic mush and swamp your entire track. There are a few interrelated factors behind this, which bear some further examination.

First, most players who have any gigging or recording experience with tube (valve) amps realize that every model has its "sweet spot," the volume level where it really starts to give up the good stuff, and that spot is usually close to half way up on the volume or gain control, and sometimes beyond. Big 50-watt or 100-watt (or even many 30-watt) amps that kick out righteous tones in a 200 to 500-seat club or hall when you get them up somewhere between 11 o'clock and 2 o'clock on the dial just don't sound anything like you want them to when they're reined in at 8 o'clock in a smaller room. Crank them up to the sweet spot regardless in a smaller room, and the confined space just doesn't let the sound blossom the way it needs to in order to sound its best. Whack a 5-watt to 15-watt amp up to its sweet spot, however, and it will bloom in just about any room, without rattling the hinges or floor studs besides.

Hand in hand with the above, the best studio microphones tend to be extremely sensitive, and are engineered to handle less-than-extreme volume levels. Yes, you can put a Shure SM57 or similarly robust dynamic mic in front of just about anything and it can take it, but many recordists prefer to tap the sonic splendors of high-end condenser or ribbon mics. A cranked 50-watter will overload the front end of a sensitive condenser mic and result in a mushy track that is distorted in all the wrong ways, and even a cranked 30-watter might blow the thin metal film element in a ribbon mic. Get a smaller amp sounding its best, though, and you can put either of these microphone types right up on it without fear, to make the most of a high-end mic translating the performance of a dynamic tube amp operating right within its sweet spot.

Also, say you do find a room to record in where you can ratchet up that 100-watter without fear of reprisal, and a microphone willing to handle it (some name artists do record this way, of course, and many mics can take the punishment). As often as not, the results on tape, or hard drive, aren't anywhere near as "big" sounding as you would hope. Recording a big, loud amp without extreme attention to details such as microphone technique (which often requires multiple mics, skillfully and strategically positioned), the application of studio compression, and other esoteric tools in the experienced engineer's arsenal, too often translates to a rather flat, characterless mush in the track. In short, it's just a lot easier to make a small amp sound good, and once you get it down in the track, physical size becomes irrelevant. What really matters is crafting a lively, original tone that sits right in the mix, and one that comes back out of the listener's speakers sounding as big as you want it to sound.

Today, the makers of the better hand-wired tube amps recognize that many discerning pros are going to use small amps in the studio, and there are some stunning models available. The smaller of the hand-made options—what I'd consider the Super-Duper-Champs, none of which are direct copies of anything—include models like the Carr Mercury, TopHat Portly Cadet and Prince Royale, Dr Z Mini-Z, Cornell Romany, Cornford Harlequin, and plenty of others. I'm sure I have forgotten a few good ones too, but while there's a pretty good selection available, it's not all that big a list. The choice in slightly larger amps is even greater, although many of these get you quickly up to small-gig volumes.

The sub-10-watt format is a fun end of the vintage market to explore, too, and one that is usually more available to the musician on a budget. You can find B- and C-list amps from the likes of Kay, Harmony, Airline, Wards, Oahu, Supro, and National (lots of the Valco brands) for peanuts, and these are frequently fantastic-sounding little studio blasters when you get them into good condition. Put any of these in front of a good microphone, and the sound can be enormous.

Even cranked up, these small amps might sound a little lean to you in the room if it's anything other than bedroom-sized, but into the mic and down on the track, they will have impressive girth and punch. You really have to try it a few times to start to believe the magic. The more pleasing harmonics, punchy midrange, and that richness of an amp being pushed hard but without the mush or fuzz of a pedal will often help them sit better with other instruments in the mix, too. Often, in the exact same recorded tune, a big amp's sound overwhelms the frequency range of the track as a whole, while simultaneously sounding like it has been compressed down to a blur. The smaller amp in its place will sound open, airy, dynamic, multi-textured, and fat. It's an exciting discovery that opens up a lot of possibilities; after all, who wants to drag around that double-stack anyway?

In considering the recorded amp verses the live rig, you need to take into consideration the mechanics of the human ear, which is to say our perception of frequency in relationship to volume levels, and decide where you want the dynamics involved in that to be best perceived: in the studio live room, or in the living-room, in the car, or on the dance-floor where the listener is enjoying the playback from your CD. In the case of recording a large amp in the studio, for a heavy-sounding track in particular, even the lower levels of your playing will tax the ability of your mic and preamp to handle the signal without clipping, and more aggressive playing will certainly go into the red. This allows less space for the light and shade of dynamics. Use a smaller amp, however, one that lets the mic and preamp be set so they are sensitive to the players' subtler passages but are still capable of capturing the heavier attack without distorting, and you can bring a much more dynamic performance to the mix.

And, if you still can't get the small amp/big sound concept through your head, look at it like this: you will be recording that amp through a microphone diaphragm that might be maybe a little over an inch (25mm) in diameter at most, and probably much less than an inch, sending a sound down a thin wire to be stored digitally or magnetically, and eventually reamplified through household speakers that, these days, are going to have maybe a six-inch (150mm) diameter at best, or through headphones with speaker diameters of less than half an inch (13mm). Listen to 'Smells Like Teen Spirit' on a good pair of headphones, and it still sounds pretty damn big. When it comes to recording, we often need to radically shift our perception of size to make the most of the job.

MICS FOR SMALL AMPS

So much of this still comes down to the fact that the smaller amp allows you a much broader selection of microphones, which means a wider palette of colors in the recording process. Any guitarist who does a lot of recording should put nearly as much thought into his mic and preamp selection as he or she does into perfecting the guitars-effects-amps chain. Some mics, even types that are perfectly good in certain situations, will render your carefully crafted rig into an entirely different beast. Others in their place might capture subtleties and offer a flattering frequency presentation that really brings "your sound" alive. It's magic when you find a mic that makes your amp sound as warm, rich, airy, and alive in the recorded track as it does in the room, and that discovery instantly changes your ability to record compelling guitar tracks.

Using a low-watt amp to record allows you to place more sensitive microphones, such as this Audio-Technica condenser, right up close to the speaker.

Of course a good mic can fall into two categories: it can render your guitar-amp sound accurately, or it can color it slightly in a way that proves preferable to the "real thing." The good old Shure SM57, with its prominent mid hump, has undoubtedly recorded a lot of classic rock tracks, and often it's still going to be just the ticket for that punchy, aggressive part where emphasized midrange snarl is desired. With the smaller amp, however, you can try out other options like the full range of condenser mikes that are so sweet with vocals but distort too easily with loud guitar parts, or the ribbon mikes that capture such a warm, natural sound in this application. My own recording world came alive when I found a used STC 4038 (a model now made by Coles) for sale in London a few years ago. For me at the time, $500 felt like a lot for a used microphone, but it turns out to have been an enormous bargain. Nothing else I had tried was able to make my tweed Deluxe sound like a tweed Deluxe on the track, or my Matchless Lightning sound like a Matchless Lightning. So I added up what I'd spent on guitars and amps in recent years, and decided that spending a fraction of that to help them sound their best on record was really a small price to pay (fortunately, I got a great drum overhead in the bargain, too). I'm getting off track a little here, and I don't mean to send you off on any mad search for expensive microphones, but it all goes toward considering the entirety of the sound chain in any quest to perfect your guitar tone—and when you are in the studio, that includes microphones, preamps, compressors, the recording deck or interface, and much more.

CRANK IT DOWN

But maybe you still love the tone of your bigger rig, and want to squeeze that into a smaller bottle, so to speak. The shift away from the large professional studio and into the home project studio has sent countless players scrambling for ways of making their big amps quieter, without simply turning down the volume. What if you've already got a Vox AC30 that produces the sound of your dreams at 2 o'clock on the dial, but neither the neighbors, your family, nor your microphones are at all happy with the situation? The dream solution would be to find a means of retaining that same sound, but at a far lower decibel level. Sounds like magic, but there are quite a few ways of doing this. Outwardly, you might imagine the possibility of squeezing that full-throttle power tube signal on its way to the speakers so that the amp is still running "cranked," but only a conversational volume level is coming out of the cab. Alternatively, hey, lock the thing in a padded room, so that anyone not locked in there with it hears no more than a muffled whisper at best. These are exactly the means that the majority of "cranked but quiet" tricks use to achieve such goals.

Some of these solutions come in the form of output attenuators, tube converters, simple half-power and pentode/triode modifications, power scaling and master voltage systems, and isolation boxes. It is worth looking at each in some detail.

OUTPUT ATTENUATORS

Want to run your amp near full-tilt, but send just a portion of that volume-creating wattage to your speakers? The output attenuator is the way to do it. Such units are placed between the amp's speaker output and the speakers themselves, and carry a large resistor or some form of silent-speaker-like device to soak up a portion of the output power. The remainder is passed along to the speakers themselves, at a level determined by the user.

Attenuators have been around for some time, but they have become more popular in recent years, due either to the fact that they have become better and more reliable, or to the trend for lower stage and studio volumes (probably some confluence of the two). The obvious function of the attenuator is to bring big amps down to the volume levels of the kinds of small amps that I have discussed in this chapter already. This opens them up to the same kinds of recording applications, enabling their use in smaller studios, with sensitive microphones, and so forth. Many players, however, have also been using them a lot more for gigs, to knock off just 6dB or so to suit a large-room amp to a smaller room, or to drop their sound down a little bit early on in the night, when the room is empty, and then bring it back up to full output with the flick of a knob or twist of a switch—without changing the sound and distortion character—when the place is packed and the bodies are absorbing more sound.

They do, however, by the nature of their operation, sometimes make your rig sound not *exactly* like the same loud amp only less loud. Driving your speakers at different levels obviously makes them perform differently; any speaker's reaction and interaction to and with the amp is a big part of the amp's overall sound, and these speakers sound differently when driven hard than they do when driven gently. Speakers usually contribute a portion of the "broken-up" sound of any cranked amp's distortion content; speakers with high power-handling ratings usually still break up a little when played hard, and speakers with low power-handling ratings break up a lot. Squelch the signal running from amp to speaker, and clearly you will cut down on this "speaker distortion," and perhaps eliminate it entirely. For some sonic goals, speaker distortion is not desired anyway, so this could be another bonus of the attenuator. For others—classic rock'n'roll, vintage blues, garage rock styles—speaker distortion can contribute a lot to that over-the-top, edge-of-freakout overdrive sound of a cranked amp.

Another, perhaps less obvious, problem with output attenuators is that the human ear responds differently to the frequency spectrum at different volume levels. In short, even though the attenuator is allowing your amp to pump the very same output-tube distortion portion of its overall tonal palette to your speakers at a lower volume level, the mere fact of that lower volume will change the way your ear perceives the frequencies that make up that sound, via a microphone used to record it. Put another way, given a rig where you're not getting any speaker distortion at full volume anyway, the amp's tonal and harmonic spectrum will still sound different to you at 84dB than at 96dB—meaning, different in more ways than just quiet vs loud. The audible results of medium to heavy attenuator settings are usually apparent in a rounding off of high-end detail, a generally slightly muted tone overall, and some lost dynamics. Some players don't hear these detractive factors, some do, and some attenuators exhibit them more than others. Whether they render such a device useful, or useless, is up to you.

Some players worry about attenuators damaging their amps, but the better models really should have nothing in their own function that is inherently bad for your amplifier. The simple fact that you are likely to be running your amp harder with an attenuator attached means that all components will be under more of a strain, tubes/valves in particular, and will be liable to burn out faster. This is just the same as if you were playing in that large auditorium every night anyway, and were turning the amp up to the same higher volume without an attenuator. The amp is still pumping as much voltage through its system and running its tubes and transformers as hot as it would be when normally cranked, but the attenuator is converting a lot of that energy to heat to be dissipated through a large heat sink, rather than sending it all to the speakers. As far as the amp itself is concerned, however, same volume levels, same wear and tear. If that's where an amp sounds best, many players figure that replacing output tubes more frequently is a small price to pay. But the fact that the amp doesn't sound as loud can make it easy to forget that you are nevertheless driving those tubes and components pretty hard, so anyone using an attenuator night after night should keep an extra sharp eye out for maintenance issues.

TUBE CONVERTERS

These were something of a craze when they first hit the market a few years ago, seen most often from the THD brand, and more recently from TAD and others. Tube converters most commonly take the form of a direct plug-in adaptor that changes 6L6 or EL34 output tubes to lower output EL84s without any further modification to the amp, but there are even variants for converting 6V6s. These don't have a whole lot more output than EL84s in the first place, but the thinking is that you might prefer the tonality of the latter, which is considered to have a crispy, compressed "British" flavor in some circuits, with slightly earlier breakup.

The sonic and volume-related changes that tube converters can offer can be considerable. The overall result is pretty impressive for the relatively low cost of the items. Given that the output tubes play a very big part in the sonic signature of any amplifier, inserting a pair of THD Yellow Jackets or TAD Tone Bones really can be "like getting a whole new amplifier," as THD's company literature states. A 50-watt amp in the Fender or Marshall style, with a pair of 6L6 or EL34 output tubes, will yield an output of around 20 watts with the yellow jackets in place. This can obviously bring a large-room amp down to bar-gig and studio levels. Be aware, though, that the relationship between wattage and apparent loudness isn't a direct correlation. All else being close to equal (sonic character, speaker performance, cab type), a 20-watt amp still sounds significantly *more* than half as loud as a 50-watt amp, not *less* than. But the converters definitely offer a quicker onset of output tube distortion, and usually that is the real goal. For the cost of a pair of converters, it's a fast-track to a significantly different sonic signature. I have tried these in some excellent 6L6 and EL34 based amps, however, that only sounded fizzy and overly compressed with the EL84s. In others, the Yellow Jackets offered an excellent alternative. Do not expect a magical AC15-conversion in whatever amp you pop them into, but they can make an interesting and useful volume-dropping or tone-altering option in many cases.

If you are really looking for a smaller amp and find yourself playing your larger amp with the Yellow Jackets or other converters installed all the time, I'd argue that you probably ought to sell the thing and get the amp that's designed from the ground up to do what you're looking for. The general principle to good, solid tone is to travel the simplest and most direct road that gets you there. On the other hand, if you love the sound you get with converters in place and wouldn't want to change it one jot, fine; or if you can only afford one amp, but have the need of cranked-up sounds at very different volume levels and with different output tube signatures, that works too. Either way, they're a cool product that can be a lot of fun.

POWER-REDUCTION MODS

There are a number of modifications available, both simple and complex, to reduce an amp's output power. Some involve actual rewiring of portions of the circuit, and some involve no surgical intervention of any kind.

The simplest of these can be achieved with many grid-biased (aka fixed bias) amps carrying four output tubes in two push-pull pairs. By removing one tube from each side of these pairs (that is, removing either the two inside or the two outside tubes, but never two from one side), the power of the amp can be approximately halved. Removing two tubes also changes the impedance relationship between the remaining output tubes and the speaker, however, as seen via the output transformer, so ideally you will make another change here, too. On amps with multiple output impedance selections, drop the impedance by half when continuing to use the same speaker cab. If you're running a 16-ohm cab and you pull two tubes, switch your selector to 8 ohms; if you're running an 8-ohm cab, switch it to 4 ohms, and so on. Rather than a selector, some amps have dedicated outputs at different impedance ratings, so just re-plug the speaker connection to a different jack—same result. If the amp has just one output impedance, as is the case with most older Fenders, you can either run different speakers to create the desired load, or just tough it out. In truth, most Fender output transformers will pretty easily tolerate an impedance mismatch of a factor of two in either direction (ie, halved or doubled). Frequency response and power might change somewhat, but you are seeking that anyway by pulling two tubes. If the result works for you, sonically, without an impedance switch, you are probably okay to go with it. Marshall amps are reputedly not as happy with an impedance mismatch, but fortunately the larger Marshall models generally carry impedance switches to match 4-, 8-, and 16-ohm loads.

Given the ability to compensate impedance-wise, this technique still doesn't instantly create, for example, a 50-watt amp that is exactly the same as the four-tube, 100-watt version of itself in every regard other than power. The two remaining output tubes are now feeding a much heftier output transformer than most 50-watt amps would normally carry, so even when the amp is cranked up high there is likely to be less output transformer saturation in the amp's overall brew of distortion. Again, if you try this technique and the sound really works for you, who cares. The other side of the coin is that this bigger-than-standard "50-watt" output transformer (meaning the 100-watt iron) should give you fat lows and a firm response overall. Also, note that you can't do this in cathode-biased amps with four output tubes, such as a Vox AC30, because the tubes share a single bias resistor, the value of which would need to be doubled when only two EL84s were used. Some such amps do, however, have a half-power switch which puts two of four tubes on "standby" while simultaneously doubling the value of the bias resistor. Matchless's C30 range—which includes the DC30 and SC30 combo and HC30 head—has a switch to do exactly this, as does the more recently released TH30 model from Orange.

A trick achieved with a little more intervention is the pentode/triode switch, already used by a number of amplifier makers in the form of a "half-power switch." It doesn't exactly halve the power, and changes the output tubes' tonal character in some other ways besides, but this mod is relatively simple, and certainly offers a faster path to output-tube distortion, with a definite drop in volume levels. The pentode/triode switch involves some fairly simple rewiring of the output tubes to make the pentode tube types think they are behaving as triodes. It doesn't actually turn them into triodes, but more "mock triodes" really. In any case, this triode mode makes the amp break up a little more quickly, and also induces a creamier, smoother, more midrange-dominant sound in the tubes. This can also be heard as a lack of sparkle and chime, with noticeably attenuated highs, so it doesn't suite every player's taste. Fortunately, the mod is simple and easily reversed, so things can be undone if you find you don't like the result. Be aware that this—like any internal modification—involves working around high voltages, so it should only be undertaken by a qualified professional amp tech. The work simply involves installing a sturdy DPDT on/on toggle switch, using one half of the switch for each side of the push-pull set (a single switch functions for 2, 4, or 6 tubes, since the significant connections will be tied together), lifting the output tubes' screen grid's connection to its DC voltage supply, and switching it between that supply (standard pentode mode) and a new connection made to the plates of the tubes (triode mode). Any good repairman should be able to install such a switch in about 15 minutes (not including the time it takes to pull your amp's chassis from its cab), plus the drilling of an appropriate hole to mount the switch. This can sometimes be located in the hole for a spare output socket that you are not using, or if you aren't entirely sure you will like the results, see if he can safely wire up the switch "free floating" first so you can hear the results, then drill and permanently mount it if you are happy with it.

Many amp makers and modifiers also use techniques to reduce the DC voltages supplied to the tubes within the amp, and thereby decrease the output level. One early version of this is called "power scaling" by the Canadian company that invented it, London Power, while more recent incarnations are 65amps' "master voltage" and Mojave Ampworks's "power dampening." The theory behind these is that the variable output reduction achieved by lowering operating and bias voltages at the tubes themselves (a trick that can take a 30-watt amp down to as little as a single watt in some cases) retains the same tonal characteristics of these tubes at any given gain setting, only with less volume. In practice, most do sound a little different dialed down to, say, five watts than they do at full volume, and issues of speaker interaction and distortion as discussed in regard to attenuators come into play too, but these do constitute other valid solutions to the volume problem.

ISOLATION CABINETS

If your concern is primarily for containing high volumes while recording—mainly, I suppose, to avoid annoying the neighbors, family members, your engineer, or whomever—there's another fairly popular solution to the problem: the isolation box. This is essentially a shrunken version of a vocal booth in a professional studio; a crate of the minimum size necessary, rendered as close to soundproof as possible, and loaded with a speaker and a microphone. Connect amp to speaker and crank up to whatever levels said speaker will handle, and the microphone inside the box picks up everything, while noise levels outside it are reduced to a whisper. Sounds simple, and in many ways it is. Commercial examples exist, or you can build your own with readily available and fairly obvious materials.

Isolation boxes can provide a great recording tool in some situations, and if you really need the sound of your amp cranked up high, unattenuated, miked-up through a roaring speaker, this is one way to do it. Of course that roaring speaker is unlikely to be the same one mounted in the cab the amp usually plays through, for one thing, and these rigs have a range of other drawbacks: they can be both boomy and over-compressed, because there is rarely enough air around the speaker to let the sound really breathe; they are difficult to either plan out or to acoustically tune, until you have built one, tested it, and perhaps discarded it for a larger or smaller box, which itself will be just another trial-and-error effort; and they make everything sound much like a closed-back cab, so a classic Fender combo sound is difficult to achieve.

They do, however, generally present high-saturation overdrive or over-the-top grungy amp filth pretty well, and usually work fine for hot rock leads or chunky, bottom-heavy rock power-chord rhythm parts. Also, another benefit of the iso cab is that, as well as keeping all the noise inside, they keep unwanted external noises out. In other words, whilst not bothering the neighbors, you can also record without them bothering you—likewise for street noise, screaming children, ringing telephones, and so forth.

You need a tough mic inside the box because you are not attenuating output level, just containing it. Therefore this volume-squelching solution doesn't allow the use of sensitive recording mics the way small amps or attenuators do. You also need a very high-powered but guitar-voiced eight-inch (200mm) or ten-inch (250mm) speaker, unless you can build a box big enough to hold a 12-inch (300mm) and its internal baffle. The bigger the speaker, however, the more air space you need around it for a semi-natural sound. As simple as it is, it's a tough item to get sounding perfect, but maybe perfect isn't absolutely necessary. A rough-shod DIY job is usually good enough for rock'n'roll, and will soon have you laying down some wailing, cranked tube amp sounds on your formerly anemic tracks. Some professional studios even have custom-built isolation boxes big enough to contain an entire 4x12 cab, but if you have noise issues in your home studio in the first place, you aren't likely to have the space available to contain something like this.

Demeter has offered an isolation box for many years, the SSC-1 Silent Speaker Chamber, as has Randall in the form of its simply-named Isolation Cab. Newcomer AxeTrak provides the most compact version of the breed that I have encountered, and it comes loaded with both speaker and microphone. Players have made their own through the years by using either temporary solutions like locking a cab in a closet full of blankets, pillows and other padding, or in a large flight case, or by building their own along the most obvious lines imaginable.

Build a wooden crate large enough to house your proposed speaker with some air space on all sides, line the inside with dense foam, embed a "floating baffle" into the foam in one corner, lodge a sturdy dynamic microphone in the other (either just wedge it there or mount a short boom stand with some vibration-dampening material), close the lid, and wail away. I'm not walking you through this project in greater detail because the means of achieving the end are as diverse as you can imagine, and by the time you put extreme effort into designing and building the "perfect" isolation cabinet, you might as well have devoted your time to something more profitable, if you ask me. Slap together a box out of some thick plywood, chipboard or MDF, line it well, cut some notches for speaker wire in and mic cable out, and get to it. Usually you need to do a lot of lid on/lid off to experiment with both speaker and mike placement before you get it right, and achieving a semi-natural sound almost always requires some EQ at the board. The freedom of full-power playing and recording that these things offer can be a real kick, though, so this is often effort well spent if you plan to record a lot of loud rock guitar.

In addition to being miked and tracked for recording, iso boxes have some other useful applications. Since like-rated speakers in a parallel setup divide an amp's power output in half between them, you can use the box as a load for all sorts of applications. If you want to drop the wattage reaching a particular speaker cab by half, parallel it with an isolation cabinet carrying a speaker with the same impedance rating. Mike up the "open" cab, which can now be cranked a little higher, and you'll find you've taken a bit of the excessive volume off the overall level. A little creative thinking reveals some other great uses for them.

In addition to bringing big-amp volume down to small-gig and studio levels, all of these avenues to quieter cranked sounds have another major benefit to them: your hearing is precious, and the less aggressively you assault it, the longer you'll have it. Plenty of great volume-reducing solutions exist, many of which retain all or at least an appreciable portion of an amp's original voice and distortion characteristics, and as such these products and techniques render sheer volume a purely quantitative phenomenon. When the quality of your tone is preserved—but at lower volume levels—you will very likely be a happier player in the long run, and hopefully one who can hear the playback, too.

Compression and EQ for electric guitar

The amount of compression you will want to apply to your guitar tracks (if any) varies as greatly as those sounds themselves, and settings for crunchy aggressive rock rhythm and clean jangly pop tones will be very different. Heavily overdriven amplifiers produce a natural compression of their own, but do often require a little compression in the DAW to sit well in the mix of a heavy rock tune, where you might run all guitars through a stereo bus with a comp plug-in helping to glue them all together. Clean guitars have a spikier feel without any added compression, and might need slightly more intense comp settings to smooth them out, so they don't appear to jump out of the track too harshly.

As far as both comp and EQ are concerned, though, you still want to do your best to achieve the right sound and dynamics through amp adjustments and mic placement. A well-miked amp should yield a track that requires no EQ at all, ideally, and perhaps just a little light compression to help the part sit in the mix. As with any instrument, you don't want to go straight to heavy compression out of habit and destroy the life and dynamics in your guitar tracks.

LIGHT GUITAR COMP SETTINGS

RATIO: **2:1**
THRESHOLD: **–4dB**
ATTACK: **20ms to 25ms or auto**
RELEASE: **20ms to 30ms or auto**
KNEE: **Soft (depending on the part)**

"CRUNCHY POWER CHORDS" GUITAR COMP SETTINGS

RATIO: **5:1**
THRESHOLD: **–12dB**
ATTACK: **10ms or auto**
RELEASE: **100ms or auto**
KNEE: **Hard (depending on the part)**

"SMOOTHED-OUT CLEAN" GUITAR COMP SETTINGS

RATIO: **6:1 to 8:1**
THRESHOLD: **–16dB**
ATTACK: **1ms or auto**
RELEASE: **100ms or auto**
KNEE: **Soft (depending on the part)**

As already mentioned, the best-case scenario is that you don't need to EQ your guitar tracks at all. Inevitably, though, many will benefit from a touch here and there, and the application is just as likely to be reductive as additive. If your guitars sound boomy and muddy and appear to be swamping other instruments in the mix, try reducing a few dBs somewhere in the band between 100Hz and 250Hz (on the other hand, if they totally lack body and muscle, a slight boost in that band might give them more chunk). Going even lower, if the guitar sounds are interfering with the bass track and giving the overall tune too much low-end resonance, apply a high-pass filter to eliminate anything below 80Hz (a guitar's low-E string produces a frequency of 82.42Hz, so you don't really need anything below that to be heard fully; if you are tuning down to drop D or below, though, or recording a seven-string guitar, you will need to re-think this frequency range). If your highs are too glassy or harsh, or you've got more hiss in the track than you would like, try rolling off a little in the neighborhood of 4kHz.

If you recorded the amp with an old-school ribbon mic, you might need to add some highs to bring out the sparkle and presence, if you didn't already do so while tracking (try moving a little boost of a few dBs through anywhere from 4kHz to 12kHz to see what brings out more sparkle in the tone, without adding too much noise). A mix that includes more than one rhythm guitar but which has both sounding a little lifeless can often benefit from the addition of some presence to each, but at different points in the frequency spectrum: try nudging one at around 2.5kHz and one at around 3.5kHz and see if that helps them to pop a little better. Whatever EQ you find it necessary to apply, it's usually a good idea to go easy and avoid cutting or boosting by more than just a few dB, or you risk creating odd-sounding peaks and nulls that will "honk" when the guitar hits chords or notes that fall directly within that range.

Recording acoustic guitars

They both have "guitar" in their name, and you tune and play them the same way, but as recorded instruments go, electric guitars and acoustic guitars are approached very, very differently. If your mic selection is limited you might be using the same tool on both, but most professional studios will choose completely different mics as starting points for electric and acoustic guitars, and their placement will be dictated differently too. And, while many "electro-acoustic" guitars have built-in pickups these days, often with onboard preamps that allow you to plug straight into the board or interface, I would argue that you are even less likely to DI an acoustic than you are an electric, that is if you want it to sound anything like the real acoustic instrument that it is.

While you can fluff your mic placement on electric guitar amps a little, or rush your technique, and still come away with useable tracks in many cases, great acoustic guitar tone is all about careful mic placement and usage. That is, after you've got a great-sounding acoustic guitar in the first place. And that doesn't have to mean an expensive acoustic guitar. High-end acoustics can indeed sound exquisite, and the craftsmanship that many of the better luthiers put into their instruments does yield some breathtaking tones. But if all you've got on hand is a mid-level import, a fresh (but broken-in) set of strings, a good set-up, and good playing—and recording—technique should still yield good results.

Also, since you will be recording acoustic guitars "in the air" in an acoustic space, a good-sounding room will greatly benefit the effort. Try to avoid setting up in any room, or portion thereof, where you hear any unduly emphasized resonances or reflections, and add a little extra treatment to the walls (and any particularly low ceilings) of a room that seems to be fighting you sonically.

MIC CHOICES FOR ACOUSTIC GUITAR

If a low-budget copy of a ball-end dynamic mic is the one and only tool in the box, sure, that's what you're going to use—and don't let it stop you from making satisfactory acoustic guitar recordings. Traditionally, though, condenser mics have been the tool of choice for acoustic guitars. Condensers have the fidelity and sensitivity to capture the nuances of the acoustic guitar, along with the crucial high-end detail and low-end solidity, and they also provide the output level needed to adequately capture this often-quiet instrument without inducing the noise inherent in a cranked preamp. Condenser mics also offer the advantage that they can be placed at some distance from the guitar, which enables the sound to "breathe" before it heads down the pipe, meaning you capture more of a "big picture" tone from the instrument, rather than a focused slice of one part of it.

The high-end detail afforded by small-diaphragm condensers has often made them the mic of choice on acoustic guitars, although the unforgiving clarity of digital recording has found more and more recordists enjoying large-diaphragm condensers for this application, and plenty have been turning to ribbon mics, too. A good ribbon mic, with a little high-end boost if necessary, can capture a deep, rich, warm acoustic tone that often cures any ills in the form of "coldness" or "brittleness" heard in some condenser mics. To make a ribbon work on acoustic, however, you do need a clean, high-gain preamp, or you are likely to be weighed down with noise.

SINGLE-MIC TECHNIQUES

As with miking guitar amps, the best way to find the right place to put your acoustic guitar mic is to listen in a number of different positions to the sound your guitar produces (while another guitarist plays it for you), record a little of it with a mic placed there, and listen back. One important tip at this point, however, and perhaps the most important

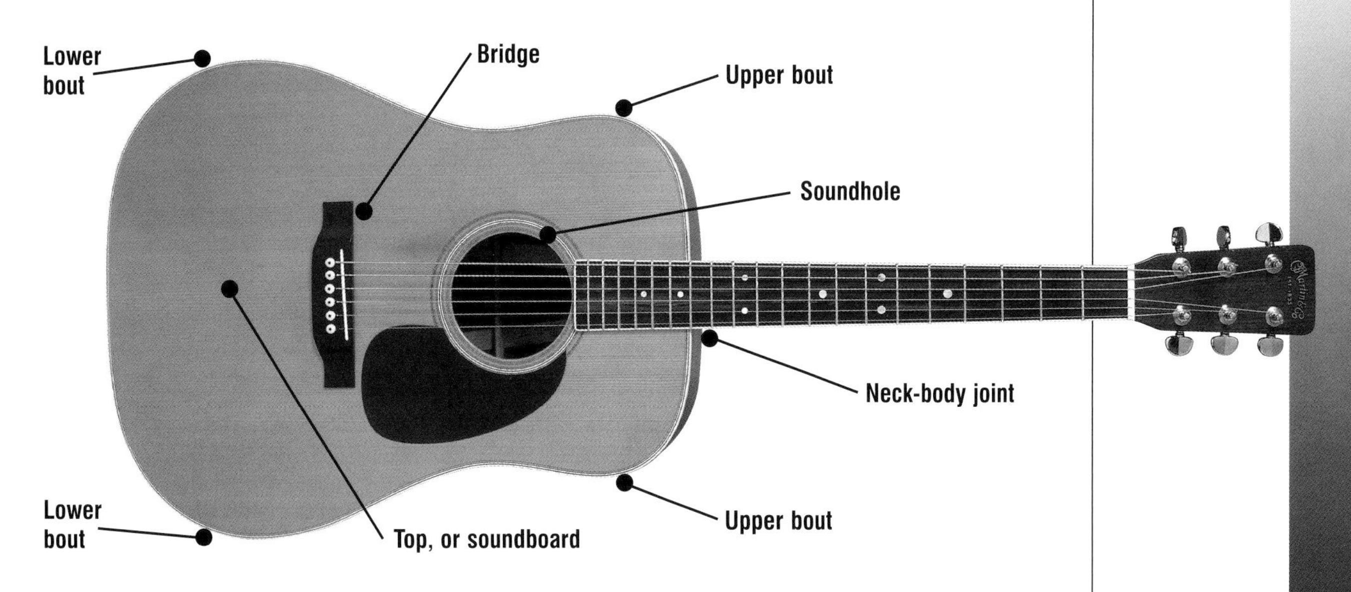

thing to get down from the start, is that you should not place the microphone pointing straight into the soundhole. Do this, and you capture a woofy, muddy, booming sound that is pretty loud, certainly, but not really representative of your full acoustic guitar tone in any other way. For beginning recordists this can take some getting used to, because of course whenever you take a guitar with no onboard pickup to an acoustic gig the sound engineer points an SM57 right into the soundhole. Even in these circumstances this technique doesn't produce the most flattering acoustic tone, but it does tend to capture the most volume from an acoustic in a live situation, and that's a compromise that we are often willing to live with at a small club gig.

An acoustic guitar's sound isn't produced from the sound hole alone, and in fact that is really just the point where sound that is reflected from the backside of the top and off of the back of the guitar escapes the guitar's body, as well as a necessary vent that allows the resonant surfaces of the guitar's body to flex freely. A lot of the tone is produced in the area around the bridge and the broad portions of the lower bout (the larger rounded section of the top), while other frequencies are produced in the region of the upper bout where the fingerboard joins the body. Along with these, the sound coming off the back of the guitar has its own tone, too. Usually you will want to use a technique that captures a blend of a few or all of these sounds in order to accurately represent the full picture.

One of the most popular traditional studio techniques for recording mono acoustic guitar involves placing a microphone at around the 12th fret, a few inches away from the fingerboard, and aimed back toward the end of the fingerboard (at the body end), but not into the soundhole. This captures a bright, lively acoustic tone with a good, rounded body and some string sound for added jangle. To mellow out this sound slightly, try moving the mic slightly lower, and more toward the meat of the upper bout, firing more directly at the guitar's top rather than at so much of an angle (test the tone achieved by aiming at both the bass and treble side of the upper bout, which will be quite different).

Another position that captures a full, woody, and

ABOVE LEFT: One classic "one-mic" technique is to position a small-diaphragm condenser such as this AKG C451 at around the 12th fret, firing toward the body of the guitar. LEFT: Aiming a condenser (in this case, an AT4033) at the guitar's body behind the bridge often captures a full, warm, resonant tone.

RIGHT: A mic pointed at the edge where the guitar's top and side meet will sometimes produce a tight, edgy tone that is effective in certain situations. BELOW RIGHT: A large-diaphragm condenser mic placed at "ear position" firing over the performer's right shoulder can sometimes achieve a very realistic acoustic-guitar sound.

somewhat less jangly tone is found by pointing a mic at the guitar's top in the region of the lower bout just below and behind the bridge. Moving the mic further down and away from the lower end of the guitar and aiming it at the edge of the body, where the top meets the side of the guitar, can produce another interesting tone, one which is usually heard as being a little more edgy and cutting, with a snappy upper-mids presence.

I have also discovered by trial and error that a rich, full, yet crisp tone can often be had by positioning a mic about head-high with the performer, some six inches (150mm) down the shoulder from his or her right ear and 10 inches (250mm) out from his or her face, and firing down toward the bass side of the lower bout of the instrument. Another even quirkier, but occasionally successful, placement is sometimes found by positioning a mic similarly, but firing from behind the player, aimed over their right shoulder. Unsurprisingly, this one achieves a modicum of the sound that the player is used to hearing (which isn't necessarily the best tonal picture of the instrument, just the one you are stuck with from the player's perspective, but sometimes it's a useful technique).

MULTI-MIC TECHNIQUES

As with recording guitar amps, you can often achieve a broader, more multi-dimensional sound from an acoustic by carefully positioning more than one microphone. Be aware, however, that two mics are not always better than one: in some cases you might want the straightforward, less harmonically saturated (less "frequency range-dominating," if you will) sound of just a single microphone, when you want to have a driving acoustic rhythm guitar part in a busy mix where other sounds are more prominent, for example. With that caveat, if you want to coax the richest, deepest, most "in-the-room" acoustic guitar sounds onto your recording, you will often turn to two or more mics to do it.

Obvious candidates for multi-mic acoustic guitar recording are found in our basic stereo mic techniques, as discussed in detail in Chapter Three: Studio Approach. The spaced or AB pair, coincident or XY pair, near-coincident pair, baffled-omni pair, and M-S pair are all classics for capturing rich stereo acoustic guitar tracks. These are particularly good starting points when you are looking to achieve a broad, realistic soundstage for the instrument in a mix that will be primarily acoustic based, or will have the acoustic guitar as a central focus. As with the single-mic techniques, avoid making the guitar's soundhole the central focus of your stereo mic set-up, unless the mics are placed far enough out from the guitar—say, three feet (1m) or so—that the boominess emanating from that dark sepulcher blends smoothly into the overall tone of the instrument. Otherwise, try positioning a coincident or M-S pair about a foot (300mm) out from the 12th fret, aiming slightly toward the neck/body joint for a bright, jangly sound, or behind and slightly below the bridge for a fuller, deeper tone. Alternatively, turn your M-S relationship on its side, with the figure-eight side mic aiming toward ceiling and floor to get a stereo spread that's bass-bout on one side, treble-bout on the other. A spaced stereo pair can obviously be set with one mic in each of these neck/bridge positions. As with any mic set-up, tweak your positions, listen, and adjust to find the optimum placement.

I mentioned the baffled-omni pair (aka "dummy head pair") as one of our stereo miking options here, and you can also achieve this one without the usual dummy head or Jeklin disc by expanding my "over the shoulder" single-mic technique from above. Set your mic stands behind the guitarist, and position each of two mics a few inches out from the ear (firing slightly downward toward an imaginary point about 10 inches/250mm in front of the guitar if you are using cardioids or figure-eights rather than omnis), and shoot. To increase the low-end body in your acoustic tracks, use this technique with the performer set up facing a corner of your room, to make use of the corner-loading effect that we explored in Recording Bass. The mics firing over the guitarist's shoulders will also pick up the bass-heavy reflected sound from the corner, and add significant weight to the tracks.

"DUAL MONO" ACOUSTIC GUITAR

Strictly speaking, a true stereo image should capture identical left and right images of a sound source, as the above techniques do. If you use two different mics, and/or place two mics in very different and unequal positions around the sound source, you aren't really recording in stereo, but in "dual mono." Which is not to rule out such a technique at all: I have often had great results from this kind of mic placement, and have probably found two different, and differently placed, mics more useful in the final mix on many occasions than precisely positioned stereo set-ups of matched mic pairs. Consider that an acoustic guitar produces very different tones from different parts of its body and neck anyway, and it's clear that you might get some interesting results from placing different mics at different points around the guitar and either blending them entirely together in mono, or positioning them L-R to some degree across the field.

Look back at the single-mic positions discussed above and consider that you can use a combination of any two of these. Even when used in "pseudo stereo"—that is, two

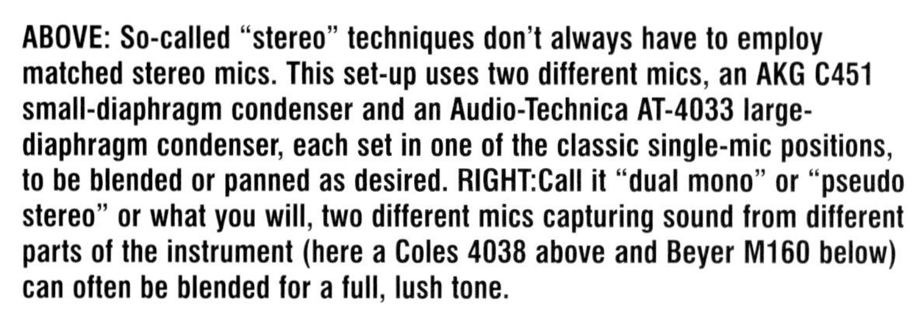

ABOVE: So-called "stereo" techniques don't always have to employ matched stereo mics. This set-up uses two different mics, an AKG C451 small-diaphragm condenser and an Audio-Technica AT-4033 large-diaphragm condenser, each set in one of the classic single-mic positions, to be blended or panned as desired. RIGHT:Call it "dual mono" or "pseudo stereo" or what you will, two different mics capturing sound from different parts of the instrument (here a Coles 4038 above and Beyer M160 below) can often be blended for a full, lush tone.

differently-recorded points of the guitar panned in stereo—you can often yield a big and sonically pleasing sound from this technique. Of course you need to be aware of phase cancellation issues with such techniques, and to do what you can to minimize them. My own favorites of such placements have come from a mic aimed just slightly behind and below the bridge and another aimed at the edge of the top and back at about 11 o'clock on the front of the lower bout, and one mic aimed at the body edge on the treble side of the lower bout and one aimed at the meat of the top in the region of the bass side of the upper bout.

FRONT-AND-BACK MIKING

Another non-stereo two-mic technique that can produce some nifty results uses one mic aimed at your position of choice on the front of the guitar, and another set up firing at the portion of the *back* of the guitar the emerges from the player's side, under their strumming arm. A big part of any acoustic guitar's overall tone emanates from its back, and blending this mic with a traditional front placement can often yield lots of depth and dimension. Because the two mics are firing in opposite directions, you will usually need to reverse the phase on the back mic, unless you are using different mics which are already reverse-phase of each other. To get even more lively back-of-guitar tone into the

An AKG C451 condenser mic positioned to record the sound from the back of the acoustic guitar.

mic, have the guitarist hold the instrument slightly away from their body while playing—if it doesn't impede their performance to do so—to avoid damping the resonance of that part of the instrument.

Compression and EQ for acoustic guitar

To an even greater extent than with the electric guitar, the ideal is to avoid comp at all with the acoustic, if you aim to retain the natural breath and dynamics of the instrument. A little light comp might be needed to help it sit right, but a well-recorded acoustic guitar should need very little by way of dynamics processing (and will be treated to a little light mastering comp in the mixing process in most cases anyway).

ACOUSTIC GUITAR COMP SETTINGS

RATIO: **2:1**
THRESHOLD: **–4dB**
ATTACK: **20ms to 25ms or auto**
RELEASE: **20ms to 30ms or auto**
KNEE: **Soft (depending on the part)**

The same goes for EQ, although some gentle boosts and reductions here and there are occasionally useful. You are likely to want to apply a high-pass filter to shelve off anything below 80Hz if you didn't do so at the mic pre when recording, and a boomy guitar (the result of getting too much direct-from-soundhole tone into the mic) can often benefit from losing just a couple dB at around 125Hz. If the acoustic track is part of a big, complex mix as a driving strummed rhythm instrument with a lot of other instruments taking more prominence, you can even try raising your high-pass filter up to anywhere between 150Hz and 300Hz, so you just get the "cut" of the guitar without the low-end woof that can interfere with bass and kick. A dull acoustic might benefit from a very light boost around 5kHz to bring more sparkle to the strings, as will one recorded with a ribbon mic that exhibits much proximity effect, or is just too warm to reveal the desired high-end detail.

Recording resonator guitars

Resonator guitars, best known under the National and Dobro brands, have made a major resurgence in popularity in the past decade or more, which means more and more people are recording them, too. Although they have the word "guitar" in their name, and are acoustic instruments, certainly, they behave very differently from traditional acoustic guitars, and require a different approach from your mic technique.

To begin to understand how to best mike up and capture the sound of a resonator guitar in the studio, we first need to understand how such instruments produce their sound, and where it comes from. The term "resonator guitar" covers a few camps, but all of them use a thin speaker-like cone (or cones) made of spun aluminum to help produce their distinctive tone. Resonator guitars, or "resos" for short, produce their sound through the vibrating strings' interaction with the cone, which resonates inside the body and amplifies the sound of the instrument (that is, amplifies it in the acoustic sense, without anything having to be plugged in). Resos were developed at a turning point in the evolution of the guitar, when players in orchestra settings were seeking more volume in order to be heard over the horns and drums, and before the amplified electric guitar had become a practical alternative. A traditional single-cone "biscuit bridge" reso, as originated by National Guitars in the late 1920s, has a cone that opens into the body of the guitar and rises to its peak at the bridge, where a round wooden disc the shape of a biscuit supports a notched saddle over which the strings pass. A Dobro works somewhat the reverse of this, with an "inverted" cone that opens outward toward the top of the guitar, and a more intricate "spider bridge" that carries the string vibration from the bridge saddles to the cone itself. The third major type of reso is the "tri-cone," another type originated by National Guitars in the 20s, which uses three smaller cones that speak into the body of the guitar, with a T-shaped bridge piece that caries the string vibration to the peaks of all three aluminum cones.

A Beyer M160 aimed at the resonator cone to capture a lively, "zingy" tone.

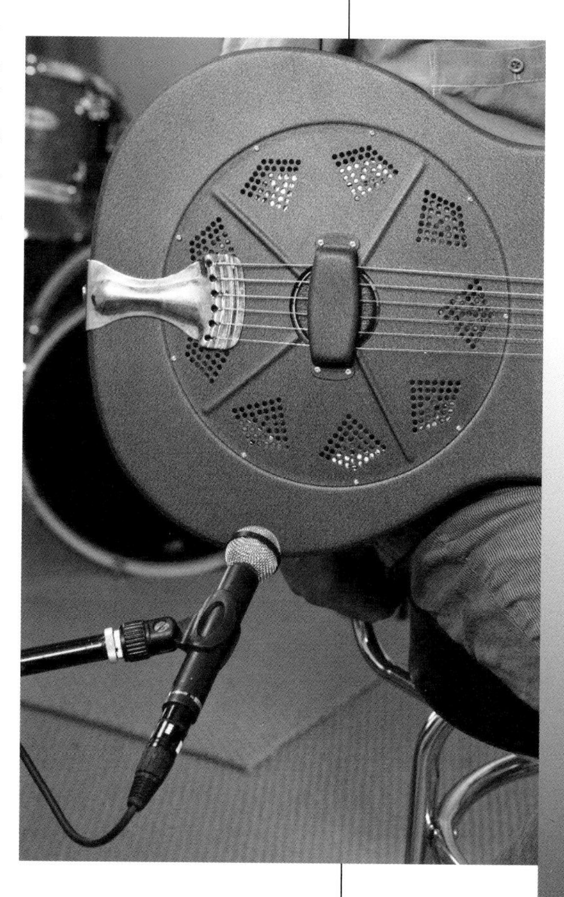

From these descriptions you can already begin to visualize a major component of the resonator guitar's sound production, and however it is configured—biscuit bridge, spider bridge with inverted cone, or tri-cone—a significant portion of the instrument's tone emanates from the cone itself (or cones themselves). Placing a microphone a few inches in front of the cone aimed slightly below or behind the bridge captures the metallic zing and twang characteristic of the resonator guitar, and this is a component you will very likely want to have in your recorded sound in some proportion or other. This is what shouts "reso" loud and clear, and also gives the cut and spank that distinguishes a Dobro from an ordinary acoustic guitar. For precise mic placement, use your ears as you have learned to do with recording standard acoustic guitars; move around the instrument in the region of the cone, stick a mic where you hear the most suitable sound being produced, and record a little to listen back to. Large and small-diaphragm condensers are popular choices for capturing the full fidelity of the tone here, but a ribbon mic will mellow it out in a lovely way if you don't want too harsh an edge on the attack of the instrument.

If you've only got one mic, or want a reso tone with a very high zing-to-warmth ratio, this mic placement might do just fine. But to understand the whole picture, we need to move on to see what other tones bloom from these complex instruments. While the cone(s) and cover plate take the position where a standard flat-top acoustic guitar's sound hole would be located, all resonator guitars do have further sound holes of another type, positioned both sides of the neck in the body's upper bout. These generally appear in one of three forms: f-holes, dual small round sound holes with steel mesh covers, or larger sound holes covered with a latticework grille (or occasionally something more unusual). While the distinctive metallic treble frequencies emanate from the resonator cone, a mic—or ear—placed near these further sound holes will detect a richer, bassier tone that is lush with reverberant frequencies that have bounced around inside the body after leaping from the underside of the cone. Aim a second mic at one of these sound holes and you capture a warmer, mellower tone with far less of the attack and zing of the cone itself, or place a mic in each position and blend the two sounds for a deep, spacious resonator sound that is probably the most accurate representation of the real instrument.

A mic aimed at the f-holes, in this case a Coles 4038, will record a warmer, deeper tone from a resonator guitar.

If you only have one good microphone to record with and want a full, blended sound rather than one that's heavy with either treble or bass, place the mic further away from the guitar and in a position that accurately reflects the full tone of the instrument. You can also achieve excellent full recordings of reso guitars by using any of the stereo miking techniques discussed above, and by placing the pair at a slight distance so it captures a good, airy, in-the-room balance of cone tone and sound-hole tone.

Of course, guitarists play resos in two different positions, upright and lap-style, and this will also influence your mic placement to some extent, although the instrument itself

Recording a resonator guitar played "lap style" obviously requires different mic positioning than one played upright. Here, two Audio-Technica condenser mics, an AT4033 left and an AT2050 right, are positioned to capture a good blend of cone and body tone from this National-Resophonic Delphi guitar.

produces its tone similarly in either position. The majority of players use a slide of some sort to play resonator guitars, too, and you can accentuate the distinctive sound of the bar or bottleneck slide moving on steel strings by aiming a mic at the middle of the neck. Capturing the "ghost notes" produced behind the slide when strings aren't adequately dampened (a sound some players try to avoid) can even add excitement, authenticity, and an eery dimension to your overall recorded reso sound. Experiment, move those mics around, and record what works best for your track. These are odd beasts indeed, but they can make some glorious sounds.

Resonator guitars tend to exhibit a decent amount of natural acoustic compression, and can often live with little or no compression at all. Also, you will ideally mic them so that little or no EQ is needed, although you might want to reduce some low-end woof if that is cluttering your tracks. If you feel you need to apply comp or EQ, the starter points given in "Comp and EQ for acoustic guitar", above, are good starting points

CHAPTER 7

RECORDING VOCALS

However much care you put into recording the other elements in your music, the vast majority of listeners will still pay the most attention to the vocals, so it follows that you want to devote some serious attention to getting these right. That being said, techniques for recording vocals are more straightforward than they are for drums, guitars, pianos, and many other instruments; essentially you put the right mic through the right preamp in front of the singer in question, and hit "record". Sound simple enough? Sure, and on paper it is. But there are a lot of fine points to investigate, and we can extrapolate the process out to explore several nuances that will help to make the difference between "so-so" and "superlative" vocal tracks.

In truth, getting the vocals just right can be one of the most involved, and occasionally frustrating, parts of any recording project, even in the professional studio. It requires a lot of finesse, and flexibility. There aren't any hard and fast rules, and whatever captures a vocal that works for you in the track is a valid way to go. There are, however, a lot of pitfalls you can avoid along the way by following "likely winners" rather than "probable losers" in your vocal-recording techniques.

Even before you get down to the engineering side of the job, a big part of any successful vocal recording session lies in keeping the singer comfortable, confident, and at ease with the process. Recording the lead vocal to any project is probably the most "on the spot" job in the studio, and it's easy to get nervous or edgy, especially when things aren't going smoothly. If you aren't singing these tracks yourself, establishing comfortable conditions, clear and accurate headphone monitoring, and an easy-going work environment will go a long way toward getting good results from the person who is. Also, once you have things set up and are starting into your run-throughs to let the singer get into the tune and warm up a little, go ahead and hit that record button regardless—and if you want to be sneaky about it, you don't even have to tell them you are doing so. Singing take after take is hard work, and many singers tire pretty quickly. There's usually a limited window for getting the best take before energy, emotion, and pitch begin to slip, and when they do, it's often too late to work your way back without a good long break. If you happen to capture a lively, spontaneous performance during what the singer thought was a warm-up pass, great. Even capturing just a few keepable phrases from that effort will put you ahead of the game.

For recordists who do sing their own vocals, well, here's another benefit of the home studio: you can wail like a canary all day, experiment with attitude and approach through take after take, and there's no one there other than you to hear your clunkers.

The downside of this scenario, though, is that there's no one there other than you to hear your clunkers. Unless you are entirely confident of your own abilities to hit pitch consistently, and to achieve the tone and attack that the song demands, an objective set of ears will be invaluable to getting the best vocal takes for the project. If you really need to track the vocals all on your lonesome, run them by a band-mate afterward, or at least audition them for a trustworthy pair of ears, and insist on an entirely objective opinion. It can be extremely difficult to objectively assess the pitch and placement of one's own voice in a track, especially after repeated takes, so it's important to throw your ego out the window and take some constructive criticism.

Vocal mic choices

The large-diaphragm condenser is the clear favorite for tracking vocals, and nine out of ten vocals you hear on the radio—and probably far more—will have been recorded through such microphones. LDC mics offer the clarity and frequency range to capture the full range of the human voice with good balance and definition, along with the sensitivity necessary to provide an adequate output on softer passages with the singer positioned an adequate distance from the mic.

Classics from Neumann, AKG, Sony and a few others would be your dream picks, but as a home recordist with what we must assume is a limited collection of mics, you probably want to start with whatever is the best LDC in your cupboard. Some professional engineers have different favorites for male and female vocals—mics that they feel flatter the frequency range of the different sexes, while also smoothing out any trouble spots in there too. In truth, any good condenser should capture either male or female vocals well when used right. Among the starter range of true pro-quality condensers, the AKG C414 will do good service on most vocals, and a somewhat more affordable Audio-Technica AT4033/CL gets plenty of raves, as do the progressively more pocket-friendly AT2035 and AT3035. Reasonably priced mics such as Rode's NT1 and NT2 have become standards in many home studios, too. Handled right, the even cheaper sub-$100 condensers that abound these days can also provide satisfactory results—or will have to, if that's all you've got.

If your selection is extremely limited, even a decent dynamic mic will get the job done. There are notable occasions when major artists have achieved magic through humble hand-held dynamics in the studio. Bono of U2 has frequently used a Shure SM57 (and possibly an SM58) for vocals in the studio, both Bjork and PJ Harvey are purportedly enamored of recording with SM58s, and Chris Cornell tracked several great Soundgarden vocals through an old Shure Unidyne dynamic mic, the precursor to these models. So, the dynamic doesn't have to be the "that's all I've got" choice; if you're finding the likely condenser mic too brittle, bright, cold, or just too "present" in the mix (and gentle comp and EQ tweaks aren't doing the trick), the simplest thing might be to try a good old dynamic microphone. Also, these can be great tools for curing the bouncing, thrashing and head-banging that many heavy metal vocalists seem to display when tracking. If you can't get that screamer to hold still and maintain a consistent distance from your usual big condenser mic (or if they keep overloading it), clamp a hand-held dynamic into their mitts, run it through your best mic pre, and go for it. The results might not knock you out when soloed, but they will often sound great in the track, and the bonus of allowing the aggressive singer free rein with their performance will often outweigh any limitations in the fidelity department.

Another favorite for curing potentially cold, brittle condenser-miked vocal tracks is the ribbon mic. While most standard ribbons are less sensitive in terms of output than condensers, many have a lovely, sonic sensitivity that can sound very deep, rich, and natural. The right ribbon mic can be a great cure for a strident, harsh, or screechy voice, too, especially when you want it to sit in a more retro or vintage-leaning track (but hell, a ribbon can help a great smooth, warm singer sit beautifully in a retro-styled track, too). Not that these guys are in any way strident or screechy, but David Bowie is known to have recorded many of his classic vocals through a Beyer-Dynamic M160, and alt-country artist Steve Earle, also a noted producer, has long been a fan of singing through vintage RCA 44 and 77 ribbon mics.

Given the low output of all but the newer active ribbon mics, you will need a good, quiet preamp with plenty of gain to make a ribbon work just right on vocals, especially in a song where there is lots of space for any extraneous noise to be heard. Unlike the hand-held dynamic mic that is made to be nearly swallowed during performance, a ribbon mic only sounds right when placed a good foot (300mm) or so from the singer, so you can't rely on screaming down the mic to produce adequate levels here, either. Also, you will often want to add a little high-end sparkle to any ribbon mic vocal track with a slight EQ boost, but frequently it doesn't take much (and it's arguable that ears used to modern recordings made with condenser mics have been trained to tolerate too much high end, too).

As whacky as it might seem, doubling a "plain old" dynamic mic with a condenser (in this case a Shure SM57 and an Audio-Technica AT4033) can sometimes get good results. Even an SM57 or SM58 or other similar dynamic mic used on its own will occasionally prove to be just the tool your session requires.

As with many of our techniques in the Recording Guitars chapter, you can approach vocals with a two-mic technique, too, especially if you aren't sure which will work and want to A/B the results in your early sessions. If you're setting up your best LDC anyway, try mounting a sturdy dynamic mic like an SM57 or SM58 (a Beta 58 can sound great, too) so it's either just shy of touching the end of the side-firing condenser and angled more directly toward (or slightly above) the singer's mouth, or altogether closer to the singer's position. Track both side by side, and either choose from your favorite, or blend the two, allowing the dynamic mic to bring a little more grit and drive to the clarity and fidelity of the condenser mic.

Vocal mic placement

With either a large-diaphragm condenser mic or a standard ribbon mic, as a general rule, you will want to position the singer so their lips are approximately 10–12 inches

(250–300mm) back from the grille of the microphone. These mics like to have some air between singer and capsule or ribbon to sound their best, and getting in too close will hamper their performance considerably in many cases, as well as inducing boomy lows thanks to the proximity effect. With some condensers, you can go in a little further (if loud passages in the vocal part allow), but you are rarely going to want to be closer than six inches (150mm), unless there's a particularly moody low-whisper section in the vocal and you need to capture that intimate, breathy effect.

Good placement and distance are also important factors in maintaining accurate levels while tracking. It's a good idea to mark the floor with tape once you have found the magic spot and instruct the singer to keep his or her toes on the line, but even so you are likely to need to employ some diplomacy to get them working with you in the effort, rather than against you. If the singer doesn't already have good mic technique gleaned from live and recording experience, urge them to lean back a couple inches and aim slightly off-mic when they hit the big crescendos, and to lean in a couple inches when they go into the sexy soft parts. Keep an eye out for the natural tendency of many singers to keep inching forward, and offer a gentle reminder between takes if they are getting in too close.

In addition to the mere distance from the singer, you usually want to position the mic level with the performer's mouth, or occasionally slightly above it, aiming very slightly down, to encourage them to open up the throat and project. Many mics sound their best when sung into from slightly off-axis (that is, from a slight angle), which also helps to reduce breath sound. In any case, you should always use a pop screen when recording vocals, to reduce the likelihood of errant plosives, and, when using a ribbon mic, to keep that thin aluminum ribbon safe. If you have a spare stand available, it can be helpful to mount this pop screen separately to avoid rattling or weighing down the mic stand, and position it about two to three inches (50-75mm) from the grille of the mic.

Some old-school engineers will also tell you

ABOVE LEFT: In most cases, the singer should stay six to 12 inches away from the capsule of a condenser mic (pictured here, a Red 5 Audio RV15 tube mic). LEFT: A pop screen is doubly important when singing into a fragile ribbon mic, such as this large-geometry AEA R84.

that aiming a ribbon mic slightly downward produces a little extra magic, especially in the high-end reproduction. The theory is that such an angle tensions the ribbon slightly through the sheer pull of gravity, and thereby allows it to capture more high-end detail than a slack ribbon. Worth a try.

As for positioning a dynamic mic for vocals, you can stand-mount the thing and let the singer get as close in as they normally would live on stage, or even put it in their hand and just let 'em go at it.

In-room position and acoustic environment

Tracking vocals is one recording situation where you really don't want much room sound interfering, unless you have a really good sounding space that you know will complement the mix—a very rare occurrence in the home studio, and one you are not likely to be able to discern until it's too late. Even acoustically-designed professional studios use an enclosed and heavily damped vocal booth for many of their vocal sessions, to avoid capturing washy reflections that can't be subtracted further on in the process and might conflict with the desired reverb and room sound of the song as a whole.

For this reason, you will want to pay extra attention to your room treatment in the vocal-recording room, and to performer position too. Position your singer toward—but not quite in—the center of the room, and avoid mounting the vocal mic close to any particularly reflective surfaces, to the front and back of the mic in particular (the latter if it's a figure-eight mic), but immediately to the side, too. Avoid singing toward or in front of any bare windows, and cover any in the room with a thick quilt or a leaning mattress just for good measure. If you have reflective surfaces that aren't permanently treated and which you just can't get away from, add some extra damping there, even if only temporarily, to cut down reflections.

As an alternative to increasing levels of damping in the room itself, you can create a barrier between reflective surfaces and the microphone by placing a gobo behind the mic (or a mini-gobo right up close to it, as discussed in Chapter Three: Studio Approach), or by using one of the nifty "portable vocal booths" that are available today, or by concocting your own. I have sometimes strapped a mini-gobo right to the back of a figure-eight mic that was picking up too many long reflections from the back of the capsule or ribbon in a large room and instantly converted it into a very effective, and far more neutral, vocal-recording mic. Temporary vocal booths take the form of products like Primacoustic's FlexBooth, a wall-mounting, fold-out isolation product; Auralex's more expensive Max-Wall booth, constructed of several acoustic panels included in a multi-pack, or affordable MudGuard, a free-standing isolation shield; or SE Electronics' Reflexion Filter, a half-pipe-shaped product following a somewhat similar concept, made from perforated metal lined with absorbing material, that can be mounted on a stand behind the mic to surround and block it from room reflections.

On a few rare occasions you might find that your room echoes or reverberation suit the music you are recording, such as a slap-back reflection echo in the vocal of a rockabilly song. If it seems like the natural ambience of your space is working just as it is, track some vocals without these added precautions applied, and run up a rough mix to see how the sound sits in the track. Otherwise, damping natural ambience will usually make it easier to craft just the right ambience for the project as a whole at the mixing stage.

Monitoring vocal tracking

A poor or inadequate monitor mix will put a singer on edge more than any other factor (other than, perhaps, a large audience). Also, given the nature of the instrument and the preamp levels required to capture it adequately, vocal mics are likely to be set "hotter" than mics used on just about any other instrument, other than the softer acoustic stringed varieties perhaps. For this reason, monitoring during tracking has to be considered from the perspective of avoiding spill into the vocal mic, as well as that of providing a comfortable and representative backing for the performer to work with.

If you have the luxury of a separate live vocal room to work with, and a fairly well isolated control room, you will be able to follow the vocal takes through the studio monitors, if you aren't doing the singing yourself. Even so, it's important to keep those levels down to avoid letting any of the backing track spill into the sensitive vocal mic in the room next door (it's amazing what these things will often pick up). Otherwise, you and the singer will both have to wear enclosed headphones, with totally closed backs that sufficiently prevent any sound from escaping. If two of you are listening simultaneously—engineer, singer—you will either need a multi-channel headphone amp, or a means of patching the signal from one device with a headphone out (the interface) to another (a mixing desk or tape machine).

However much you want to hear what's going on yourself, be sure to cater the rough mix to the singer's requirements, as regards the balance of live vocal to backing tracks, the general balance of individual instruments, overall volume, and so forth. Some singers will perform better with a little reverb added to their vocal in the monitor, too, but be certain to configure this in your DAW, mixer, or interface so the reverb is only heard along with the vocal being tracked, rather than recorded. It can take some effort to perfect that monitor mix, but when tracking vocals in particular, it's worth taking time to get it right, rather than blasting on through hoping for the best, then wondering later why your usually competent vocalist was having so much trouble hitting pitch. Part of your role as a home recordist when working with others rather than just tracking your own parts is to "play producer" and create the best possible working environment for your musicians. Apply a little extra patience here and craft a mix that will have your performer working in their comfort zone.

Backing vocals

Backing vocals are as important as any instrument in the track, but unless the performance is a genuine duet or multi-vocalist lead part, you will want them to be tucked in behind the lead vocal. Often you will simply use the same mic you used to track the lead vocal, but there are other nifty ways of approaching this task. Using a different mic can sometimes help to add the color and contrast that can make a backing vocal "pop" in just the right way, enough to be noticed without requiring a volume level that finds it competing with the lead vocal.

If you are layering several backing vocals, there are different ways to optimize them. depending on what you are trying to achieve. Multiple b-vox parts performed by different singers taking different harmonies can often be best achieved using the same mic, which can help to glue them together. To achieve the thick, layered "choral" style backing vocals with the same singer layering track upon track, changing the mic for each new track is often the way to go. The different character imparted by each mic, when confronted with the same voice, often helps to lend definition to what might otherwise be a sonic wash. That way such epic b-vox efforts will feel thick and multi-dimensional rather than just swampy.

If you have more than one singer doing backing vocals in a band, and they are already experienced at singing their parts this way live, you might even consider the good old "all around one mic" approach. Tracking individual backing vocals separately will obviously give you more control over balancing the levels in the mix, but if two, three, or more performers are used to singing with reference to each other's harmonies, and already do so well on stage, it can be tough to know where to start in stripping them down and doing the parts one by one. A large-diaphragm condenser or large ribbon mic is best for this job, because one of these will best capture the width of the sonic picture coming at it. An omni mic is ideal for this application, although a good cardioid should do fine if you don't spread your singers too widely, and they can even stand either side of a figure-eight mic. Set your singers up around it, let them go to it, and if it works, it works. Or, if you want to hear that multi-voice backing in stereo behind the lead vocal, set up a coincident or near-coincident pair and shoot it that way.

Recording levels, and tracking with compression

After nailing a suitable sound, a big part of the job of recording usable vocals has to do with capturing consistent signal levels. I have advocated doing without a compressor in the tracking process if you can't afford a decent sounding outboard hardware compressor. Better, usually to simply add it as a plug-in later in the DAW as necessary. But the extremes of signal level produced by the average vocal performance make it a great candidate for a little distortion-preventing comp during recording.

Put another way, it can be extremely difficult to set a good average level for a vocal performance, unless it's a fairly flat and even performance to begin with. If you set your mic pre to just avoid clipping your interface's input in the louder sections, the quieter sections barely register; if you set it to bring out the quieter sections, more aggressive passages blast into the red. The solution? Well, traditionally it has been to use a compressor in line after the mic pre (or as a channel insert), set to pull down any loud notes that might slam your meters, and to expand any soft passages to bring them out better. If you have a decent sounding hardware compressor, this is one place where you might give some consideration to using it. You don't want to squash and pump your vocal tracks so hard during recording that everything sounds the same and you rob them of their natural dynamics; but use the comp as a safety net, and you can apply a little more via plug-in later in the process to tweak or sweeten the track as desired.

Alternatively, you can still forego tracking through a compressor and add any necessary comp "in the box" while mixing, but you need to be extremely careful with your recording levels to do so. Old-school engineers still rave about the beauty of "tape compression" achieved by hitting analog tape with a hot signal. But anything approaching the 0dB mark on your digital-recording meter and the clipping that this represents will result in nasty distortion and an unusable track. The power and clarity of 24-bit digital recording make it easy to record low-level signals and boost them to acceptable volume levels in the DAW. With this in mind, we avoid digital clipping simply by recording a much, much lower signal than you would normally be happy with—something averaging around –12dB to –14dB but not peaking above –7dB at any time—to prevent any chance of an accidental overload spoiling an otherwise perfect take. To make this work, you also need a quiet mic pre, and a low-noise signal chain in general all the way from mic to interface, so that when you boost the levels in the DAW you don't heap on a lot of hiss and hum along with the vocal track.

COMPRESSOR SETTINGS FOR VOCALS

RATIO: **2:1 to 4:1**
THRESHOLD: **–7dB to –10dB**
ATTACK: **1ms (fast)**
RELEASE: **300ms to 500ms or auto**
KNEE: **soft**

Whether tracking through a hardware compressor to avoid overs, or adding a plug-in in the DAW to smooth a vocal track and add a little sonic mojo, it's best to start with some fairly gentle compression, and increase things from there as necessary. If you really want to thicken up a vocal to suit a heavy-feeling track, you might push the ratio up to 6:1 or even 8:1, then adjust the threshold so it isn't smashing everything that comes through, but just reducing the loudest passages. Most vocal tracks can use at least a little compression, but giving it more than necessary can prove a quick way of ruining the dynamics of the performance.

EQ SETTINGS

Ideally, you will have captured a good, balanced vocal tone by using the right mic and preamp for the job, your singer won't have any annoying frequency peaks, and you can dispense with EQ altogether. If a little extra presence and cut is required, try gently boosting a fairly wide band somewhere in the 4kHz to 6kHz region. As with most instruments that aren't key to the low-end content of the material, you might also set a high-pass filter to dump any low-end junk below 80Hz if you didn't already do so during recording. You can also tame any boomy or woofy resonances in the vocal track by slightly reducing a band in the region above that—check anything up to about 300Hz (or, conversely, if the track sounds a little emasculated, you might try boosting in that region instead). If your singer does have any annoying frequency peaks, you can find them by first boosting a narrow band and sweeping it throughout the frequency range of the vocal to find the point where "annoying" becomes "unbearable," then reducing that spot slightly.

CHAPTER 8

RECORDING PIANO AND OTHER INSTRUMENTS

Having come this far in our exploration of mic techniques for recording different instruments, it's clear that several of them have fairly broad applications. Mics and mic placements used, for example, to record acoustic guitars can obviously be adapted to record mandolin, banjo, ukulele, violin, and other acoustic stringed instruments. Those used to record traditional drum kits might easily be applied to other forms of percussion, and so on. Even with all of these, a few tweaks and adjustments with the specific instrument in mind will help to hone your tracks. And of course there are some major instruments that haven't yet been touched upon—keyboards, both acoustic and electric, and horns—that are very much their own animals. This chapter will deal with these in an effort to help you become a well-rounded recordist, and to handle more than just the bare-bones rock set-up.

Recording acoustic piano

Even a brief examination of the size, construction, and sonic range of the acoustic piano leads pretty quickly to a few resounding conclusions: these things can be beasts to record accurately, and there are as many ways of doing so as there are days in the month. Your approach will depend on how you define "accurately" as regards the sound of the piano, and that should vary depending on the sound and feel that are desired for the track as a whole, and what "picture" of the piano will best suit it.

Just by placing your mic(s) in different positions around the instrument you can make it sound like half a dozen or more different pianos, since the sound of these things emanates from so many different places. To compound that, a technique that might sound great for one track can easily sound entirely wrong for another. Microphone positioning will determine whether your piano sounds warm or bright, ambient or dry, containing mostly string tone or blending in the percussive element of the hammers. Let's examine a few likely starting points on both grand (or baby grand) and upright (also known as console) piano, which are quite different instruments from the recording engineer's perspective. You can adapt these and use your imagination to discover further variations and original placements besides.

ACOUSTIC GRAND PIANO

Many techniques for recording grand and baby grand pianos were developed with classical music in mind, and seek to maximize the resonance and room sound of the instrument. Dry this out just a little, and you are moving into good jazz-piano territory. We aren't dealing with classical music much in this book, since it is largely irrelevant to the notion of "home recording," but it is entirely conceivable that you might want to record "classical-style" for solo piano performances, for piano-and-voice singer-songwriter compositions, or simply to capture the full depth and breadth of the instrument in more atmospheric tracks.

In a small room, a spaced pair of mics shooting inside the raised lid, a few feet back from the strings, might provide as much ambiance as you can muster.

Traditional techniques for recording a grand piano in a classical composition rely on distance and depth, which also requires a spacious room. You're unlikely to keep your concert grand in the laundry room, but many do live in rooms that are barely large enough to contain the distant-miking techniques that are used in larger studios to adequately capture the full breadth of the instrument. A starter placement for a classical or ambient solo rock/pop piano sound in your semi-restricted space might include a spaced stereo (AB) pair of large-diaphragm or small-diaphragm condenser mics or large-geometry ribbon mics placed six to eight feet (1.8–2.4m) high, about ten feet (3m) apart and five feet (1.5m) from the piano, aiming toward the strings in the top of the case with the lid open to its highest position. (Dynamic mics generally just don't hack it on grand piano, but if that's all you've got, so be it.) Taking this further back, you can also try a coincident XY pair aimed approximately at where your ear tells you the piano sounds its best. An M-S pair similarly positioned can also yield good results.

You can get an even greater sense of space, even in a medium-sized room, by adding a more distant mic or two to your main stereo pair. Place it on or near the opposite wall or corner from the instrument (after first walking the room to listen out for the ideal spot) and blend in as much as you need with the primary pair.

Conversely, though, it can sometimes be difficult to bring your mics in tight in order to get a lot *less* room sound with any of the traditional stereo pairs, unless you have good omni mics to work with. Once you get a pair of cardioid or hyper-cardioid (or even figure-eight) mics right in over the strings of a grand piano, each is likely to focus too tightly on a narrow grouping of strings, thus accentuating two bands left and right of middle-C, rather than presenting a balanced L–R stereo spectrum. You can cut the room down somewhat with a cardioid pair positioned a couple of feet above the strings of the piano, with the lid raised to its highest position or removed, one mic over the treble strings, one over the bass strings. Play with the precise positioning to achieve a realistic stereo balance; sometimes you will get better results by placing the bass-string mic further from the hammers than the treble-string mic, so each captures the vibrating strings at a relatively similar point along their length.

For a good blend of room and direct sound in your tone, and a full stereo piano sound that's great for jazz, try bringing any of the above stereo set-ups in to within a couple of

ABOVE: Experiment with moving condenser mics around to different positions above the strings to achieve an accurate stereo sound that isn't too tightly focused on specific groups of notes, unless you want to accentuate those notes in the recording. BELOW: Even positioned so they hover just above the strings, a pair of large-diaphragm condenser mics placed under the lid of the piano will usually capture a lot of natural resonance and ambience.

feet of the top of the piano and experiment with placement for desired frequency blend and stereo field. Some engineers also get great results by placing two condenser or ribbon mics in the curve of the piano's body, a couple of feet apart, with the right mic (as viewed when facing the curve from the side of the instrument) aimed across toward the bass

strings, and the left mic aimed slightly left toward the treble strings. The size and construction of the grand piano means that it produces a lot of depth and reverberation within its own body (if you doubt this, step on the sustain pedal and hit a big chord), so you don't always need a lot of room depth to capture a sweet, natural reverb in your piano tone.

Plenty of recordists achieve semi-close-miked piano with a pair of boundary mics, either the affordable Radio Shack model with its Crown element (slightly modded, when possible) or a more expensive but still good value model from Beyer-Dynamic or another name-brand mic manufacturer. Tape them to the underside of the lid, one over the bass strings and one over the treble strings, about half way down the length of the piano, with the lid open to its short-stick position, and check this stereo spread for balance in your DAW. For a little more string ambience, move them slightly further away from the player; for more percussion and hammer sound, move them toward the player. For more isolation, yet still pretty good natural reverb and resonance from the instrument itself, you can close the lid entirely; and if you only need a mono track, a single boundary mic placed in the middle of underside of the lid often gets great results too.

To capture a not overly ambient sound, and one that presents a pretty accurate picture of the tone of the piano as heard from the player's perspective, you can use a variation of our baffled omni or "dummy head" technique. The technique traditionally calls for a pair of omni condenser mics positioned near the ears of the pianist (keep them far enough from his or her head that they won't be knocked by any movement during the performance). You can reduce the room sound somewhat, and still get a fairly balanced picture, by using a pair of cardioid mics instead, placed in the same positions and firing into the edge of the open piano lid.

FOCUS YOUR PIANO MICS

In many cases, the piano part played for any given track will be inherently restricted to a narrow range of the keyboard, rather than stretching from the first key to the eighty-eighth. You can use this to your advantage in setting up the mics. A piano part that forms just one of several instruments in a mix that also includes bass, guitar, drums, and perhaps others, will often be composed so as not to step on too many toes in the mix, and might therefore be constrained to just two or three octaves. When this is the case, you can hone your stereo piano-miking technique by focusing more closely on the strings which are actually sounded, rather than spreading your mics wide enough to capture the entire range of the instrument and possibly ending up with the crucial notes in the scale falling through a hole in the middle. Confer with the pianist to ascertain the limits of the range of the part, check the internal workings of the piano to ensure you know which strings will come into play, and tighten your miking focus to best capture them.

Mics placed either side of the performer's head will often achieve an accurate and versatile tone.

An interesting dual-mono mic technique that some engineers have used in several slight variations involves placing one mic above the strings near the center of the piano, or in what you determine to achieve the best balance from all keys, and another underneath the piano, aiming up at a slight angle. In most cases, you will need to reverse the phase of the under-piano mic, but you can experiment with this in the DAW. These two tracks can be blended into a mono track that adds plenty of woody warmth to a clear, full string sound, or panned half-left, half-right, for an interesting stereo effect.

UPRIGHT PIANO

The very different geometry of the upright (or console) piano means you can throw most of the above-mentioned mic positions right out the window. Many of the same principles still apply, however, regarding capturing a good, balanced stereo image and using ambient vs dry miking techniques, even if these qualities are achieved in different ways. Even when miking an upright from above or in front, as with several of these techniques, it's a good idea to pull the piano some distance out from any wall against which it is placed, if possible, to give free rein to the sound emanating from the back of the soundboard and to minimize any standing waves created by the reflective surface of the wall itself.

The simplest, and one of the most obvious, ways of miking an upright is to open the lid at the top and place a spaced stereo AB pair, coincident XY pair, or M-S pair a short distance above it, firing in toward the hammers and strings. This will capture a fairly percussive, possibly somewhat "plonky" tone that is also pretty bright, and might suit some recordings where you are looking for such a voice. Since the strings of an upright are mounted on a vertical plane, though, and most of the resonance occurs further down the case of the instrument, it can often be difficult to capture adequate low-end from such placements, if you're looking for a full-bodied piano sound.

Removing the upper panel from the front of the piano, above the keys, if you are able to do so, opens up the sound of the instrument considerably. Thus configured, the piano can be miked with your favorite stereo or mono set-up from a foot or two above the pianist's head, with mikes aiming down at an angle to a point roughly a foot above the keys. Alternatively, try the same baffled omni or "dummy head" technique described above for use on grand piano, with your mics of choice placed either side of the performer's head, a safe distance out so they aren't in the bang-bang zone, and aiming slightly downward.

If you can remove the lower-front panel also (or alternatively), you can capture a very different voice by miking an upright below the keyboard. Position a spaced stereo pair with one mic either side of the piano stool, with the mics about a foot and a half (500mm) off the floor and aiming at an upward angle toward a point at the strings just beneath the keyboard. Since the hammers are at the top of the piano, this will give you less of the percussive hammer action. It will also capture a fuller low end, since it focuses on more of the speaking length of the bass strings, while also missing much of the direct vibration of the treble strings, which are mounted higher up on the soundboard. (With any mics below the keyboard, listen out for squeaky or thumping pedal sounds, and deal with them as best you can if necessary.) For a "best of both worlds" effort you can even place one mic below the keyboard and one above, with the lower mic just left of the stool and the upper mic just right of the pianist's head. These can paint a slightly odd picture panned for full-width stereo, putting the mellow low end on one side and the percussive, more present high end on the other. Alternatively, you can pan them in fairly tight, maybe eleven o'clock/one o'clock, or position them in a dual-mono mix that favors one side of the stereo field with several other instruments in the spectrum—for example, the low-register mic at around two o'clock and the high-register mic further right at four o'clock—to produce a piano sound that isn't literally "stereo," but is deep and effective nonetheless.

If you can pull the piano out from the wall, some good sounds can be had by miking the soundboard at the back of the instrument, too. A spaced stereo pair will work fairly close in if you don't want a whole lot of room sound, or these and any of the other classics will do good service further out if you want more ambience. A lot of people ignore this side of an upright piano, but a deep and well-balanced sound can be achieved from these positions, and you can always add a third mic placed above the opened top cover pointing down toward the hammers if you want to blend in a more percussive sound with this stereo image.

PZMs or other types of boundary mics can also work well on uprights. Try taping either a single mic or a stereo pair about two and a half feet (750mm) apart on the underside of the opened top lid. While you're at it, leave them there and close the lid for some interesting internal tones. Alternatively, to get them further along the strings" speaking length, tape them on the inside front panel of the piano (in other words, the opposite side of the panel that the pianist stares at while playing), but if this is a removable panel you'll need to make sure it isn't loose and rattling, and imparting that noise into the mics. Some recordists also achieve good results by taping boundary mics to the soundboard, the large wooden surface (usually spruce) that runs behind the strings and adds resonance to the piano tone, but it can be tricky to get them in there in the first place.

Compression and EQ for acoustic piano

The balanced nature of any well-built acoustic piano should ensure that it produces no major spikes in output level when miked correctly, and no troublesome frequency peaks or nulls either. For this reason, compression, if necessary at all, is most likely to be used gently, to help the instrument sit well in the mix. But you might still require it to tame any sections that jump out in volume because the part strayed closer to the close-mic positions or because the performer simply "went for it." EQ might only be needed to correct unflattering room resonances or less-than-ideal mic technique, but can also be used to craft the voice of the instrument to suit the mood and feel of the composition as a whole.

As an acoustic stringed instrument with its own soundboard and other resonant components, a piano has its own built-in elements of compression, so if it sounds good in the track just as it is, don't feel you need to use any at all just for the sake of it. But having said all that, if you do want to make a piano part thick, even, and creamy, with less of the instrument's natural dynamics, squashing it with some heavy compression used as an "effect" is the way to go.

COMPRESSOR SETTINGS FOR PIANO

RATIO: **2:1**
THRESHOLD: **–7dB to –10dB**
ATTACK: **around 150ms or auto**
RELEASE: **around 250ms or auto**
KNEE: **soft**

EQ SETTINGS

If the piano is part of a dense mix, and seems to be adding some low-end woof and clutter as a result, you might start by using a high-pass filter to dump anything below 80Hz, although you won't want to do this if you rely on any low notes in the piano part itself. To bring out more sparkle and shimmer from the instrument's copious overtones, to suit a poppier track, for example, try boosting it in the 20kHz range with a shelving filter. Conversely, to mellow it out for a warmer tone, do the reverse and pull things down a little in that range. If you want to add firmness to the low end without increasing the

TIGHTEN UP YOUR PARTS!

A keyboard part can take up a lot of sonic space in a full band mix, and can touch a little of just about everything in the frequency range from the rumble of a bass guitar's low E (and below) to the shimmer of a crash cymbal. If the keyboard parts you are recording feel too "weighty" for the track, get the player to tighten up his or her part and focus on the part of the keyboard that really needs to be heard in order to make its statement in the song. They don't need to have ten fingers on the keys at all times, stomping on other instruments in the process; very often, more compact chords and simple melody lines will do just fine.

Listen to any great Hammond organ player working within a band context, and they will be playing just enough to make their musical statement within the overall arrangement, working little dyads and triads (two- and three-note chords) and playing the tone of the instrument, rather than showing how many notes they can hit at once. This approach can be counter-intuitive for many players who learned their skills in formal piano lessons, where it's taught mainly as a solo instrument or as a lone accompaniment to another voice or soloist. But work with them on the notion of filling a specific part in a broad range of voices—an orchestral approach to the band arrangement as a whole, really—and your tracks will benefit as a result.

boominess of the track as a whole, give the piano a little boost in the 100Hz to 250Hz range. Anything above that, up to around 4kHz, constitutes the midrange of the instrument, where its real punch and body live, so you can increase the weight of the track by homing in on a band in this range and giving it a little boost.

Recording Hammond organ

When we talk about techniques for "recording Hammond," we're really talking about "recording a Leslie cabinet." We will look at some tricks for recording electric keyboards below, but a proper Hammond organ, although "electric" in the sense that you plug it in to make it work, must be treated as an acoustic instrument in the sense that it needs to be miked. The effect of a Leslie rotating speaker cabinet in the air is an essential part of this instrument's sound. The classic "Hammond" really constitutes the pairing of Hammond B3 organ and Leslie 122 tone cabinet, although people get great results from C3, C2, A100, M3, and RT3 Hammond models too, as well as Leslie 145, 147, and other tone cabinet models. Also, plenty of organists use Hammond simulators, like those found in the popular Nord Electro models and others, but still run them (via adaptors and appropriate preamps) into Leslie cabinets or similar rotating-speaker units to achieve "that sound." So miking the Leslie is still key to recording these keyboards.

Being the monster that it is, a Leslie cab (and we'll use that name to refer to any similarly designed rotating-speaker cabinet) can be miked from a myriad different positions. The Doppler-effected sound of these cabs is created by two different components within them, a lower and upper rotor that spin independently at slightly different speeds. You really need to mic both of these to capture the sound adequately, or mike the cabinet from enough of a distance that the two are blended realistically as they might be heard in the room. Ambient miking (room miking) at a distance of more than five or six feet (1.5–1.8m) will often add too much room sound to this instrument, however, making it more diffuse than most tracks would like, so positions are usually from close to semi-distant.

Also, the difference in tone produced by the upper and lower rotors often leads engineers to use different types of microphones on each. The upper rotor, which consists of a pair of horns that rotate around a tweeter, is the "treble" unit, while the lower rotor, a rotating drum with a larger "woofer" speaker firing down into it, is the bass unit. As you might imagine, there can be some benefit to miking each with a mic that specializes in capturing its particular frequency range.

Many engineers will make the most of a Hammond's vast soundscape through a Leslie by putting one mic on the lower rotor, perhaps a Shure Beta 52A or AKG D112 positioned just a few inches from the central louvers, and a pair of small-diaphragm condensers such as AKG C451s or C480s a similar distance from two different points in the upper-rotor vents to capture the higher frequencies in stereo. These can be at 180 degrees from each other on opposite sides of the cab, or just around 90 degrees apart. Traditionally, the lower-rotor mic is panned right up the middle with the upper-rotor pair panned left-right according to their placement, but you can also move the entire Hammond "picture" toward the left or right of the mix as a whole by panning them, for example, lower-rotor at three o'clock, left upper-rotor mic at noon, and right upper-rotor mic wide right.

To mellow out your upper-rotor sound, you might try other dynamic mics there, or a pair of ribbon mics, provided you keep them out of any wind blast zone from the rotors. A ribbon can sound great on the lower rotor too—as can a large-diaphragm condenser if you want more crispness and fidelity from that position. Moving your mics of choice back a few feet obviously brings more ambience into the sound by admitting more room reflections. With any semi-distant miking techniques, you should have the Leslie cab positioned away from any walls, so any reflective walls aren't whacked disproportionately back into the mic, throwing off the balance of the room tone you capture. It's a good idea to place it closer to the center of the room in any case.

For a more focused sound in a song where you don't want the Hammond to take up too much space, you can place one mic each on the upper and lower rotors, and either blend them in mono, or give them just a little separation in the stereo picture (again, placing them to left or right rather than across the center of the mix if you prefer) to create at least some sense of space. Or mike the entire cab with just a single mic a little further back in the room, say four to six feet (1.2–1.8m), to get a realistic sound that still presents plenty of rotor motion in a single track (larger ribbons like the Coles 4038, AEA R84, Royer 121, or more affordable Alctron types *et al* are great for this application).

Whether or not you compress or EQ your Hammond will depend on what you are trying to achieve with it, and it's such a mammoth tone-producing beast that the settings will vary greatly with your requirements. As ever, mike it right and you might not need any treatment at all.

Recording electric keyboards

First, I should point out that I'm not even getting into MIDI in the studio, which isn't "recording" as such, but a means of programming, arranging, and triggering sounds from keyboards or between a range of electronic components and instruments. It's an entirely valid creative avenue, don't get me wrong, but it's something you will use as an element of your musical style, not a "recording technique" as such. There are plenty of great resources for learning about MIDI's benefits as a creative technique, and its usefulness in workflow management. Recording an electric keyboard as played "live," however, is a different matter, and one that requires techniques that might be related to those used to record other instruments. And even if you are generating those parts from MIDI programming, you still need them to *sound right* in the track, which is what we're all about here.

Most electric keyboards are designed to be plugged straight into your interface and recorded direct, without an amp. The tones in digital keyboards are usually modeled to sound "real" when reproduced in this way, and in theory shouldn't require any further processing. Regardless of this fact, many of them seem to like a little something going on from keyboard output to interface input, and you often get better tracks by putting in a little more thought than the "plug and play" scenario might imply.

Unless they are buried far back in the mix in a song with a lot of other instruments going on, keyboards tracked straight in can often sound a little flat and artificial (and even within a busy mix that can still be a drawback). Frequently, some careful processing between keys and interface will do the trick: try running the signal through an outboard compressor starting with a fairly gentle setting (the starter points for piano will work fine, with some alterations in attack and release times depending upon the attack and sustain of the sound you are using, and the part you are playing), and that should help it sit in the mix a little better. If you want to fatten it up further, squash it with a heavier ratio of 10:1 or so and a more sensitive threshold setting and see if you like the results. You will really need to listen to the keyboards in the track in some good monitors or headphones, or record some and play them back in a representative rough mix, to get an idea of whether this is working or not. Just listening to the processed signal in solo doesn't really tell you anything.

If you have a tube mic preamp, or even a solid-state unit with some character to it, try running the signal into that before hitting the compressor to give a little more analog juice to the sound. Be sure to lower the keyboard's own output level, and run through a line-level input on the pre if it has one, because you will be boosting the signal through the pre before hitting the compressor. Often this kind of treatment is enough to add the body and personality that some DI-ed keyboard tones, however "realistic" they might seem, tend to lack when recorded. If you don't have any such outboard units you can always add some plug-in compression in the track, and an analog preamp-style treatment too, but it's a good idea to get the improved voice in the track in the first place, if you can.

Amping up a keyboard and miking the result is another good way to get some "air" and character into the track. Ideally you want to use a keyboard amp, or a bass amp at a pinch. It should have a line-level input, too, or you are likely to experience front-end distortion and unwanted noise. Set your keyboard signal so it isn't pushing the preamp stage of the amplifier too hard and causing any unwanted clipping there, then try miking the cab using any of the techniques discussed in the Recording Bass and Recording Guitars chapters. Choose your mic according to the frequency range in which the keyboard part dwells: if it's a bass-heavy part, a dynamic mic like a Shure Beta 52A or AKG D112 might be best, but for a fuller response, a sturdy large-diaphragm condenser that's

ARE STEREO KEYBOARD TRACKS REALLY NECESSARY?

Electronic keyboards played in stereo in the headphones can sound pretty damn cool, and it's tempting to print all that lush depth and dimension into your tracks. If you're recording electronic music, or a song in which that keyboard part shines as the star, the central focus of the arrangement, that can work great. On many other occasions, however, a big, lush stereo spread just isn't necessary, and can actually get in the way of the rest of the instruments in the mix. Often, a mono keyboard track will provide more than enough sonic information to make the necessary statement, when it is recorded right in the first place. If you want more width in the keyboard sound than one track allows for, though, you can imply some stereo with a range of other mixes, without panning the tracks wide left-right. Try panning the tracks to two slightly different points on the left and right, something like two o'clock and four o'clock, and you will still feel plenty of space between them, or pan one slightly left at eleven o'clock and one further right at three o'clock, to create a semi-stereo sound of sorts that still leans to one side to give the keyboard its own place in the mix, while leaving room for something else to dominate on the other side.

When using these other mixing approaches with keyboard parts that were recorded from stereo outs, listen for any loss of level or depletion of sound in general as you bring the tracks closer together across the stereo field. Some keyboard sounds produce an artificial stereo spread by processing the left and right outputs out of phase of each other through reverb or delay or some other effect, and these will cancel each other out as you bring each side closer to center in the mix.

able to take semi-close miking might be preferable. A ribbon mic will yield some thicker, warmer results that might do the trick if you're seeking a less clinical sound.

If you are miking an amp, try to record a second DI-ed track of the keyboard part alongside it, either processed through some outboard comp as described as above, or just straight in as a "safety." You can take this DI-ed signal from the stereo output of the keyboard itself, but before doing so consider whether you really want two sides of a stereo sound processed and recorded slightly differently (one through a miked amp, one direct), or in fact whether you want a stereo keyboard sound at all. If you're going for a mono keyboard track in the first place, take your DI from a DI box between keys and amp, so you've got the same signal happening in both tracks. As discussed in the sidebar, a stereo keyboard track isn't always a good idea, "just because you can," unless you want that wide L-R spread for very conscious creative reasons.

MIDI keyboards

Often these days, electronic keyboards used in recording take the form of MIDI keyboards, or MIDI-triggered plug-in instruments, rather than instruments that are played live in real-time as you roll in record mode with the red light on. MIDI tracks provide enormous flexibility, for the solo recordist in particular. One benefit is that they can be edited and looped with ease; another is that they can be assigned to trigger any desired MIDI sound that you have available (from a plug-in instrument in the DAW, or an external MIDI instrument or module), rather than a sound that is locked in at the initial time of recording the track, as with anything recorded as a standard audio track. As such, you can tweak the sound of your MIDI piano, organ, synth or what have you long after recording the part in the MIDI track itself, or select an entirely different instrument to produce the sounds of that part. On top of all of this, MIDI instruments offer a "what you hear is what you get" product: their sound won't change according to mic technique or other engineering techniques, and will consistently come back out of the box in the same sonic form as it went it ... unless you change it yourself, of course.

More detailed information on the use of specific MIDI instruments, whether hardware or plug-in based, will be found in the user's manuals supplied with the products themselves. Incorporating them into recording in the DAW, however, is usually fairly simple. Most systems in use these days (even fairly basic programs like GarageBand) have MIDI tracks that can be created, recorded, and manipulated in the DAW's editing window, and which will carry the MIDI information required to trigger the instruments of your choice. In most DAWs, MIDI tracks are created from the same menu that allows the creation of audio, auxiliary, and master tracks. Rather than constituting a holding place for recorded audio, though, they carry recorded MIDI information that any other MIDI instrument should be able to understand, when connected correctly.

MIDI can be recorded into a MIDI track in a couple of different ways. It can be performed in real time on a MIDI controller (a MIDI-capable keyboard connected to your audio interface), with the MIDI track record-enabled and your song rolling in record mode the same way you would record an audio track. Note that the ultimate sound produced by the MIDI track won't necessarily be a sound from the MIDI-capable keyboard that you use to record it—unless you route it back to that keyboard to trigger one of its sounds during mixdown—but can generally be any MIDI instrument with an input that is fed by your recorded MIDI track. Otherwise, a MIDI track can usually be created by programming or editing the information in the track's editing window, locking each note to the tempo grid (timebase ruler) that you have preset for your song.

With many systems, Pro Tools for one, it's advisable to lock a performance recorded in real-time to a MIDI track to the bars and beats of the tempo grid (ruler) to that imprecisely played notes will still fall accurately to the beat, or can easily be edited to do so. To ensure this, many DAWs have an option for recording tick-based MIDI, a format that fixes MIDI notes to the relative time of the timebase. When recorded in this way, MIDI information will also move automatically with any global tempo changes made in the DAW, so notes will still start in their same relative positions in the time/bars/beats line. Such a change will not, however, alter the duration of notes, and that might need to be edited further to suit any drastic changes in tempo settings.

With most DAWs, you don't even need an external MIDI keyboard to achieve MIDI instrument sounds in your tracks. Most come with a selection of plug-in instruments—from grand pianos, to Hammond-style organs, to analog synth-style modules and more—that can be played, and recorded, with your mouse or with keystrokes. Once recorded to a track, MIDI information can be edited just like audio tracks, cut-and-pasted to a different section of the song where the same riffs need to be repeated, for example, or looped with your DAW's looping tool, the same as any drum track would be looped. Between the ease of recording information to a MIDI track, and the convenience and versatility of triggering the sounds of myriad plug-in instruments in an instrument track, MIDI really does offer virtually unlimited performance power for those who want to explore it in their recording.

Recording acoustic stringed instruments: mandolin, ukulele, violin, banjo, etc.

By this point in the book we have covered microphone techniques for recording acoustic instruments pretty thoroughly, so there's no point in rehashing all of it with respect to each of these. If you are a ukulele player (there are plenty of them around these days) who skipped forward to this section in heated anticipation, my apologies: I will offer a few specific pointers for these instruments, but for the most part I'm going to ask you to review the techniques covered under Recording Acoustic Guitars, p154, and use some common sense to apply them to your instrument of choice.

The volume levels and frequency ranges of the acoustic guitar and other instruments such as the mandolin, violin, uke, and so forth are similar enough that most of the same mic set-ups—single, multi, and stereo—will apply with a few tweaks. Adjustments will be necessary to accommodate the way each instrument produces its sound, and from what part of the body, but we have already put plenty of thought into finding the "sweet spot," so the same kind of thinking applies here, too. Similar mics are likely to work well, too, although a few exceptions will be noted below.

RECORDING MANDOLIN

Just like acoustic guitars, mandolins vary greatly in quality and tone (and quality of tone), and any sound you are trying to capture really begins with the instrument and the player. In addition, other factors such as pick (plectrum) type and thickness, string type and condition, and playing style (near the bridge for a brighter and chimier sound with more attack; closer to the neck for a warmer, rounder sound) will make a huge difference, before you even put a mic up to the instrument.

Often the go-to one-mic approach is to set up a small-diaphragm condenser such as a Neumann KM54 or AKG C451 or a more affordable Audio-Technica AT2021 or similar in front of the mandolin, a few inches out from a point near the neck/body joint and aimed slightly toward the meat of the body between the f-holes. This should capture a clear, crisp tone with plenty of high-end shimmer, the classic studio-recorded bluegrass mandolin tone. Many mandolins heard in more contemporary arrangements these days, however—bluegrass or otherwise—are leaning toward warmer, rounder sounds with some low-end weight to them. Think of the sounds on Alison Krauss's records, or to some extent Chris Thile's playing with Nickel Creek and solo. To warm up a mandolin in this manner, try a large-diaphragm condenser mic in the position described above, but further out from the instrument, perhaps 12 to 18 inches (300–450mm). Or, to add more midrange chunk to the tone, put it a similar distance out from a spot just south of the bridge, aiming at the meat of the lower bout, or about chin-high to the player, aiming slightly down.

Ribbon mics can do a great job of warming up a mandolin and adding thickness too. One likely candidate is the Beyer M160, which will still sound precise and clear, but with lots of thick ribbon character. You can try a larger ribbon mic too, for an even darker mando sound.

RECORDING VIOLIN

For violin, it's tempting just to say "see Recording Mandolin, above," although a few alterations are usually necessary. For one thing, and rather obviously, the violin—"fiddle" in bluegrass, Irish, and Cajun parlance—is held on the horizontal rather than the vertical plane in playing position, so its tone emanates from the resonating portions of the body somewhat differently.

By and large, your microphone of choice should be mounted above the instrument, at a distance that helps to diminish string squeak or any strident honk from potentially shrill notes, while also being out of range of the performer's natural movement, that slicing bow action in particular. This small instrument can produce a lot of volume, so you can get away with placing a condenser mic a good foot or two above and out from the violin. Positioning will likely be above and to the right of the violinist's face, aiming downward at the soundboard, between the f-holes. For less room sound, or less spill if you're recording other instruments into their own mics at the same time, you can come in closer and reduce mic-pre levels accordingly, but you will need to put more care into positioning to home in on the tone you are seeking. In a pinch, a good dynamic mic will even capture violin pretty well, and ribbons can work their retro-toned magic too.

RECORDING BANJO

Loud, strident, and percussive, the banjo can be tricky to track just right—that is, if you're looking for something other than loud, strident, and percussive. Those are, of course, inherent elements of this instrument's tone, but most of us want to hear our banjo as "bright and jangly" rather than "harsh and piercing," and it can be a challenge to get it there. A small-diaphragm condenser in close on the head will inevitably be rather shrill; backing off to a foot or so will open up the sound somewhat, as will moving the mic up toward the neck/body joint. A large-diaphragm condenser will often warm things up a little more, too, and can work great a little further out.

But, once again, the right ribbon mic can make a great "shrillness squelcher"; try a smaller variety such as a Beyer M160 to capture plenty of detail without the ear-piercing squawk, or smooth it out more with a larger model such as a Coles 4038, an AEA R84, a Royer R121, or even a cheapo from the Alctron/Nady/CAD camp. Like so many stringed instruments, the banjo produces sound from different parts of the structure, and you can capture it in all its glory by using two mics at once. Any of the basic stereo techniques from our Studio Approach will work pretty well if you want a genuine stereo recording, but I would also suggest a dual-mono approach with one mic near the neck/body joint, and one in front of and slightly higher than the head, aiming at a point slightly above the player's picking hand (or, conversely, below the body aiming upward at the head). Use the right mics, and blend these appropriately, and you can nail a banjo sound that's both fat and lively, without being overly shrill.

RECORDING UKULELE

See Recording Acoustic Guitars, p154, then shrink your perspective.

Recording harmonica

Harmonica pops up in a surprisingly wide range of musical contexts, but in the broad spectrum of popular music is mainly used in two very specific ways: blues style, and folk style. Each aims to achieve a very different tone from the instrument, and is therefore recorded differently too.

Folk style is the simpler of the two. Think Bob Dylan or to some extent Bruce Springsteen, performers who—on the live stage, at least—play their harmonicas from a neck harness, into the same mic they use for vocals. A little more consideration is given to their harmonica tracks in the studio, no doubt, but the approach remains simple and direct. For what we might call "high-fidelity" folk harmonica (which also means pop and country harmonica, too), a robust large-diaphragm condenser mic is the ideal candidate. Position it a good eight to 12 inches (200–300mm) back from the harmonica, and have the performer blow from slightly off-axis rather than directly into the mic—and use a pop screen too, as you would to record a vocal. Even at this distance, notes blown straight at the mic can still sound surprisingly shrill, but most experienced players will use appropriate hand-muting techniques and will naturally add dynamics to their performance.

If you want more of a close-miked sound, something of a hybrid of the distant technique above and the blues technique we'll discuss below, you can use a decent dynamic vocal mic like a Shure Beta 58, or even a good old SM57 or SM58, and let the performer cup the mic in his or her palms, behind the harmonica. With this one you will want to start with your preamp's gain set extremely low and work gradually upward, checking any climactic peaks through the course of the performance to keep from slamming your meters and clipping the signal. Running the signal through an outboard compressor for some limiting is also a good idea.

Recording proper "blues harp" is a whole different ballgame, and is really more akin to miking an electric guitar amp. The sound associated with this style of harmonica playing is produced by blowing straight into a hand-held "bullet mic," an old-fashioned desk-top dynamic mic of the type used by radio dispatchers back in the day—the Shure model 520 "green bullet" being perhaps the most famous example—which is rammed through a small tube amplifier. Combos with eight- or ten-inch speakers and vintage-style circuits are usually preferred, and these are generally cranked to produce a hot, reedy tone with plenty of natural tube overdrive. As such, the harmonica, mic, and amp really work together as the instrument known as "blues harp," rather than the tone being generated by the harmonica itself.

It all sounds rather complicated, I know, but if you have an experienced blues blower coming in to play, they should already have a harp mic and amp that work well for them, and which you can simply mike as you would a guitar amp. Close-miking is a likely starting point, since you're trying to capture that intensely "coupled" sounding response from harmonica reed to mic diaphragm to speaker, but you can always fatten it up by trying any of the distant and multi-mic techniques covered in the Recording Guitars chapter. If you're trying to achieve the blues harp sound for yourself and don't already possess the tools of the trade, try an SM57 or SM58 through a low impedance (lo-z) to high impedance (hi-z) transformer into the front end of a good small tube guitar amp. Even a little tube distortion from the thing will produce that characteristically wailing blues tone—think Little Walter, or Kim Wilson of The Fabulous Thunderbirds—and bring on the note-cracking transients and overtones that define this style of playing.

Recording horns

Horns can be intimidating to record, mainly because the average home-studio boffin encounters them less often than other instruments, and because they can product an awful lot of noise from a small package. They are really pretty straightforward to capture in practice, though, and the right mic, and good placement, should provide fairly forgiving results, provided the player and the horn are up to the job in the first place. Horns—by which we usually mean trumpet, trombone, and saxophones of various sizes, but sometimes anything from flute to clarinet to sousaphone, too—can be recorded individually or in groups, known as "horn sections," and the approach to each is somewhat different. Let's look at mics and placements to capture their individual characteristics first, then consider a few good techniques for capturing a horn section that plays tightly together.

The Coles 4038, a large ribbon mic, is a classic for recording smooth, rich horn parts.

TRUMPET

An instrument with one of the loudest decibel-per-pound ratios out there, this member of the brass family packs incredible punch and projection, and as such, needs to be treated with care. The vast majority of the sound of the trumpet comes out of its bell, and on the live stage we generally see a soloist jamming the big end of his horn right onto a dynamic mic. In the studio, a little more finesse, and distance, is usually preferred, and will capture a better and more representative tone besides. Even so, you want to aim the mic right into the bell, or set it to fire upward from a height of a few inches below, at a distance of around 12 inches (300mm) from the end of the horn. Neumann's U87 is a classic for this application, but any condenser with a similarly flat frequency response and the ability to capture high SPLs (with pad engaged, if necessary) should do a good job. That said, a condenser mic can sound overly bright on trumpet in many tracks, and you might want to tame this at its source with other mic choices.

Several good ribbon mics will eat up trumpet and sound gorgeous in the process, yielding silky highs and warm midrange and lows. The Coles 4038, which was designed to be used on, among other things, instruments in the BBC's orchestras, is a classic for horns of all types. Other large ribbons can do a great job—from the more expensive Royer R121 and AEA R84 to the affordable Alctron/Nady/CAD types—and even smaller models like the Beyer M160 can sound great. Even though a trumpet doesn't put out quite the blast of wind that its volume levels, or common cartoon images, might imply, it's a good idea to keep any ribbon mic a good foot (300mm) or more from the bell of the horn.

TROMBONE

Another brass instrument that similarly belts its thing straight out the horn at the end, the trombone can be recorded with similar mics to those used on the trumpet, but also works in a lower register. Given this, you might want to tweak your mic choice to opt for more of a low-end specialist, if you have one to play with. But if you're lucky enough to have a quality condenser of any kind, that's a good place to start. The larger ribbon mics will work wonders on trombone, too. The only major note for 'bone vs trumpet is that you might want to move the mic back to somewhere in the 18-inch (450mm) range.

SAXOPHONE

Saxes of various sizes—baritone, tenor, alto and so on—will sound quite different, of course, but they all produce their sound in a similar manner, as to some extent do the clarinet and other reed-driven members of the woodwind family. A portion of the sound comes out the bell, certainly, but some also emanates from the reed itself (at the mouthpiece) and from the body of the instrument, where it escapes through the holes beneath the keys as they open. The mics mentioned above in the Trumpet section make good choices for the sax, too, but will capture a more representative sound when positioned a little higher, perhaps four to eight inches (100–200mm) above the bell, around 12 inches (300mm) out, and firing toward the middle of the body of the horn.

RECORDING THE "HORN SECTION"

The job of tracking a horn section can be even scarier than recording individual horns, but it really doesn't need to be any more complicated. The magic of a tight horn section—traditionally consisting of three pieces, trumpet, sax, and trombone, but sometimes bigger or with a different line-up—is in the way the musicians play together and harmonize "live," on the spot, rather than in overdubbing tracks the way you would layer guitar parts or vocal harmonies performed by the same singer. A good horn section, one that has performed live together, should be experienced at working as a tight unit, and is ideally recorded that way.

With good players and good-sounding horns, the job can be as simple as putting up just one good mic and letting them go at it. Any of the above choices, other than the smaller ribbons, will do a good job; go for an open-sounding large-diaphragm condenser for greater clarity and fidelity, and a large ribbon mic for a more retro soul, jazz, or rhythm and blues vibe. Set up the players from about three to five feet (1–1.5m) from the mic with the trumpet in the middle and all close enough to each other to present a tight sonic picture but not so close that they're elbowing each other as they play. For a little more breadth and air, and more room sound besides, use a condenser set to omni and spread the horns in more of a semi-circle around the mic. You can also pair any of these all-into-one techniques with individual closer mics as described above for more control in the mix (with baffles between the musicians for even more separation).

A condenser mic positioned between the "bell" and the mouthpiece of the saxophone to capture the full tone of the instrument.

Alternatively, if you really want stereo horns in your mix, try a coincident or near-coincident pair a few feet out, or even an M-S pair, to which you can also add individual mics. Try spreading the players to different widths around a semi-circle in front of the mics to play with the sense of separation between each horn. And remember, just because you record in stereo doesn't mean you have to pan wide left-right, resulting in a song that sounds like the sax and trombone are each standing against the walls at opposite ends of the room with the trumpet in the middle. Tightening it up to more of a ten o'clock/two o'clock spread will keep your horn section punchy and tight and more "up the middle" when you really want these tracks to drive the songs. For a more orchestral or atmospheric feel, though, the wider pan might do just the trick.

CHAPTER 9
MIXING

Mixing and mastering are the dark arts of recording—or perhaps "dark and darker"—and both processes can be enigmatic at best, and utterly baffling at worst, for the newcomer to recording. In principle, each is a fairly simple process, but you need to develop new skills as well as the "ears" to do the best possible job.

In truth, these major steps on the way to finishing any project require objectivity, and therefore should ideally not be undertaken by a musician involved in the recordings. Many experienced producers and engineers even turn these over to specialists who were not involved in recording the project, in order to put them before "fresh ears" and an outside perspective that isn't biased by any sonic choices made along the way or muddled by repeated listenings to the songs involved. But this type of "handing it over" goes against the very notion of DIY home recording, which is what this book is all about. So we are going to accept that, for reasons ranging from budget to artistic control, we will often need to be doing these things ourselves. Later in the chapter, however, we'll discuss taking either or both of these jobs out of house, if you can afford it, and the likely benefits of having a professional mix and/or master your project.

Even if you do take these jobs to a pro at some point, you will want to go as far as you can with your own rough mixes, and perhaps some pseudo-mastering too, to provide early examples to bandmates. These are essential for providing something representative to listen to in order to make sure all the parts really do work in the songs, that they are recorded correctly, and so on. So whatever your resources, a basic understanding of the mixing and mastering processes is indispensable to the home recordist. And, in even introducing the "take it to a pro" option, I don't want to imply that you can't get valid results on your own: you absolutely can, and many musicians do produce great-sounding, broadcast-ready and fully releasable mixes all the time. So let's dive in, and find out what steps are likely to get us there.

What is mixing?

In simple terms, mixing (also called "mixdown") involves blending the multiple tracks that constitute your recording of any song into the two stereo tracks, left and right, that will be heard by any end listener via the final medium of distribution, whether that's a CD, vinyl, or an MP3 or other digital format distributed online. Important basic elements of this job include setting the ideal relative volume levels for each track, and putting each of these in its desired place in the stereo field. In practice, though, the fine points of mixing involve a lot more than that, and include compressing individual tracks as necessary so they both "sit" well in the mix and gel as a whole, using EQ to carve out space for each individual instrument within the frequency range of the entire composition, adding any desired effects, and more. As such, this job we call "mixing" is approached in several different steps, or layers, which build up to construct the final picture that will stand as our "mix" (a process made much simpler these days by the mix automation available in all good DAWs).

Achieving a great mix can often involve overcoming something of a Catch 22: you want the entire thing to sound cohesive and "of a piece," yet each instrument ideally needs to have a little of its own space, so it can be identified within the whole. Getting that balance just right is the key to a good mix, however else you want things to sound. The most important thing to remember during mixing is that anything you do to one instrument will affect the listener's perception of any other instruments in the arrangement. For example, increasing the level (volume) of a guitar will get in the way of anything else operating in the same frequency range, or conversely, reducing it will make other instruments seem more prominent; adding reverb to one instrument will make others sound relatively drier in comparison, and on and on. To put it more precisely, you simply can't have everything in your mix sounding huge, deep, wide, warm, and sparkly all at the same time or it will just be a big mushy mess. In order to make your mix really work it's worth planning ahead as regards the sonic space that each instrument in the arrangement will fill. Whether you do this mentally or, better yet, actually chart it out to some extent with pen and paper, list everything in the mix and take note of any instruments that might be fighting each other, and plan to EQ and pan those slightly differently so everything at least has some place to poke through.

Let's look at those "layers" within the job of mixing as a whole, and see how they build up to get you toward the final product. Most of this section will address mixing "in the box" in your DAW, keeping the signal entirely within the computer, which is how the vast majority of home recordists work these days, but we will also touch on using outboard gear to bring external analog effects into your project.

PRE-MIX: PREPARING YOUR TRACKS

Before you launch into the actual mixing, you need to get the individual tracks or groups of tracks that represent each instrument into their final shape. Ideally you will have done a little of this during the recording process, in order to hear your tracks edging toward their completed form after landing the takes you decided to keep. But there is usually still a lot of work to be done preparing individual tracks for final mixdown before you can adequately begin to judge levels, EQ, effects content, stereo pan, and so forth—all of the critical decisions that will follow this prepping step.

A good first step in track prep is to phase-align any tracks that might require it. I'm not referring to merely checking that multiple mic or mic and DI tracks of the same instrument are not in a reverse-phase relationship; that is also important, but it can be quickly checked and cured with a phase reverse button (often found on a "trim" plug-in). Phase alignment has to do with dragging audio regions to line up their waveforms with those of other tracks representing alternative mics used to record the same take. The object is to minimize the potentially detrimental effects of phase cancellations that occur when sound waves from the same source reach two or more different mics (or your ears)

Dragging one bass track into alignment with another in Pro Tools's editing window.

at slightly different times. Some engineers go wild in the DAW these days and phase-align anything that has more than one mic on it, moving drum overheads to line up precisely with the snare track, a distant mic and close mic on a guitar amp, and so on. Occasionally this kind of attention to detail can yield punchier sounding tracks, but it can also exacerbate the problem, possibly creating worse phase issues than you had in the first place. Detrimental results can come about because any time you are aligning a distant mic and close mic used on the same source, the distant mic is also capturing a significant amount of room sound, reflections that arrive at the mic at different times from different points in the room. Distant mics are used in the first place precisely to capture the depth that this distance and room sound adds to the sound, and messing with that can often yield odd results. In short, multi-miked sources that are miked with the right technique in the first place shouldn't require a lot of messing around with, phase-wise, and they certainly weren't doing this kind of tweaking to get classic tracks of the 60s and 70s sounding their best.

Certain instruments with a defined attack, and those with a lot of low-end content in particular, such as bass guitar and kick drum, do often benefit from phase alignment. For a concise explanation of how to do this, refer to "Phase-aligning bass tracks" in Chapter Five: Recording Bass. Any time you track both a miked bass cab and a DI track, you should check the phase of the bass tracks according to these instructions, and in most cases they will need a little adjustment. Kick drums recorded with more than one mic might need similar lining up, and will sound punchier and more solid with a little such attention. If dragging a distant mic's region forward to match the time position of the kick's close mic

Using the "strip silence" function in Pro Tools: above, the waveform of a kick-drum track with the parameters defined, and below, the individual regions that remain after the noise between them has been stripped.

doesn't improve matters, you can also try this technique: put the track back the way it was, then cross-fade each individual hit in the distant-mic track so that you eliminate the front edge of the attack, but fade in in time to hear all the decay of the ring of the kick drum. (To do this you need to have split these tracks into individual regions using the "strip silence" function in your DAW, which removes background noise below a threshold determined by you and replaces it with silence, breaking the track into segments as it does so.) That way you combine the tight, punchy attack of the close mic and the broad, resonant ring of the distant mic, for a full kick sound overall.

You can try messing with phase alignment of multi-miked guitars and other instruments too (although this should never be necessary with pure stereo mic techniques, such as any of our coincident, AB pair, or M-S techniques, and so on). But sometimes dragging these tracks around will just create deeper issues that can be more and more confusing to correct. Several phase-alignment plug-ins do exist, though, that can sometimes neatly zero in on phasing troubles between tracks and tighten them up in an easily dial-in-able, and totally undoable, manner. Check products such as the Voxengo PHA-979 or Little Labs IPB plug-ins (the latter also available as a DI-style analog hardware box, the product on which the plug-in was based).

Sometimes confused with phase-alignment, "time-alignment" is the process of tightening up tracks in the rhythmic sense prior to mixing. Once you have chopped up drum beats and bass-guitar notes using strip silence, for example, you can drag them into perfect alignment so your rhythm section sounds totally in the pocket with a tight, precise groove. To do this, you first need to carefully determine which part is actually on the groove, or where the groove is if none are, so you aren't realigning things further off the actual beat. Alternatively, some DAWs have a nifty and complex function that will automatically detect the rhythm of a track in BPMs (Pro Tools' "Beat Detective," for example) and use this to quantize and adjust the rhythm of the session as a whole. There are, of course, several steps to this process, some of which can be fairly complicated the first time you approach it, but your DAW's user's manual should lay it all out for you.

It's also extremely important to clean up any unwanted sounds or noise that remains in the quiet passages of many of the tracks in your session. These might range from the vocalist mumbling or talking between lines, to amp hum that's present in passages when the electric guitar isn't playing, to undesirable sonic clutter that you would have tried to reduce while tracking in the good old days of analogue, but which someone like me told you you could wait to do in the DAW before mixing ... which means now. That clutter might include any spill from one drum into the mic of another that would have been squelched by a gate "the old-fashioned way," such as snare rattle between beats of the kick drum. Occasional occurrences such as the coughing singer can be removed by simply selecting and deleting the section manually in your editing window.

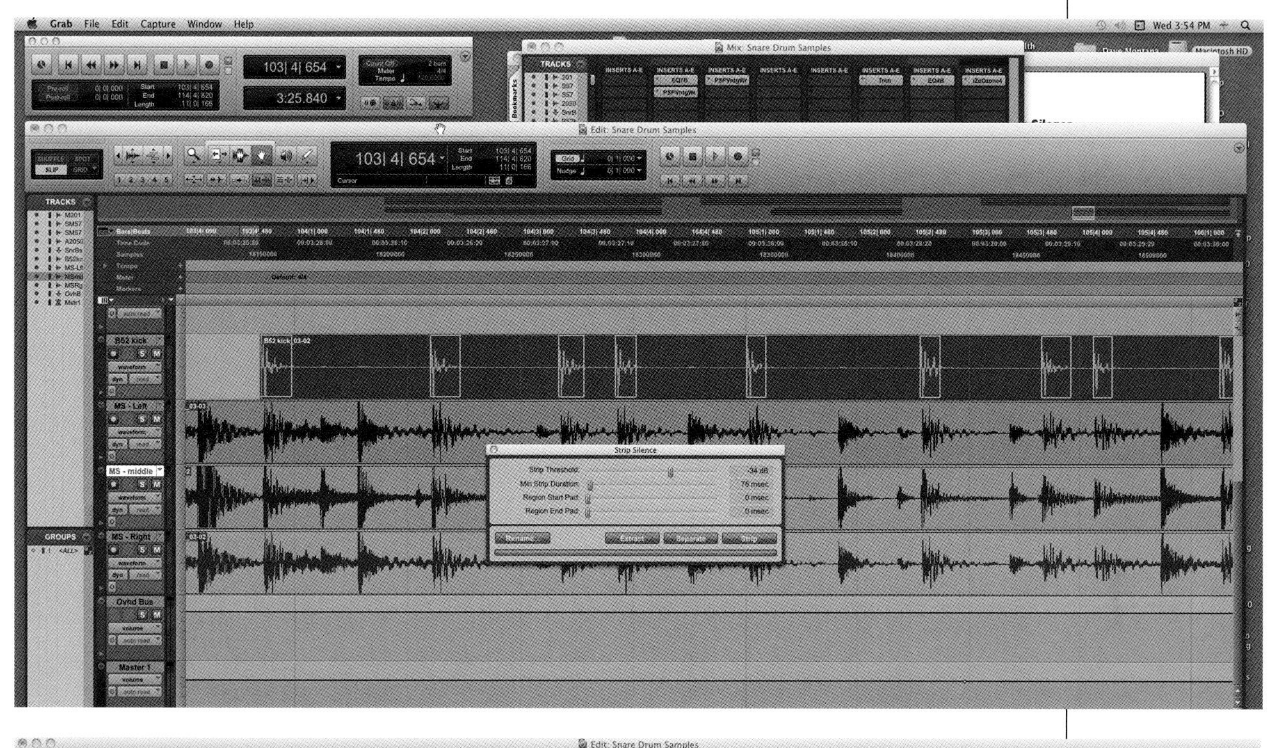

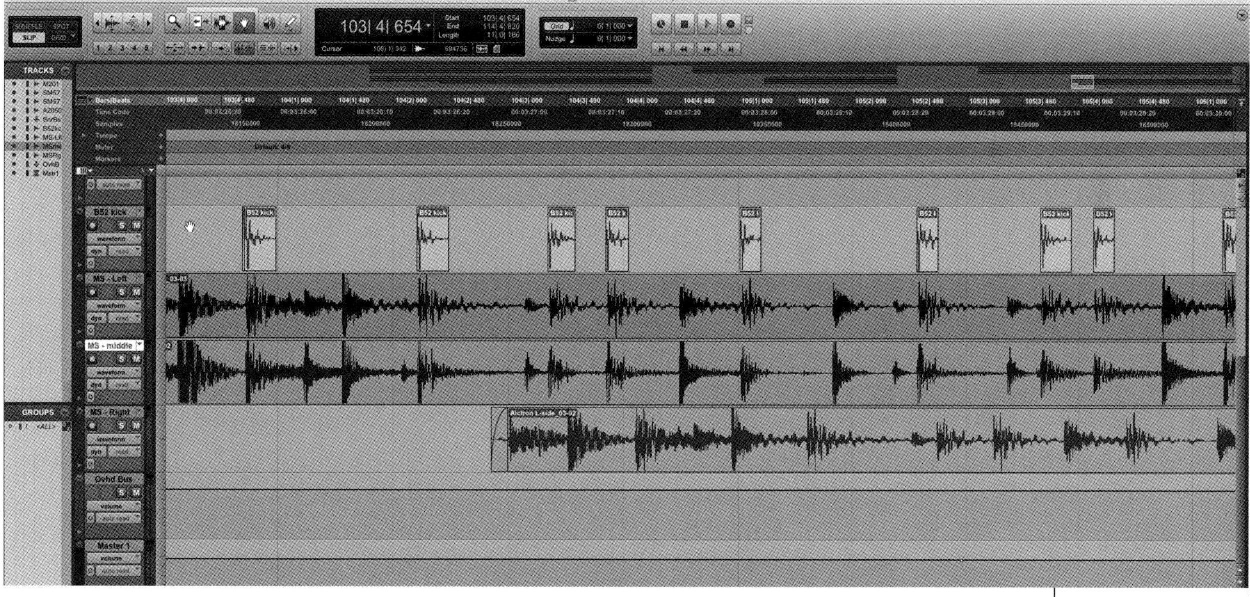

Regular or more plentiful noise can be more quickly and efficiently dealt with by using the strip silence function. It functions much like a gate processor would, stripping away background noise below a certain threshold and replacing it with silence. But the beauty of applying it in your DAW is that it will do its job non-destructively, so that you can "undo" it if you aren't happy with the results.

This tool might have slightly different parameters and settings in different DAWs, so whether you're working in Pro Tools, Logic, Digital Performer, Cubase or whatever, you will need to consult your manual for the precise details, but all should have similar functions and applications. It can work extremely well when applied to tracks where the musical information has a strong attack and a fairly short decay, such as a kick track, a snare, maybe a chunky power-chord guitar track, or bass track without too much tail on the notes. On tracks with a broader dynamic range, lots of quieter passages, and long note decays, you will need to check the results of the strip silence function to ensure that it hasn't chopped off anything essential to the performance. If it has, you can simply "undo" it, set the parameters to a lower threshold, and try again. Many examples of this tool also provide user-definable parameters to ensure you don't miss the attack and decay of a note, as found in the Region Start Pad and Region End Pad sliders in the Pro Tools strip silence window, which help you retain the initial thump and the following resonance of a kick-drum hit, for example. Alternatively, a gate plug-in used on the individual track (as you might already have guessed) will do much the same thing as the strip silence function, but I find strip silence to be more sensitive in many cases, and to offer more editing control over the results.

Once you have removed all of the sonic clutter, you should apply "cross-fades" to any starts and ends of regions that might induce unwanted pops and clicks. A cross-fade is a fading up or down of the volume level in an audio region, and can be applied in the editing window to any and all regions that require it, without the need for touching the track fader itself. Cross-fades can be extremely short, or long and gradual, as desired, and they enable individual regions of sonic information in a track to register smoothly during playing back or when bouncing to disk. Without them, an abrupt start to a region—even one that appears to begin with a few milliseconds of "silence"—might induce an audible "click" in your final mix. Cross-fades are also essential for smoothly joining together any drop-ins or paste-ins where new sonic information was added to the original take in a track. These can be made to work seamlessly, so that, for example, the cross-fades between the start and end of a drop-in segment happen so quickly that they aren't heard as a gap in the track, but bring the one part down and the other up just enough to avoid any odd click or pop as one audio region rolls into the other. Zoom in on the region in your editing window until the waveform is enormous, and draw a tight cross-fade between the segments that brings the level down and then back up again during the natural gap between notes, however swiftly that gap might pass in real time, and you have achieved a smooth and silent join between them.

The pre-mix stage is also the time to apply effects and processor plug-ins on individual tracks, as necessary, and to establish their basic settings. You won't really know how these will make your tracks sound—that is, whether they will work as desired, or will even be necessary—until you start the critical process of listening back to the mix as a whole. But you can take some educated guesses at this point and prep, for example, the drum tracks with some compression, some EQ on kick and snare, a little comp and gentle reverb on guitars, a delay on lead vocals, and whatever else you feel will work for the track.

Going beyond this, it's a good idea to set up any bus channels that you are likely to use, grouping together tracks representing either multiple mics or DI inputs of the same instrument or different but similar instruments that you will want to treat with the same effect or processor plug-in. For example, many recordists will group all drum tracks together to a stereo bus, in which they insert compressor and reverb plug-ins to give the stereo drum mix a little overall treatment as a group. Similarly, you might want to group all electric guitars, a selection of acoustic instruments, multiple mics used to capture a single acoustic guitar, or what have you. In addition to giving a desired uniformity of treatment to like-sounding tracks, this can be a great way of saving processor speed if weighty plug-ins are slowing down your computer, since you can use one instance of the plug-in on a bus track rather than, for example, five instances on individual guitar tracks.

To set up a bus channel, use your DAW's "new track" function and designate the new track as a mono or stereo bus (sometimes selected as an "auxiliary" track), then select the input for the new channel (for example, "bus 1-2"), and designate its output as whatever you are using for your master fader. Change the outputs of all tracks that you want to go through this bus to "bus 1-2," and they will now be routed through anything you put on that channel before going to the master fader. Label your bus tracks accordingly ('drum

A bus routed to an auxiliary channel in the Pro Tools mixer.

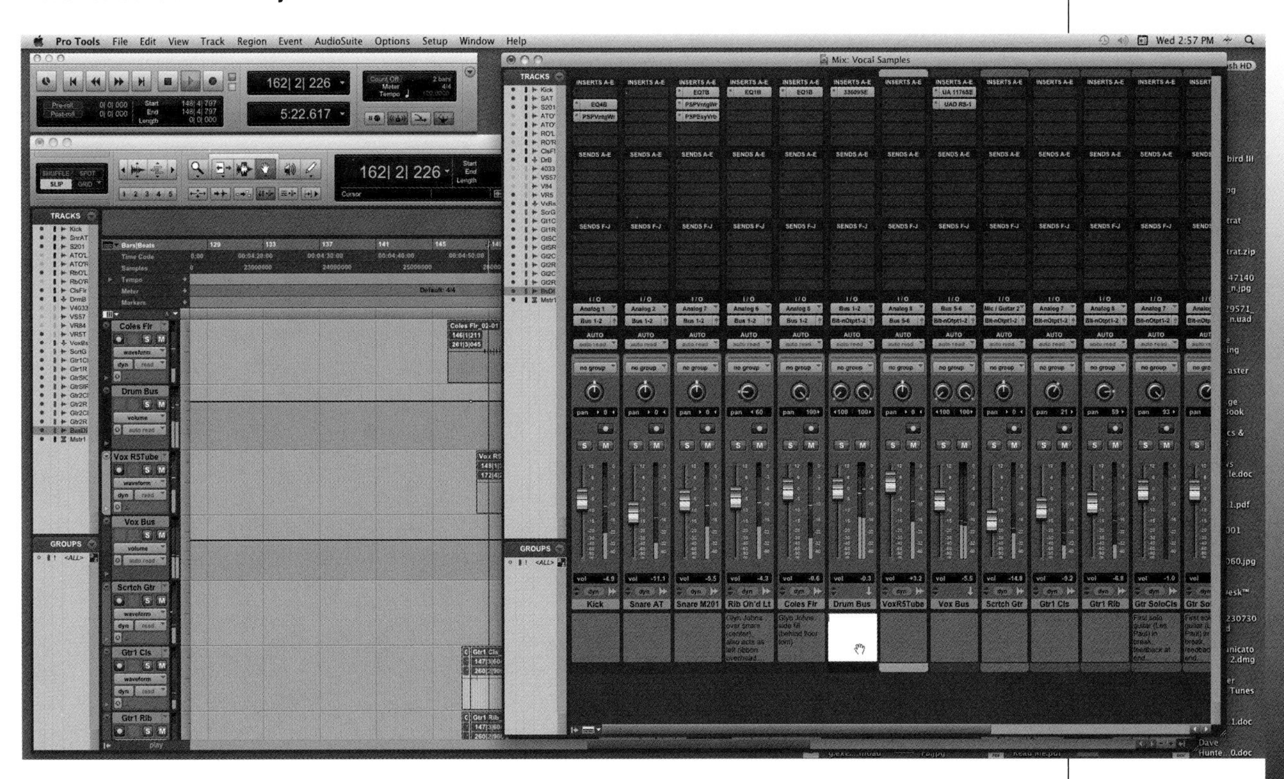

bus" or "guitar bus"), and be sure to establish them as stereo tracks for any group that will be panned in stereo. The faders and pan controls on the individual tracks that constitute any group will still establish the signal level and left-right relationships of these tracks relative to each other, and any plug-ins inserted in them will be processed *before* anything applied to the bus track, but the fader on the bus track makes a great way of adjusting the volume level of the group as a whole, so you don't have to tweak each individual track once you have your desired balance established if, for example, you just want to "make the drums a little louder" overall. As such, these "sub mixes" make it a lot easier to adjust the final mix, since you will be able to bring any large group of tracks up or down in relation to the rest of what is going on, and you can comp or EQ them and add any reverb, delay, or other effects as a stereo group too, if desired.

MIX ORDER

There is no universal right answer to the question "which instrument do you mix first?" Your answer will depend on your tracks, what you are hoping to achieve, and the way you like to work. Even so, it's worth discussing a few of the likely scenarios here and examining how approaching things in a different order might affect your perspective on the song as a whole. The reality is, you will need to select a place to begin one way or the other, but to get everything just right you will most likely need to follow your chosen mix order a certain distance down the road, then go back and tweak several elements once tracks approached later in the process come more clearly into focus. For example, I have heard several authorities on getting great bass sounds say that you should mix the bass last, but in order to get to that "last" position, it might be most productive to start with drums, then bring the bass in to complete the foundation of the song, then layer on everything else. This isn't to say that mixing bass last doesn't work, but essentially you might actually need to do the job twice: mix bass early to get your foundation working, then mix it again at the end to get it sounding its best with everything else in the track. Of course, you could apply this logic to every instrument in your arrangement—and the vocal, guitars, keyboards or whatever will only sound their best once you know how everything else sounds, right?—but once again, you have to start and end somewhere, and those points can't be *everywhere*.

If you want to be told where to begin, most mix engineers are likely to advise you to start with the drums, although there is something to be said for beginning with whatever is the central performance of the song, its main focus, which nine times out of ten will be the lead vocal. Before considering either of these approaches, though, let's look at the very real necessity of *starting with everything*. Which is to say, you really won't know how anything will sound until you put a little of everything up in the mix. Begin with a rough, dry mix with everything in your "best guess" position regarding level and pan, and just listen to the arrangement as a whole for a few passes. It's important to get this into your head early in the mixing process, I believe, and to absorb the concept that you really can't make viable decisions on the sound of any instrument as it is heard in "solo" mode. You can solo tracks to conduct close listening checks on how any processing or EQ settings change their sound in the comparative A/B sense, but to decide whether any change works you need to hear the track or tracks in the context of the song as a whole. Many engineers are crazy for working in "solo" mode, and tweak tracks endlessly with nothing else going on in the mix; but often you can get away without soloing certain tracks at all, since their sound within the broader mix is all that matters. Inevitably you will solo things anyway, if only because it's kind of cool to hear how subtly or dramatically your changes in parameter settings alter the sounds on the track. But try to keep this "don't make decisions in solo" principle in your head, and your mixes will be better for it, whatever order you approach them in.

A lot can be said for starting with the drums for your final mix, whatever form they are in—live kit, stereo loop, MIDI tracks. Whatever genre you are working in, the drums (if there are any, at least) will form the backbone of the rhythm, and that will be one of the main elements that listeners latch on to, even if only subconsciously while their more conscious attention is following a vocal or instrumental melody line. Following this logical order, it makes sense to proceed to bass next, to complete the foundation of the song, then to add rhythm guitars and keyboards (or acoustic guitar, mandolin, banjo and so forth in a folk or bluegrass arrangement), horns or other ensemble or "pad" instruments, extra percussion (tambourine or shakers or other hand percussion), lead guitar or other major solo instruments, lead vocals, and backing vocals. Done in this order, each following instrument makes the most sense in the context of what you have already laid down behind it, but anything can be re-tweaked to perfect that "bed" as your perspective changes with the addition of each track. Different types of music might require different approaches, of course. For example, a dance track might work best if you get the kick drum thumping just right on its own, then get the bass working with it before bringing in other percussion tracks, then add any featured synth loops or samples, and so on.

There's a certain logic to beginning with your featured performance—let's say lead vocals, since that's most often the case. This is the part that will draw the average listener to the song, and is really the make-or-break track within the whole (if you are working with instrumental music, substitute whatever is your main melodic focus). Of course, provided you have already recorded a lead vocal that can be made to work one way or the other, you have no way of knowing *how* to make it work until you hear it within the context of the mix as a whole. Reverb, echo, and EQ settings, for example, are fairly pointless until you hear how the delays react with the rhythm of the track, and how the EQ affects your perception of guitar or keyboards, and so on. You can focus your main attention on mixing the vocals, certainly, but that doesn't necessarily mean you have to start with them. As discussed above in this section, you really need to be listening to a little of everything in order to make any decisions about the viability of individual tracks.

With this in mind, the order in which we are going to tackle the final mix elements of individual instruments isn't set in stone, but follows the most likely approach for a rock song, in the broad sense.

SIGNAL FLOW: BUS AND AUXILIARY ROUTING

The signal flow from one type of channel to another in the DAW is designed to mirror the routing of an analog mixing desk, but if you don't already have some experience working with that piece of hardware the internal connections can be baffling. The different types of tracks used by most DAWs were covered in Chapter Three: Studio Approach. Let's look in a little more detail at the ways that your signal can be routed from one to another of these, to take it, for example, from the recorded audio on an audio track, to effects processing on an auxiliary track (perhaps alongside a group of like-processed audio tracks), to final overall level control on a master fader.

There are three main ways that the signal can leave an audio track: via its output to the main stereo outputs that are governed by the master fader, via its output to a bus that takes it to an aux track, or via its send to a bus that also takes it to an aux track. The first two options are selected from the output menu of the audio track, and the latter is designated from a send port located above the track's fader. Audio routed via a send taps off a parallel path of that signal, sending a new branch to an aux track, while the original signal also still follows through the output of the audio track itself (either to the main stereo outs, or another aux). A "sub mix" of a group of like instruments in a mixer is called a "bus," and that's also the term used in the DAW to designate the numbers used to internally link tracks together. To select which aux track you want to route a send's parallel signal path to, you chose the same bus channel number (or numbers, for stereo) that are designated as the input of the aux that you want to process it in. To route signal to an aux from the track's output, you similarly select the bus designated as the desired aux track's input.

Any individual aux track is used either as an auxiliary track to hold effects and processors to which audio is routed via a send, or as a bus group to which several tracks

Mixing drums

There's a lot to be said for starting with the drums, whether you are working with a group of tracks representing a recorded live drum kit, or with either a simple stereo loop or a handful of tracks of sampled or MIDI-triggered drums. If the raw tracks represent anything more than a stereo pair you will ideally already have grouped these tracks into their own stereo bus with some individual track plug-ins selected, if not yet set up, and perhaps a stereo plug-in or two on the bus as well, as discussed in Pre-Mix: Preparing Your Tracks. If you haven't already done so, this is a good place to start. Samples or loops of pre-recorded tracks shouldn't need any treatment as regards between-the-beat noise on individual tracks, and any looped drums in stereo tracks will already have gone a long way toward preparing final elements of the mix for you, since these are usually professionally recorded and mixed before you acquire them.

are routed together via their outputs. The main difference is that only a portion of the signal goes via the send, as determined by the setting of the "send level" control on the individual audio channel, whereas the entire signal goes via the track's output. Regardless of how it receives such signals, the aux track will blend it all back into the main mix via its own output, which is usually set to the stereo pair that represents the main outputs of the mix as a whole, after processing it through whatever effects plug-ins are loaded into its inserts. If this signal has come from the sends of individual audio tracks, it will be mixed in alongside the unprocessed signal that also comes from those tracks' outputs, in proportion to the setting of the aux track's fader (which, as such, essentially acts as an 'effects depth' control). If it comes from the outputs of a group of audio tracks, the signal from the aux will represent the entirety of those tracks in the mix, and therefore the overall level of these signals will be determined by the aux track's fader.

The audio tracks in most DAWs have several sends available to them, and these can be used to route the signal to more than one aux track for processing by different effects plug-ins, when you want that signal treated separately by two different effects, rather than by the sound of one effect going into the other, for example. Or, two or three different effects or processors can be loaded into an aux track, if audio tracks need treatment by a chain of different effects (delay into reverb, for example). In the good old days, an analog studio might only have had one "best" reverb or delay unit, so everything that needed a little of that sound was tapped off via a send to a channel into which that effect was inserted. These days we can, in theory, insert our best reverb plug-in directly on as many different audio tracks as we like, but doing so uses a lot of processing power, and might crash your mix now and then, or at least slow things down. Retaining the old method of routing to major shared effects on auxiliary tracks is a great means of preserving processing power and keeping things running smoothly.

The first job in preparing any live drums, though, and one that, once again, you should have tackled in your pre-mix prep, will be to apply a gate or strip silence function to individual drum tracks that have any hint of extraneous noise or spill from other drums. Even if the spill or noise heard on certain individual tracks isn't a problem when everything is playing in the mix (big noises help to make small noises disappear in this way), any lingering signal other than that representing the focus of the track itself might become a bigger problem when you add further processing such as compression, EQ, reverb, or delay, and will likely start to conflict with your treatment of other tracks in the drum mix. It's a good idea, therefore, to apply a gate or strip silence to any close-miked kick and snare tracks, for example, as well as any individual tom tracks. A hi-hat track, if you have one, might also have a fair amount of spill from the snare in particular, but if it's a steady part (straight eighth notes is pretty typical) you might not hear much of the extraneous noise going on in between, and it might be hard to effectively chop out that many regions anyway.

Overheads or room mics, on the other hand, should usually be left without a gate or strip silence function, since they are intended to pick up the entire drum kit, and to provide some depth and ambience in the process, and stripping away their quieter passages is only likely to mess with this effort, unnaturally trimming the decay of cymbal crashes and drum ring, for example. If any of these more distant mics are picking up noise from other sources in passages when you want total silence from the drums, you can trim these manually in your DAW's editing window.

Starting points for comp and EQ suggestions for individual drums were already given in the Recording Drums chapter, and now is a good time to apply some of these. Just as it's impossible to gauge the effectiveness of the sound of any instrument track in isolation, it's also hard to know how your individual drums are working when you hear them by themselves, but you do have to start somewhere.

The kick is a logical place to start, and it's a good idea to begin by tweaking it to achieve what you feel will work for you once everything else is brought up in the mix. Once you have a good clean "thump" in the attack and some resonance in the tail, bring the snare up and craft your ideal perception of crack and body in that track. These two drums will form the backbone of your song's rhythm, with major assistance from the hi-hat for many musical styles, so bring that one up if you have an individual track for it, and get these three sitting so they give a pretty good impression on their own of what your drums are doing for the track. At the risk of over-emphasizing this point (a risk I'm willing to take), try to remain aware of the fact that your kick and snare simply aren't likely to sound very good out of context of the rest of the mix. Time and time again I have been frustrated by my seeming inability to get enough of a deep "thump" from the kick or a sharp, driving "crack" from the snare while crafting their comp and EQ settings in "solo" mode, only to find that they sounded pretty damn good as part of the whole when I brought up the rest of the mix. It's important to note here, too, that you really won't fine-tune the sound of the kick until you start working more closely with the bass guitar (which we will approach in the next section, below), so you will be coming back to this one again later to get it just right.

At this stage, it's worth introducing another variable of drum mixing, and another inevitable choice that will have to be made out of two possible priorities at this point. Do you base your drum sound around the kick and snare tracks (along with toms and hi-hat if you have them on individual tracks), and bring up the overheads as necessary, or let the overheads be the foundation and bring in the kick and snare (etc) mainly to give body and presence to the overhead tracks? Either is valid, and the choice really depends on what you are trying to achieve. A more classic or "retro" rock or roots sound might work with the overheads taking precedence, and the kick and snare coming in to add as much punch as necessary. A more contemporary sound is often achieved by getting the individual drum tracks in sharp focus, then adding the overheads to create as much ambience and cymbal presence as necessary. If you are new to drum mixing, it's probably a good idea to try it both ways to see what works for your track. I often find the difference is really pretty subtle and my songs would actually work either way, but each approach definitely lends a slightly different sound and feel to any song.

Other choices to be made at this point involve both your stereo width and stereo perspective. If you have recorded your live drums in any of the mono techniques discussed, these decisions will be moot, and your overall mixing effort will probably be easier, too. Even with some "mono" set-ups, however, you can make some stereo decisions to enhance the overall sound. A simple three-track set-up representing kick, snare, and a single overhead can still be grouped to a stereo bus for a little room reverb that aids the impression of stereo width from three drums panned right up the middle. Or, you might find that you have recorded both a mono overhead and a single front-of-kit mic, and that panning these slightly left-right actually works well in the mix, even though it's nowhere close to a genuine stereo recording technique.

Otherwise, for any true stereo drum mixes—even those that constitute just four drum tracks with kick, snare, and a pair of overheads—you will need to decide both how wide to pan the stereo ingredients, and from what perspective the listener is hearing the drums, that of the drummer, or that of the audience.

A full-width stereo drum mix can sound impressively big and roomy, will certainly work for some musical styles, and can be a seductive temptation for newcomers to home recording, with a major, "Wow, listen to *that*!" factor. For others, it can sound too big, literally: do you want a drum kit that sounds as wide as your living room in an indie or roots song? Probably not. Pulling your stereo drum spread a little tighter up the middle, anywhere from 9-and-3 o'clock to 10-and-2, will not only add focus and punch to the drum sound, it will open up space at both sides of the stereo field for other instruments to shine. Often, when used in the right context, the result of a tighter stereo drum image such as this isn't a "smaller" drum sound, but a bigger one, since it will benefit from the weight and body of that more centered sound. On the other hand, wide stereo works for certain styles too, and especially when individual toms were recorded in a big rock or fusion track. That big drum roll that goes from left to right (or vice versa) is an undeniably cool feature, sure, so if that sound works to enhance the ends of your song as a whole, go for it.

To revisit the snare here for a minute, most advice simply says "pan it up the middle," and that will hold true for nine out of ten instances, or maybe ninety nine out of a hundred, but we are bound by the so-called "rules" here, are we? A thick snare up the middle makes sense for traditional rock in any of its forms, certainly, but several other styles—from indie to country to roots rock, or anything that isn't relying on overly heavy processed drums—can sometimes sound pretty nifty with the snare tweaked to just slightly off-center, say just eight or ten per cent to the drummer's left. The result shouldn't sound too noticeably "off center," but will reposition the snare just enough that it registers in a slightly different place when you listen to the mix as a whole, without taking it too far out of the solid center of the track. If you think this might give your drum mix a little more dimension, and possibly more realism, give it a shot. If it depletes your snare sound, put it back.

Drum tracks in Pro Tools's mixer, with the overheads split into three M-S stereo tracks: M-S left, M-S middle, and M-S right (note the Trim plug-in in the M-S right insert, used to reverse the phase of this track).

Perspective-wise, you need to decide right from the start whether the end listener will hear your drums' stereo elements from the drummer's perspective (that is, rolling from left to right with a right-handed drummer), or from the perspective of the audience in front of a live stage (drums rolling from right to left). Either is legit, it's just a matter of preference. The important thing here is consistency. If you have a simple four-track drum part with kick, snare, and two overheads, the job is an easy one once you've decided which perspective to follow: decide how wide you want your stereo spread, and put the overheads there. Although the snare is on the drummer's left from the perspective of any stereo mics, such as the overheads, the snare track itself is panned right up the middle with the kick. If you have tracked the toms and hi-hat with individual mics, you will need to ensure that you have your stereo overheads the right way around with respect to the high-to-low tom spread, and the hi-hat should go far left (when mixing to the drummer's listening perspective).

Simple yet "high-concept" overhead set-ups such as the M-S stereo pair and the Glyn Johns technique are obviously a little more fixed in the mix process, yet there is still a little bit of room to maneuver. Any M-S stereo recording relies on a full left-right stereo spread of the two tracks taken from the side mic's signal (one the original, one a copy of it that has had its phase reversed). If you pan these two tracks toward the center, they will begin to null each other out in direct proportion to the amount they are moved toward center, theoretically vanishing entirely when both are panned to mono, leaving the mid mic on its own. To make this technique work as intended you need to keep them panned to their full widths, but that doesn't mean you need as much of this stereo spread in the final mix as you have of the mono mid mic. You can use just a little of the side tracks for ambience if you like (or, what the hell, experiment with toeing them in toward center a little to achieve the same effect of reduced stereo drum level in the mix).

The Glyn Johns set-up (described in detail in Chapter Four: Recording Drums) is a simple technique that yields the solidity of a mono overhead with some of the width and perspective of stereo drums. But it relies on bringing the technique into the mixing process and not just the tracking room. The original intention is that you start by putting the mic above the snare to the right at about 3 o'clock, then pan the "fill" mic (to the side of the floor tom) hard left; reverse these if you want to hear things from the perspective of the drummer's ears. Following the "whatever works, works" rule, however, you can also try panning both mics equally left-right, anywhere from 10 and 2 o'clock to 9 and 3 o'clock, or play with them at a full-width left-right spread if you're curious to hear how that works. The original Glyn Johns-certified pan is likely to produce the most viable results more often than not, since that is how this mic set-up was designed to work, but if something else does a better job for you, well, Johns isn't likely to come busting into your studio demanding justice.

Even if you aren't working with a lot of reverb in your mix in general, or plan to add a little to the entire mix on your master channel, drums can often benefit from a little room reverb on the kit as a whole to help give them space and presence. Of course, you might have a distant room mic or two to bring up in the mix to do exactly this in a natural way. If you have recorded in a good-sounding room with plenty of natural ambience, and these room mics enhance your drum sound rather than making it fluffy and washy, so much the better. Otherwise, consider putting a stereo reverb plug-in on your drum bus—start with something gentle like a half-second delay or a medium room, medium damping, and maybe anywhere from four to eight per cent "wet"—and see if that helps the kit sound more like it's happening in a real live space (see my more general comments on mixing with reverb later in this chapter).

Once you have found a reverb setting that enhances the drum kit as a whole, you might find you want to return to the snare track and insert a separate reverb on that, a move that can often help this crucial drum pop in the mix, even if it's getting a little something later in the chain along with the rest of the kit. The best way to find the right snare reverb is to flick through the options on your best reverb plug-in (select a mono version, obviously) and to try them with everything rolling in the track. Many reverbs will have snare-dedicated presets, and those are worth a try, but don't hesitate to scroll through the options and try a little of anything and everything. Listen to high-production recordings of the 80s and early 90s in particular, and you'll hear major reverb action on the snare tracks in many cases (sometimes you get the impression many of these engineers put more thought into snare processing than they did into recording vocals, and certainly guitars). Although many of these snares are way over the top and sound pretty dated today, your mix as a whole can sometimes survive a surprisingly extreme reverb setting on the snare, even if the rest of the mix is drier than average. The right snare reverb can sometimes come off sounding like ring and resonance from a super-mega snare itself, rather than as processing. Or, it can sometimes sound awful. Try it and see.

With some light (or occasionally heavy) compression already happening on your individual drum tracks, another dose of gentle stereo comp on the drum bus can sometimes work wonders to help glue the kit together. This might sound like extreme measures—potentially three levels of compression, if you also end up adding some on the master channel during final mixdown, or in the mastering process, as is usually the case. But if you tread carefully, and play it cautiously with gentle settings to start with, a little bus compression on the drum pre-mix can sometimes be the difference between a kit that gels and one that sounds disparate and unbalanced.

Once it's all happening pan and level-wise, you might find you don't need any further tweaking from EQ. But if necessary you can cure a boomy kick drum by reducing it slightly in the 200Hz to 250Hz range, or add some presence to the beater attack by boosting something in the 2kHz and 4kHz range if it isn't cutting through quite enough. A boost somewhere within the same range might help to give the snare more presence if it seems to be a little dull (note that the kick and snare aren't likely to require boosting in precisely the same part of that range, but you will need to sweep a fairly broad band of boost across each to see what works for that particular drum sound). Or, if the snare is somewhat "honking" and nasal sounding, you can usually fix that with a little reduction somewhere between 800Hz and 1.2kHz. Cymbals that sound harsh and piercing in your overheads can often be tamed with a slight reduction around 1kHz, and if more sparkle is required—often the case if you used ribbon mics on them—try a gentle shelf to bring them up at around 5kHz and above.

Individual MIDI-triggered or programmed drum tracks can be treated as individual live-recorded drum tracks for mix purposes, but probably won't need comp and EQ treatment to the same extent, since the samples or synthesized sounds from which they have been built will likely have been shaped with comp and EQ already. You might want to use some processing regardless, though, to make such sounds "yours" in the creative sense. Or, you might find some EQ helps them sit better in the overall mix, or that squashing them with comp will give them a little more character. Automated drum parts do take out a lot of the work, but don't assume that you should leave them untouched in every instance; sometimes monkeying around with some comp, EQ ,and reverb on samples that don't really "need it" can make all the difference between a part that sounds mechanized and one that really gels with the rest of the performance.

For loops, as with individual sample tracks, you might still want a touch (or a slathering) of EQ and comp, but you will apply stereo bus-style processors that act on the kit as a whole. As such, it might be easiest to use a few of your plug-ins' presets as starting points—settings with names like "big rock drums" or "more punch and presence"—and tweak them to work toward your desired sound. Most of the better drum samples available in loop packages will have been professionally recorded and treated, and therefore will often have some studio processing applied. But again, a little judicious extra something of your own might be just the ticket.

If you're using alternative percussion in place of a standard drum "kit," such as congas and timbales in a Latin arrangement, these are an equally good place to start since they will form the rhythmic backbone of the song. Percussion used in addition to a traditional kit, however, is more of an enhancement that is often best dealt with a little later in the process, once you have more of everything else working in the mix. Those classic little "excitement inducers"—tambourine and shaker—often sound great when mixed pretty far off to one side, which also helps to increase the perception of dimension in the mix as a whole. If your aim is to add some high-end jangle to the chunky momentum of the kick, bass, and snare, though, there's nothing wrong with putting them straight up the middle. Pay extra attention to the volume level of either of these in your overall mix, too: just a little touch of shaker or tambourine can cut through effectively and be surprisingly noticeable, while too much of either is likely to pull the listener's attention away from the rest of what's going on, rather than just enhancing the rhythmic momentum of that passage, which is usually the intention.

Mixing bass

At this stage in the game, we have already paved the road for a great-sounding bass part by recording the instrument well, eliminating any phase issues between mic and DI tracks, and applying some suitable comp and EQ (as advised in the Recording Bass chapter) to help this instrument sit well in the mix. Getting bass levels just right, however, can be notoriously difficult—as can achieving the optimum low-end content in general—and usually takes a lot of careful listening and tweaking.

Pan-wise, bass definitely wants to go straight up the middle, so that's an easy call. Ideally, you want the bass and kick drum to lock in well together, a scenario that requires as much from the original performances as from the mix itself. But you also want each to be heard against the contrast of the other, rather than being a single thump of low-end mush, and that's where your bass mixing technique comes in. It is often said that you should consider the two as a single instrument, with the kick as the attack element, and the bass guitar as the body of the note (that is, the "tail" or "decay"), and there is some sense to that. But contemporary bass tracks often have more drive and sustain than that implies, and might ultimately go beyond merely being the tail of the low-end thump that the kick provides. The main point in mixing bass guitar and kick drum is that you want them to work as an interlocking unit of sorts, but without stepping on each other's toes—which is to say, together they should dominate the low end of the mix (anything below 250Hz). But within that low zone each should have its own bands in which to poke through, while also allowing the bass more prominence as a feature instrument in its own right.

Both instruments have a great deal of low-end content, but how you use your EQ in that sub-250Hz range will determine, to a great extent, the feel of your song. For a more open pop, indie, country, or roots-based mix, a thumping kick that dominates the lowest end of the spectrum and a clear yet non-obtrusive bass that punches through a little higher up might work best. Put a high-pass filter at 50Hz on both instruments to remove ultra-low-end clutter, and give the kick a slight boost around 80Hz to bring out its "whoomph" factor. Keep the bass down a little from 150Hz and below by applying a broad-band reduction there of just a few dB, and boost it slightly around 200Hz or possibly up to 250Hz, depending on the part. Although dipping the bass down from 150Hz and below will reduce the fundamental of some notes, it will add clarity to the bass/kick combination, and the bass will still make a clean, strong impression because its overtones will cut through higher up in the frequency range. (Ampeg discovered a version of this trick when designing the 8x10 speaker cab for the legendary SVT amplifier: the 10-inch speakers aren't physically capable of fully reproducing the fundamentals of the lower notes on the bass guitar, but they excel at the early overtones, which help to give the impression that you are "hearing the big picture" just fine.)

To create a good, heavy bass sound in anything from a rock to a dance mix we reverse the above scenario somewhat and let the bass guitar form the body of the lowest frequencies, while the kick drum offers the punch at frequencies slightly above that. We can start this process by cutting everything happening in the kick below 50Hz with a high-pass filter. A little cut of 2–3dB to the bass in a narrow band around 100Hz will help the front of the kick's "boom" punch through in the attack, and you can boost the kick just slightly in the same place if even more punch is required. A light boost to the bass of 2–3dB at around 250Hz will help to make its lower-midrange grind more apparent, while still keeping it under the main body of the guitars. If the kick sounds a little boxy at this point, you might dip it down by a few dB somewhere in the 250Hz to 400Hz range, depending upon where within its resonance that "honk" is coming from (sweep a band across that range to find the culprit).

When fine-tuning either of these approaches, you will obviously need to work back and forth between the kick and bass drum in tandem, constantly checking how they interact. I have urged throughout this chapter so far that you shouldn't make any crucial decisions in "solo" mode, but you will probably want to solo bass and kick together for a while to hear how they work in unison. The idea is to focus in on how little EQ boosts and cuts in one affects your perception of the other—as a learning exercise, at least—then make your final adjustments with everything else back in the mix. Ultimately, what matters is how it all sounds when everything else is running on top of it. To that end, you can also help out the bass guitar a lot (and the kick too) by putting a high-pass filter at 80Hz on anything else in the mix that might be producing low-end clutter that muddies up your foundation. Even the rumble from a mic stand, passing traffic, a nearby AC unit, or the quirks of proximity effect can produce low-end junk on, for example, a vocal mic that normally wouldn't have anything useful going on down in that range.

Mixing bass samples, a MIDI bass part, or bass synth follows similar principles to all of the above, although much of the EQ work, and some of the compression, will most likely have been done for you by the original designer of the patch (the bass tone selected). Even so, you might need to consider further processing to make any simulated bass tracks sit just right in the mix and work with your selected kick sound, rather than just assuming you don't need to touch them.

Once you've got your bass track sounding right, getting it at the optimum level can also be a real challenge. The human ear's perception of low frequencies is even more skewed by psychoacoustics than is its perception of most of the rest of the frequency range, and a big part of the difficulty in achieving the right bass level is in perceiving an accurate level in the first place. The first steps toward making that easier were outlined in the discussion of optimizing your mixing environment and monitor placement in Chapter One: Home Studio Set-Up. If you haven't already done your best job of these crucial elements, revisit that now and create the most neutral listening environment you can possibly achieve. Low frequencies can be skewed by wall, corner, and ceiling reflections in all kinds of crazy ways, the results of which, as often as not, simply sound like the difference of a couple of notches up or down on the level slider of your bass track rather than any distortions of your acoustic space. The upshot of all this is that it can be extremely difficult to accurately gauge the sheer volume (or lack thereof) of your bass in the mix.

The best solution to this, for those of us who just can't afford professional acoustic analysis and room treatment, is to test your mix in a number of different listening environments. Take a burn or a bounce of what you feel is your best mix, low-end wise, to audition on your living-room sound system, in your car, on a boom box, in your bandmates' apartments, and wherever else you can. And when doing so, A/B it frequently with the mixes heard on professional releases in the same musical style. This comparative approach in a broad range of spaces should work toward compiling a more accurate low-end picture, and one that you can use to tweak your own mix to perfection.

Mixing guitars

Ready to explore the world of infinite variables? Time to start thinking about mixing guitars. We covered a lot of bases regarding general tones, comp, and EQ in the Recording Guitars chapter, but there are still a million and one ways to place guitar tracks in your mixes, and to really make them shine, too. Let's tackle electric guitars first, then address some options for acoustics.

The whole issue is complicated somewhat by the fact that the average song in what we might broadly refer to as "rock and pop" will often have two, three, or more guitars. As with the mix as a whole, we want them all to gel, but also we often want them to remain distinct as individual "parts." Also, these guitars can sound extremely different, and are likely to be mixed very differently if they are pristine clean or grungey ultra-fuzz, or any of an infinite number of gradations in between. Even so, it isn't difficult to outline some basic parameters for helping different types of guitars work their best in different settings and for optimizing whatever guitar tones you have tracked for your own project.

Fortunately, the ways in which we have handled other instruments should have helped us with the job of placing our guitars in the mix. We have carved all this room on the sides of the stereo picture for our guitars by keeping drums and bass fairly tight up the middle (in many of the above-mentioned mix scenarios, at least). We have also left a large chunk of the midrange free and clear, so we are already ahead of the game in providing clear sonic space in which these tracks can shine. Also, if you heeded the advice in the Recording Guitars chapter, you will have layered any electric guitar overdubs with slightly different tones each time—changing guitars, or at least pickup and amp settings whenever possible—so you should be able to build up the ideal ratio of girth and definition at this time, rather than merely piling mud on top of mud.

One of the first decisions to be made takes us partially back to the mix-prep section above: if you have used any multi-mic techniques, you now need to decide whether you blend these into a single mono track (which can receive overall processing by routing your multiple mics to a mono bus), or use them as "pseudo-stereo" (that is, dual-mono) tracks. Beyond this, you also need to decide whether you want to group multiple tracks

CREATING DYNAMICS AND EXCITEMENT IN YOUR MIX

The elements of excitement and surprise—created by the use of dynamics—are major factors in separating the attention-grabbing mix from one that's dull and lifeless. I'm not talking about using an "exciter" or "dynamics" processor plug-in, but dynamics created by the ups and downs, the light and shade, of the mix itself. Ideally you will have considered this naturally in your arrangement as you tracked the performances of each instrument, creating little "listen to that!" moments out of the introduction of a new part, or the slight change in the approach to a hook or a backing behind a chorus. But you can still create it to some extent in the mix if you didn't, and can certainly enhance it if you did.

Do you have three different rhythm guitars pounding away, and a lead guitar track on which the guitarist pretty much went full-bore throughout the three and a half minutes of the song? Introduce the guitars one at a time as the verse builds, perhaps starting with the cleanest and "airiest" of them. Hold off on bringing the third rhythm guitar in until the chorus, and introduce the lead in the background in the following verse, bridge, or second chorus. Keyboard parts can be used to enhance the second half of a verse, rather than blaring away from the start, and you can drop everything for part of a verse after the penultimate chorus to let the drums, bass, and vocals carry the momentum for half a verse. These are just examples, but you get the picture. Do what you can to create distinct introductions for each part, and moments where the basic rhythmic elements shine, too, and the listeners' ears will naturally remain more aware of all of the individual ingredients and be more attentive than they would to a monotonous mix in which everything hammers away from start to finish.

of *different* guitar parts in a stereo bus to give them a similar overall reverb and/or delay treatment, or alternatively to give each an individual flavor. There is no right or wrong answer to this one: it really depends on what you are trying to achieve with the tracks, and what type of song it is. If you want the rhythm-guitar overdubs to work as a dense layer—the typical heavy wall-of-power-chords sound—routing them to a stereo group usually makes sense, and not only allows you to help them gel with a little overall comp (even if you're applying initial comp and EQ on individual tracks) and the same stereo reverb, but also enables a sub-master level control of the overall "rhythm guitars" volume via the stereo guitar bus fader.

If you aim to blend a range of airier jangle and arpeggio and atmospheric sounds with your multiple guitar parts, it might make more sense to treat them more independently, carving more individual comp and EQ and effects settings for each. If they are all to share a similar stereo reverb plug-in, however, but at slightly different depths of "wetness," you can still route them to this at your desired proportion for each by setting up an auxiliary send on each guitar track which goes to the same stereo auxiliary channel, on which you have inserted the reverb (or other effect) in question.

With a few of these fundamental choices in place, you are ready to begin the real work of placing your guitars in the mix. If you only have one main rhythm guitar, and one track of that part, you might need to retain solidity by keeping it panned fairly close to the middle. You still don't want it dead center in most cases, or it will get in the way of your other central elements like kick and snare drum and bass guitar (and the lead vocals, yet to come). Chances are, if you have only one electric rhythm guitar in your arrangement, and one mic track of it at that, you will have another element that is helping to carry the weight—a keyboard, or a horn part—and you can balance the two across the stereo field by placing them, for example, somewhere between 10 and 2 o'clock and 9 and 3 o'clock. Pan it much wider, with so few elements working in the midrange, and you can start to get an unnatural room-wide stereo spread that is just too spacious and diffuse. If your single rhythm guitar track is part of an arrangement that has a big stereo piano or keyboard or horns sound as its focal element, however, you can often get away with panning the guitar a little further toward the center, to enhance the lushness and width of the stereo image from the keys. Alternatively, if you have a lead guitar partnering a single rhythm guitar track, you can usually pan these about equally left-right. Even if the lead isn't playing throughout the song, leaving the rhythm potentially a little "unbalanced" on its own on one side, its introduction in the fills, hooks, and solos will give some much-needed movement and dynamics to your mix. The same goes for a rhythm guitar and a harmonica in a blues tune, where the "harp" is treated like an amplified instrument.

In another of our "mix a little now, finish the job later" moves, keep in mind that with any of these techniques you won't really get the guitar mix set in stone until you hear how it works with anything else in the broad midrange of the mix, frequency wise, and with the lead vocal in particular. The job for now is to get the guitar tracks into a position that sounds solid and gels with the rest of what we have brought up in the mix so far, then to tweak each of these supporting elements to perfection once you have crafted your way close to their optimum individual tones.

If you have multi-miked tracks of a single electric rhythm guitar performance, you can either blend these into a solid mono image as mentioned above (most likely by grouping them in a bus channel and jointly controlling their level and effects processing from there), or alternatively, if you want a fat, huge-sounding rhythm guitar spread without overdubbing further takes, you can split these two (or more) tracks somewhere in the stereo spectrum. Even if these weren't tracked with a standard stereo recording technique—that is, two similar mics, equally balanced to capture the left-right images of the sound source—you can split them apart in a "dual mono" configuration that often works to create surprising depth and girth in your mix. Perhaps you miked two speakers in a multi-speaker cab, or two amps with the same guitar part coming through them, or used a close mic and a room mic, or whatever. Try panning these each side of the left-right spectrum to whatever degree you feel will work with the rest of the instruments in your mix, adjust to taste, and check out the results. They don't by any means have to be panned to equal degrees left and right either; I have had great results from placing, for example, a close-mic track at around one to two o'clock and a semi-distant or room mic track anywhere from four o'clock to full-right. That way you can achieve a guitar with plenty of solidity, yet its own very natural stereo depth and airy room sound. This also gives you a big, multi-dimensional guitar sound from a single take, while leaving room on the other side for a different instrument, whether it's an acoustic guitar, a keyboard, or whatever. And remember, you certainly don't have to use equal levels from each mic—balance them as best suits the overall picture you are trying to paint.

If you have two multi-miked guitars, you can do something like the above, panning one mic from each nearer to center, and another further out for ambience. Another nifty trick, though, is to criss-cross these mics by putting the close mic from guitar A at ten o'clock and its distant mic at four o'clock, with the close mic from guitar B at two o'clock and its distant mic at eight o'clock. Often you will want to keep the distant-mic levels down quite a bit in relation to the close mics in this scenario. If the sounds work well together you can create a lot of width and natural ambience from just two electric guitars.

There are a lot of tricks that can help you create big, thick electric guitar tracks for heavy rock mixes. Instead of compressing all of your guitars together in a grouped bus, you can EQ them there as necessary and add a touch of room reverb if desired, but send them out from there to another stereo auxiliary channel (while retaining the output of the original bus to the master fader) where you can squash the hell out of them with compression without dulling the attack and dynamics of the original performances. Used in this way, "parallel compression" offers a great means of slamming out a wall of guitars without just layering up the mud.

Another thing worth trying is opening up a few other auxiliary channels on which you give each of the different rhythm guitar tracks some more extreme effects treatment, without treating the original. You can try plug-ins for electronic doubling, pitch shifting, chorus, a good old rotary speaker simulator, or whatever. Anything that helps you thicken up the aural space by creating a new sonic impression of the original track, without adding the clutter that can often come from simply layering more and more of the same thing. Get creative with your panning of the original and effected tracks, and you can really move a lot of air with what started out as just a take or two on rhythm guitar.

So far I have mostly advocated keeping multiple guitar tracks partially left-right, but some mixes can work great with two different guitars panned full-width in either direction, or nearly so. Done wrong, or in the wrong setting, this can sound too broad, with each guitar sitting unnaturally isolated out on either fringe. Done right, though, it can be a great way to give two fat, chunky guitars plenty of room to breathe without each muddying up the other toward the center of the spectrum. Often, a wide pan like this works best when you have heavy, busy drums and a fat, snarly bass track up the middle. When trying more extreme options such as this, be sure to check the mix's pan both in headphones and on the monitors, because you will get a different stereo impression from each. You want your mix to work well with both, given all the earbud listeners out there these days.

What you do with EQ will depend on how your guitar tracks sound in the raw, and what else is happening in the track that you need to make them fit in with. At the very least, you should dump everything below 80Hz with a high-pass filter, if you didn't do so when recording, to open up space for the bass. If you are looking for chunky, gut-thumping power-chord rhythm sounds, you might not want to lose any more low end than that from the rhythm guitars. On lead guitars, you can usually move that filter up to around 150Hz to clear up more room for the bass and kick, unless your lead dips down to lots of low-string twang, thrash riffing, or any bottom-dwelling seven-string stuff. If, one the other hand, none of your guitars has a whole lot going on down low, and giving them all a high-pass filter at 250Hz or so doesn't appear to weaken them in any way, that can be a great way of really opening things up for your bass and kick so they can make a solid impression. As a result, the guitars will often appear to breathe more freely in their own space, too. Otherwise, while guitars live in the midrange, you won't want them interfering with your lead vocal's share of that zone either. Putting guitars slightly to the side and the vocal up the center will help in that regard, but you will ultimately want to assess what part of that broad midrange zone works best for vocal and guitar. Make sure it isn't precisely the same band for both, and give each a little room to roam in the mix.

Mixing acoustic guitars (and acoustic string instruments)

Mixing acoustic guitars might seem to be a whole different ball game from mixing electrics, but a lot of the same rules often apply in terms of overall levels and finding appropriate space in the stereo field. Although the general tone of different acoustic guitar performances might not vary as much as that of electric guitars (which run the gamut from clean to filthy), acoustic guitars are used in very different ways. An acoustic track might be a rhythm track within a large mix, in the same way an electric rhythm guitar track is used; or it might be a solo or featured instrument that either carries a tune all on its own or provides a deep, rich accompaniment to a vocal performance. You will of course have recorded acoustic guitars with such diverse roles somewhat differently, and you will also account for them very differently in the way you mix them.

An acoustic rhythm-guitar part can often be achieved with a single track representing one mic. If that mic was placed right, it should give you the punchy, jangly "thrum" that we often seek in an acoustic rhythm-guitar part, and one that will easily be placed within the rhythmic elements of the mix without stepping on the toes of other melodic instruments. You might have used more than one mic to achieve a full sound with some ambience, and these can be blended together to achieve a tightly focused position in a busy stereo mix. Alternatively, give them a little more space to carry more weight in a less cluttered mix, depending on what you are trying to achieve, using some of the techniques discussed in relation to electric rhythm guitars, above.

An acoustic guitar track that's a featured part of a song, or the central element of a folk, singer-songwriter, or "acoustic" performance, can usually do with more space, depth, and ambience. If you recorded the thing right in the first place, you can now give more play to multiple mics by placing them judiciously across the left-right field for a full stereo sound. If you used any of our basic stereo recording techniques, these can obviously be placed full-width, or toed in somewhat to nine to three o'clock or even ten to two o'clock to lessen any perception of a "hole in the middle" that might arise from a wide spread. Stereo tracks can still be set "off balance" too, if you like, if your track has other instruments happening that will benefit from favoring their own side of the stereo field.

Any of the non-stereo but multi-miked techniques discussed in the Recording Guitars chapter can also be mixed across the stereo field as desired. Just because it ain't "stereo" in the technical sense doesn't mean it can't be moved around in your spectrum, with each of a pair of different mics used either equally left-right, or again, off balance in any mix that works with your arrangement as a whole. I've had great results from different mics positioned at the upper and lower sections of the guitar's lower bout, for example, panned halfway left and right in the mix, or favored center-right at something like 11 o'clock and four o'clock.

If you didn't apply a low-pass filter on the mic(s) or mic pre when recording, it's a good idea to use an EQ plug-in to do so now and cut everything below 80Hz at least; usually you can push this to 100Hz, sometimes even 150Hz, without disemboweling your guitar track. There might not seem to be much going on down there in your acoustic rhythm part anyway, but the instrument can put out some subtle low-end rumble that is worth eliminating before final mixdown. If you dump that, then find your guitar still sounds too boomy, you should try cutting the low-mids somewhere between 150Hz and 350Hz, with 200Hz being the usual culprit. Sweep a fairly narrow band in that region to find what works. Then, if the part needs more high-end shimmer, try applying a high-frequency shelf to its upper reaches to gently raise everything above 5kHz or so. You can tweak the upper-highs sense of zing and air by boosting a little further way up in the 12kHz to 16kHz region. gain, experiment with the precise point to find what works; and note that this might sound bright and lively on its own, but pushing it too hard will interfere with the shimmer of your cymbals in the full mix. If the track sounds tinny and shrill, a slight reduction somewhere in the 2kHz to 3kHz ballpark should do the trick.

The acoustic guitar shouldn't require a lot of compression when recorded well, at least if you simply want it to sound "good and normal." You can use comp to craft a thick, smooth rhythm track, or to enhance the jangle of a part with a lot of arpeggio work, starting with some of the settings suggested in Recording Guitars. In most cases, though, even if you feel you need some comp to help the acoustic sit in the mix, start with gentle settings and proceed cautiously.

Other "folkier" acoustic instruments like the mandolin, banjo, violin, and so forth can largely be treated as we have the acoustic guitar. They will need their own space in the mix, naturally, but where—and how prominent—that is will depend upon each instrument's role in the arrangement, and the style and context of the song as a whole. A bluegrass tune, for example, will usually have all the instruments on a par during any vocals, with each of the soloists stepping up separately but equally when their turn comes around. A folkie singer-songwriter arrangement, on the other hand, might treat an acoustic guitar as more of a rhythm instrument throughout, with a fiddle or mandolin peaking in and out as it takes solo and fill duties.

Mixing keyboards and other instruments

This is a pretty broad umbrella, I know, but having come this far in our mix we have already covered a lot of bases as regards carving space for different instruments within the sonic field by using frequency range, stereo panning, and basic volume level. Most of what you are likely to deal with will be subject to similar principles.

Acoustically recorded keyboard instruments, such as the piano and the Hammond organ with Leslie tone cabinet, will likely be mixed in some manner that you anticipated when recording them, either using some form of stereo technique, or focusing them more narrowly across the field as part of a busy mix.

We seem to be coming out the other side of an era in which Hammond organ has been an essential part of almost any commercial rock or pop track. Often it has been used as only a marginal element within a fairly dense arrangement, perhaps just a few briefly glimpsed accelerations and decelerations of that rotary speaker to signal "hey, we're hip enough to know how cool a Hammond is." If you're packing it in like that yourself, with multiple guitar tracks and other elements going on simultaneously, you might want to place your own Hammond track in a fairly tight window anywhere from around 50 per cent right or left to full pan one way or the other, balancing it with another instrument on the other side. Even mixed as a single track (or a mono sub-mix of multi-miked tracks), the Hammond can still make itself felt in a dense mix, thanks to its inherent thickness of tone, and the multi-dimensionality that the Leslie speaker implies, even when heard in mono. Alternatively, a wide stereo pan of a Hammond in a supportive role can keep it heard out there on the atmospheric fringes without needing to have it too high in the mix, leaving lots of room center stage for your lead vocals, or your featured soloing instrument.

For that huge, "star-of-the-show" Hammond sound that often suits anything from gutsy roots and blues to classic 70s rock, and certainly an organ trio in a somewhat different context, you can go hog-wild with your multi-miked recording of the Leslie cab and space your tracks to your desired width across the stereo field. The Leslie can sound great with a single mic on the low rotor placed straight up the middle with the bass and kick (and, in the context of a traditional organ trio, even replacing the bass at times), and two stereo mics recorded either side of the upper rotor spread anywhere from nine and three o'clock to full width. Even if you just used one mic each on the upper and lower, a stereo pan of these can still sound mammoth. With the three-mic approach, consider compressing the center (lower-rotor) mic on its own, then routing the stereo mics to the same bus on a stereo channel for compressing via a stereo plug-in. If you recorded a room mic or two as well, you can often get away without any reverb, and craft a sound that is truly hypnotic.

Your piano mix will be dictated by the prominence of the part, much as were our suggested mixes for acoustic guitar above. A grand or console piano that's used as just one decorative element among many can be placed as a single track, or a mono sub-mix of two, slightly to one side of center, or further out if you have a lot going on and plenty of candidates to balance it out on the other side. With a big stereo piano that is the central focus, or at least one of the main elements in a more "open" arrangement, you can go to town as we did with the acoustic guitar and Hammond organ in similar circumstances. Alternatively, even if the piano is just comping chords as a "pad" for vocal and/or other more prominently featured instruments, you can also go with a full left-right pan of your stereo recording to put a lot of sonic excitement out at the edges, leaving the featured performances most of the middle ground for the sake of their punch and solidity.

There should be a lot to say about an instrument this size, and with such sonic potential, but the significant comments on EQ and compression were covered pretty thoroughly in Chapter Eight. A good-sounding piano that is played well should really benefit from some crafting and attention to detail in the mix, rather than just being subjected to any supposed "basic settings" or Mixing Piano 101-style advice. Otherwise, I would mainly want to note that piano can be an extremely obtrusive instrument if mixed poorly; if you are getting a lot of peaks jumping out and stomping on other elements of your arrangement, apply enough gentle compression to rein these in and smooth out the overall performance a little. Also, if your recording technique was one of the more close-miked set-ups, a good stereo reverb plug-in on an auxiliary channel, or in a bus to which you have grouped your multiple piano mics, can really open up the sound of a good piano track.

Other acoustic stringed instruments will be handled much as the acoustic guitar (as detailed above), in ways that will of course vary greatly depending upon your song and arrangement.

Horns can be treated in ways as diverse as can the electric guitar, or any other instrument really. A prominent sax part in a rock'n'roll song, or a big Springsteen-esque arrangement, will be placed in the mix much as would a lead guitar part, although obviously EQ-ed and compressed slightly differently, according to your requirements (perhaps not so differently, in fact). Another horn that is meant to blend in as more of a supporting element in a pop-rock or jam-band context might be carved in a little more tightly, but pushed up for any solos. Both of these would, however, most likely be a single track or mono group of multi-miked tracks panned to one side or the other of the stereo field. A horn section, on the other hand, will be treated very differently, depending on its prominence in the arrangement. A stereo recording of a section of three or more horns that tracked an arrangement together can sound great with something like a nine to three o'clock or ten to two o'clock stereo pan, so it achieves some width, but retains that girth and solidity up the middle. Or, for something with a little more ambience, a full left-right pan can work as part of a lush mix, and still leave room for solid individual instruments in the center third of the stereo field.

Mixing vocals

In 99 out of 100 mixing situations, the lead vocal will take center stage in the arrangement (instrumental tunes obviously being the major exception, alongside thrash-metal and some types of dance music, perhaps). The vocal carries the melody and therefore defines the "song," and it's the musical element listeners will latch on to more than anything else, even if everything else is extremely important in setting the context and creating excitement for the mix as a whole. As discussed above, however, that doesn't mean that you have to mix the vocals first, by any means; but you should probably begin the mixing process with your lead vocal's requirements in mind.

Fortunately, as important as the lead vocal is, the textbook directives for mixing it are pretty simple as regards panning and level, and 90 per cent of the work will have been done in getting a good recording of a good vocal performance in the first place. On some occasions you might be blending two tracks of different mics used to capture different characteristics, as described in the Recording Vocals chapter, but this will be the exception rather than the rule. Whatever you do, though, you are most likely going to pan the lead vocal straight up the middle, and more often than not you will make it the most prominent sound in the mix, too. Regarding the latter, I feel it's important to tack on the qualification "if only slightly." There's no quicker way to ruin an otherwise great mix than to make the lead vocal just too hot. That will have it jumping out of its instrumental bed rather unnaturally, while also robbing the rest of the arrangement of much of its energy and dynamics. But these are considerations that will be made for every element in the mix—they're just that much more crucial when deciding the final level of the vocals. There's no formula or meter reading to tell you "what's right" volume-wise. You have to use your ears, compare carefully with several commercial releases from bands working in a similar style, and be ready to seek second opinions from objective ears that haven't been dulled by the mixing process.

Otherwise, the spice and nuance of a creatively mixed lead vocal come in the subtle (or not so subtle) use of processors and effects. A little light compression is likely to be useful to help the track "pop," especially if you didn't record through any comp in the first place (and if you did, sometimes a little more doesn't hurt). Start with the settings suggested in the Recording Vocals chapter, and be sure to tweak them with everything else up in the track so you can hear how the results work in the mix, rather than in solo mode. Sure, you can squash the hell out of a vocal track if you need to, and that will often thicken it up and add perceived "punching power," but the braver and more creative approach is to go very light on compression, or avoid it altogether, and if you recorded a good performance well in the first place, with the right mic and no overtly "hot" sections, it can often sit great just as it is. Other than standard compression, or in addition to it, you might find you need to use a de-esser plug-in (which is really a more narrowly focused type of compressor) if your track has a lot of snakey hiss on it. These can really help to clean up sibilance in a performance, although over-use can leave a track sounding just as unnatural as leaving it off altogether.

A little EQ often helps, too, and be sure to apply your EQ plug-in before your compressor plug-in on the track, so you are compressing a sound that has already had its frequency shaped, rather than the other way around. The first thing you should do with the EQ is a treatment we have given all of the other non-bass instruments in the mix, in order to keep them out of the way of the kick drum and bass guitar. If you didn't record the track with a high-pass filter set on the mic or preamp to roll off some low frequencies, you can do that now to remove anything below 60Hz with a deep-voiced male singer, or higher than that—maybe up to 100Hz or a little above—with other vocalists, depending on the range of the part. You can often also remove 3 or 4 dB from somewhere in the 140Hz to 250Hz range to help give more prominence to the "punch zone" of your kick and bass. You don't usually need to add anything to the meat of the vocal itself, and doing so will often result in a muddy, boxy sounding midrange hump within the track as a whole if it's boosted too high. But for a poppy or contemporary vocal sound you can sometimes do with adding presence and the perception of "air" by boosting it by just a few dB with a shelving EQ set to start at anywhere from 10kHz to 15kHz or so. That should feel like it gives the upper end of the part more room to breathe, and provides some shimmer that enables the vocal to stand out without having to have its overall level boosted too far beyond that of everything else.

Reverb and delay can also go a long way toward helping a vocal part shine. You probably don't want to make the mistake of slathering on lots of deep, long reverb settings that leave the vocal sounding like it was recorded in a cathedral while the rest of the band was playing in a small room next door. Use just enough to increase the feeling of presence in the part. The ideal vocal reverb, other than where you want the reverb to be noticed for conscious creative reasons, tends simply to make the listener feel they are hearing the performance in a live space rather than in a small, dry, heavily treated vocal booth, and isn't much noticed as a "reverb effect" in the track as a whole. A mix, or blend, of around 10 per cent wet to 90 per cent dry is a good starting point (and you can often do with a lower wetness). That should keep it from sounding like you recorded your vocals in an Alesis showroom.

In cases when reverb can make a vocal sound washy and less present rather than more present—always a danger—a short delay can often work wonders. Frequently, this can add a little magical something that listeners don't consciously hear as "echo," but which helps to give the lead vocal the prominence it needs. Sometimes a roots or retro vocal part will work with a delay setting as short as a traditional "slapback" sound—often considered to be super-short, in the 60ms to 100ms range, but as high as 150ms in old-school rockabilly practice. That will help to both thicken up the vocal and give it something special to raise it above the other instruments in the mix. Keep it to a single repeat, and don't dial in your echo depth so that repeat is too prominent. Bigger rock mixes often benefit from slightly longer delays; try to time something to the tempo of the track, if you can. Even so, you still usually don't want multiple repeats fading off into the distance, unless that's the effect you are specifically seeking.

Other more dramatic effects can sometimes lend depth and dimension to lead vocals. A little modulation from a chorus or a phaser or rotary speaker plug-in (or a good hardware unit if you have it) can often sound great when used right. Done well, this is, once again, the kind of thing the listener doesn't consciously register as "an effect," but hears as part of the style, presence, and multi-dimensionality of the lead vocal part (the treatment of the vocals of James Mercer with The Shins often shines with a little added modulation, which works great within the context of their music). If you want to put a little extra craft into this sound, you can use your chosen effect plug-in (or outboard analog unit) on a separate auxiliary channel, and even make it a stereo effect if that works without cluttering the mix too badly. Set up the aux channel, link to it on a send from the main vocal track, and designate its output as whatever your master pair is called. You can then blend your desired quantity of the effect using the "send level" control and the aux track's fader, and still retain the unaffected sound of the original track in the mix.

Ultimately, because it's worth repeating, you want to get the vocal sounding its best within the track as a whole, and anything you do to it in solo mode really is irrelevant. Listen carefully to the entire mix while working to finalize the vocal, check it at different overall volume levels, and take frequent quiet breaks to cleanse your ears. Once you think you've got it right, try running the whole track back again with the vocal turned *down* just a little further; if it's still prominent and distinctive, consider whether the lower setting for this crucial track gives your overall mix more character and energy, and go with whatever makes the best sounding song as a whole.

Mixing backing vocals

Backing vocals can be extremely simple to mix in, or a royal pain in the ass, depending on the parts and the song you are weaving them into. If the harmonies are sung well, and weren't recorded with any glaring frequency spikes or oddities, you can usually just tuck them in a few notches below the lead vocal, dispense with EQ altogether, treat them to just a little of the same reverb but, often, on a slightly lesser depth ("wetness") setting, and leave it at that. With multiple harmonies recorded on separate tracks, spreading them just a little bit in the stereo spectrum often sounds good, if the parts are equal enough in weight that the result doesn't sound off-balance. You usually don't want to pan them to extremes, either. Something in the 10-to-2 o'clock zone usually works, but sometimes a tighter pan of around 11-and-1 o'clock for a pair of backing vocal harmonies keeps it all sounding more like a unit.

While EQ is usually unnecessary (other than adding a high-pass filter if you didn't record with one), a little compression usually helps, and if anything you might give the backing vocals a little heavier compression than the lead vocal in order to keep them from jumping out at any point, unless of course they smoothly resist doing so anyway. The best approach to this is usually to group all backing vocals to a stereo bus track and treat them there. If the vocals were tracked "backing singer" style with two or more singers around a single mic or a stereo pair, however, you can just drop your plug-ins directly into that track and treat as needed. Pan a stereo group to the width suggested above, unless you're looking for a wide, room-filling backing harmony as a creative choice.

In songs with just a single backing vocal, it can still often be effective to pan that track slightly off center, to give a little space both to it and to the lead vocal that it supports. Consider putting it slightly opposite another supportive instrument with a similar range, such as a lead guitar, keyboard, horn, or harmonica part that plays fills between vocal lines. If, on the other hand, the backing vocal is a close-harmony part performed by the lead vocalist—the type of part intended to be heard as more of a thickening of the lead vocal than as a separate voice—you might want to try that right up the middle with the lead, treated similarly, but tucked just slightly beneath it, level-wise. As such, this is really a form of double-tracking, but one in which the lead vocalist sings plenty of close harmonies to the original part (often with some unison notes, too), to give dimension to the lead vocal as a whole. Listen closely to the recorded work of Dolores O'Riordan of The Cranberries, Chris Barron with The Spin Doctors, and Sinead O'Connor, and you will detect subtle self-harmonies rippling beneath lead vocal tracks that just wouldn't sound the same without them.

Mixing with outboard analog effects

If you possess any good-sounding, old-school analog effects units that you would like to bring into your digital mixing efforts, there are plenty of ways of achieving this. The most straightforward method is to use them on an auxiliary track. Just as we have discussed using some plug-in effects and processors on auxiliary channels in your DAW, you can assign auxiliary channels routed from the DAW to analog outputs on your multi-channel interface (provided you are using something more advanced than one of the very basic units). From there, route the interface's analog output to the input of your effect or processing unit, then go from its output back to an analog input on the interface, which should be assigned to the input of a new audio track for recording. (Note that if your analog effect has a high-impedance input designed to work best with a guitar plugged straight into it, rather than a low-impedance line-level input, you will often get cleaner results by using a low-impedance to hi-impedance converter, or by routing the signal from the interface's low-impedance analog output to the low-impedance *output* of a DI box—using an adaptor cable as described in the Re-Amping sections in Recording Bass and Recording Guitar, if necessary—and linking the high-impedance *input* of the DI box to the input of the analog effects unit, to show it the high-impedance signal it prefers to work with.)

The best means of bringing your analog effect into the picture isn't to "mix with analog effects," as you would have during mixdown in the good old days, bringing in the sound of such effects as you run your final mix in real time. Instead, record your analog-effects-laden "auxiliary" as you would record any live-instrument track. Route, for example, your lead vocal to an analog tape echo such as a Maestro Echoplex, a Roland Space Echo, or a modern Fulltone Tube Tape Echo, run through the track a few times to get your delay and repeat settings just right, then record-enable your new track (perhaps labeled "vocal echo') and record a pass of the entire part. You can afford to record it fairly "wet" (that is, with a high depth setting on the effects unit) because you will control the final amount of effects by blending it in with the "vocal echo" track's fader. If you want to change effects settings for different parts, you can even record this effects track in stages. Now you have an entirely new track that represents the effected sound and can be blended in to the final mix in whatever proportion you desire, just as you would any plug-in effect placed on an auxiliary channel.

Similarly, you can also route multiple tracks—groups of guitars, drums, backing vocals, or several different instruments that want a little touch of the same reverb or delay—to the same effect, using it as you would an effect on an auxiliary channel of an analog mixing desk. Of course, you can also run different instruments or groups independently through the effect on successive takes, using slightly different depth and delay settings if desired, to use the effect on more than one source in your mix, and with independent control over each.

The majority of such effects are mono, so the most straightforward route is to route them back to a mono track for recording the effected sound. If you do have a stereo unit, like an old plate reverb or an analog delay line with stereo outputs, you can obviously route these back to a stereo audio track for recording. But what if you want to route stereo mics or instrument groups through your mono analog effect? No sweat—it's easily done, and just takes a little more effort. Route your stereo track or instrument, or the left and right outputs of a stereo bus that groups together several tracks, to a stereo pair of analog outputs on your interface, and retain the left-right pan that you intend to hear in the final mix. Set up two new mono audio tracks to record to, and pan them hard left and right in advance. Route the interface's analog output that represents the left side of your stereo group through the mono effect as above and back to your new record-enabled "left" audio track. Run a pass, and record the left side of your effects sound. Now, move the cable from the interface's analog out representing "left" to the one representing "right," and the input from the one assigned to your new "left" audio track to the one representing your new "right" audio track, which you now record-enable. Run another record pass, and you have now "printed" a stereo effect on two channels representing the left and right of that sound according to your mix. If you want slight differences in the delays of the left and right signal of, for example, an analog tape delay, you can alter the head position slightly between the two record passes, checking them first to make sure they work together. With a reverb, different delay times heard on the left and right sides of a stereo effect can sound extremely unnatural, so you probably want to use the same settings both times. The mere fact of running the different sides of a stereo instrument or bus independently through the effect still makes it a genuine "stereo signal" in the end.

If you have a more basic DAW and interface, you can often still achieve some success with analog outboard effects if you work at it, provided your system can run signal at its stereo outputs and stereo inputs simultaneously, while recording from the latter, without any time delay between them. In this instance, you mute everything in the mix other than the instrument or group of instruments that you want to run through the external effect, and set up a new audio track to record the new sound to, as described above. After you have "printed" your pseudo auxiliary effect, you un-mute the rest of the mix, and blend the effects track in as desired.

Alternative reverb sources

A genuine room-reverb sound can be a great way of bringing some real-life ambience into an otherwise "in the box" recording, and often proves an excellent means of making it sound a little more "human," "organic," or whatever squishy adjective you want to apply to it. Going beyond the method described above for recording an analog effects unit on its own track or tracks, capturing genuine room reverb requires that you play back your final mix, or the instruments that you want to receive the effect, in a live space with good reverberant qualities. Then you record the sound of that—at a distance from the source—back to your DAW. A reflective basement or a large bathroom is often ideal for these purposes, or a bare living room that you have emptied in preparation for painting. You can even take the effort out of house to a public or commercial space to which you are allowed access (a church, a gym, a swimming pool), and achieve it with a makeshift portable recording and playback system, which might perhaps comprise a laptop and a couple of mics, and two powered speakers for playback.

As you can probably guess, this "live room reverb" is achieved in a process similar to that used for recording analog effects, detailed above. The differences are that your interface's analog output goes to a powered speaker for live playback (or any decent home stereo system), and the input back to your record-enabled audio track comes from a microphone into a mic pre. For stereo reverb, you clearly just run stereo analog outs into two speakers, and record this with two well-matched microphones. Experiment both with speaker and mic placement in your chosen space, and face both of these ends of the play-record chain slightly away from each other, or entirely back-to-back if you like (maximizing reflections from hard walls and floors), aimed into corners, and so forth, to hear how different positions change the natural reverb that this technique creates.

For a nifty twist on this live-reverb technique—one that is usually best when used subtly, but which can provide some interesting results—try aiming your playback speaker at the soundboard of an acoustic stringed instrument, and positioning a mic to record the results. A piano works great for this, if you can aim the speaker and mic into the top of a grand or remove the front panel of a console piano (place a heavy weight on the sustain pedal to let the strings ring freely). A resonator guitar also yields some haunting sounds, since the resonator cones in these are extremely sensitive to acoustic vibrations, and even a standard acoustic guitar can give you some interesting results with a thin mic aimed right inside the sound hole. When using either of these guitars, try tuning to an open chord that represents the key of the song to which you are applying this effect, and you will hear all kinds of eerie, resonant string sounds and harmonic overtones that are in tune with your track. For a stereo effect, simply track the results twice, as described in the above section on Analog Effects.

Final mixdown

Well, we're here. Bit by bit we have crept up on the final step of the mixing process, and are on the verge of sending our work out as the stereo signal that will represent the "song" to any listeners who hear it. Essentially all that remains to be done to set our final mix in stone is to "bounce" it to a two-track interleaved stereo file (as opposed to separate left and right files). This is usually accomplished in the digital realm by rendering the file to disk, a process often called "export" or "bounce to disk" in the DAW. Or you can record it in real time to a new stereo audio track. A final few tweaks and techniques are worth consideration, though, and will help you achieve the most professional-sounding results from your efforts.

MASTER CHANNEL PROCESSORS AND EFFECTS

In addition to any effects and processor plug-ins used on individual channels and group buses, recordists often mix with additional plug-ins inserted in the stereo master track, through which every signal passes on its way to the mixdown. Any such processing should be used judiciously, so that you don't end up stamping your project with a sound that is too heavy-handed. But a little master compression and reverb can often provide the finishing touches that help a mix sound like a "glued together" whole, rather than a jumble of individual parts. Even some multi-band master EQ can sometimes work toward restraining troublesome frequencies heard in the mix as a whole, or can add anything that might be missing, from low-end girth to midrange punch or high-end sheen.

Before running with any plug-ins on a master track, though, check whether the inserts occur pre- or post-fader. The latter is often the case (as it is in Pro Tools), but you usually won't want it that way in your final mixdown. That's because any changes in master fader settings will change the way plug-ins placed after the fader, which receive their input from it, react to the signal (for example, if you lower the signal coming into a compressor, it won't just "sound quieter," but will compress that signal very differently). If that's the case with your DAW's master fader, see if you can reset the inserts to "pre-fader," and if not, you can always set up an auxiliary track to behave as a master track. To do so, create a new stereo auxiliary track, then select a new stereo bus to assign as the input of your new stereo auxiliary. Change the output of all tracks that previously went to your master track (that is, any individual audio tracks, MIDI instrument tracks, any buses or any other form of auxiliary tracks) so that they now go to the stereo bus that represents the input of your new auxiliary track, which you might want to label "sub master." You can now move any plug-ins from the inserts of the master track to this auxiliary track that now represents your "sub master" and set the master track's fader to 0dB (that is, unity gain, sometimes labeled "U", and meaning no change in signal level rather than "no output"). Note: if you are operating this way, assume the use of the term "master track" in the following paragraphs to refer to this stereo auxiliary track that is acting as your master track.

The use of compression in the master track will depend on whether or not you are mastering the session after the mix, either by running it through a mastering program separately, post-mix, or by taking it to a professional mastering engineer (both of which are discussed further in the Mastering chapter). Compression, limiting, and EQ are all major tools in the mastering engineer's box, and the more of them you use during your own mixdown, the less effective they will be as applied during the mastering process, where you really want them to shine.

Compression is definitely used as something of a creative sonic tool in the mixing process too, and you shouldn't necessarily cut off that avenue if you are taking your mix for further mastering elsewhere. If you do use it in such a situation, though, prepare to go easy and avoid slamming the final master-track level. As explained further in the

Mastering chapter, you need to leave the mastering engineer enough headroom to more effectively boost your final signal as necessary.

While you might have reverb on some individual instrument tracks, or shared among groups in auxiliary tracks, it can sometimes be useful to put a touch of reverb on the master track, too, to give the overall mix the sense of existing in the same performance space. Overdoing this can make a song sound distant and, well, rather dated, unless you are doing it for conscious creative reasons. Several contemporary producers advocate avoiding reverb entirely, either on instruments or the master. Steve Earle, who is a busy producer as well as an artist in his own right, told me during an interview several years ago that he never uses reverb in his mixes, on anything. I was surprised to hear it at the time, but a return listen to two of his latest albums as of that time—*El Corazón* and *Transcendental Blues*—confirmed it. They are dry as a bone. And you know what? They sound just right that way: very present, alive, and real. Imagine, on the other hand, My Morning Jacket without reverb, on their first several albums at least. They pile it on as a creative choice, and it works extremely well in that context.

I suppose what I'm really getting at here is that you don't want to go to the reverb simply because it's a powerful and impressive tool, and seems like an easy way of "making your mixes sound professional." It's just as likely to be a quick way of doing exactly the opposite; but it can certainly also work for you, when used right. Listen carefully, proceed in small doses, and always do lots of comparative listening to what other respected contemporary artists working in your genre are doing sonically.

If you are bouncing this mix as an example to be shared with band mates or friends for final comment before bouncing a final version for professional mastering, you can use a mastering plug-in on the master track to give it some final sheen and a modicum of professional-grade treatment. Software like iZotope's Ozone and IK Multimedia's T-RackS, or one of UA's powered mastering plug-ins, can help you get close to a "mastered sounding" product. They offer convenient presets that you can turn to if you haven't yet acquired the experience to set up all the parameters yourself, or are just in a hurry (see the Mastering chapter for a more considered approach to the real deal).

These mastering plug-ins are useful in other ways, too. I always monitor my mixes for a time through some relatively gentle and universal settings on a mastering plug-in when I'm getting close to the final stage. I do that even when I'm ultimately going to take the song to a professional mastering engineer, because it's sometimes difficult to know how the final product will really sound until you hear the effects of mastering. In this way, a mastering plug-in on the master track can help you get a better idea of the likely sound of the finished effort, even if you don't intend for anyone but you to hear it in that context. Once you get it right, bypass (or entirely remove) the mastering plug-in, adjust your master fader level for appropriate headroom, and go for it.

On some occasions, depending on the speed of your system, using a mastering plug-in on the master channel in this way will simply demand too much processing power from your computer, particularly when you are also running other individual track and bus plug-ins throughout the mix. In such a case, it's a good idea to bounce your mix without the mastering plug-in in place, then reload the new stereo file into a new session in your DAW, and run that through the mastering plug-in to hear how it affects your mix.

MIX AUTOMATION

In the good old days before the DAW, and before automated mixing desks (or when your band couldn't afford to work in a studio with an automated mixing desk), the final mixdown was often an "all hands on deck" situation. Once you had made the creative choices and planned what was to be done, if the mix required much movement of the level faders or pan knobs, any on-the-fly changes of effects for guitar solos or vocal parts, or the muting of more than a track or two to silence tracks during quieter musical moments, it was often necessary to recruit band members to lean over the desk and assist. With four, six, or eight hands hovering over the controls, the mixing process became as much of a performance as any of the musical performances tracked during recording. Missed cues were commonplace, and all you could do was roll the tapes back—the multi-track and master both—and go for it again.

These days, automation makes the final mix a breeze. In fact, you now inch so gradually toward the final moment, which is now performed as a "bounce to disk" rather than a real-time recording from one tape to another, that it often kind of sneaks up on you in the end. "Check the reverb on the lead vocal one more time, record the automation of the fade-out of that last guitar solo, and ... hey, we're done." You hit "export" or "bounce to disk," wait for the file to copy, and you've finished.

But I'm getting ahead of myself a little. The main point about automation is that you should use it. The user instructions with your own particular DAW will tell you specifically how to use its various automation functions, but the ease and convenience of being able to do so at all is an enormous boon to the contemporary recordist. With most DAWs, you can record automated movements and changes in real time as the "play head" rolls and you listen to the mix, and change them ad infinitum later in the editing window. Or you can just "draw" them in your editing window in the first place, if you have enough experience with the parameters involved to graphically visualize what is required. It's an amazing feature, and one that has virtually erased the "make or break" anxiety that used to go hand-in-hand with the final mixdown.

Automation also makes it easy to make dynamic level changes throughout the course of the song, as necessary. Individual or grouped instrument tracks can obviously come up or down slightly to introduce solos or to enhance quieter passages. You can also bring the entire mix up by automating a slightly higher setting of the master level fader at the start of the song, for example, so an early section with fewer instruments in the mix doesn't sound thin and wimpy, and bring it all down slightly so it doesn't overload—but retains comparable overall level—when other, heavier instruments are brought in. The creative power that this hands-freeing function offers really is just about limitless, so use it to your advantage.

And having said all that, just because you can pan tracks back and forth robotically, have levels bopping up and down, and achieve several different effects settings in the course of a single rhythm-guitar part doesn't mean you should. Overdoing it with the automation is a sure-fire way to signal a "Pro Toolsed" recording. It ends up sounding like you're cheating—and sounding like an amateur at it at that. Use automation to make any changes that need to be made, and to make them smoothly, and it will remain the extremely useful tool that it is.

DIGITAL FORMAT AND SETTINGS

Before you run that final bounce—or, as is often the case, in the course of doing so—you need to make a few decisions regarding digital file format (also known as "delivery format") and settings. The form that these take will depend on a combination of factors, including the end medium by which any listener will access them (MP3? High-resolution digital audio? CD?) and whether or not the file will be subject to any further mastering, either by you or by a professional mastering engineer.

Another of the beauties of automation, discussed in the section above, is that you can easily crank out different versions of the exact same mix to match different format and processing requirements. Simply by running your "bounce to disk" function again, and changing the parameters presented in the options windows before you click "OK," you can, for example, burn your mix as an MP3 with a mastering plug-in in the master track and a fade at the end, for immediate circulation online or as an email attachment to bandmates; as a 16-bit/44.1kHz AIFF file with mastering insert and fade out for burning demo CDs; and as a 24-bit/88.2kHz WAV with no mastering plug-ins, no fade out, and a little more headroom in the final master level for taking to a professional engineer for mastering. Give due consideration to the end product, and how it will be used, and set your parameters accordingly. You can always pop out another rendition in the future as required.

One more decision that the "export" or "bounce to disk" settings window often asks you to make is whether you want to create "stereo interleaved" tracks or "multiple mono" tracks. If you want to be able to play the final result on a conventional commercial digital music player of some sort without further conversion or processing, you will want a stereo interleaved track (which is created as a single file, but with two distinct audio tracks, left and right). For some purposes, multiple mono tracks, which come out as two separate files with an "L" and an "R" attached to their respective names, are easier to work with in further processing. If you get it wrong—producing unplayable multiple mono files when you were intending to bounce to interleaved stereo—hey, it's automated. Just run it again!

BOUNCING OR RECORDING YOUR MIX

There is much debate about whether your mix will sound better "bounced to disk" (aka "shared," "exported," or "rendered") or recorded in real time to a new stereo audio track. Opinions weighing in on one side of the fence or the other seem to differ depending on

TAKE YOUR MIX TO A PRO

While this book is resolutely about doing it yourself, there are definitely still advantages to be had by tapping a trained and experienced professional for your mixing work. If you are recording a project for commercial release, even as an independent, self-released CD, and have invested a lot of time, blood, sweat, and tears in the effort—and no shortage of creative energy, not to mention your hopes and dreams—the added expense of taking it to an experienced mixing engineer is often an investment worth making. The cost of this can vary tremendously, of course, and might run anywhere from a minimum of $1,000 for the two days required to do a quick but effective mix of a ten-song release, to several thousands and several days of work. If you have already saved a lot of money by doing the recording yourself, though, consider that as a boost to your budget, a strategy that might make it more feasible to spring for professional mixing.

In addition to the experienced and objective ear that a professional engineer brings to the job, you will often also gain access to a studio full of top-quality gear. Very possibly this will include several outstanding vintage analog outboard units and a big analog desk, all used in an "out of the box" mixdown of the type that you couldn't begin to approach in your DAW-based home studio. The correct use of such equipment can bring warmth and depth to a mix, which is otherwise extremely difficult to acquire in the digital realm. Even if your engineer mixes entirely "in the box," as you most likely would at home, his or her experience should constitute an important final point of "checks and balances" for your project. And the digital gear used and the technique applied are still likely to be superior to what you have access to in your own project studio.

If and when you do take your mix to a pro, be sure to inquire about the required track format ahead of time. If you aren't already recording on a digital system with which the pro's studio is compatible, they will usually want you to bounce down your final version of each individual track to a high-resolution WAV or AIFF file. You will need to first remove all effects and major processing that you have added in your rough mix so that the mixing engineer can add them to his or her taste (if these plug-ins constitute critical creative choices for you, you can bounce alternate tracks with and without them). And you must give the tracks that comprise each song the exact same starting point, of course, so they can load these into any DAW they might be working with themselves or using to feed their analog system. Also check whether they prefer to work with "stereo interleaved" tracks or "multiple mono," and set your parameters accordingly when exporting. Discuss these things in detail with the engineer or their technical assistant, ensure you understand their requirements, and get your part of the work done well before your mix date, all of which prep work will pay off in a more efficient session.

the DAW in question, and on the number and type of plug-in processors being used. The best suggestion is to try both and hear for yourself. The extra time invested in doing it both ways only accounts for the length of the song you are mixing, so it's a quick process, and worth the effort.

First, employ the "bounce to disk" function, or whatever your DAW calls it, and set the format to remain the same as that in which you have been recording (for example, 24 bits and 88.2kHz, or whatever your DAW and interface are set to). Give that file a name that will represent the "A" of your A/B comparison, and go for it. Once the bounce is completed, return to the same starting point, and send your main two-track stereo outs to a stereo bus that you designate as the input of a new stereo audio track, which you should name to represent your "B" of the comparison, if possible. Record-enable that track, and run the mix, recording it in real time to your new stereo "master" track. Locate the real-time recorded mix in your session's "audio files" folder and leave that folder window open, then close the session, and open a new session with only two stereo audio tracks in it. Load your "A" version of the mix into one, and your "B" version into the other of the stereo tracks, mute one, and play a little. Scroll back, swap the mutes, and play the other. Do you hear a difference between them? In theory, they should be exactly the same, but if you detect any difference (more "openness," greater "depth" or "dimension" in one or the other), that's your preferred method for final mixdown. Try it for several other mixes as you work through your material, and if one method is consistently superior to another, you know what to go for.

MIXING TIPS CHECKLIST

- Take frequent listening breaks to refresh your ears

- Change your listening volume occasionally, from soft to loud or vice-versa, rather than always monitoring at the same level. Different volume levels will reveal different responses from different parts of the frequency range, the low end in particular

- Review crucial points like reverb depths, vocal level, and bass content

- When you think you've got it all down, put it away overnight—or for a few days—and come back with totally fresh ears to assess it anew

- Take your mix to different listening environments (living-room hi-fi system, car stereo, boom box) via a CD, MP3 player, or flash drive played through a laptop, and assess it there.

CHAPTER 10

MASTERING

The process known as "mastering" really involves several different processes, and has changed considerably, both in theory and in practice, between the early days of the vinyl era and the dominance of digital production in recording today. In the 40s and early 50s the mastering engineer was part of an in-house studio attached to a record label, and was responsible for accurately transferring the master tape to the lacquer master that would be used to press vinyl albums. It was all about the ears, and less about the use of the gear in between—other than, of course, "cutting" the lacquer correctly. In the 60s, 70s, and 80s many studios, and therefore mastering engineers, worked independently, and the role became both more corrective and more creative, with mastering engineers commonly adjusting EQ, compression and limiting, and occasionally other factors during the mastering process.

Today, for any purely digital release, mastering is entirely about this processing, and far less about achieving the correct "master," from which to press the final product. Even so, the mastering engineer is definitely responsible for getting the digital format correct, achieving your final track order, and embedding any text and relevant codes that will be on the CD itself.

To put it succinctly, the job of mastering is still a highly technical one, and one that usually requires a lot of skill, training, and a substantial apprenticeship. As such, it is virtually impossible for the home recordist to achieve the kind of results that a true professional will give you, and the best advice is simply this: take it to a professional. A professional will have facilities far above anything you are likely to be able to set up at home, the listening environment itself being foremost of these, and will have the skill and experience to use them. In addition to simply making your work sound better, he or she will offer a final and objective set of ears, and possibly save you from disasters like having too much or too little bass in your mix, inappropriate lead-vocal levels, and so forth.

Of course, professionalism costs, and we can't always afford it. That is perhaps the first reason that you are likely to do it yourself. I would suggest that a second reason is found in the fact that the prevalence of reasonably affordable and user-friendly mastering software has meant an increase in pseudo-professional mastering engineers who claim to offer "professional results" for far less money, but really don't do a whole lot more with your mixes than you can learn to do yourself. That's not to say that the better practitioners in this range can't be of service: they might know how to use the programs better than you do, will perhaps have set up a better listening environment, and will at least offer an unbiased pair of ears. And there's a lot to be said for each of these points. The trouble is, it can be hard to judge the skill level of a fly-by-nighter such as this compared to the established professional mastering engineer with a known reputation. If you're tempted to go with the budget guy, I would suggest you perhaps proceed like this: make your own best effort at mastering a few of your final mixes, then negotiate with the proposed out-of-house engineer to master just a song or two for a bargain price, as a "tester" of sorts. Take the results and your own masters to several friends, bandmates, and fellow musicians, and gauge their feedback on the quality of each. From there, you decide the road to take.

To cover all the mastering options, we will look at what's required to do the job ourselves, as well as discussing in detail the preparation necessary for you to take your mix to a seasoned professional. By tackling the latter of these first, we will also be prepared to have our mixes in the best shape for self-mastering.

Pre-mastering preparation

To make the best job of mastering your mix, a mastering engineer needs to receive it in the best format and in the right condition. This means "exporting" or "bouncing" your final mix with the correct parameters as regards resolution and format, and ensuring—as far as possible—that there are no glitches or digital overloads in any of the files. If there are, you must make notes to remind you where they happen, and use these warn the engineer in advance. The following list presents the most likely steps you will need to take to have your mixed files ready for delivery. All are essentially final steps in your own mixing process, but also constitute your own efforts toward the mastering process. You should also discuss these procedures with the engineer who will be doing the work to find out if they suggest any changes to them, or have anything else to add.

- Remove any bus processing from your master track (master fader), unless you are using some light bus compression and reverb as essential parts of your creative voice. Even when you are using these, it's a good idea to run an alternative version of your mix without them in case the mastering engineer can improve upon your efforts. Definitely avoid any limiting, master EQ, stereo imaging or exciter plug-ins at this stage.

- Provide enough headroom for the mastering engineer to work with, so they have room to boost your tracks as necessary with compression and limiting. Keep peaks to around –3dB or –4dB or below, and average levels around –12dB to –14dB or so.

- Undo (or disable the automation on) any fade-outs on your master track at the end of any song. A mastering engineer can achieve better fades for you. Note the precise time where you would like the fade to begin, and the time by which you would like the fader to reach zero output (ie, the end time).

- When bouncing your mix, retain the highest bit rate available, such as 24 bits, and retain the frequency rate that you worked with in the session (most likely 48kHz, 88.2kHz or 96kHz). Again, confirm these with the mastering engineer.

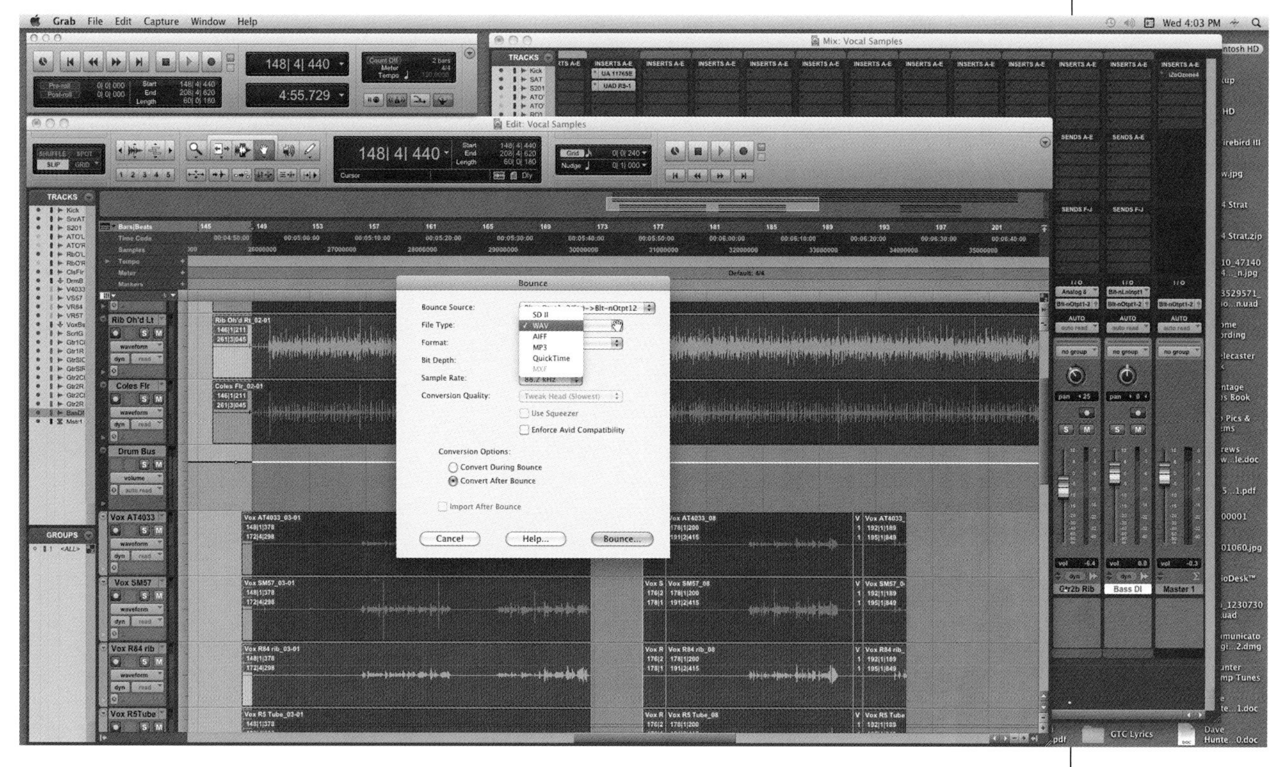

Selecting the digital format for a "bounce" in Pro Tools.

- Confirm the desired format. Most mastering engineers can work with a wide range of formats—most commonly WAV, AIFF, or SD II, but sometimes others—but if they have a preference for any reason, and you can just as easily bounce your mix to that format, go with it.

- Ask whether your mastering engineer prefers to receive mixes as "stereo interleaved" or "multiple mono" files. Most can work with either, but will often express a preference for one over the other.

- Also confirm all details regarding delivery format with the production house, if you know who it will be, so you can advise your engineer accordingly.

- Bounce multiple versions of each song: one with the vocal at the volume level where you feel it should be in the track, another with it just a touch louder, a third with it just a touch lower than your perceived "normal." If you have any doubts about your ability to perceive low-end content accurately in your listening environment, you can do the same regarding the bass level, or the level of any guitar solo or other musical moment that you aren't entirely confident with. Present the mastering engineer with your own "normal" mixes first rather than

expecting them to choose from several variations, or it will cost you in time and money, and have the others available if they express a desire to hear different levels. Keep a written log of which mix is which as you bounce them, and be sure you can relate the name of the file to the intended variation, rather trying to guess whether it's "vocal normal" or "vocal up" just by listening.

- Prepare other details needed for the final product, such as the precise song sequencing, the correct text for song titles and CD title, any ISRC song-identification codes if you are embedding these in the digital metadata, and so forth, so the mastering engineer can enter these onto the master CD, and your backup.

- Finally, it's usually a good idea to bring two copies of all files, a working copy and a backup, to your mastering session. By the time you have all of this in its final pre-mastering form it will represent a lot of data. You can load it to a portable external hard drive, a laptop computer, or a series of CD-ROMs. Have an alternative source ready if there's a glitch in any of your original masters.

Mastering it yourself

It would take an entire book to teach the art of mastering. Of course that book would need to be written by an experienced professional mastering engineer... and then you would need to work as one yourself for several years before you could be sure of having it down. With that in mind, offering a mere section of a chapter called "Mastering It Yourself" is a little like publishing a pamphlet entitled "Perform Your Own Open-Heart Surgery." At least doing your own mastering bears no life-threatening risk, only a substantial risk of blowing your creative efforts in this final, crucial step. But you *can* do it yourself without entirely voiding everything you have worked so hard to achieve, if you proceed slowly and cautiously, and, in applying most processes, err on the side of less rather than more. At the very least, you should be able to get your final mixes sounding a little bit bigger, deeper, and shinier than they did before you mastered them, and that is at least something.

While mastering involves the use of several powerful processors to shape the final sound of a mix, the most crucial tools of the job are your own ears. Right up alongside that, of course, is the accuracy of your listening space, because your ears can't give you accurate feedback on frequency information that is skewed by an inaccurate room. This was discussed in some detail in Chapter One: Studio Set-Up, and it is arguably more important here than at any other step in the process, if only marginally so as compared to its importance to successful mixing. As with my suggestions for checking your mix in other listening environments, if you have any doubts at all about the neutrality of your room, or the quality and accuracy of your studio monitors, check any and all work you do by listening on different systems, in different rooms, to build a "composite opinion" of sorts on the success of your efforts. You should also spend plenty of time listening to commercially produced and mastered CDs on your studio monitors, particularly those in genres similar to the mixes you intend to master yourself. Choose CDs you are familiar with from your car and home stereos, and note any glaring differences in EQ and general tonality that might signal trouble spots in your own acoustic environment.

As with the majority of the effects you will have applied during mixing, your mastering processors will be used as plug-ins on a master channel strip. Rather than doing this in mixdown, however, as discussed in the preceding chapter, you will do this as a new and isolated step in itself, devoting full processor speed and power, and your full attention, to the effort of mastering. Before undertaking this step, though, ensure once more that you have taken the relevant steps to prepare the tracks for your own mastering, just as you would prepare them for a professional mastering engineer, as regards format, bit rate, headroom, and so forth.

LOADING YOUR MIX

To do the best job of your own mastering, approach it as if you are a mastering engineer yourself. Open an entirely new session in your DAW, and start by loading a single stereo audio track in place if you are working with a stereo interleaved file (which is probably the simplest way to go with your own mastering), or two mono audio tracks and a stereo auxiliary track if you are working with multiple mono files. The only difference in your procedure between the two will be in where you place your processor plug-ins, but the job of mastering will otherwise be exactly the same. Some DAWs convert stereo interleaved files to two mono files when importing them; check yours to discover if this is the case. If so, you are probably better off working with multiple mono files in the first place, rather than subjecting your audio to that further unnecessary stage of conversion. Make a note of this when mixing, and bounce appropriately.

With a stereo interleaved file, load the mix into your stereo audio track with an "import audio" function or by dragging and dropping it into the editing window (or by whichever method you commonly use with your DAW). With multiple mono

Pro Tools tracks set up to load in the left and right bounces for mastering, with plug-ins on a stereo aux track, and dithering on the master fader.

files, load your "L" file into mono audio track one and pan it hard left, and load your "R" file into mono audio track two and pan it hard right, and be sure that both are lined up at the same starting point. Now, from your stereo auxiliary track's input menu, select a stereo bus to designate as the input, and select that as the output from each of your "left" and "right" audio tracks. The output of the stereo aux track should go to whatever you use as your main output pair, which will be the default with many DAWs.

When loading the mastering processors that will be discussed below, you put them in inserts in the stereo audio track when working with a stereo interleaved file, and in the stereo auxiliary track when working with multiple mono tracks, leaving the faders and insert windows of the two audio tracks holding your "L" and "R" files untouched. Next, whichever way you are working, add a master fader, if one isn't sitting there already, and if possible, set it to have the inserts post-fader (the master fader in Pro Tools works this way anyway). You will later use one of these post-fader inserts for your dithering plug-in, which wants to happen absolutely last in your signal chain when mastering, while this master fader will be the last level-setting link in the signal chain before that occurs. The inserts on your stereo auxiliary track, on the other hand, where all other mastering processors will be loaded, occur pre-fader, which is exactly where you want them.

The tools of mastering

Let's look at the types of software plug-in that you are likely to use to master your own work, many of which mirror the hardware that professional mastering engineers have used in major studios for decades. The main tools are EQs, compressors, and limiters, while mastering reverb, stereo imaging, harmonic exciters, and loudness maximizers (another form of limiting) are also sometimes used. A separate dithering plug-in is often placed last of all, after the master fader, to convert the digital bit depth used for recording to the bit depth required for CD production.

You can do your own mastering by loading individual plug-ins to achieve each of the essential jobs, but as often as not any home recordist will use an all-in-one mastering package which includes versions of some or all of these tools, linked together in a single powerful plug-in. Packages like iZotope's Ozone, IK Multimedia's T-RackS, Bias Peak Studio and Steinberg WaveLab are among the popular software mastering plug-ins out there. You can also investigate the more powerful packages that require either an additional external hardware device or an internal computer card, such as TC Finalizer or one of Universal Audio's powered mastering plug-ins. (It's worth noting here that the folks at iZotope have produced an excellent PDF on mastering, which applies to the company's Ozone software product in particular, but also offers a lot of good general advice on the art of mastering with plug-ins. It's available free from the company's website, and elsewhere, to customers and non-customers alike, and should easily be found by searching the net for "ozone mastering guide.")

The presets screen in iZotope's Ozone mastering plug-in.

ORDER OF INSERTS

There is no fixed order in which all of the tools used in mastering should always be placed, although certain functions do need to be used in the penultimate and final insert positions. Mastering engineers will often run them EQ > compressor > limiter > dither, the first two slots being interchangeable but the last two not. A limiter (or loudness maximizer, as it often is today), if used, should always be the last signal-processing tool before the master fader, while the dither is a bit-depth converter that always comes after the master fader, and can't do its job properly otherwise. If mastering reverb is used it can be placed before or after the compressor, and some occasions might call for comp before EQ. If a harmonic exciter and/or stereo imaging are used, they are likely to come after the compressor (or reverb) but before the limiter. Each processor will sound and behave a little differently depending on where in the order it is placed, so you can experiment with different chains to create different sonic results. The user's information included with any plug-ins you use yourself should include further tips on these matters.

The multi-band compressor screen in iZotope's Ozone mastering plug-in.

MASTERING EQ

The types of EQs used for mastering are usually graphic (or paragraphic) EQs, with multiple bands for imposing powerful control over several different bands of the frequency range. Each band of a multi-band EQ such as this is essentially a single filter, which can boost or cut frequencies by a number of dBs within a range that is determined by the user. Each band can also be set to any of several different EQ shapes, each of which influences how the level and width of cut or boost "carves" its place in the frequency range as a whole. A "bell" (or "peak filter") raises or lowers the gain of the target frequency, in a band shaped like a bell curve that has a width (or "Q") determined by your Q setting, so the boost or cut rises or declines gradually or sharply to or from the target frequency according to that setting. A high-pass or low-pass filter attenuates everything above or below your determined frequency, respectively, as we have already seen with the frequent use of high-pass filters to cut unwanted low-end clutter (the names can be confusing: a high-pass filter cuts lows by letting the high frequencies "pass" through it). High and low shelving filters, the final two of the five major shapes, work a little like bell and high/low-pass filters combined, shape-wise. They don't cut everything above or below your determined frequency like a pass filter, or curve gently to and from it like a bell, but boost or cut a level "shelf" of frequencies in a band of adjustable width, by a number of dBs that you also determine.

Multi-band EQs such as this provide a powerful mastering tool by enabling you to use these shapes in any desired combination to essentially "draw" the shape of the frequency response of your stereo mix as a whole, cutting any troublesome spikes and boosting regions that need a little push, all with the same processor.

The first job of determining any EQ settings for mastering is to listen to the mix without any master EQ applied and try to determine whether you have any problem frequencies. It's worth knowing at this stage, though, that you won't entirely craft the listener's perception of frequency with this multi-band EQ as you might think; a multi-band compressor will also play a big part in emphasizing certain instruments or frequency bands within the overall range. So, do you hear anything that jumps out as harsh or irritating, any low-end mud or boominess, or any boxy or nasal sound in the midrange? This is the time to deal with it.

As we did so often in the recording and mixing stages, you might deal with irritating low-end rattle and boom (even that which is barely detectable) by applying a high-pass filter that cuts everything below 30Hz, or even 40Hz. Some thumping club mixes might have essential information happening down there, but most mixes will not. Harshness is often found in the 1kHz to 3kHz range, and is dealt with by applying the right kind of cut somewhere in that region. Muddiness is found somewhere between 100Hz and 250Hz or so, or possibly a little higher. Midrange boxiness can often be located in the 500Hz band, but sweep below and above that if you fail to nail it in that position. You'll notice that we are talking about gain reduction on everything so far (always start with just a little), but you can often increase the sense of liveliness and excitement in a mix by boosting the high frequencies a little with a wide bell shape in the 12kHz to 15kHz range.

All of these are just examples, and your mix might differ entirely. Also, you will frequently find that different songs require very different EQ treatments, although a batch of tunes recorded in the same place, and in similar ways, will often need similar starting points in your multi-band EQ treatment. If you are entirely unsure of where to begin, experiment with any available presets in your plug-in that aim to address specific genres of music, or specific EQ goals (these might be called "heavy rock" or "thumping dance"). In general, though, mastering EQ is likely to be used to cut more than to boost, and these cuts—as well as any necessary boosts—should always be fairly gentle. You should probably start by cutting or boosting by just 2 or 3dB in most instances, and if you have to go as high as 4 or 5dB anywhere (other than your 30Hz high-pass filter) then there is probably something significantly wrong with your mix in the first place. Also, with any bell shaped bands you want to keep your bell fairly wide (a low Q point) so you don't cut or boost in any steep peaks, which will sound extremely unnatural (a high Q can be a great tool for fixing a major problem in a specific instrument track prior to mixing, but shouldn't be used in mastering). Remember, too, that we are going to shape things considerably with the use of multi-band compression, and possibly a harmonic exciter, so you don't need to try to correct and improve everything here in the EQ stage.

MASTERING COMPRESSION

Straightforward stereo units that apply the same amount of compression to the entire frequency range might sometimes be used in mastering, but the job will usually be tackled by complex multi-band compressors capable of compressing different parts of the song's frequency range in different ways. Such compressors might offer three or four bands, each of which can be independently set to all the parameters of a standard compressor, such as ratio, threshold, attack, and release. Usually you can also determine the positioning of each band within the frequency range, that is, where one band ends and the other begins. You can use one band to focus on adding punch and emphasis to the low end, mainly represented by the kick drum and bass guitar, another to smooth out the midrange, and yet another to add air to the highs, and so on.

The settings for such multi-band mastering compressors are even more diverse, and potentially complex, than those for multi-band mastering EQ, given you have so many parameters to consider with each band, as well as the placement of each band within the frequency range. A good place to begin, though, is by working hand in hand with your EQ to identify the cut-off points of frequency bands that might want to be treated differently (an EQ with a graphic frequency display of your mix is a big help here), then using the suggested compression starting points given in the individual chapters of this book that address instruments found in those parts of the frequency range. We are talking master compression here rather than individual track or bus compression, sure, but the approach to each is usually determined by considerations of frequency range in the first place. For the most part you will want to begin with low ratios and long attach and release times. In fact, the only major addendum I would add here is that you should err on the side of gentle comp in all instances, and seek to subtly influence the overall impression of punch, smoothness, and presence in your mix, rather than trying to slam or squash any regions, or the mix as a whole. If you are looking to do these things as a creative choice, that's a job more appropriate for individual track or bus compression, not mastering compression.

Once again, look to any presets in your mastering plug-ins as starting places if you feel baffled by the variables of multi-band dynamics. To make the most of what this tool has to offer, you will ultimately need to fine-tune compressor settings yourself, but appropriate presets can often provide good starting points. What's more, you can check the specific parameter settings and band cut-off points used by such presets to learn how they are creating the sounds they are creating.

MASTERING REVERB

Not a "must use" certainly, mastering reverb can be useful when you want to give the stereo mix as a whole the feeling of being recorded in the same space, or in any live space at all, if that sense is lacking from the original work. As often as not, no mastering reverb will be required, and if you didn't have enough reverb on the mix as a whole from the individual instruments that required it (or groups sent to an aux reverb track), you might have added a little on your master or sub-master track during mixdown anyway, as discussed above. If a project reaches the mastering stage, though, and sounds as if it needs a little more air and dimension to sound its best, mastering reverb can be just the ticket.

There isn't a whole lot to be said about this tool that you won't already have learned from working with other reverb plug-ins, except that many reverbs designed for use in mastering will offer you the ability to treat only certain parts of the frequency range, to use the reverb where it is most effective and avoid it where it will only clutter your sound. Typically the ultra-low-end of any mix won't need, or want, any reverb, and will sound washy and diffuse if you use it there. Think of the high-pass filter you applied to so many non-bass instruments, and work this into your reverb cutoff, designating a starting point at 50Hz, 100Hz, or even 150Hz to avoid a washy low end. Highs can sound noisy, unnatural, or "hyped" with added reverb, too, so you might set your high-point cutoff at 5kHz or so. Adjust these according to your own requirements, and remember to go light on the wet/dry blend, too, for the most natural sound. When adding reverb to such a broad spectrum of the mix, something as light as just six per cent or eight per cent "wet" can already start to sound fairly effected.

LIMITERS AND LOUDNESS MAXIMIZERS

Each of these tools does somewhat the same thing, and while many compressors often include limiter functions, limiting is also frequently used independent of mastering compression, as a further step unto itself, to raise the final volume of the mix to its loudest possible level without clipping. In modern mastering this type of limiting often takes the form of a loudness maximizer, which is a type of limiter designed to do just what it says.

Upon going into this subject, I should point out there has been something of a competition in recent years to produce the loudest possible CDs, squashing all dynamics in the process. The result is a master where everything is as loud as everything else and runs right up against the max the entire time, remaining just the tiniest hair short of clipping. The theory is that the louder the mix, the more attention-grabbing the song will be. More thoughtful mastering engineers, though, and better producers in general, are tending to rebel against this. They realize that you can easily destroy the life and dynamics of a performance by going to such extremes, and that doing so can just as quickly produce a piece of music that is as aurally irritating and off-putting as it might be attention-grabbing. I make this point because many home recordists have access to loudness maximizers that can slam their tracks just as powerfully as those used in professional mastering studios and can just as easily make them sound like dung in the process.

A loudness maximizer can be a good tool for helping your mix compete with the volume levels of other (but less extreme) commercially produced tracks, and you can still employ it in a way that retains plenty of natural feel and dynamics in your performances. So be clear about your creative objectives before you go in and blast all your hard work to kingdom come in the name of sheer volume. Also, be aware that many amateur recordists will tell you that you need to make your song as loud as possible to have it sound its best on the radio, if you have the good fortune to get any airplay; but broadcast compressors used to retain specific average broadcast levels will flatten out louder tracks and boost softer ones anyway, so this theory is largely hokum.

In brief, a loudness maximizer works by limiting the peaks in your mix so that when these are raised to 0dB, just under the point of clipping, everything else gets louder along with it. The extent to which these peaks are squashed, and everything else is therefore boosted, determines how severe the process is, and the resultant sound along with it. If you want to use this tool to increase the impact of your master, I would advise going gently to avoid killing the natural dynamics of your tracks. And remember, most of the classic rock, jazz, country, blues, and rock'n'roll recordings of the 40s, 50s, 60s, 70s and even 80s were mastered with no limiting, and certainly no loudness maximizing. They might sound a little softer when played back-to=back with contemporary recordings, but chances are they often sound more "real"—and simply better, too—so just turn up the stereo if you want them louder.

HARMONIC EXCITERS AND STEREO IMAGING

These additional tools are occasionally used to add extra sparkle and width to a master, and they can be extremely seductive processors. Be forewarned that it is easy to over-use either or both, and sometimes difficult to realize that you are doing so. As the ear gets more and more attuned to the added harmonic excitement or wider stereo image created, the pre-excitement/widening version heard by clicking "bypass" begins to sound more and more flat and dull. Rest your ears for a while, come back and listen to the mix with these processors "bypassed" first, though, and you might then hear the enhanced version as hyped, harsh, and artificial. What I'm edging toward saying, I suppose, is that either or both of these can be great ways of adding sparkle to a mix that truly is harmonically flat and dull, or adding some stereo imaging to one that is too narrow and one-dimensional, but over-use is likely to sound unnatural, and using them at all on a track that already achieved good use of stereo space and lively harmonic sparkle in the mix is probably unnecessary.

Both of these are usually pretty simple to use in the basic sense, and until you take the time to get into the deep editing of either, you are likely to begin with presets and tweak parameters gently. Controls and parameters will be somewhat different depending on the exact software you are using, but should be easy enough to root out with assistance from the user's manual or "help" menu.

Harmonic exciter plug-ins today usually offer multi-band treatment so you can hone regions that need extra harmonic shimmer and leave others untreated. Likewise, the more creative stereo imaging plug-ins today offer multi-band stereo widening so you can, for example, enhance the stereo image of the lower mids slightly, the upper mids and highs considerably, while leaving the lows untreated and solidly dead-center, or whatever works for your mix. Again, go easy, if you use these at all—and if your mix sounds great without them, be proud that you have achieved shimmer and excitement and depth and stereo width during previous steps in the recording and mixing process, and leave it at that.

DITHER

Dithering is the process of converting a higher bit rate used for recording and mixing to the lower rate that is standard for audio CDs, 16-bit/44.1kHz. All DAWs today will offer their own dithering, which is used when you elect to burn your 24-bit mix as a 16-bit file as one of the parameters offered in the "bounce to disk" window. Often, however, a mastering engineer will elect to use a superior dithering plug-in to do this job, and bypass the built-in dither functions of the host DAW. When this is the case, dither should be placed *last* of all, even after the master fader, in a post-fader insert slot. Check the information with your DAW or dither plug-in for precise instructions if you are using this processor in your own work.

Going for it!

Once you have set your parameters, listened carefully to the results of each (checking the mix with each plug-in in "bypass" in turn, too, just to be absolutely certain of whether you need that treatment or not), you are ready to "record" your master of the mix in question. If you removed any automated master fade-outs during mixing, you should determine them now and automate them into your master fader. Since you are most likely doing this in the DAW that you recorded and mixed in, the process will be the same as the "export" or "bounce to disk" function you used for your final mix, although some of the settings might be different. At this point, you most definitely want a stereo interleaved WAV or AIFF file, and obviously you also want to retain the 16-bit/44.1kHz format that your dithering plug-in is giving you, too. Or, if you aren't using a separate dithering plug-in after your master fader, set your "bounce to disk" parameters to those settings. Hit "OK," and go for it!

As with mixing, you can keep your mixes loaded in your mastering program and bounce them again to different formats for alternative forms of delivery, direct to MP3 for use online, or with a 24-bit depth for some form of high-resolution distribution.

Preparing a CD master

If you are delivering a CD master for commercial duplication or replication, you will need to undertake a few more steps to have that in the right shape for their requirements. This will be a rough guide to what is likely to be required, but you should always check any requirements with the production house you will be working with.

The basic requirements of a CD master is that it carry 16-bit/44.1kHz audio, with individual audio tracks sequenced in the order in which you intend them to run on your final product. In short, it should be an audio CD that can be played in any conventional commercial CD player. Such a master can fairly easily be created by loading your mastered tracks into software such as Toast or Nero or any of several other alternatives out there, and sequencing them in the order of your choosing. More advanced programs will allow you to set the gap between tracks independently, perhaps allowing a little more time before or after a mellow song, or a little less when you're looking to create an attention-grabbing start to an explosive song. Many of these packages will also offer fade and cross-fade options, as well as the ability to "normalize" tracks—that is, balance their respective maximum volumes across the entire CD—according to one of a few different parameters. As ever, check the instructions with the system you are using for the specifics on these processes.

Some programs will also let you add CD text such as album and song titles and metadata such as ISRC codes, none of which are required for replication of a standard "playable" audio CD, but which contribute to a more professional commercial package.

When you are ready to burn, use a high-quality CD blank, and choose the slowest burn speed available on your computer to avoid errors in the disk. Close all other programs to let your computer concentrate on the work at hand without any stops and stars. Also, be sure to "finalize" the CD by selecting to "close" the session or burn with a "disc at once" option. Once you have burned your master, burn another straight away as a backup. Listen to the master in its entirety on a standard CD player, a different one from that on which you burned it, and double-check all delivery requirements with the manufacturer in question before sending it off.

Congratulations. You have produced a CD!

ON THE CD

On the CD

The sound examples on the CD included with *The Home Recording Handbook* were all recorded in my own home project studio, other than the piano examples, which were recorded at the Portsmouth Music and Arts Center in Portsmouth, NH. My studio is by no means a "professional studio" in the common sense, and although fairly well equipped for a home studio, it is really outfitted no better than the studios of thousands of home recordists around the world. You can achieve such recordings at home yourself, with a little care and effort, and can probably even do better.

Having said that, the majority of the raw examples included here were not engineered to "sound their best," as they would be if recorded as part of a specific song; they are designed to exhibit the many variables of microphone type and placement. They should be taken, therefore, not as examples of "exemplary recordings" in the broad sense, but as examples of how different techniques result in different sounds. Where possible, other than where noted, excerpts were recorded in a single pass with an array of microphones set up to capture the performance from different locations. The notes included with these examples will tell you which mics were used and in what positions. For the sake of brevity, the mic abbreviations in the notes represent the full make and model names of these microphones used in the recording:

4038 = Coles 4038 ribbon mic, figure-eight.
Alctron = Alctron RM-8 ribbon mic, figure-eight.
AT2021 = Audio-Technica AT2021 small-diaphragm condenser mic, cardioid.
AT2050 = Audio-Technica AT2050 large-diaphragm condenser mic, switchable polar patterns, omni/cardioid/figure-eight (cardioid used here).
AT4033 = Audio-Technica AT4033a large-diaphragm condenser mic, cardioid.
Beta 52 = Shure Beta 52A dynamic mic, cardioid.
C451 = AKG C451E small-diaphragm condenser mic, cardioid.
M160 = Beyer-Dynamic M160 ribbon mic, cardioid.
M201 = Beyer-Dynamic M201 dynamic mic, cardioid.
NT1 = Rode NT1 large-diaphragm condenser mic, cardioid.
R84 = AEA R84 ribbon mic, figure-eight.
RV15 = Red 5 Audio RV15 large-diaphragm tube condenser mic, cardioid.
SM57 = Shure SM57 dynamic mic, cardioid.

For the sake of parity, mic preamps were the standard channel pres in a Mackie 1604-VLZ Pro mixer, except when ribbon mics and condenser mics were tracked together, in which case AEA TRPs were used for the ribbons to keep them safe from phantom power.

All examples were recorded via a MOTU 828 MkII with Black Lion mod and Black Lion Microclock to Pro Tools 9 on a Mac Pro computer. The only exception here is the piano examples, which required a portable rig and were recorded to GarageBand on a MacBook laptop computer.

The tunes in the individual examples are all copyright of the musician performing them, as noted in the headers to each section, and are the original compositions of that particular artist. They cannot be copied, sampled, re-arranged, or re-recorded without the express written consent of those individual composers. All electric and acoustic guitar parts were performed by the author. Instruments and amplifiers used, where applicable, are also noted in the headers to each section.

Drum examples

KICK DRUM

Let's start off with several techniques for miking the kick drum, as discussed in Chapter Four: Recording Drums. These were performed by the author (definitely *not* a professional drummer) on a Mapex kit with a 22-inch kick drum, Remo heads, and Zildjian cymbals. Kick mics (and kick set-up) change as noted, although an M201 on snare and a 4038 mid and Alctron side overheads in M-S stereo were used throughout to capture the rest of the kit. Separate takes were required for each reconfiguration of the kick-drum head. Note that the first few kick hits in each example are of just the kick mic soloed; the overhead and snare mics are brought in for the "whole kit" section, and the individual kick hits at the end are the sound with all mics in. Drum variables include a full uncut front head, front head removed with and without internal damping, and a front head with a "port hole" cut out.

■ TRACK 1
'KICK HEAD-ON B52'

Uncut front head, Beta 52 three inches (75mm) in front, off-axis.

■ TRACK 2
'KICK HEAD-ON AT2050'

Uncut front head, AT2050, three feet (900mm) from the front, straight on. Note how using this mic changes the entire kit sound each time, because it picks up a little of everything.

■ TRACK 3
'KICK BATTERHD SM57'

SM57 aimed at the contact point of the batter head, just a few inches out, with uncut front head.

■ TRACK 4
'KICK H-O BTRHDSM57+AT2050'
Uncut front head with an AT2050 three feet (900mm) back, with some SM57 on the batter head mixed in.

■ TRACK 5
'KICK HEAD-HOLE B52'
Front head on with "port hole" cut out, Beta 52 aimed into the hole (no internal damping).

■ TRACK 6
'KICK HEAD-OFF B52'
Front head removed, Beta 52 a few inches inside drum, pillow for damping (not touching batter head).

■ TRACK 7
'KICK HEAD-OFF AT2050'
Front head removed, AT2050 three feet (900mm) in front of drum, pillow for damping (not touching batter head).

■ TRACK 8
'KICK HEAD-OFF SM57'
Front head removed, SM57 alone, inside drum a few inches from inside of batter head, pillow for damping (not touching batter head).

■ TRACK 9
'KICK HD-OFF B52+SM57'
A blend of the Beta 52 and SM57 as positioned above, pillow for damping (not touching batter head).

■ TRACK 10
'KICK HD-OFF NOPLW B52'
Front head removed, Beta 52 a few inches inside drum, no internal damping.

■ TRACK 11
'KICK HD-OFF NOPLW AT2050'
Front head removed, AT2050 three feet (900mm) in front of drum, no internal damping.

■ TRACK 12
'KICK W-1X12CAB'

Using a speaker cabinet as a "microphone," as described in the Recording Drums chapter. Front head on with port hole, 1x12 speaker cab with Celestion G12-65 speaker at 8 ohms positioned directly in front of kick, wrapped in quilt for isolation.

TRACK 13
'KICK B52HOLE+1X12CAB'

Again, using a speaker cabinet as a "microphone." Front head on with port hole, 1x12 speaker cab with Celestion G12-65 speaker at 8 ohms positioned a few inches front of kick with Beta 52 in the port hole, wrapped in quilt for isolation; mic and cab mixed in approximately equal proportions.

SNARE DRUM

Next, a selection of the snare-miking techniques covered in the Recording Drums chapter. Notes for this one are largely as per kick drum, above, although these mics were all set up together and required only one performance. The snare is the Mapex snare included with the kit, Remo head with only minimal damping from gaffer tape. The first few individual hits of the snare are the snare mic(s) alone, while the remainder of the example (from the entrance of the full kit) includes the mics on the rest of the kit. The same M-S overhead set-up is used as on the kick examples above, with a Beta 52 in the hole in the kick-drum head.

TRACK 14
'SNARE M201'

M201 at the side of the snare, a few inches in over the rim and aiming slightly down toward the center of the head.

TRACK 15
'SNARE SM57 ABOVE'

SM57 at the side of the snare, a few inches in over the rim and aiming slightly down toward the center of the head (mounted side-by-side with the M201).

TRACK 16
'SNARE SM57 UNDER'

SM57 mounted beneath the drum, aimed at the wire snares on the resonant head (not a great sound on its own).

TRACK 17
'SNARE AT2050'

AT2050 at the side of the snare, about two inches (50mm) above and two inches (50mm) back from the rim.

TRACK 18
'SNARE M201 + AT2050'

A blend of the M201 and AT2050 in their positions as noted above.

TRACK 19
'SNARE SM57 OVR + SM57 UNDR'

A blend of the SM57s above and below the snare, with the "below" mic slightly lower in the mix (note snare rattle on the tom rolls).

DRUM OVERHEADS

The Mapex kit played by Rick Habib this time, recorded in a single pass by a selection of mics in different positions. A pair of AT2021s and a pair of Alctrons are mounted together in a typical "spaced pair" stereo overhead configuration (that is, one of each mic left and right) mounted about four feet above the snare and the floor tom. A further ribbon mic, a 4038, is mounted off the back edge of the floor tom for use with the Alctron above the snare in a Glyn Johns configuration. An M201 and Beta 52 are on the snare and kick respectively at all times. Minimal bus EQ and comp is applied to the entire kit so it sounds somewhat the way you would expect to hear it in a recording. Note: Rick is a right-handed drummer, but rather unusually, plays his hi-hats and ride cymbal with his left hand, so the ride is positioned just over the snare and hats on left of the kit (drummer's perspective), which might confuse your stereo imaging slightly).

TRACK 20
'DRUMS OHS CONDENSERS'

The AT2021s as a stereo pair.

TRACK 21
'DRUMS OHS RIBBONS'

The Alctrons panned in the same stereo mix as the AT2021s above (no EQ added).

TRACK 22
'DRUMS OHS RIBBONS EQ'D'

The Alctrons as above, but with a little high-end track-insert EQ added to each, 3dB peaking at around 10kHz, as might often be added to "sweeten" the highs of ribbon mics.

TRACK 23
'DRUMS OHS GJ'

Glyn Johns stereo mix, Alctron mic (same as OH) over snare, 4038 as "side fill" behind floor tom, no added EQ.

DRUMS IN THE MIX

■ TRACK 24
'DRUMS BB EXCERPT

A section of the song 'Blood And Bone' by The Molenes, Zach Field on an Eames kit, tracks loaded in and roughly mixed in the "pre-mix" before delivery to Paul Q. Kolderie and Adam Taylor for final mixing and mastering. Refer to example #29 'Bass In BB Section' in the Bass section below for reference to the final mix.

Refer also to 'Building the mix' below to hear the above 'Drums OHs GJ' Glyn Johns mic technique used in a full mix.

Bass examples

BASS DI + AMP

These tracks are taken from Andrew Russell's bass parts on The Molenes' song 'Blood And Bone' from the CD *Good Times Comin'* (©Dave Hunter, 2010). Andrew is playing a mid-70s Fender Precision Bass with Jason Lollar vintage-wind pickup, with tracks split to a direct feed via a passive DI and to a small Ampeg tube combo set for some midrange grind and miked with a Shure Beta 52, using the dual-path technique frequently recommended in Chapter Five: Recording Bass. Both tracks were recorded through a little gentle compression.

■ TRACK 25
'BASS DI 1'

The DI track on its own.

■ TRACK 26
'BASS AMP 1'

The amp track on its own.

■ TRACK 27
'BASS 1 BOTH PREALIGNED'

Both DI and amp tracks together, equal fader settings, tracks *not* realigned for phase.

■ TRACK 28
'BASS 1 BOTH REALIGNED'

Both DI and amp tracks together, equal fader settings, after realignment for phase (note how the bass is fuller and tighter here).

■ TRACK 29
'BASS IN BB SECTION'

The same section of the song, both bass tracks in, after final mixing and mastering by Paul Q. Kolderie and Adam Taylor.

BASS DI + PLUG-IN

Examples of a bass performance from a rock session, Andrew Russell on the Precision Bass again. Note: These tracks are used again in full context in the 'Building the mix' example, below.

■ TRACK 30
'BASS 2 DI'

The Precision Bass, straight in.

■ TRACK 31
'BASS 2 PLUG-IN'

The same DI-ed track as above, copied to another track, with an amp-simulator plug-in added for some crunch.

■ TRACK 32
'BASS 2 DI+PLUG-IN'

The two tracks blended (amp plug-in track about 30 per cent lower than the straight DI) to achieve a thick, greasy overdriven bass sound in a circumstance where you might not be able to crank a real amp to achieve such tones (which is to say, the kids were asleep).

Electric guitar examples

CLEAN ELECTRIC GUITAR

Recorded in one pass with multiple mics set up, as specified in the notes. The guitar is a 1957 Fender Telecaster, the amp a Matchless SC30 on the 12AX7 ("clean") channel through its original Matchless-spec Celestion G12H-30 speaker. No pedals are used, but all tracks are run through just a little gentle bus compression to help them sound as they would in a mix. Note the considerable difference between individual mics and mic positions, as well as the distinctly different sounds created by blending multiple mics, as discussed in Chapter Six: Recording Guitars.

■ TRACK 33
'GTR CLEAN SM57'

SM57 one inch (25mm) from speaker grille cloth.

■ TRACK 34
'GTR CLEAN M201'

Beyer M201 one inch (25mm) from speaker grille cloth (mounted side-by-side with the SM57).

■ TRACK 35
'GTR CLEAN M160'

Beyer M160 ribbon mic 16 inches (400mm) from the speaker.

■ TRACK 36
'GTR CLEAN R84'

AEA R84 ribbon mic two feet (600mm) from the speaker.

■ TRACK 37
'GTR CLEAN 4038'

Coles 4038 ribbon mic two feet (600mm) from the speaker.

■ TRACK 38
'GTR CLEAN ALCTRON'

Alctron RM-8 ribbon mic two feet (600mm) from the speaker.

■ TRACK 39
'GTR CLEAN C451'

AKG C451 condenser seven feet (2.1m) back and five feet (1.5m) high as a room mic.

■ TRACK 40
'GTR CLEAN NT1'

Rode NT1 condenser seven feet (2.1m) back and five feet (1.5m) high as a room mic.

■ TRACK 41
'GTR CLEAN MULTI CDC'

SM57 close-mic panned center, C451 seven feet (2.1m) back panned 80 per cent left, NT1 seven feet (2.1m) back panned 80 per cent right (L-R mic levels down to –7dB).

■ TRACK 42
'GTR CLEAN MULTI RRR'

Three ribbons: M160 16 inches (400mm) back panned center, R84 two feet (600mm) back panned 80 per cent left, 4038 two feet (600mm) back panned 80 per cent right (L-R mic levels down to –7dB).

DIRTY ELECTRIC GUITAR

A grungy riff with some simple lead thrown in, recorded with a Gibson Custom Shop 1957 Les Paul Goldtop Reissue (aka R7) with Wolfetone Dr Vintage humbucking pickups (bridge pickup selected), through the "Modern" channel of a TopHat Emplexador MkII with an open-back 1x12 cab with Celestion G12-65 speaker. Note: the SM57, M201, and M160 were bundled together in the same position.

■ TRACK 43
'GTR EGRUNGE 57'

SM57 close.

■ TRACK 44
'GTR EGRUNGE M201'

Beyer M201 close.

■ TRACK 45
'GTR EGRUNGE M160'

Beyer M160 close.

■ TRACK 46
'GTR EGRUNGE SM57BACK'

SM57 in the back of the cab (not a great sounding track on its own).

■ TRACK 47
'GTR EGRUNGE 4038'

4038 18 inches (460mm) from the amp.

■ TRACK 48
'GTR EGRUNGE 57FTBK'

The close SM57 at front paired with the SM57 in the back of the cab, both right up the middle. Blended together, the SM57s at the front and at the back help this little open-back 1x12 cab to approximate the sound of a big closed-back cab.

ELECTRIC GUITAR: MULTI-SPEAKER MIKING

The Recording Guitars chapter examines how you can achieve different sounds by putting individual mics on different speakers in multi-speaker extension cabs, which is put to the test here. They are recorded with the Les Paul through the Matchless SC30 (EF86 "high-gain" channel) patched into a TopHat 2x12 extension cab with one Celestion Alnico Blue and one G12H-30, with matching SM57s close on each speaker, and a single Coles 4038 ribbon mic positioned about three feet (900mm) back and three feet (900mm) high, aiming at the point between the two speakers.

TRACK 49
'GTR MULTI SM57-BLUE'
SM57 close on Celestion Alnico Blue (left speaker in the cab).

TRACK 50
'GTR MULTI SM57-G12H30'
SM57, close, G12H-30 (right speaker in the cab).

TRACK 51
'GTR MULTI 4038-MIDDLE'
The Coles 4038 aimed dead center (this one is a little nasal, perhaps from some phase cancellation).

TRACK 52
'GTR MULTI BLUEL-H30R'
Both SM57s now, panned 50 per cent left (Alnico Blue) and 50 per cent right (G12H-30).

ELECTRIC GUITAR: TWO AMPS
You can often produce a big, rich sound from just one guitar take by running it through two amps simultaneously. Here, a Matchless SC30 1x12 combo and a boutique "hotrodded tweed 5E3-style" combo are placed side by side, both set clean, each miked with an SM57 close and an Alctron RM-8 three feet (900mm) back. The guitar is a Fano alt de Facto JM6 with Lindy Fralin P-90 pickups. A "clean" tone results, but one with plenty of bite, depth, and multi-dimensionality.

TRACK 53
'GTR TWO AMPS FULL'
SC30's SM57 panned 12 per cent left, Alctron panned 65 per cent left; 5E3-style amp's SM57 close panned 12 per cent right, Alctron panned 65 per cent right.

TRACK 54
'GTR TWO AMPS IND-TOGETHER'
The same performance as above, but waveforms edited to give you solo segments from individual mics, then together, then individually again, as follows:

0:00—0:04 – SM57 on Matchless.
0:04—0:06 – Alctron on Matchless.
0:06—0:09 – SM57 on "tweed" combo.
0:09—0:11 – Alctron on "tweed" combo.
0:11—0:16 – All four tracks together, both amps in.

0:16—0:22 – Alctron on "tweed" combo.
0:22—0:27 – SM57 on "tweed" combo.
0:27—0:29 – Alctron on Matchless.
0:29—0:32 – SM57 on Matchless.
0:32—0:51 – All four tracks together, both amps in.

DOUBLE-TRACKED ELECTRIC GUITARS

These are some quick edits from the rough mix of a song still in progress called 'The Cut' (working title; ©Cara Morse & Dave Hunter, 2011), using a different guitar and amp for each in order to increase the effectiveness of the layering, as discussed in the Recording Guitars chapter. The first example is recorded with a Gibson Custom Shop 1957 Goldtop reissue with Wolfetone Dr. Vintage pickups, through a TopHat Emplexador MkII on the "Modern" channel; the second is a Fano alt de Facto SP6 with Fralin pickups (T-style bridge) through the "high-gain" (EF86) channel of a Matchless SC30. Both were miked with an M201 close and an Alctron RM-8 back about two and a half feet (750mm). A little gentle comp and light reverb is applied in the mix, and they are run through the iZotope Ozone mastering plug-in on the master fader for that "on the CD" sound. The third example is the two guitars together, the Les Paul/TopHat panned M201 25 per cent right, Alctron 75 per cent right; the Fano/Matchless panned M201 25 per cent left, Alctron 75 per cent left.

Note: Also listen to 'Building the mix' below to hear these guitar parts in the context of an entire rough mix.

■ TRACK 55
'GTR THE CUT LP'

The Les Paul and TopHat combination for a classic "Marshally" rock rhythm sound.

■ TRACK 56
'GTR ROCK CUT FANO'

The Fano (single coil pickup) and Matchless; still thick and meaty, but a little more cutting.

■ TRACK 57
'GTR ROCK CUT BOTH'

Used together, panned L-R, the two contrast well, but pair up for a thick, heavy rhythm part constructed of just two guitar takes (with two mics on each).

SMALL AMP

Small, low-wattage amps can often make extremely effective recording tools. Here we have a few takes with the Telecaster, then with the Les Paul, through a small single-ended Two Stroke combo with one ten-inch (250mm) and one eight-inch

(200mm) speaker (which was used as noted below) and a single 6V6 output tube installed for about five watts of power.

TRACK 58
'GTR SMALL SEMI-CLEAN'

With the Telecaster, transitioning through three different mics:
First – M201 half an inch (12mm) from grille.
Second – Alctron ten inches (250mm) from speaker.
Third – C451 four inches (100mm) from speaker.

TRACK 59
'GTR SMALL GRITTY-8'

The Tele again, amp set a little grittier, through the eight-inch (200mm) speaker, same mic transitions as above.
First – M201 half an inch (12mm) from grille.
Second – Alctron ten inches (250mm) from speaker.
Third – C451 four inches (100mm) from speaker.

TRACK 60
'GTR SMALL GRITTY-10'

Same as "Gtr Small Gritty" but through the ten-inch (250mm) speaker.

TRACK 61
'GTR SMALL BLUESY'

Amp cranked to around 3 o'clock, with the Les Paul this time; ten-inch (250mm) speaker, same mic transitions as above.

GUITAR MIC ACROSS THE SPEAKER

These are four separate but successive performances of the same riff to show how different the same mic will sound when moved to slightly different positions across the space of the same 12-inch/300mm speaker (the amp is the Matchless SC30, the speaker its Celestion G12H-30). The same M201 dynamic mic is used for each, one inch (25mm) out from the cone, positioned as follows:

TRACK 62
'GTR CLOSE EDGE'

At the outer edge of the cone (right side).

TRACK 63
'GTR CLOSE 1INCH LEFT'

Moved another inch (25mm) left toward center.

■ **TRACK 64**

'GTR CLOSE 3INCH LEFT'

Moved three inches (75mm) left of the right edge.

■ **TRACK 65**

'GTR CLOSE CENTER'

Almost dead center.

Acoustic guitar examples

SEVEN CONDENSER MICS

The following examples were recorded using seven different condenser mic positions (both large-diaphragm and small-diaphragm) with a 1996 Froggy Bottom H-12 flat-top acoustic, played fingerstyle ("with a little bit of nail"), with well broken-in D'Addario strings. All are simultaneous mics and positions of the same take except 'Acstc Gtr AT2050 Body,' which was recorded before moving that mic to its new position (a successive take though, which sounds very similar).

■ **TRACK 66**

'ACTSC GTR AT2021 NECK'

AT2021 positioned around four inches (100mm) out from the 12th fret (the neck/body joint), aiming slightly in toward the body of the guitar.

■ **TRACK 67**

'ACTSC GTR AT2021 BODY'

AT2021 positioned around four inches (100mm) out, aiming at the lower bout of the body below and slightly behind the bridge.

■ **TRACK 68**

'ACTSC GTR C451 NECK'

AKG C451 positioned around four inches (100mm) out from the 12th fret (the neck/body joint), aiming slightly in toward the body of the guitar (strapped together with the AT2021).

■ **TRACK 69**

'ACTSC GTR AT4033 NECK'

The sound of a large-diaphragm condenser mic positioned similar to the SDCs at the 12th fret.

■ TRACK 70
'ACSTC GTR NT1 BODY'

Same position as 'Actsc Gtr AT2021 Body.'

■ TRACK 71
'ACSTC GTR AT2050 BODY'

Same position as NT1.

■ TRACK 72
'ACSTC GTR RV15 OVRSHLDR'

The RV15 tube condenser mic, positioned at the back of the performer, firing from over the right shoulder at a slightly downward angle.

■ TRACK 73
'ACSTC GTR AT2021 STEREO'

Matching AT2021 small diaphragm condensers at neck and body, panned 50 per cent L-R respectively.

■ TRACK 74
'ACSTC GTR C451-RV15 STEREO'

Actually a "pseudo stereo" mix, with the C451 at the neck panned 70 per cent left, the RV15 over the shoulder panned 30 per cent right, and the faders balanced so there's an equal L-R balance at the outputs.

■ TRACK 75
'ACSTC GTR AT33-NT1 STEREO'

A "stereo" mix with two different large diaphragm condensers, with the AT4033 at the neck panned 40 per cent left, the NT1 at the body panned 40 per cent right.

Vocal examples

FEMALE VOCALS

As discussed in Chapter Seven: Recording Vocals, different mics will yield significantly different results on vocals, and some might be more suitable for certain singers than others. Here, four different mics are set up at the same time, tracking Cara Morse singing 'The Cut' (working title; ©Cara Morse & Dave Hunter, 2011). The SM57 is closer to the vocalist, hence the occasional plosive "pop." Some gentle comp is added courtesy of a UAD 1176 plug-in, and gentle reverb with a little slap-back echo courtesy of the UAD RS-1 Reflection Engine plug-in (plate). All tracks are also run through the iZotope Ozone mastering plug-in on the master fader for that "on

the CD" sound. No EQ other than where noted. Note: To hear these vocal tracks further in context, listen to the 'Building the mix' examples, below.

■ TRACK 76
'VOX FEMALE AT4033'
The AT4033 large-diaphragm condenser mic at 12 inches (300mm) away.

■ TRACK 77
'VOX FEMALE SM57'
A Shure SM57 about four inches (100mm) away. A surprisingly usable sound from an affordable dynamic mic.

■ TRACK 78
'VOX FEMALE R84'
An AEA R84 ribbon mic, 12 inches (300mm) away, no EQ compensation.

■ TRACK 79
'VOX FEMALE R84 EQ'
Same mic and position as above, but with some high-end EQ added to sweeten the highs of a notoriously "warm" ribbon mic.

■ TRACK 80
'VOX FEMALE RV15'
The Red 5 Audio RV15 tube condenser mic, 12 inches (300mm) away.

■ TRACK 81
'Vox Female In Context'
Ultimately, hearing any vocal recording in isolation doesn't tell you much about how it will work in the track, so now we will hear each mic in succession, in the rough mix, one per phrase: AT4033, SM57, R84 (with EQ), RV15.

MALE VOCALS

■ TRACK 82
'VOX MALE FOUR MICS'
This is the first verse of the song 'Blood And Bone' from the album *Good Times Comin'* by The Molenes (©Dave Hunter, 2010), with the vocal re-tracked through four different mics. They are heard in the track for context, with just a little treatment to help them "sit" like a real recording.

0:00 – The AT4033 condenser from 12 inches (300mm).
0:33 – The SM57 from 4 inches (100mm).
0:48 – The RV15 tube condenser from 12 inches (300mm).
0:57 – The R84 ribbon mic (no high-end EQ added).

■ TRACK 83
'VOX MALE RIBBON EQ'D'

Starts with the RV15 tube condenser for comparison, then goes to the R84 [from 0:10] with high-end EQ added to increase the sense of air and presence. Sounds much better this time!

■ TRACK 84
'BLOOD AND BONE'

Here's the full song, as mixed and mastered out of house in Camp Street Studio by Paul Q. Kolderie and Adam Taylor, with the R84 that it was originally recorded on, and analog reverb/delay treatment (a fully analog mix, in fact). Dave Hunter guitars and vocals, Andrew Russell bass, Zach Field drums.

Piano examples

Recorded with different mics, as noted, on location to GarageBand using the Mackie mixer for mic pres. Performances by Elissa Margolin on a Yamaha G2 grand piano.

■ TRACK 85
'PIANO MONO RIBBON'

A single Alctron RM-8 ribbon mic located in the "curve" of the piano, firing at an angle into the open lid on full stick, about four feet (1.2m) out from the center of the strings.

■ TRACK 86
'PIANO XY AT2021'

Two AT2021 in a coincident XY stereo pair, about six feet (1.8m) high and eight feet (2.4m) back from the open lid of the piano on full stick, firing at the middle of the "curve."

■ TRACK 87
'PIANO AT2021 INSIDE LOW'

Matched AT2021s inside the piano just a few inches over the strings, left channel mic over the bass strings, lid on the short stick.

TRACK 88
'PIANO LDCS UNDER LID'

AT2050 near treble strings (right channel), AT4033 near bass strings (left channel), mics hovering part way under lid from the "curve" of the piano.

TRACK 89
'PIANO MONO LDC FRONT'

A single AT2050 large-diaphragm condenser set to cardioid, positioned at the front of the piano, above the keys and the performer's head, firing into the center of the piano with the front board (the music stand support) removed.

Sax examples

These examples were recorded all from the same performance, with four mics set up simultaneously. Sax played by Russ Grazier, Jr., on a Yamaha YAS-62 alto saxophone. No treatment other than some gentle mastering dynamics applied on the master fader.

TRACK 90
'SAX AT2050 18INCHES'

The affordable AT2050 large-diaphragm condenser set to cardioid, about 18 inches (450mm) out and aiming at midpoint between bell and mouthpiece.

TRACK 91
'SAX BETA 52 4INCHES'

Shure Beta52 dynamic mic, pointing into bell from four inches (100mm) away.

TRACK 92
'SAX 4038 18INCHES'

The large figure-eight Coles 4038 ribbon , about 18 inches (450mm) out and aiming at midpoint between bell and mouthpiece.

TRACK 93
'SAX M160 10INCHES'

A Beyer M160 ribbon, cardioid, ten inches (250mm) out and aiming at about a third of the distance from bell to mouthpiece.

TRACK 94
'SAX MULTI-MIX'

M160 up the middle, AT2050 50 per cent left, 4038 50 per cent right, some mastering reverb added for kicks (note the uneven reverb delay created by having the figure-eight mic panned to one side).

■ TRACK 95
'SAX DOS RIBBONS'

M160 panned 16 per cent right, 4038 panned four per cent left, same mastering reverb as 'multi-mix.' This one sounds like it jumps right out of the monitors and into the room with you.

Building the mix

■ TRACK 96
'MIX CUT BUILDING'

This is an excerpt from the rough mix of a song with the working title 'The Cut' (©Cara Morse & Dave Hunter, 2011), featuring Cara Morse on vocals, Dave Hunter on guitars, Andrew Russell on bass, and Rick Habib on drums. You can find individual track examples lifted from this throughout the examples above, but this one builds up the different instruments one by one to paint the entire picture. For the vocal track (which comes in after the solo), I decided to use the RV15 tube condenser mic track from the multiple 'Vox female' examples above. The two rhythm guitar tracks are the same as detailed in the 'Double-tracked electric guitars' examples above, and the same amps are used for the solos—Les Paul and TopHat panned toward the right (recorded on additional tracks), Fano and Matchless panned toward the left—but a basic Xotic Effects EP-1 booster pedal is stomped on for a slight gain boost for each solo. Drums are the Glyn Johns mic set-up used in the 'Drum overheads' examples, and the bass is a blend of the two tracks recorded with the mid-70s Precision Bass in the 'Bass DI and plug-in' examples.

Tracks are added to the mix as follows:
0:00 – Drums
0:13 – Bass
0:20 – Right guitar (Les Paul/TopHat)
0:32 – Left guitar (Fano/Matchless)
0:43 – First guitar solo, Les Paul, right
0:49 – Second guitar solo, Fano, left
0:55 – Third guitar solo, Les Paul, right
1:02 – Fourth guitar solo, Fano, left
1:15 – Vocal

ROUGH MIX/PRO MIX

The following are two mixes of the song 'Rockin' Monophonic' from the album *Good Times Comin'* by The Molenes (©Dave Hunter, 2010), recorded in the author's home studio. The musicians are Bruce Derr on pedal-steel guitar (re-amped through a DIY Leslie cab), Dave Hunter on guitars and vocals, Andrew Russell on bass and harmony vocals, Zach Field on drums. The first is the rough mix done entirely "in the box" for final checking and distribution to band members prior to the pro mix, with a quick iZotope Ozone plug-in preset loaded just to give it a pseudo-mastered feel. The second is the final product after mixing and mastering by Paul Q. Kolderie and Adam Taylor at Camp Street Studio, running the tracks out of Pro Tools to an entirely analog Tweed Audio mixing desk built in the 1970s and vintage outboard processors, reverbs, delays and so forth, then mastering through TC Finalizer. Kolderie has worked with Radiohead, Pixies, Buffalo Tom, Uncle Tupelo, The Lemonheads, and several other respected artists, and certainly knows his chops, as does Taylor, formerly his partner at Camp Street (now closed, sadly). As discussed in Chapter 9: Mixing and Chapter 10: Mastering, however good you get at doing it yourself (and that's the idea here, right?) there are definite benefits to taking it to a pro, especially when it's your own work and you hope to benefit from an objective ear.

The rough mix is the honest-to-goodness final working mix that was bounced back before this book was even a glimmer in the author's eye, and has not been tweaked with reference to Kolderie and Taylor's final master mix. The entire band was extremely pleased with the final mix, but in hindsight, the rough mix doesn't sound too bad either, especially considering it would inevitably have been given some final tweaks and touches if it were to be the master itself. Listen to the two, and see what differences you can hear between them. Is there anything you would have changed on either if you were mixing them yourself?

■ TRACK 97
'ROCKIN' MONO ROUGH MIX'

The home-studio, in-the-box rough mix.

■ TRACK 98
'ROCKIN' MONOPHONIC'

The professional mix, mastered.

Index

Words *in italics* indicate album titles unless otherwise stated. Words 'in quotes' indicate song titles. Page numbers in **bold** indicate illustrations.

A

B

C

D

E

F

G

H

Acknowledgements

The author wishes to thank all the musicians who participated in the recording of the sound-sample CD bundled with this book, including Andrew Russell, Zach Field, Bruce Derr, Cara Morse, Rick Habib, Russ Grazier Jr., and Elissa Margolin. Thanks also to my editor John Morrish; Nigel Osborne, Tony Bacon, Mark Brend and the entire team at Jawbone Press, and to designer Paul Cooper and photographer Jerry Monkman. The good folks at Audio-Technica USA, AEA, Matchless Amplifiers, TopHat Amplifiers, Fano Guitars, Koll Guitars, and Hahn Guitars were all extremely helpful during the course of the writing and recording, as were Katie Grazier and, again, Russ of the Portsmouth Music & Arts Center (PMAC). Thanks too to "the pros," such as Paul Q. Kolderie and Adam Taylor, formerly of Camp Street Studio (aka "the studio formerly known as Fort Apache"). Finally, heartfelt thanks to Flo, Freddie and Jess Hunter for putting up with the studio in the attic.

Other great books in this series:

PLAY CLASSICAL GUITAR
ISBN 978-0-87930-657-1

THE FIDDLE HANDBOOK
ISBN 978-0-87930-978-7

THE PIANO HANDBOOK
ISBN 978-0-87930-727-1

THE PIANO IMPROVISATION HANDBOOK
ISBN 978-0-87930-977-0

PLAY ACOUSTIC
ISBN 978-0-87930-853-7

THE ELECTRIC GUITAR HANDBOOK
ISBN 978-0-87930-989-3

THE BASS HANDBOOK
ISBN 978-0-87930-872-8

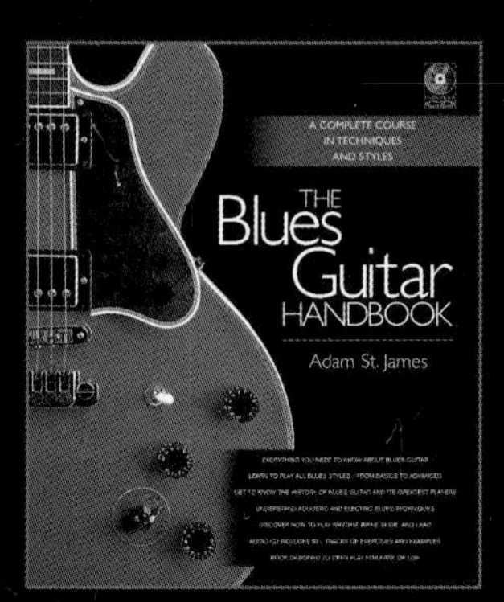

THE BLUES GUITAR HANDBOOK
ISBN 978-1-61713-011-3